Turbo Algorithms

A Programmer's Reference

Related Titles of Interest

Turbo Language Essentials: A Programmer's Reference, Weiskamp, Shammas, and Pronk
Turbo Libraries: A Programmer's Reference, Weiskamp, Shammas, and Pronk
Power Graphics Using Turbo C, Weiskamp, Heiny, and Shammas
Introducing C to Pascal Programmer's, Shammas
Advanced Turbo C Programmer's Guide, Mosich, Shammas, and Flamig
The Turbo C Survival Guide, Miller and Quilici
C Programming Language: An Applied Perspective, Miller and Quilici
C Wizard's Programming Reference, Schwaderer
Turbo C DOS Utilities, Alonso
Quick C DOS Utilities, Alonso
Turbo C and Quick C Functions: Building Blocks for Efficient Code, Barden
Power Graphics Using Turbo Pascal, Weiskamp, Heiny, and Shammas
Applying Turbo Pascal Library Units, Shammas
Programming with Macintosh Turbo Pascal, Swan
Turbo Pascal DOS Utilities, Alonso
Artificial Intelligence Programming with Turbo Prolog, Weiskamp and Hengl
Mastering HyperTalk, Weiskamp and Shammas

Turbo Algorithms

A Programmer's Reference

Keith Weiskamp
Namir Shammas
Ron Pronk

WILEY

John Wiley & Sons, Inc.
New York • Chichester • Brisbane • Toronto • Singapore

Publisher: Stephen Kippur
Editor: Katherine Schowalter
Managing Editor: Ruth Greif
Copy Editor and Proofreader: Brown Editorial Service

Turbo BASIC, Turbo C, Turbo Pascal, and Turbo Prolog are registered trademarks of Borland International, Inc.

Library of Congress Cataloging-in-Publication Data

Weiskamp, Keith.
    Turbo algorithms: a programmers's reference / Keith Weiskamp, Namir Shammas, Ron Pronk.
        p.   cm.
    Bibliography: p.
    ISBN 0-471-61009-7
    1. Programming languages (Electronic computers)   2. Algorithms. I. Shammas, Namir Clemet, 1954-   . II. Pronk, Ron.   III. Title.
    QA76.7.W44   1989
    005.1'3--dc20   88-31892
                                                                CIP

Printed in the United States of America
89 90 10 9 8 7 6 5 4 3 2 1

Contents

Section 2 Searching Techniques   49

Section 3 Mathematical Algorithms

Section 4 String Processing with Word Strings   153

Section 5 String Processing with Token Strings   203

Section 6 List Processing with Singly Linked Lists   227

Section 7 List Processing with Doubly Linked and Circular Lists 271

Section 8 Stacks and Queues   **317**

Listings

Preface

Once you learn how to write program statements and where to put every comma and semicolon, what are you left with? A lot of code that is worthless unless you have some solid data structures and algorithms to back you up. Let's face it, trying to solve a practical programming problem without having the right data structures and algorithms is like trying to build a house without a hammer and a box of nails.

Our goal in writing this book is to provide you with a solid reference of the major algorithms, from sorting and searching to data representation with AVL trees, that you'll need to write useful programs. Because we have implemented major algorithms in each of Borland's Turbo languages, you'll be able to compare the similarities and differences between the languages.

This book is the third volume of a three-part reference series for programmers using Borland's Turbo languages. We designed each volume to cover a key area of programming with the Turbo languages. The first book, *Turbo Language Essentials*, presents the fundamentals of programming with Turbo BASIC, C, Pascal, and Prolog. The second book, *Turbo Libraries*, covers the major functions, procedures, and predicates available with each of the four languages. This book, *Turbo Algorithms*, shows you how to write useful algorithms and flexible data structures.

Who Should Read This Book

If you use any of Borland's Turbo languages and you want to further develop your programming skills, you'll really benefit from this book. Professional programmers who need to port programs from one language to another will find the book to be an especially valuable resource. Because the same algorithms are implemented in each language, you'll be able to compare languages easily.

If you're like most serious Turbo language programmers, you want not just another user's guide, but rather a complete reference book that helps you find key information quickly. To fill this need, *Turbo Algorithms* presents each language with useful examples and provides you with numerous programming tips and techniques.

What You'll Need

To use this book you'll need one or more of the Turbo language compilers. You'll also need an IBM PC, XT, AT, PS/2, or a compatible computer system. All of the code examples that we present are designed for use with the latest versions of the Turbo language compilers, including the recently released versions: Turbo BASIC, Turbo C 2.0, Turbo Pascal 5.0, and Turbo Prolog 2.0.

A Look Inside

We've designed the book so that you can find information easily and quickly. Each section starts with a solid overview of the algorithms presented, followed by a description of the routines used to implement the algorithms in each Turbo language. We've arranged the book so that it progresses from the simpler algorithms to the more complex. The major algorithms and data structures are presented in 10 sections. Here is a breakdown of each section:

Section 1: *Sorting Techniques* presents an assortment of the major routines for sorting data in each Turbo language. This section starts with the popular insertion sort and takes you through the shellsort, quicksort, radix sort, and the heap sort.

Section 2: *Searching Techniques* explores the major algorithms for sorting data. This section uses arrays and lists as the primary data structure to implement searching algorithms for heuristic, binary, indexed, and hash-based searches.

Section 3: *Mathematical Algorithms* presents an assortment of useful mathematical algorithms from transcendental functions to integration.

Section 4: *String Processing with Word Strings* shows you how to design and code a useful set of string processing routines in each Turbo language. In this section, strings are represented and processed as sequences of words.

Section 5: *String Processing with Token Strings* expands on the material covered in Section 5. Here strings are represented and processed as general token strings.

Section 6: *List Processing with Singly Linked Lists* covers all of the major algorithms you can perform with singly linked lists. We explore different methods for representing singly linked lists from the use of arrays in Turbo BASIC to the use of pointers, records, and structures in Turbo C and Pascal.

Section 7: *List Processing with Doubly Linked and Circular Lists* continues the coverage of list processing algorithms by introducing doubly linked and circular lists. These structures help improve the performance of the algorithms presented in Section 6.

Section 8: *Stacks and Queues* shows you how to implement and process basic stack and queue data structures. The algorithms presented cover both array-based and linked-list-based stacks and queues.

Section 9: *Binary Trees* presents techniques for representing and processing binary trees. You'll learn how to use programming techniques such as recursion and dynamic memory allocation to implement the binary tree processing algorithms.

Section 10: *AVL Trees* explores a powerful variation of the binary tree—the AVL tree. We present algorithms for adding elements, deleting elements, searching for elements, and balancing trees.

How to Use This Book

This book is packed with material on techniques both for programming with the Turbo languages and mastering algorithms. We'll start with the more basic topics and then progress to more advanced ones. As you use the book, try as many of the examples as possible. Because each language is so highly interactive, you can quickly learn the subtleties of programming by running the examples and modifying them.

If you take a minute to glance through this book, you'll notice the following set of icons are used to represent the four Turbo languages:

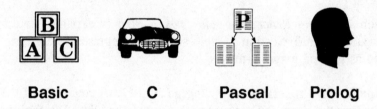

Basic   **C**   **Pascal**   **Prolog**

These icons are included to help you quickly locate the technical discussions on the language that you are working with. In addition, you'll find numerous tips in the left and right margins. We've used the following icon to label the tips:

T<small>IP</small>

Notational Conventions

Because *Turbo Libraries* covers four languages under one cover, we've tried to keep the notational symbols as simple and consistent as possible to avoid any unnecessary confusion. To help you detect any program statements or specials symbols, we've put all of the language keywords, symbols, functions, procedures, variables, constants, and so on in bold type.

Whenever general programming statements are introduced, we use the following format:

```
<function name>( [<argument 1,> <argument 2,> ... ] )
{

  [<declarations>]

  <statements>

  return(return value);
}
```

The language reserved words and symbols such as return and { } are
placed in normal type, and the identifiers that must be supplied by the
programmer are placed inside angle brackets and set in italics such as
<function name>, *<statements>*, and so on. The symbols [ ] are used
to indicate optional parts. Bold type is used for language terms, parts
of syntax lines, and other code components as they occur in the text.

Acknowledgments

We'd like to take this opportunity to thank all those very special people out there whose help was invaluable in getting this book and the other Turbo Reference books out. The list of names, in no special order, goes something like this : Dan Shafer (for inspiration), Mike Floyd and Jeff Duntemann (for their excellent technical feedback), Teri Zak, Katherine Schowalter, Ruth Greif (for great taste and an eye for detail), Nana Clark, Frank Grazioli, Stephen Kippur, Nan Borreson, Bill Gladstone, Ted Reed, Rob Mauhar, Lenity Himburg, Norm and Lois Atkin, Loren Heiny, Bryan Flamig, and the guy who drives out to the desert to pick up packages.

Turbo Algorithms

A Programmer's Reference

Sorting Techniques

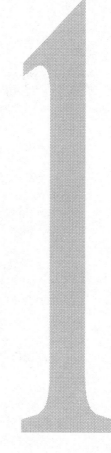

Introduction

In our first look at techniques for developing algorithms with the Turbo languages, we'll concentrate on sorting methods. Because sorting operations are critical to most applications from databases to operating systems, you'll find that the algorithms covered here can be used in many of your own programs. Computer scientists have developed many sophisticated sorting algorithms over the years. Unfortunately, we can't cover them all in this section. We'll limit our discussion to the more popular and practical algorithms. This section starts by examining the simpler algorithms such as the insertion sort; then it explains the more complex algorithms.

The following is the complete set of sorting algorithms covered.

- Insertion sort
- Shell-Metzner sort
- Quicksort
- Radix sort
- Heap sort

For each sorting method we present a complete, general explanation of the algorithm with examples to help you see how the algorithm works. After presenting the algorithms, we include documented calls to the sort routines in the four Turbo languages, along with a set of program listings for each language at the end of this section. You can use the sorting routines as they are provided, or you can modify them to suit your own needs. We suggest that you compare the sorting implementations language to see how the general algorithms are coded.

Sorting Overview

Without the ability to sort data, we couldn't write applications such as databases, spreadsheets, and operating systems. Fortunately, sorting is a simple concept to understand. To perform a useful task most computer programs require internal data, such as arrays, or external data, such as files. And in most cases, the data used must be arranged in a special order. The technique of ordering data is called *sorting*.

Data is typically sorted in one of two orders: ascending (increasing) or descending (decreasing). For ascending order, the following formula defines how each element in a data set is sorted:

e1 <= e2 <= ... <= en

where **e1**, **e2**, and so on represent the sorted data elements. For descending order, on the other hand, this formula defines how elements are ordered:

e1 >= e2 >= ... >= en

The implementations of the sorting algorithms that we'll present in Turbo BASIC, C, and Pascal are designed for the most part to work with arrays of strings, because strings are most frequently involved in sorting. The Turbo Prolog implementations use lists as the primary data structure. Sorting with other types is similar and requires a few changes.

You can modify any of the sorting routines presented in this section so that they can work with data types other than strings.

TIP

The Insertion Sort

The insertion sort is one of the simplest sorting algorithms to understand and implement in any programming language. As its name implies, the *insertion sort* method sorts the data elements in a list by inserting them one at a time into proper order. The basic algorithm incorporates the following three steps:

1. Take the first two elements of the list and arrange them in a sorted order (ascending or descending).
2. Take the next element (third) and insert it in its sorted position in relation to the already sorted elements.
3. Repeat step 2 for each element in the list; that is, insert element four in its proper order, then element five, and so on.

To see how this sorting algorithm works, look at an example. Consider an unordered list of abbreviated state names with the following initial order:

WA   VA   MI   MA   AL   AZ   CA   OR   NY   NJ

We'll sort this list in an ascending order. The first member, WA, is assigned to the first position until it is replaced by another element. The partially sorted list looks like this:

WA | VA MI MA AL AZ CA OR NY NJ

Note that the bar symbol delimits the sorted sublist from the unsorted one. The second element, VA, is selected and compared with the members of the sorted sublist (in this case just WA). The sort moves element VA to the first position and element WA to the second position. The list now looks like this:

VA WA | MI MA AL AZ CA OR NY NJ

The third element, MI, is selected and the comparisons continue. Element MI is moved to first position, displacing elements VA and WA by one position. Repeating the process with element MA, it becomes the first element and moves the sorted sublist one position to the right. The list becomes:

MA MI VA WA | AL AZ CA OR NY NJ

The above insertion process repeats until all of the elements are examined. The fully sorted list is

AL AZ CA MA MI NJ NY OR VA WA

As shown, the insertion sort is characterized by its ability to maintain a sorted list when new elements are added without re-sorting the entire list.

Insertion Sort Implementation

The implementation of the insertion sort is very similar in Turbo BASIC, C, and Pascal (see Listings 1.1, 1.2, and 1.3). Each program uses a nested **WHILE** loop to sort an array of strings in ascending order. The first **WHILE** loop repeats until each element in the array is examined. Here we are showing the loop initialization in Turbo Pascal to provide you with a reference.

```
WHILE (i <= NumData) DO BEGIN
   ...
```

The variable **NumData** stores the number of elements in the list.

The inner **WHILE** loop, on the other hand, performs the steps of the insertion sort. The following loop repeats as long as the following two conditions are true:

```
WHILE (j < i) AND nomatch DO BEGIN
    ...
```

The variable **i** keeps track of the current position in the array (the element that is being sorted) and the variable **j** serves as a counter that is incremented from the beginning of the list to the position of the element being sorted. Before the inner **WHILE** loop starts, **j** is initialized to 1. After each iteration of the loop, this variable is incremented by 1. The loop repeats until one of two conditions is met:

1. A[i] < A[j], that is, an element whose value is less than the element being sorted is found.
2. A[i] = A[j], that is, an element whose value is equal to the element being sorted is found.

If the **A[i] < A[j]** condition is true, as illustrated in Figure 1.1, the algorithm must move element **A[i]** to position **A[j]** and then slide the elements from **A[j]** to **A[i-1]** up one index as shown in Figure 1.2. The code that rearranges the array is

```
tempo := A[i];
FOR k := i-1 DOWNTO j DO
    A[k+1] := A[k];
    A[j] := tempo;
```

Notice that it is necessary to save the element stored in **A[i]** before the array is rearranged. These simple operations are the only ones required to keep an array in a sorted order.

A different strategy is required to implement the insertion sort algorithm in Turbo Prolog, because Turbo Prolog does not support arrays. The data is kept in a list that is sorted recursively. Instead of starting at the beginning of the list and working to the end, we'll use a recursive clause to get to the end of the list; then we'll sort and insert each element as we work our way back to the top of the list. Examine the code in Listing 1.4 to see that two clauses are required. The first, **insertsort**, is responsible for controlling the recursion; the second, **insert**, performs the sort and insert.

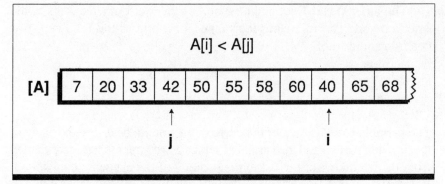

Figure 1.1. Comparing two array elements

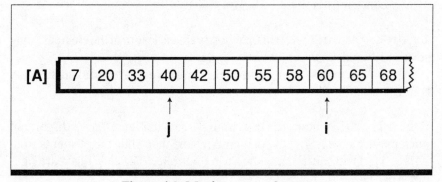

Figure 1.2. Moving array elements

The Shell-Metzner Sort

The *Shell-Metzner sort*, which is commonly called the *shellsort*, incorporates a powerful extension to the simple insertion sort. Instead of comparing and exchanging only adjacent elements, the shellsort also compares and exchanges elements that are far apart. Because of this feature, it is much more efficient for sorting larger lists of data. The sorting technique used resembles the operation of piling sea shells on top of each other.

The basic algorithm requires the following steps:

1. Divide a list into two equal-sized lists.
2. Compare and exchange each element in the first list with the corresponding element in the second list. That is, compare element 1 in the first list with element 1 in the second list, compare element 2 in the first list with element 2 in the second list, and so on.

3. To further sort the list, the elements that are closer together are compared and sorted.

4. Repeat step 3 until the list is completely sorted. Each time step 3 is repeated, the distance between the elements compared is reduced.

As you can see from the general description, this algorithm is more complex than the insertion sort. We'll use the same list of abbreviated state names that we used to explain the insertion sort method.

WA   VA   MI   MA   AL   AZ   CA   OR   NY   NJ

Since the list has 10 elements, the shellsort method starts by comparing elements that are 5 elements apart. This divides the list into two sublists:

WA   VA   MI   MA   AL   AZ   CA   OR   NY   NJ
_____   _____

 1   2   3   4   5   1   2   3   4   5

The elements having the same index number are compared and exchanged, if necessary. Thus, elements WA and AZ are compared and exchanged, to give

AZ   VA   MI   MA   AL   WA   CA   OR   NY   NJ
_____   _____

 1   2   3   4   5   1   2   3   4   5

Similarly VA and CA are compared and exchanged. The process is repeated for the other sublist elements. After the first pass is completed, we end up with the following semiordered list:

AZ   CA   MI   MA   AL   WA   VA   OR   NY   NJ
_____   _____

 1   2   3   4   5   1   2   3   4   5

Although this list is not completely sorted, we have little left to do to arrange the list. Use steps 1 and 2 of the algorithm so that the members that are five elements apart are ordered. Next, reduce the distance of compared neighbors by one half. Using integer division, that number is reduced to two (5/2). The new set of sublists becomes:

AZ	CA	MI	MA	AL	WA	VA	OR	NY	NJ
1	2	1	2	1	2	1	2	1	2

Now, the elements AZ and MI are compared but not exchanged. The next elements compared are CA and MA; they are in the correct order, so they are not exchanged. Next, elements MI and AL are compared and exchanged because MI is greater than AL. After the first round of comparisons is completed (with OR and NJ being the last elements compared), the new list is

AZ	CA	AL	MA	MI	OR	NY	NJ	VA	WA
1	2	1	2	1	2	1	2	1	2

As you can see, the list is still not in order. Thus, a second round of comparisons is required. The first elements compared, AZ and AL, must be exchanged. Likewise, the OR and NJ elements are exchanged. At the end of this round, the list looks like this:

AL	CA	AZ	MA	MI	NJ	NY	OR	VA	WA
1	2	1	2	1	2	1	2	1	2

Because elements were exchanged in this last round, a third round of comparisons is required. After the third round, the members two elements apart are in the correct order. Next, the algorithm reduces the increment between compared elements from two to one. As you can see, the shellsort sorts the list from the outside in. This means that neighboring elements are now compared. The rounds of comparisons begin by examining elements AL and CA, then CA and AZ, and exchanging the last two. The process is repeated for the remaining list elements. Additional rounds of comparisons are conducted until no elements need to be exchanged. The sorted list is

AL   AZ   CA   MA   MI   NJ   NY   OR   VA   WA

Because of the complexity and number of steps involved in this algorithm, you might at first think that it is not very efficient. In reality it is efficient, because each pass through the list requires a minimum number of comparisons and exchanges. As the algorithm compares elements that are closer together, the number of exchanges is reduced because the ordering of data improves.

When you use the shellsort algorithm, keep in mind that you can change the increment sequence for comparing elements. Our example used a 5-2-1 sequence; however, we could have used a 5-3-2-1 sequence as well. The only requirement is that the last comparison use an increment of 1. Experiment with different sequences to find the most efficient one for the data you are sorting.

TIP

Shellsort Implementation

Like the insertion sort, the procedural implementations (Turbo BASIC, C, and Pascal) are similar. Again, nested loops are used to carry out the search. The shellsort, however, is slightly more complex than the insertion sort and therefore requires three nested loops. The outer loop repeats from one to the size of the array being sorted, and the second-level loop divides the list in half with each iteration. The innermost loop performs the actual comparisons and swaps elements if necessary. The code for this operation is actually very similar to the code used in the insertion sort. It is shown here in Turbo Pascal:

```
IF A[i] < A[j] THEN BEGIN
    {swap members}
    tempo := A[j];
    A[j] := tempo;
    inorder := FALSE;
END;
```

The shellsort algorithm does not work efficiently in Turbo Prolog, because lists cannot be divided quickly. In a procedural language such as Turbo Pascal, we can easily get to the middle of a list once we determine its index. In Prolog, a list can only be accessed sequentially.

An alternative algorithm to try is the popular *bubblesort*. This algorithm introduces a technique of exchanging elements to sort a list. The basic technique involves comparing two adjacent elements and then swapping them if they are out of order. In Turbo Prolog, this algorithm is easy to implement. In our implementation shown in Listing 1.4, we make use of the useful **append** predicate to select elements from a list. The main predicate, **bubblesort**, is recursive and makes calls to **append** until the list is sorted.

Quicksort

Just as the shellsort is an improvement over the insertion sort, the *quicksort* is an improvement over the shellsort. Many programmers are convinced that the quicksort is one of the best sorting algorithms ever invented because it meets the two important criteria for an algorithm; it is fast and it is easy to implement in most languages.

The quicksort algorithm introduces a clever divide-and-conquer strategy that enhances its efficiency. The basic strategy consists of selecting a median or partition element from a list. This partition element is then used to divide the list into two sublists, one with elements less than the partition element, the other with elements equal to or greater than the partition element. To sort the list completely, the division is repeated for each sublist. That is, the algorithm selects a partition element in each sublist and divides the sublist into smaller sublists. As you can see by this description, this algorithm has a recursive nature.

Here is a summary of the steps required to sort a list with the quicksort method:

1. Select a partition element in a list and divide the list into two sublists. (The list is divided by putting all elements less than the partition element in the first list and all of the other elements in the second list.)
2. Select a partition element in each sublist and divide each sublist into more sublists.
3. Repeat step 2 until each sublist has one or zero elements.
4. Using recursion, create an ordered list by piecing together an element from each sublist.

Let's next study an example to see the quicksort in action. We'll start with the following unordered list:

WA VA MI CA MA OR NY AZ AL NJ

First, the partition element is selected. We'll pick MA, which is the middle element or true median. The list is then divided into two sublists. The left sublist contains all elements that are less than MA, and the right sublist contains the elements that are greater than MA, as shown:

```
CA   AZ   AL                                    ←——left sublist
            MA                                  ←——median
                WA   VA   MI   OR   NY   NJ  ←——right sublist
```

This process repeats recursively on each sublist. For example, the right sublist is split by selecting OR as the median. The nested left sublist has three elements, whereas the right one has only two elements, as shown:

```
MI   NY   NJ                 ←——left subarray
            OR               ←——median
                WA   VA   ←——right subarray
```

This process continues until each nested sublist contains one or zero elements. When this requirement is met, the algorithm rolls back and builds ordered sublists and eventually produces a completely sorted list.

Recursion plays an important role in the quicksort method. Keep in mind, however, that this algorithm can be implemented without using recursion. In fact, we've provided both a recursive and nonrecursive implementation of the quicksort in Listings 1.1, 1.2, and 1.3 for Turbo BASIC, C, and Pascal so that you can compare the two approaches.

When using the quicksort algorithm, you can "fine tune" it by experimenting with different methods for selecting a partition. In both our example and implementations for the Turbo languages, the middle element is selected as the partition element. As an alternate method, you could select the partition element by choosing a value at random or taking a value other than the middle element.

Quicksort Implementation

The implementation of the recursive quicksort algorithm in BASIC, C, and Pascal uses the routines **RecQuickSort** and **Sort**. The **RecQuickSort** routine is the high-level routine that calls **Sort** to perform the recursive sorting algorithm. Each time **Sort** is called, a median is selected and the array is divided in half. The sorting continues as **Sort** calls itself recursively with either half of the array. To keep track of the left and right positions of the array section being sorted, two index pointers, **i** and **j**, are used. The sorting is actually performed inside a **Repeat** loop that continues until the left index pointer **i** advances past the right index pointer **j**.

The nonrecursive version is slightly more complex. In this implementation, a stack-like data structure is used to keep track of the different subarrays as the main array is subdivided. This data structure is shown in Figure 1.3. Notice that it contains two columns: left and right. The two components store indexes to reference the left and right positions of a subarray. Each time the array of data is subdivided, the new left and right positions are pushed on this stack structure. Keep in mind that an array is sorted by dividing it into smaller and smaller subarrays. After one of the inner subarrays is sorted, we need to return to an outer subarray. Therefore, by storing the positions of each subarray in the stack structure we can easily retrieve the positions of each subarray.

Radix Sort

The *radix* sorting method is useful for sorting numbers. In fact, it is especially well suited for sorting binary numbers. It can also be used with non-numeric data, such as strings, if the data is first converted to a numeric representation.

The radix sort is different than the other sorting methods presented because it processes data by breaking it up into its parts and then sorts the

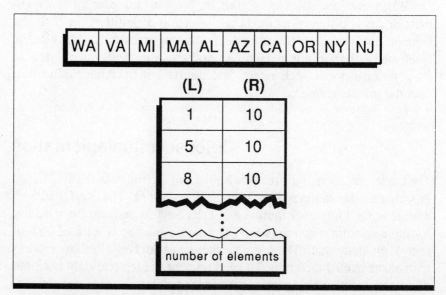

Figure 1.3. Data structure used to implement the quicksort

data by comparing the parts instead of the whole data element. For instance, to sort the following elements using standard sorting techniques:

Saul   Mary   John

we would compare each complete string to determine the proper sorting order. If, on the other hand, we wanted to sort the following numbers with the radix method:

100   500   201   309

we would break each number into its three-digit sequence and compare each digit separately. That is, we would compare the 1 in 100 with the 5 in 500, the 5 with the 2 in 201, and so on.

Let's examine an example to see how the radix method works to sort a set of numbers. Consider this list of three-digit numbers:

132   213   321   231   111   232   112   221   123

The first step is to create bins for the least significant digits for each number. Normally there are 10 bins; however, we'll only need 3 because none of the numbers contain a digit larger than 3. The numbers are arranged in bins of 1s, 2s, and 3s, as follows:

1s ⟶   321   231   111   221
2s ⟶   132   232   112
3s ⟶   213   123

This arrangement brings some initial order to the set of numbers. The next step is to repeat the previous operation using the next significant digit (that is, 10s). The bins of 10s, 20s, and 30s are

10s ⟶   111   112   213
20s ⟶   321   221   123
30s ⟶   231   132   232

Notice that in creating the new bin lists, the elements from the previous ones were selected according to their position in the lists. Next, the process of bin arrangement goes one step further to arrange the most significant digits, the hundreds. The new bin lists created are

```
100s ──→ 111   112   123   132
200s ──→ 213   221   231   232
300s ──→ 321
```

By joining the latter bin lists, we obtain the following sorted list of numbers:

111   112   123   132   213   221   231   232   321

Radix Sort Implementation

Because the radix sort algorithm is designed to work with arrays, we'll only include implementations for the procedural languages (Turbo BASIC, C, and Pascal). Of course, this algorithm could be implemented in Turbo Prolog with lists; however, it would not be very efficient.

In each implementation shown in Listings 1.1, 1.2, and 1.3, three array structures are used to perform the sort. The first array, **bin_matrix**, is a two-dimensional array that represents the bins needed to sort digits. The **bin_count** array keeps track of the frequency of each digit in a sort. **Numbers** is the structure used to hold the numbers as they are being sorted.

The best way to see how these arrays are used is to explore an example. Figure 1.4 shows how a list is sorted. The original list is stored in the **Numbers** array. Because this illustration represents the first pass of the sort,

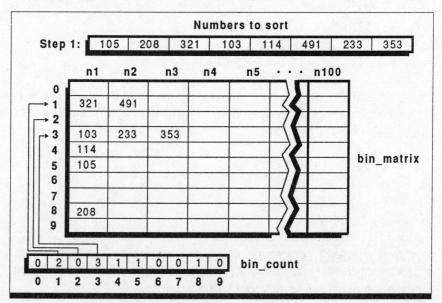

Figure 1.4. Radix sort example: Step 1

all of the numbers are arranged in the **bin_matrix** according to the 1s digit. The **bin_count** array keeps track of the number of entries stored in each bin in the matrix. For example, two numbers, 321 and 491, are listed in the 1s digit bin in the matrix; therefore the value 2 is stored in **bin_count[1]**.

Keep in mind that Figure 1.4 only shows the first pass of the radix algorithm. Once we have stored this information in the arrays, we can continue to sort the numbers using the 10s digit. But before we sort with the 10s digit, we need to transfer the numbers stored in the **bin_matrix** array into the **Numbers** array. This operation is performed with the following loop:

```
FOR j := 0 TO 9 DO
    IF bin_Count[j] > 0 THEN
        FOR k := 1 TO bin_Count[j] DO BEGIN
                INC(i);
                { copy from bin to numeric array }
                Numbers[i] := bins[j,k]
        END;
```

Here the **bin_count** array directs the exchange. After this loop executes, the **Numbers** array is modified as shown in Figure 1.5. This figure also shows how the numbers are next sorted in the **bin_matrix** array by the 10s digit. The numbers are then once again transferred to the **Numbers** array

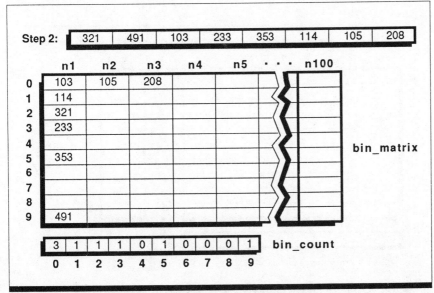

Figure 1.5. Radix sort example: Step 2

as shown in Figure 1.6. The **bin_matrix** in this figure shows how the numbers are then sorted by the 100s digit. Because the numbers only contain three digits, we are done sorting. The final step required is to transfer the numbers in the **bin_matrix** to the **Numbers** array. The result produced is the list:

103   105   114   208   233   321   353   491

Heap Sort

The last sorting method presented is the heap sort. It operates by treating a set of data as if it were stored as a "special" binary tree. This binary tree is characterized by the fact that its root is the smallest element. The left and right child nodes of the root are the second and third largest elements, respectively. An example of such a binary tree is shown in Figure 1.7.

To obtain a sorted list, the *heap tree* is visited width-first from the left nodes to the right nodes. To perform the sort, a list is used to represent the tree. This list has the following properties:

1. The root is the first element of the list.
2. The root must be less than its left and right child.

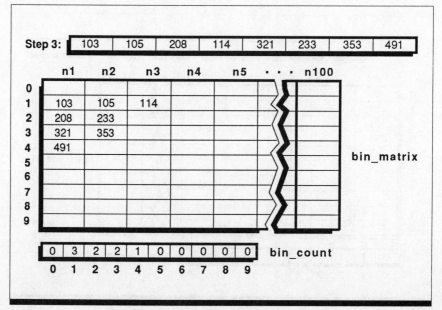

Figure 1.6. Radix sort example: Step 3

3. The left child of a node N is located in element 2*N.
4. The right child of a node N is located in element 2*N+1.
5. The parent of node N is located in element N / 2.

To see how the heap sort method works, consider the following list of state abbreviations:

MA   AZ   WA   AL   OR   CA   PA   DE   MI   HI

This list is equivalent to the heap tree shown in Figure 1.8. Notice that this tree structure violates the rules of a sorted tree. That is, the root node MA is not the first sorted element of the list. The first major change consists of rearranging the list in the form shown in Figure 1.9. Notice that the last element in the original list of states becomes the root of the heap tree. This new tree representation is equivalent to the following list:

WA   OR   PA   MI   HI   CA   MA   DE   AL   AZ

In the next steps, the initial heap, created in Figure 1.9, is gradually adjusted to put its elements in ascending order. The trick, in every step, is to move the root (currently the first array element) to the highest unordered heap node (also the last unordered array element). Then the tree is readjusted

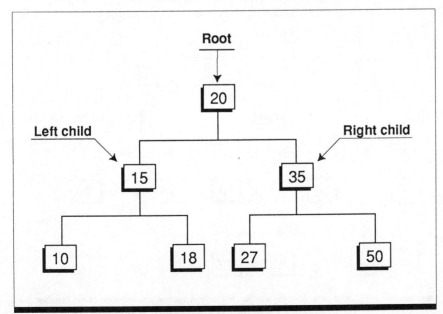

Figure 1.7. Binary tree used for the heap sort

to move the next highest element to the new root. The effect of this operation is to sort the list from the tail end as we work our way to the front. The first time the steps are applied to the heap, the root, WA, is swapped with the node AZ. After adjusting the nodes, the heap looks like the tree shown

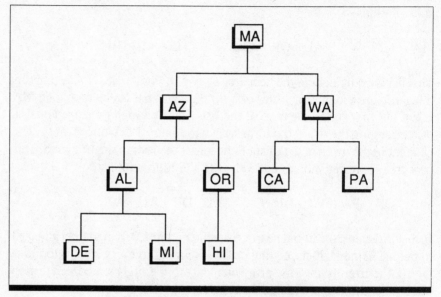

Figure 1.8. Heap tree for unordered list

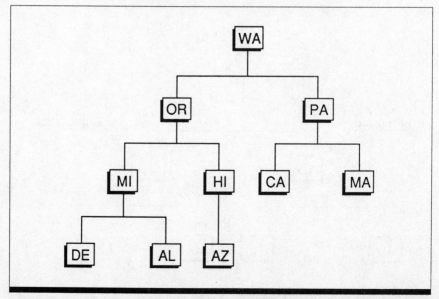

Figure 1.9. Sorting the heap tree: Step 1

in Figure 1.10. Notice that the sorted nodes of the heap are enclosed in braces.

In the second pass, the new root, OR, is swapped with the node AL, and the heap is readjusted, yielding a new root as shown in Figure 1.11.

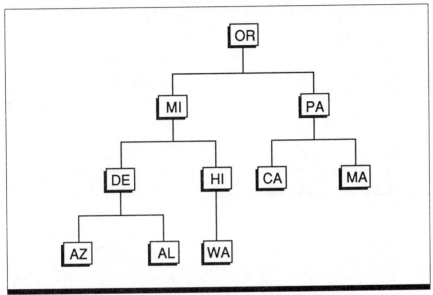

Figure 1.10. Sorting the heap tree: Step 2

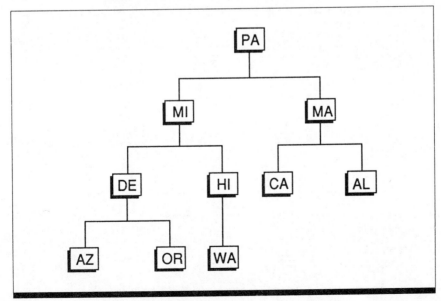

Figure 1.11. Sorting the heap tree: Step 3

The very first step in each heap sort iteration parallels the array representation shown in Figure 1.12.

Once a new root is established, the heap is readjusted to ensure that the next largest array member is at the head of the array. In the third pass, the new root, PA, is swapped with the node AZ, and the heap is readjusted to yield a new root, as shown in Figure 1.13. The above steps are repeated

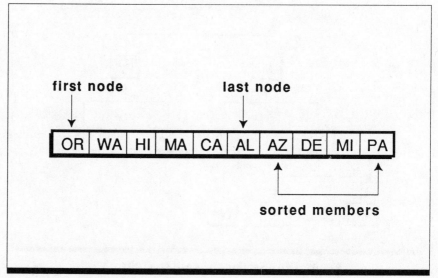

Figure 1.12. Heap compared to an array structure

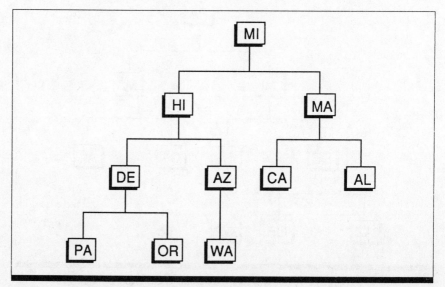

Figure 1.13. Changing the root of the heap tree

until the heap is completely sorted. The sorted heap is shown in Figure 1.14. You should now be able to see that this heap structure is simply a representation of the following sorted array:

AL, AZ, CA, DE, HI, MA, MI, PA, OR, WA

Selecting a Sorting Method

Each sorting method presented so far is designed for a different sorting problem.The quicksort works well for most applications because of its flexibility and speed. The insertion sort method is a good choice when you are working with data that is already partially sorted. You can easily adapt this sorting method by implementing a routine that enables you to insert data into a sorted list.

If you are sorting a small data set, the shellsort is recommended because of its simplicity. It does not require the additional overhead for recursion, as does the quicksort, so the shellsort is ideal for applications where memory space is limited. If you're working with numeric data, consider using the radix method.

The last sorting method covered, the heap sort, should be considered if you need to sort large data sets that are greatly out of order. This algorithm always takes the same amount of steps to sort a set of data even if the "worst-case" condition occurs.

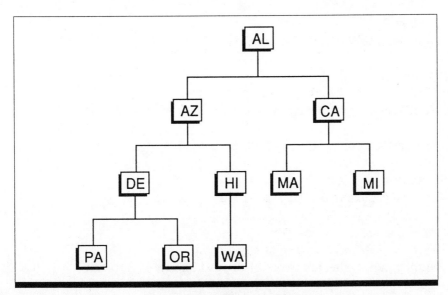

Figure 1.14. The sorted heap

The Sorting Implementations

Listings 1.1 through 1.4 present implementations of the five sorting methods discussed in this section. All of the routines presented work with strings except the radix sort routines, which sort numbers.

Turbo BASIC

The Turbo BASIC sort routines require the **OPTION BASE 1** statement. The routines determine the size of the sorted array using the built-in **UBOUND** function. If the supplied number of elements exceeds the actual array size, the sort count is reset to the array size.

InsertSort

Performs the insertion sort on an array of strings.

Syntax:
```
SUB InsertSort(A$(1), NumData%)
```

Parameters:
A$()   the array of strings to sort.
NumData%   the number of elements in array **A$()** to sort.

ShellSort

Performs the Shell-Metzner sort on an array of strings.

Syntax:
```
SUB ShellSort(A$(1), NumData%)
```

Parameters:
A$()   the array of strings to sort.
NumData%   the number of elements in array **A$()** to sort.

RecQuickSort

Performs a recursive quicksort on an array of strings.

Syntax:
```
SUB RecQuickSort(A$(1), NumData%) STATIC
```

Parameters:
A$()   the array of strings to sort.
NumData%   the number of elements in array **A$()** to sort.

Performs a nonrecursive quicksort on an array of strings. **QuickSort**

Syntax:
```
SUB QuickSort(A$(1), NumData%)
```

Parameters:
A$()   the array of strings to sort.
NumData%   the number of elements in array **A$()** to sort.

Performs a heap sort on an array of strings. **HeapSort**

Syntax:
```
SUB HeapSort(A$(1), NumData%)
```

Parameters:
A$()   the array of strings to sort.
NumData%   the number of elements in array **A$()** to sort.

Performs a radix sort on a set of integers. **IntRadixSort**

Syntax:
```
SUB IntRadixSort(Numbers%(1), NumData%, Digits%)
```

Parameters:
Numbers%()   an array of positive integers to sort.
NumData%   the number of elements in array **Numbers%()** to sort.
Digits%   the number of digits used for sorting. This must vary
                 between 1 and 5.

Turbo C

The Turbo C routines require the following declarations:

```
#include <string.h>
#define STRING 81
enum boolean { FALSE, TRUE };
```

The macro-based constant, **STRING**, defines the maximum size for sorted strings—80 characters long. For longer or shorter strings, you can adjust the value of **STRING** accordingly. The enumerated boolean type is declared for implementing boolean variables in Turbo C. The **string.h** file is required to prototype the **strcmp**() and **strcpy**() functions used extensively in the Turbo C sort functions. The Turbo C routines are covered next.

insertsort()

Performs the insertion sort on an array of strings.

Syntax:
```
void insertsort(char a[][STRING], unsigned numdata);
```

Parameters:
a[ ][ ]   the array of strings to sort.
numdata   the number of elements in array **a[ ][ ]** to sort.

shellsort()

Performs the Shell-Metzner sort on an array of strings.

Syntax:
```
void shellsort(char a[][STRING], unsigned numdata);
```

Parameters:
a[ ][ ]   the array of strings to sort.
numdata   the number of elements in array **a[ ][ ]** to sort.

recquicksort()

Performs a recursive quicksort on an array of strings.

Syntax:
```
void recquicksort(char a[][STRING], unsigned numdata);
```

Parameters:
a[ ][ ]   the array of strings to sort.
numdata   the number of elements in array **a[ ][ ]** to sort.

quicksort()

Performs a nonrecursive quicksort on an array of strings.

Syntax:
```
void quicksort(char a[][STRING], unsigned numdata);
```

Parameters:
a[ ][ ]   the array of strings to sort.
numdata   the number of elements in array **a[ ][ ]** to sort.

Performs a heap sort on an array of strings.   **heapsort()**

Syntax:
```
void heapsort(char a[][STRING], unsigned numdata);
```

Parameters:
a[ ][ ]   the array of strings to sort.
numdata   the number of elements in array **a[ ][ ]** to sort.

Performs a radix sort on a set of integers.   **intradixsort()**

Syntax:
```
void intradixsort(unsigned numbers[], unsigned numdata,
                  unsigned digits);
```

Parameters:
numbers[ ] an array of unsigned integers to sort.
numdata   the number of elements in array **numbers[ ]** to sort.
digits   the number of digits used for sorting. This should vary
                between 1 and 5.

Turbo Pascal

The Turbo Pascal routines are packaged in the **SORT** unit library. The following constant and data types are declared and exported by the library unit:

```
CONST MAX_SORT_ARRAY_SIZE = 100;
TYPE  SortType    = STRING[80];
      SortRange   = 1..MAX_SORT_ARRAY_SIZE;
      SortArray   = ARRAY[SortRange] OF SortType;
      RadixDigits = 1..5;
      RadixArray  = ARRAY[SortRange] OF WORD;
```

The library unit is used to ensure that the above constant and data types are always available to the programs that use the sorting routines. The size of the sorted array can be adjusted by changing the **MAX_SORT_ARRAY_SIZE** constant. In addition, the **SortType** can be altered to handle other data types or strings of different maximum lengths. The Pascal sort routines are covered next.

InsertSort   Performs the insertion sort on an array of strings.

Syntax:

```
PROCEDURE InsertSort(VAR A : SortArray; NumData : WORD);
```

Parameters:

A   the array of strings to sort.
NumData   the number of elements in array **A$**() to sort.

ShellSort   Performs the Shell-Metzner sort on an array of strings.

Syntax:

```
PROCEDURE ShellSort(VAR A : SortArray; NumData : WORD);
```

Parameters:

A   the array of strings to sort.
NumData   the number of elements in array **A$**() to sort.

RecQuickSort   Performs a recursive quicksort on an array of strings.

Syntax:

```
PROCEDURE RecQuickSort(VAR A : SortArray;  NumData : WORD);
```

Parameters:

A   the array of strings to sort.
NumData   the number of elements in array **A$**() to sort.

QuickSort   Performs a nonrecursive quicksort.

Syntax:

```
PROCEDURE QuickSort(VAR A : SortArray; NumData : WORD);
```

Parameters:

A   the array of strings to sort.
NumData   the number of elements in array **A$**() to sort.

HeapSort   Performs a heap sort on an array of strings.

Syntax:

```
PROCEDURE HeapSort(VAR A : SortArray; NumData : WORD);
```

Parameters:

A   the array of strings to sort.

NumData   the number of elements in array **A$()** to sort.

Performs a radix sort on a set of integers.   **IntRadixSort**

Syntax:
```
PROCEDURE  IntRadixSort (VAR Numbers  :  RadixArray;
                             NumData   :  WORD;
                             Digits    :  RadixDigits);
```

Parameters:

Numbers   an array of unsigned integers to sort.

NumData   the number of elements in array **Numbers** to sort.

Digits   the number of digits used for sorting. This should vary
              between 1 and 5.

Turbo Prolog

The Turbo Prolog code shown in Listing 1.4 includes versions of the insertion sort, bubblesort, and quicksort algorithms. We've omitted the radix and heap sort implementations, because these algorithms work more efficiently with languages that support random access data structures such as arrays. We've used the following domain declaration to allow all of the sorting routines to work with lists of symbols:

```
domains
    symlist = symbol*
```

You can add other domain definitions to support other data types such as strings or numbers.

The complete set of Turbo Prolog sorting predicates is covered next.

                                                                              insertsort

Performs insertion sort on a list of symbols.

Syntax:
```
insertsort (List, SortedList)     (i,o)
          (symlist, symlist)
```

Parameters:

List   the number of elements in the list to sort.

SortedList   the returned sorted list.

bubblesort   Performs a recursive bubble sort on a list of symbols.

Syntax:

```
bubblesort(List, SortedList)      (i,o)
          (symlist, symlist)
```

Parameters:

List   the number of elements in the list to sort.

SortedList   the returned sorted list.

quicksort   Performs a recursive quicksort on a list of symbols.

Syntax:

```
quicksort(List, SortedList)       (i,o)
          (symlist, symlist)
```

Parameters:

List   the number of elements in the list being sorted.

SortedList   the returned sorted list.

• Listing 1.1. Turbo BASIC sorting routines

```
OPTION BASE 1

SUB InsertSort(A$(1), NumData%)
' perform an insertion sort on the array A$(1)..A$(NumData%)
LOCAL tempo$, i%, j%, k%, nomatch$
IF NumData% = 0 THEN
    EXIT SUB
ELSEIF NumData% > UBound(A$(1)) THEN
    NumData% = UBound(A$(1))
END IF
i% = 2 ' start with the second array element
DO WHILE (i% <= NumData%)
' start with the first element of the current sorted subarray
    j% = 1
```

```
        nomatch$ = "TRUE"
        DO WHILE (j% < i%) AND (nomatch$ = "TRUE")
            IF A$(j%) >= A$(i%) THEN
                nomatch$ = "FALSE"
                tempo$ = A$(i%)
                FOR k% = i%-1 TO j% STEP -1
                    A$(k%+1) = A$(k%)
                NEXT k%
                A$(j%) = tempo$
            ELSE
                INCR j%
            END IF
        LOOP
        INCR i%
LOOP
END SUB ' InsertSort


SUB ShellSort(A$(1), NumData%)
' perform a shellsort on the array A$(1)..A$(NumData%)
LOCAL i%, j%, skip%, inorder$
IF NumData% = 0 THEN
    EXIT SUB
ELSEIF NumData% > UBound(A$(1)) THEN
    NumData% = UBound(A$(1))
END IF
skip% = NumData%
DO WHILE skip% > 1
    skip% = skip% \ 2
    DO
        inorder$ = "TRUE"
        FOR j% = 1 TO NumData% - skip%
            i% = j% + skip%
            IF A$(i%) < A$(j%) THEN
                ' swap members
                SWAP A$(i%),A$(j%)
                inorder$ = "FALSE"
            END IF
        NEXT j%
    LOOP UNTIL inorder$ = "TRUE"
LOOP
END SUB ' ShellSort
```

```
SUB Sort(A$(1), Left%, Right%)
' "local" recursive subroutine called by RecQuickSort
LOCAL i%, j%, median%, data1$
i% = Left%
j% = Right%
median% = INT((Left% + Right%) / 2)
data1$ = A$(median%)
DO
   DO WHILE A$(i%) < data1$
      INCR i%
   LOOP
   DO WHILE data1$ < A$(j%)
      DECR j%
   LOOP
   IF i% <= j% THEN
      SWAP A$(i%),A$(j%)
      INCR i%
      DECR j%
    END IF
LOOP UNTIL i% > j%
IF Left% < j%   THEN CALL Sort(A$(),Left%,j%)
IF i% < Right% THEN CALL Sort(A$(),i%,Right%)
END SUB ' Sort


SUB RecQuickSort(A$(1), NumData%) STATIC
' subroutine used to perform a recursive quickSort
IF NumData% = 0 THEN
   EXIT SUB
ELSEIF NumData% > UBound(A$(1)) THEN
   NumData% = UBound(A$(1))
END IF
CALL Sort(A$(),1,NumData%)
END SUB ' RecQuickSort


SUB QuickSort(A$(1),  NumData%) STATIC
' Procedure to perform a nonrecursive quickSort
STATIC left%, right%, i%, j%, median$, stack.height%
DIM lstack%(50), rstack%(50)
IF NumData% = 0 THEN
   ERASE lstack%, rstack%
   EXIT SUB
```

```
ELSEIF NumData% > UBound(A$(1)) THEN
    NumData% = UBound(A$(1))
END IF
stack.height% = 1 : lstack%(1) = 1 : rstack%(1) = NumData%
DO
    left% = lstack%(stack.height%)
    right% = rstack%(stack.height%)
    stack.height% = stack.height% - 1
    DO
        i% = left% : j% = right%
        median$ = A$((left% + right%) \ 2)
        DO
            WHILE A$(i%) < median$
                INCR i%
            WEND
            WHILE median$ < A$(j%)
                DECR j%
            WEND
            IF i% <= j% THEN
                SWAP A$(i%), A$(j%)
                INCR i%
                DECR j%
            END IF
        LOOP WHILE i% <= j%
        IF i% < right% THEN
            stack.height% = stack.height% + 1
            lstack%(stack.height%) = i%
            rstack%(stack.height%) = right%
        END IF
        right% = j%
    LOOP WHILE left% < right%
LOOP WHILE stack.height% <> 0
ERASE lstack%, rstack%
END SUB ' QuickSort

SUB Sift(A$(1), Root%, Nodes%)
' "local" routine that adjusts the array A$(), treated as a heap
LOCAL j%, pivot$, resume.loop$
resume.loop$ = "TRUE"
pivot$ = A$(Root%)
j% = 2 * Root%
```

```
DO WHILE (j% <= Nodes%) AND (resume.loop$ = "TRUE")
    IF j% < Nodes% THEN
        IF A$(j%) < A$(j%+1) THEN INCR j%
    END IF
    IF pivot$ < A$(j%) THEN
        A$(j% \ 2) = A$(j%)
        j% = 2 * j%
    ELSE
        resume.loop$ = "FALSE"
    END IF
LOOP
A$(j% \ 2) = pivot$
END SUB ' Sift


SUB HeapSort(A$(1), NumData%)
' perform a heap sort on the array A$(1)..A$(NumData%)
LOCAL i%, j%
IF NumData% = 0 THEN
    EXIT SUB
ELSEIF NumData% > UBound(A$(1)) THEN
    NumData% = UBound(A$(1))
END IF
FOR i% = (NumData% \ 2) TO 1 STEP -1 ' convert array into heap
    CALL Sift(A$(),i%,NumData%)
NEXT i%
FOR i% = (NumData% - 1) TO 1 STEP -1
    ' swap members i% and i%+1
    SWAP A$(i%+1),A$(1)
    CALL Sift(A$(),1,i%) ' regenerate the heap
NEXT i%
END SUB ' HeapSort


SUB IntRadixSort(Numbers%(1), NumData%, Digits%)
' perform a radix sort on the numeric array Numbers%(1)..Numbers%(NumData%)
LOCAL exponent%, i%, j%, k%, numeral%
DIM bin.Count%(0 : 9), bins%(0 : 9,1 : UBound(Numbers%(1)))
IF NumData% = 0 THEN
    ERASE bin.Count%, bins%
    EXIT SUB
ELSEIF NumData% > UBound(Numbers%(1)) THEN
```

```
      NumData% = UBound(Numbers%(1))
END IF
exponent% = 1
FOR numeral% = 1 TO Digits%
    IF numeral% > 1 THEN exponent% = 10 * exponent%
    FOR i% = 0 TO 9
        bin.Count%(i%) = 0 ' reset the bin counters
    NEXT i%
    FOR i% = 1 TO NumData%
        k% = Numbers%(i%)
        j% = (k% \ exponent%) MOD 10 ' j% is in 0..9
        INCR bin.Count%(j%)
        bins%(j%, bin.Count%(j%)) = k% ' store number in the bin
    NEXT i%
    ' reorder integers in original array
    i% = 0
    FOR j% = 0 TO 9
        IF bin.Count%(j%) > 0 THEN
            FOR k% = 1 TO bin.Count%(j%)
                INCR i%
                ' copy from bin to numeric array
                Numbers%(i%) = bins%(j%,k%)
            NEXT k%
        END IF
    NEXT j%
NEXT numeral%
ERASE bin.Count%, bins%
END SUB ' IntRadixSort
```

• Listing 1.2. Turbo C sorting routines

```c
#include <string.h>
#include <stdlib.h>

#define STRING 81
enum boolean { FALSE, TRUE };

void insertsort(char a[][STRING], unsigned numdata)
/* perform an insertion sort on the array a[0]..a[numdata-1] */
```

```
{
    char tempo[STRING];
    unsigned i, j, k;
    enum boolean nomatch;

    if (numdata == 0) return;
    i = 1; /* start with the second array element */
    while (i < numdata)   {
    /* start with the first element of the sorted subarray */
        j = 0;
        nomatch = TRUE;
        while (j < i && nomatch == TRUE)   {
            if (strcmp(a[i],a[j]) <= 0)   {
                nomatch = FALSE;
                strcpy(tempo,a[i]);
                for (k = i; k > j; k--)
                    strcpy(a[k],a[k-1]);
                strcpy(a[j],tempo);
            }
            else if (strcmp(a[i],a[j]) > 0)
            j++;
        } /* while  (j < i && nomatch == TRUE) */
        i++;
    } /* while i <= numdata   */
}

void shellsort(char a[][STRING], unsigned numdata)
/* perform a shellsort on the array a[0]..a[numdata-1] */
{
    char tempo[STRING];
    unsigned i, j, skip;
    enum boolean inorder;

    if (numdata == 0) return;
    skip = numdata;
    while (skip > 1)   {
        skip /=  2;
        do {
            inorder = TRUE;
            for (j = 0 ; j <= (numdata - 1 - skip); j++)   {
```

```
              i = j + skip;
              if (strcmp(a[i],a[j]) < 0)   {
                  /* swap members */
                  strcpy(tempo,a[i]);
                  strcpy(a[i],a[j]);
                  strcpy(a[j],tempo);
                  inorder = FALSE;
              } /* if */
          } /* for */
      } while (inorder == FALSE);
  } /* while skip > 1 */
}


void sort(char a[][STRING], unsigned left, unsigned right)
/* "local" recursive subroutine called by recquicksort */
{
    unsigned i, j, median;
    char data1[STRING], tempo[STRING];

    i = left;
    j = right;
    median = (left + right) / 2;
    strcpy(data1,a[median]);
    do {
        while (strcmp(a[i],data1) < 0) i++;
        while (strcmp(data1,a[j]) < 0) j--;
        if (i <= j) {
            strcpy(tempo,a[i]);
            strcpy(a[i],a[j]);
            strcpy(a[j],tempo);
            i++;
            j--;
        }
    } while (i <= j);
    if (left < j)   sort(a,left,j);
    if (i < right) sort(a,i,right);
}


void recquicksort(char a[][STRING], unsigned numdata)
/* procedure to perform a recursive quicksort */
```

```
{
    if (numdata == 0) return;
    sort(a,0,numdata-1);
}

void quicksort(char a[][STRING], unsigned numdata)
/* perform a nonrecursive quicksort on the array a[0]..a[numdata-1] */

{
    struct indexrec {
        unsigned left;
        unsigned right;
    };

    unsigned i, j, lt, rt, stack_height;
    char median[STRING], tempo[STRING];
    struct indexrec *stack;

    if (numdata == 0) return;
    /* adjust size to match the run-time size of array */
    stack = (struct indexrec*) malloc(numdata * sizeof(struct indexrec));
    /* initialize stack */
    stack_height = 1;
    stack->left = 0;
    stack->right = numdata-1;
    do {
        lt = (stack+stack_height-1)->left;
        rt = (stack+stack_height-1)->right;
        stack_height--;
        do {
            i = lt;
            j = rt;
            strcpy(median,a[(lt + rt) / 2]);
            do {
                while (strcmp(a[i],median) < 0)   i++;
                while (strcmp(median,a[j]) < 0)   j--;
                if (i <= j)  {
                    strcpy(tempo,a[i]);
                    strcpy(a[i],a[j]);
                    strcpy(a[j],tempo);
```

```
                    i++;
                    j--;
                } /* if */
            } while (i <= j);
            if (i < rt)   {
                stack_height++;
                (stack+stack_height-1)->left = i;
                (stack+stack_height-1)->right = rt;
            } /* if */
            rt = j;
        } while (lt < rt);
    } while (stack_height != 0);
    free(stack); /* free dynamic data */
}


void sift(char a[][STRING], unsigned root, unsigned nodes)
/* routine that adjusts the array a[], treated as a heap */
{
    unsigned j;
    char pivot[STRING];
    enum boolean resume_loop;

    resume_loop = TRUE;
    strcpy(pivot,a[root]);
    j = 2 * root;
    while (j <= nodes && resume_loop == TRUE)   {
        if (j < nodes) {
            if (strcmp(a[j],a[j+1]) < 0)   j++;
        }
        if (strcmp(pivot,a[j]) < 0)   {
            strcpy(a[j / 2],a[j]);
            j *= 2;
        }
        else
            resume_loop = FALSE;
    }
    strcpy(a[j / 2], pivot);
}


void heapsort(char a[][STRING], unsigned numdata)
/* performs a heap sort on the array a[0]..a[numdata-1] */
```

```
{
    int i;
    char tempo[STRING];

    if (numdata == 0) return;
    for (i = (numdata/2)-1 ; i >= 0; i--)   /* convert array into heap */
        sift(a,i,numdata-1);
    for (i = (numdata - 2); i >= 0; i--)   {
        /* swap members i && i+1 */
        strcpy(tempo,a[i+1]);
        strcpy(a[i+1],a[0]);
        strcpy(a[0],tempo);
        sift(a,0,i); /* regenerate the heap */
    }
}

void intradixsort(unsigned numbers[], int numdata, unsigned digits)
/* performs a radix sort on the numeric array
   numbers[0]..numbers[numdata-1] */
{
    unsigned exponent, j, k, numeral;
    int i;
    unsigned bin_count[10];
    unsigned *bins[100];

    if (numdata == 0) return;
    if (numdata > 100) return;
    /* create bin matrix using the bins pointers */
    for (i = 0; i < numdata; i++)
        bins[i] = (unsigned *) malloc(numdata * sizeof(unsigned));
    exponent = 1;
    for (numeral = 1; numeral <= digits; numeral++)   {
        if (numeral > 1)   exponent *= 10;
        for (i = 0; i <= 9; i++)
            bin_count[i] = 0; /* reset the bin counters */
        for (i = 0; i < numdata; i++)   {
            k = numbers[i];
            j = (k / exponent) % 10; /* j is in 0..9 */
            bin_count[j]++;
            *(*(bins+j)+bin_count[j]) = k; /* store number in the bin */
```

```
    } /* for i */
    /* reorder integers in original array */
    i = 0;
    for (j = 0; j <= 9; j++)
        if (bin_count[j] > 0)
        for (k = 1; k <= bin_count[j]; k++, i++)
            /* copy from bin to numeric array */
            numbers[i] = bins[j][k];
    } /* for numeral */
    for (i = 0; i < numdata; i++)
        free(bins[i]);
}
```

• Listing 1.3. Turbo Pascal sorting routines

```pascal
UNIT SORT;
CONST MAX_SORT_ARRAY_SIZE = 15;
TYPE SortType = STRING[80];
    SortRange = 1..MAX_SORT_ARRAY_SIZE;
    SortArray = ARRAY [SortRange] OF SortType;
    RadixDigits = 1..5;
    RadixArray = ARRAY[SortRange] OF WORD;

PROCEDURE InsertSort(VAR A      : SortArray; { in/out }
                        NumData : WORD        { input });
{ performs an insertion sort on the array A[1]..A[NumData] }

PROCEDURE ShellSort(VAR A      : SortArray; { in/out }
                       NumData : WORD        { input });
{ performs a shellsort on the array A[1]..A[NumData] }

PROCEDURE RecQuickSort(VAR A      : SortArray; { in/out }
                          NumData : WORD        { input });
{ performs a recursive quicksort on the array A[1]..A[NumData] }

PROCEDURE QuickSort(VAR A      : SortArray; { in/out }
                       NumData : WORD        { input });
{ performs a nonrecursive quicksort on the array A[1]..A[NumData] }
```

```
PROCEDURE  HeapSort(VAR A        : SortArray;  { in/out }
                        NumData : WORD          { input });
{ performs a heap sort on the array A[1]..A[NumData] }

PROCEDURE  IntRadixSort(VAR Numbers  : RadixArray;     { in/out }
                            NumData  : WORD;           { input }
                            Digits   : RadixDigits     { input });
{ performs a radix sort on the numeric array A[1]..A[NumData] }

{***********************************************************************}
PROCEDURE  InsertSort(VAR A        : SortArray;  { in/out }
                         NumData : WORD          { input });
{ performs an insertion sort on the array A[1]..A[NumData] }

VAR tempo : SortType;
    i, j, k : WORD;
    nomatch : BOOLEAN;

BEGIN
   IF NumData = 0 THEN EXIT
   ELSE IF NumData > MAX_SORT_ARRAY_SIZE THEN
      NumData := MAX_SORT_ARRAY_SIZE;
   i := 2; { start with the second array element }
   WHILE (i <= NumData) DO BEGIN
      { start with the first element of the current sorted subarray }
      j := 1;
      nomatch := TRUE;
      WHILE (j < i) AND nomatch DO BEGIN
         IF A[i] <= A[j] THEN BEGIN
            nomatch := FALSE;
            tempo := A[i];
            FOR k := i-1 DOWNTO j DO
               A[k+1] := A[k];
            A[j] := tempo
         END
         ELSE IF A[i] > A[j] THEN
               INC(j)
      END; { WHILE  (j < i) AND nomatch }
      INC(i);
   END; { WHILE i <= NumData  }
END; { InsertSort }
```

```
PROCEDURE ShellSort(VAR A         : SortArray;  { in/out }
                        NumData : WORD         { input });
{ performs a shellsort on the array A[1]..A[NumData] }


VAR tempo : SortType;
    i, j, skip   : WORD;
    inorder : BOOLEAN;


BEGIN
    IF NumData = 0 THEN EXIT
    ELSE IF NumData > MAX_SORT_ARRAY_SIZE THEN
        NumData := MAX_SORT_ARRAY_SIZE;
    skip := NumData;
    WHILE skip > 1 DO BEGIN
        skip := skip DIV 2;
        REPEAT
            inorder := TRUE;
            FOR j := 1 TO NumData - skip DO BEGIN
                i := j + skip;
                IF A[i] < A[j] THEN BEGIN
                    { swap members }
                    tempo := A[i];
                    A[i] := A[j];
                    A[j] := tempo;
                    inorder := FALSE
                END; { IF }
            END; { FOR }
        UNTIL inorder;
    END; { WHILE skip > 1 }
END; { ShellSort }


PROCEDURE RecQuickSort(VAR A        : SortArray;  { in/out }
                        NumData  : WORD         { input });
{ performs a recursive quicksort on the array A[1]..A[NumData] }


VAR k : WORD;
    median, tempo : SortType;


PROCEDURE Sort(Left,              { input  }
               Right : WORD       { input  });
{ local recursive routine that is the heart of the quicksort routine }
```

```
VAR tempo, median : SortType;
    i, j   : WORD;

BEGIN
    i := Left;
    j := Right;
    median := A[(Left + Right) div 2];
    REPEAT
       WHILE A[i] < median DO INC(i);
       WHILE median < A[j] DO DEC(j);
       IF i <= j THEN BEGIN
          tempo := A[i];
          A[i] := A[j];
          A[j] := tempo;
          INC(i);
          DEC(j);
       END; { IF }
    UNTIL  i > j;
    IF Left < j THEN Sort(Left,j);
    IF i < Right THEN Sort(i,Right);
END; { Sort }


BEGIN
    IF NumData = 0 THEN EXIT
    ELSE IF NumData > MAX_SORT_ARRAY_SIZE THEN
       NumData := MAX_SORT_ARRAY_SIZE;
    Sort(1, NumData)
END; { RecQuickSort }


PROCEDURE QuickSort(VAR A        : SortArray;  { in/out }
                       NumData : WORD         { input });
{ performs a nonrecursive quicksort on the array A[1]..A[NumData] }

{$R-}
TYPE indexrec = RECORD
       left, right : WORD;
    END;
    loc_stack_array_type = ARRAY [1..1] OF indexrec;
    loc_stack_ptr = ^loc_stack_array_type;
```

```
VAR i, j, lt, rt, stack_height : WORD;
    median, tempo : SortType;
    stack : loc_stack_ptr;

BEGIN
    IF NumData = 0 THEN EXIT
    ELSE IF NumData > MAX_SORT_ARRAY_SIZE THEN
        NumData := MAX_SORT_ARRAY_SIZE;
    { adjust size to match the run-time size of array }
    GetMem(stack, NumData * Sizeof(indexrec) );
    { initialize stack }
    stack_height := 1;
    stack^[1].left := 1;
    stack^[1].right := NumData;
    REPEAT
        lt := stack^[stack_height].left;
        rt := stack^[stack_height].right;
        DEC(stack_height);
        REPEAT
            i := lt;
            j := rt;
            median := A[(lt + rt) div 2];
            REPEAT
                WHILE A[i] < median DO INC(i);
                WHILE median < A[j] DO DEC(j);
                IF i <= j THEN BEGIN
                  tempo := A[i];
                  A[i] := A[j];
                  A[j] := tempo;
                  INC(i);
                  DEC(j);
                END; { IF }
            UNTIL  i > j;
            IF i < rt THEN BEGIN
                INC(stack_height);
                stack^[stack_height].left := i;
                stack^[stack_height].right := rt
            END; { IF }
            rt := j;
```

```
        UNTIL lt >= rt;
    UNTIL stack_height = 0;
{$R+}
END; { QuickSort }


PROCEDURE Sift(VAR A      : SortArray;  { in/out }
                   Root,                { input  }
                   Nodes : WORD         { input });
{ adjusts the array A[], treated as a heap }


VAR j : WORD;
    pivot : SortType;
    resume : BOOLEAN;


BEGIN
    resume := TRUE;
    pivot := A[Root];
    j := 2 * Root;
    WHILE (j <= Nodes) AND resume DO BEGIN
        IF j < Nodes THEN
            IF A[j] < A[j+1] THEN INC(j);
        IF pivot < A[j] THEN BEGIN
            A[j div 2] := A[j];
            j := 2 * j;
        END
        ELSE resume := FALSE;
    END;
    A[j div 2] := pivot;
END; { Sift }


PROCEDURE HeapSort(VAR A       : SortArray;   { in/out }
                       NumData : WORD         { input });
{ performs a heap sort on the array A[1]..A[NumData] }


VAR i,j : WORD;
    tempo : SortType;


BEGIN
    IF NumData = 0 THEN EXIT
    ELSE IF NumData > MAX_SORT_ARRAY_SIZE THEN
```

```
        NumData := MAX_SORT_ARRAY_SIZE;
    FOR i := (NumData div 2) DOWNTO 1 DO { convert array into heap }
        Sift(A,i,NumData);
    FOR i := (NumData - 1) DOWNTO 1 DO BEGIN
        { swap members i and i+1 }
        tempo := A[i+1];
        A[i+1] := A[1];
        A[1] := tempo;
        Sift(A,1,i); { regenerate the heap }
    END;
END; { HeapSort }


PROCEDURE IntRadixSort(VAR Numbers : RadixArray;    { in/out }
                           NumData : WORD;          { input }
                           Digits  : RadixDigits    { input });
{ performs a radix sort on the numeric array A[1]..A[NumData] }


TYPE bin_matrix = ARRAY [0..9,1..MAX_SORT_ARRAY_SIZE] OF WORD;


VAR exponent, i, j, k, numeral : WORD;
    bin_Count : ARRAY [0..9] OF WORD;
    bins : bin_matrix;


BEGIN
    IF NumData = 0 THEN EXIT
    ELSE IF NumData > MAX_SORT_ARRAY_SIZE THEN
        NumData := MAX_SORT_ARRAY_SIZE;
    exponent := 1;
    FOR numeral := 1 TO Digits DO BEGIN
        IF numeral > 1 THEN exponent := 10 * exponent;
        FOR i := 0 TO 9 DO bin_Count[i] := 0; { reset the bin counters }
        FOR i := 1 TO NumData DO BEGIN
            k := Numbers[i];
            j := (k div exponent) MOD 10; { j is in 0..9 }
            INC(bin_Count[j]);
            bins[j, bin_Count[j]] := k; { store number in the bin }
        END; { FOR i }
        { reorder integers in original array }
        i := 0;
        FOR j := 0 TO 9 DO
```

```
        IF bin_Count[j] > 0 THEN
            FOR k := 1 TO bin_Count[j] DO BEGIN
                INC(i);
                { copy from bin to numeric array }
                Numbers[i] := bins[j,k]
            END; { IF }
    END; { FOR numeral }
END; { IntRadixSort }
END.
```

• Listing 1.4. Turbo Prolog sorting routines

```
% Turbo Prolog implementation of the insertion sort
%
% To take advantage of Turbo Prolog's recursive nature, we
% apply the insertion sort by stepping through the list until
% we get to the end; then we insert each element working
% from the end of the list to the beginning of the list.

domains
    symlist = symbol*

predicates
    insertsort(symlist, symlist)
    insert(symbol, symlist, symlist)

clauses
    insertsort([], []).                       % list is empty

    insertsort([H | Tail], Sortlst) :-        % use recursion to get to
        insertsort(Tail, Sortend),            % end of list
        insert(H, Sortend, Sortlst).          % insert each element

    insert(H, [E | Sortlst], [E | Lst2] ) :-  % check order of element
        H > E, !,
        insert(H, Sortlst, Lst2).

    insert(H, Sortlst, [H | Sortlst]).        % add element to head of list
```

```
% Turbo Prolog implementation of the bubblesort
%
% Because Turbo Prolog does not allow you to easily access a
% given element of a list without sequentially stepping
% through the list, algorithms such as the Shellsort are
% not very efficient. Instead, we have included a version
% of the bubblesort.

domains
    symlist = symbol*

predicates
    bubblesort(symlist, symlist)
    append(symlist, symlist, symlist)

clauses
    bubblesort(Lst, Sortlst) :-
        append(L1, [A,B | H2], Lst),
        B < A, !,
        append(L1, [B,A | H2], L2),
        bubblesort(L2, Sortlst).

    bubblesort(Lst, Lst).

    append([], L, L).
    append([H | Tail], L, [H | Tail2]) :- append(Tail, L, Tail2).

% Turbo Prolog implementation of the Quicksort
%
domains
    symlist = symbol*

predicates
    quicksort(symlist, symlist)
    split(symbol, symlist, symlist, symlist)
    append(symlist, symlist, symlist)

clauses
    quicksort([], []).                        % list is empty
```

```
quicksort([H | Tail], Sortlst) :-
    split(H, Tail, L1, L2),                 % split list
    quicksort(L1, Sortl1),                  % sort first sublist
    quicksort(L2, Sortl2),                  % sort second sublist
    append(Sortl1, [H | Sortl2], Sortlst).

split(_, [], [], []).

split(H, [E | Tail], [E | L1], L2) :-       % put element in right
    H > E, !,                               % sublist
    split(H, Tail, L1, L2).

split(H, [E | Tail], L1, [E | L2] ) :-      % put element in left
    split(H, Tail, L1, L2).                 % sublist

append( [], L, L).
append( [H | L1], L2, [H | L3] ) :-
    append(L1, L2, L3).
```

Searching Techniques

Introduction

In addition to sorting algorithms, efficient searching algorithms are critical to the performance of applications such as databases, spreadsheets, and operating systems. Our goal in this section is to present implementations of the major searching algorithms. The searching algorithms include methods for searching sorted and unsorted data sets. The following are the searching methods covered:

- Heuristic search
- Binary search
- Indexed search
- Hash-based search

These searching methods are representative of the fundamental searching algorithms. We'll implement these algorithms using the data structures supported by the Turbo languages including arrays and lists. Later sections present searching strategies that use more complex data structures such as linked lists and binary trees.

Searching Overview

If you've written an application such as a database, a text editor, or even a mailing list program, you're probably familiar with searching algorithms. *Searching* in this sense means the operation of locating a data element in a larger set of ordered or unordered data called a *data set*. If the data set being searched is small, the search can be simplified by checking each element in the data set until the correct element is located. This technique is called *sequential searching*. Unfortunately, the data set searched in most applications is usually too large for a simple sequential search. Therefore, we need to use other searching methods.

Before we present the searching algorithms, you should know some important terminology. The first terms are *keys* and *search key*. The keys are the data elements in a data set that are compared in a search with a target data element—the search key. In most applications, data is grouped into units called *records*. Each record contains a unique key that the searching algorithm uses to match with the search key.

In the implementations of our searching algorithms, simple arrays are used in Turbo BASIC, C, and Pascal. Because Turbo Prolog provides built-in searching features, we have omitted the implementation of the searching algorithms for this language.

Heuristic Search

Sequential searches are inefficient when used with unsorted data sets. Assuming that each key in the data set has the same probability of being searched, the average search typically must scan at least half of the unsorted data set. In many cases we can improve the efficiency of the search by rearranging the data set into a better order. However, if the data can't be reordered because it changes dynamically, we can apply a heuristic search to increase the searching efficiency.

A heuristic search applies *rules of thumb* to improve the efficiency of a search. With these rules, the search algorithm can quickly determine which elements of a data set should be ignored. The technology behind heuristic searches was developed in the 1960s by artificial intelligence researchers, who used rules of thumb to create mock-intelligent searching strategies for chess programs.

The rules applied by heuristic searches are usually based on intuitive or natural rules. To implement a heuristic search, we can employ a simple rule to enhance the standard sequential searching method. Our algorithm works by sequentially examining the keys in a data set until a match is found. If the search is successful and the matching key is not the first element in the data set, the matching key is exchanged with its previous neighbor. This forces the elements most frequently searched for to move toward the top of the data set. Assuming that some keys have greater demand than others, this method reduces the search time. The keys are dynamically sorted according to their recall-frequency. As the demand for a certain set of keys changes, the new keys are moved to the beginning of the data set. Unfortunately, during the transition period, the search efficiency drops.

Our algorithm should provide you with an idea of the type of searching methods that you can develop using rules of thumb. The technique that we used is well-suited for applications in which multiple searches are performed on the same key. You can modify the algorithm using other rules of thumb. For example, you could introduce a second storage area called a *hit list* where keys frequently searched for are placed. This hit list can then be searched before the main data set is checked. If the size of the hit list is kept small, and you are frequently searching for the same key, this enhancement can provide additional search efficiency.

Heuristic Search Implementation

The heuristic search is easy to implement in the Turbo languages. Because our algorithm is based on a variation of the sequential search method, we can perform the search with a simple **WHILE** loop that repeats until the element we are searching for is found or the end of the array is reached. This control structure, shown in Turbo Pascal, is

```
WHILE (i <= NumData) AND (ActualOccur < Occurrence) DO
BEGIN
   IF A[i] = Search_Str THEN
      INC(ActualOccur);
   INC(i);
END; { WHILE }
```

Note that two terminating conditions are checked: (**i <= NumData**) and (**ActualOccur < Occurrence**). The first condition becomes true when the end of the array is reached. The second condition tests to see if the correct number of matches have been found. The variable **Occurrence** is a parameter passed to the routine that specifies the number of matches to search for. Notice that every time a match is found, the variable **ActualOccur** is increased by one.

After the loop terminates, a decision is made to see if the element found should be moved to a new array position, as shown by the following code:

```
IF ActualOccur = Occurrence THEN
   IF i > 1 THEN BEGIN
      tempo := A[i];
      A[i] := A[i-1];
      A[i-1] := tempo;
      result := i-1
   END
```

Note that this code merely swaps the found element with its array neighbor.

Binary Search

With the heuristic search method, we can efficiently search for keys in unordered data sets. If the data set is in a sorted order, the binary search method provides a better alternative. To perform a binary search, the basic divide-and-conquer strategy introduced in Section 1 with the Quicksort method is applied.

The basic algorithm for the binary search that we'll implement works with data sets sorted in an ascending order. The steps required for the binary sort are:

1. Select the middle key of the data set and compare it with the search key.
2. If the search key matches the middle key, the search stops and the index (position) of the middle key is returned.
3. If the search key is greater than the middle key, the keys to the left of the middle key are searched. Repeat the process starting with step 1. If there are no keys after the middle key, the search halts and returns a zero value.
4. If the search key is less than the middle key, the keys to the right of the middle key are searched. Repeat the process starting with step 1. If there are no keys after the current key, the search halts and returns a zero value.

To see how the binary search method works, let's consider a practical example. Assume that we want to locate the search key Gloria in the following ordered data set:

Adam Harold Gloria Lori Mark Pete Ray Steve Zeus

First, we select the middle key, which is Mark. Because Gloria is less than Mark, we next take the keys to the left of Mark and search them as shown:

Adam Harold Gloria Lori

The middle key in this data set is Harold, and because Gloria is greater than Harold, we next consider the keys to the right of Harold:

Gloria Lori

We are only left with two keys, so we are able to locate our search key, Gloria.

Binary Search Implementation

The binary search can be coded with or without recursion. In the versions we've provided in Listings 2.1, 2.2, and 2.3, the search is performed with a **REPEAT-UNTIL** style loop as shown:

```
REPEAT
    median := (low + high) div 2;
    IF Search_Str < A[median] THEN
        high := median - 1
    ELSE
        low := median + 1;
UNTIL (Search_Str = A[median]) OR (low > high);
```

With each iteration of the loop, a new middle array index called **median** is determined by dividing the sum of the left and right array indexes (**low** and **high**) by 2. The simple **IF-ELSE** statement determines which half of the array should be examined next. Essentially, all this statement does is alter either the left or right index pointer. As the loop repeats, the gap between the left and right indexes of the array closes until the search key is located or the left index passes by the right index (**low > high**). When the loop terminates, the following statement determines the outcome of the search:

```
IF Search_Str = A[median] THEN result := median
ELSE result := 0;
```

Indexed Search

Binary search methods blindly start searching with the middle key in a data set. Whereas this may be adequate for many applications, other methods are available to increase the searching efficiency. The flexible indexed-based search method uses an additional table called the *index table* to speed up a search. The index table contains a subset of the data set elements. Each search begins with the table. Once a match is found in a table entry, the search resumes in the sorted data set itself. Using the information in the table, the searching routines can limit the scope of their search.

The indexed search table must be initialized by selecting entries from the ordered data set. The entries are selected as equidistant neighbors, regardless of the first few characters of each search key. This step must be performed whenever a data set has been modified and re-sorted.

To see how the indexed search works, let's consider an example. Assume that we want to search the following list for the search key Linda:

Alex Barry Eileen Hal Keith Linda Mark Rick Steve Thomas

The index table would store some of the keys in this list as shown in Figure 2.1. Notice that the index table has five entries. For the indexed search method to work effectively, the index table must be smaller than the list of data being searched. To find our search key, Linda, the index table is examined first. Each entry in the table is compared with the search key until an entry is found that is greater than or equal to the search key. In our example, the search stops with the key Mark. We then take the index value (7) stored with this key, along with the index value (5) stored with the preceding key (Keith) to search the original list of data for our search key. As you can see, the index table helps us narrow in on the region of the list where the search key is located.

Indexed Search Implementation

Because of the data structure and the extra code required to represent and process the index table, the implementation of the indexed search is more complex than any of the previously described searching methods. To support this search, we'll need two routines. These routines are listed in Table 2.1 for each of the Turbo languages.

Before a search can be started, the **Init_Index_Search** initialization routine must be called to set up the index table. This routine steps through

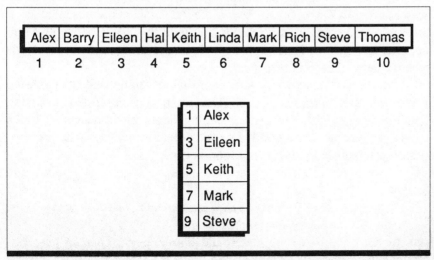

Figure 2.1. Example of the indexed search

Table 2.1. Routines used to support the indexed search

Routine	Language	Description
Init.Index.Search	BASIC	Initializes the index table
Index.Search	BASIC	Performs the index search
init_index_search()	C	Initializes the index table
index_search()	C	Performs the index search
Init_Index_Search	Pascal	Initializes the index table
Index_Search	Pascal	Performs the index search

the data set that is stored in an array and places keys in the index table. Because we can't place all of the keys in the index table, we must first determine the interval between the keys in the data set that will be represented by the index table. This calculation is accomplished with the statement:

```
skip := NumData div MAX_TABLE_SIZE;
```

where **NumData** is the number of elements in the search array (data set) and **MAX_TABLE_SIZE** is the size of the index table. Once this calculation is made, keys can be placed in the index table with a simple **REPEAT-UNTIL** style loop. Keep in mind that each entry in the index table contains two components: the key and the position of the key in the search array. In Turbo C and Pascal, the index table is represented as an array of records, and in Turbo BASIC it is represented as two arrays. More notes on the details of these implementations are included in the discussions where each language is presented.

Now that we've shown how the index table is initialized, the next step is to examine the index search itself. The search is accomplished by passing both the data set, which we've been calling the search array, and the index table as arguments. The algorithm requires that the index table be searched first. For this task, the following loop is used:

```
REPEAT
    IF Search_Str > TableArray[i].TableKey THEN INC(i)
    ELSE found_entry := TRUE;
UNTIL (i > Table_Size) OR found_entry;
```

When the loop terminates, the variable **i** indicates which index table entry should be used to access the search array. Actually, we must use this entry and its preceding neighbor to determine the range for searching the search array. This operation is performed with the following code:

```
IF found_entry THEN BEGIN
    first := TableArray[i-1].TableIndex;
IF i < Table_Size THEN
    last := TableArray[i].TableIndex
ELSE
    last := NumData;
END;
```

The variables **first** and **last** are then used to reference the search array. Finally, we locate the search key with this loop:

```
WHILE (i <= last) AND no_match DO
    IF Search_Str <> A[i] THEN INC(i)
    ELSE no_match := FALSE;
```

Hash-Based Search

Some applications require very fast searching algorithms, and methods like the ones presented earlier may not be fast enough. To overcome this problem, use a hash-based search algorithm. The basic concept behind a hash-based search method is simple; it converts a key or string of text into a unique address. You can compare this technique to that of accessing an array element, in which an integer index is used to access a member. This method eliminates the need to sequentially step through a data set to locate a key. In a hashing system, a special function called a *hashing function* generates a storage address (an index into an array or table where the data set is stored) for a key.

To implement a hashing system, the first thing we'll need is a hashing function--the heart of the hashing method. But keep in mind that a hashing function does not maintain data in any ordered fashion. In the majority of cases, the hashing function translates the search key into a unique address using techniques of random number generation. Thus, hashing functions are only as good as the random number generators they employ. The paradox with hashing functions is that they use random numbers to generate unique storage addresses for keys. In practice, however, hashing functions fail to do that, and two different keys may wind up competing for the same address. This phenomenon is called *collision*, and every hashing function must provide a method for handling collisions.

Now that we've discussed the basic concepts involved in a hashing search system, let's explore an example. Assume that we have the data set shown in Figure 2.2. Notice that this figure contains two tables of data: the hash table and the collision table. The locations of the data stored in both of the tables are determined with a hash function. The keys in the collision table were placed in this table because they collided with keys stored in the hash table. The address (index) for each key in the collision table computed by the hash function is the same as the computed address for one of the keys in the hash table. For example, let's assume that the keys John and Hal generate the same address. If the key John is already stored in the hash table and we attempt to add the Hal key, a collision occurs and the key Hal must be placed in the collision table.

We've now shown how a key is added to the hash table; let's next look at how a search key is located. Let's assume that we want to find the search key Gloria. The hash function takes this search key and produces an integer index, as shown:

hash(Gloria) $\longrightarrow$ 6

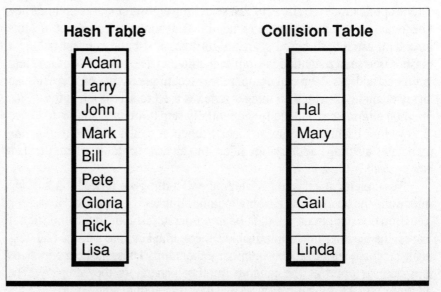

Figure 2.2. Examples of the hash and collision tables

This integer value is then used to compare the search key with the key stored in the hash table at location 6. If we wanted to search for Hal, the hash function produces the index

hash(Hal) $\longrightarrow$ 5

Now the key stored at location 5 in the hash table (Tom) does not match our search key. In this case, we must search the collision table.

Let's next examine the details of how the hash function is implemented.

Hash-Based Search Implementation

Various methods are used to implement hashing functions. The underlying strategy behind most methods is to approximate a random function that produces a unique index value for each input key. It is important to select a hashing function that provides a compromise between memory requirements and collision frequency. (If we had an unlimited amount of memory space to use for the hash table, we could implement a hash function so that each key maps to a unique address.)

The standard technique used in many hash functions is as follows:

hash(key) $\longrightarrow$ ORD(key) MOD hash_constant

Here an index is produced with the modula operator. The **hash_constant** is the size of the hash table. To produce the best results, this value should be a prime number. You can experiment with hash tables of different sizes. In general, as the size of the hash table increases, the collision rate decreases.

Our implementation of the hash function uses a variation of the previously discussed method. This calculation is shown in Turbo Pascal.

```
hash := Ord(Strng[1]);
FOR i := 2 TO Length(Strng) DO
    hash := ((hash * 64) MOD 13 + Ord(Strng[i])) MOD
MAX_HASH_TABLE_SIZE;
```

The basic technique consists of summing the ASCII values of a string. Each iteration of the loop uses the previous value of the hash calculation and adds it to the next character in the string. This calculation produces a more even distribution of the keys in a data set.

Handling Collisions

The next function we'll need is one for handling collisions. Like hash functions, many techniques have been developed by computer scientists over the years for handling collisions.

One of the more popular techniques is called the *chaining method*. With this method, colliding keys are kept in a linked list that is assigned to each entry in the hash table where a collision occurs. This technique is illustrated in Figure 2.3. Notice that the keys Thomas and Troy collided with the key Ted; therefore, they are put in a list and linked with the key Ted. With the collision system, when we search for a key, the key is first mapped to a hash table entry. If the search key does not match with the hash table entry, we search the list of collision keys.

The chaining method is popular because it is both efficient and easy to implement. In Pascal and C, the collision list can be represented with a linked list that employs pointers. The collision list could also be represented as a binary tree for greater efficiency. (For a discussion of binary trees, see Section 9.)

The Hashing Routines

Because of the complexity of the hash-based search method, we'll need to develop a set of routines in each language to implement the algorithm

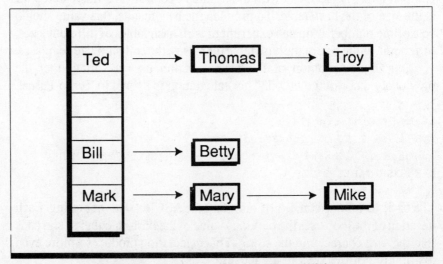

Figure 2.3. Technique for handling collisions

(see Table 2.2). Keep in mind that the hash table initialization routine must be called before any keys are added to the hash table.

Table 2.2. Hashing routines for the hash-based search implementations

Routine	Language	Description
FNHash0%	BASIC	Performs the hashing function
Init.Hash.Table	BASIC	Initializes the hash table
Insert.Hash.Table	BASIC	Inserts a key in hash table
Search.Hash.Table	BASIC	Searches the hash table
hash0()	C	Performs the hashing function
init_hash_table()	C	Initializes the hash table
insert_hash_table()	C	Inserts a key in hash table
search_hash_table()	C	Searches the hash table
Hash0	Pascal	Performs the hashing function
Init_Hash_Table	Pascal	Initializes the hash table
Inset_Hash_Table	Pascal	Inserts a key in hash table
Search_Hash_Table	Pascal	Searches the hash table

Selecting a Searching Method

Although we've only presented four searching strategies in this section, they span the range of major searching algorithms. The first method presented, the heuristic search, is well-suited for searching unordered data sets. The main advantage of heuristic searches is that you can add your own rules of thumb to fine tune the searching algorithm. Heuristic searches are also effective when you use dynamic data sets, because the data set does not require sorting when a new element is added.

If you're working with ordered data sets, the binary search is better than the heuristic search. The number of comparisons required to locate a search key is never more than log $2n$ where n is the number of keys in the data set. If a data set changes, the keys must be sorted before the binary search can be applied.

With the indexed search, we can improve the performance of the binary search using an indexed search table to store references to the data set. Keep in mind that the index table requires additional storage and maintenance overhead. If a data set is altered, it must be sorted and the index table must be updated and re-sorted. Because of these extra steps, you should stick with the binary search if you expect the data you are searching to change.

The last searching method we presented, the hash-based search, is the most efficient of the four methods. If a data set changes, no sorting operations are required. The hash-based search does require more memory overhead than the other methods. Therefore, it might not be the best choice if you're working with very large data sets. Programs such as compilers and language translators usually employ hash-based algorithms because these programs typically require small data sets.

The Searching Algorithm Implementation

The code for the complete searching routines are provided in Listings 2.1, 2.2 and 2.3.

Turbo BASIC

The Turbo BASIC searching routines are presented in Listing 2.1. The routines are self-contained and only require the Turbo BASIC **OPTION BASE 1** statement.

In the indexed search subroutine called **Index.Search**, the index search table is constructed with an array of strings, an array of integers, and a scalar variable. For the subroutine to work, the two arrays must be dimensioned to the same size.

The hash-based search is designed to work with strings. Specifically, collision is handled using strings to simulate linked lists. The method is simple, because it makes use of Turbo BASIC's support for large strings. The hash table is implemented using an array of strings, and each member is initialized with the comma character. The comma is a list delimiter. A noncolliding entry is simply appended after the original comma in the hash table array member. Another comma is also appended to prepare that entry to deal with any colliding entries. Consequently, a colliding string is appended at the end of the corresponding string-based hash table entry. This method can be modified to handle numeric data if the latter is first converted to strings.

The Turbo BASIC search routines are presented next.

Heuristic.Search   Performs a heuristic search on an unordered array. You can search for a particular occurrence of a specified string.

Syntax:
```
SUB Heuristic.Search(A$(1), NumData%, Search.Str$, _
                     Occurrence%, ActualOccur%, Result%)
```

Parameters:

A$()	the array of strings being searched and whose elements are most likely to be moved.
NumData%	the number of elements of **array A$()** being searched.
Search.Str$	the search string.
Occurrence%	the specified occurrence of the search string.
ActualOccur%	the number of times the search string has been actually encountered.
Result%	the position of the search string in the array or 0 if no match is found.

Performs a binary search on an array sorted in an ascending order. **Binary.Search**

Syntax:
```
SUB Binary.Search(A$(1), NumData%, Search.Str$, Result%)
```

Parameters:

A$()	the array of strings being searched.
NumData%	the number of elements of array A$() being searched.
Search.Str$	the search string.
Result%	the position of the search string in the array or zero if no match is found.

Initializes the indexed search table. This routine must be called before **Init.Index.Search**
Index.Search is used.

Syntax:
```
SUB Init.Index.Search(A$(1), NumData%, Table.Key$(1), _
                      Table.Index%(1), Table.Size%, Done%)
```

Parameters:

A$()	the array of sorted strings whose indexed search table is being built.
NumData%	the number of elements of array A$() being used to build the index table.
Table.Key$()	the array of table entries.

Table.Index%()	the array of table indexes.
Table.Size%	the size of the initialized table.
Done%	the flag to signal whether the table was initialized successfully. A 1 indicates success; a 0 signals failure.

Remarks:
The arrays **Table.Key$()** and **Table.Index%()** must be of the same size.

Index.Search

Performs an indexed search on an unordered array.

Syntax:
```
SUB Index.Search(A$(1), NumData%, Table.Key$(1), _
                 Table.Index%(1), Table.Size%, _
                 Search.Str$, Result%)
```

Parameters:

A$()	the array of strings being searched.
NumData%	the number of elements of array A$() being searched.
Table.Key$()	the array of table entries.
Table.Index%()	the array of table indexes.
Table.Size%	the size of the index table.
Search.Str$	the search string.
Result%	the position of the search string in the array or zero if no match is found.

FNHash0%

Obtains a hash address from a string of any size.

Syntax:
```
DEF FNHash0%(Strng$, Hash.Table.Size%)
```

Parameters:

Strng$	the string being mapped onto a hash address.
Hash.Table.Size%	the hash table size.

TIP

To obtain a hash address quickly for a very large string, just use a leading portion of it, such as:

```
FNHash0%(LEFT$(BigString$,10), 100)
```

Init.Hash.Table

Initializes a hash table by assigning commas to the **HashTable$()** array. This prepares the array for emulating a series of dynamic linked lists.

Syntax:
```
SUB Init.Hash.Table(HashTable$(1), Hash.Table.Size%)
```

Parameters:

HashTable$()   the array of strings implementing a hash table.
Hash.Table.Size%   the size of the hash table.

Inserts an element in the hash table.   **Insert.Hash.Table**

Syntax:
```
SUB Insert.Hash.Table(HashTable$(1), Item$)
```

Parameters:

HashTable$()   the array of strings used to implement a hash table.
Item$ the inserted string.

Searches the hash table for a string.   **Search.Hash.Table**

Syntax:
```
SUB Search.Hash.Table(HashTable$(1), Search.Str$, _
                  Ptr%, Hash.Address%)
```

Parameters:

HashTable$()   the array of strings used to implement a hash table.
Search.Str$ the search string.
Ptr%   the character index of the **HashTable$()** elements
that contain the matching search string. A 0 is returned if no matching occurs.
Hash.Address%   the hash table entry for the search string.

Turbo C

The Turbo C routines presented in Listing 2.2 require an include file, macros, and data types. The **string.h** is included to prototype string-manipulating functions, such as **strcmp()** and **strcpy()**.

   STRING, MAX_TABLE_SIZE, and **MAX_HASH_TABLE_SIZE** macros define the string size, maximum index table size, and maximum hash table size, respectively. You can alter these values to fine tune the search operations for strings of different sizes and use hash tables or a larger or smaller index.

The enumerated boolean type is declared to implement booleans in the C code. The structures **tableinforec** and **tablerec** are used to represent the indexed search table as shown:

```
struct tableinforec {
    unsigned tableindex;
    char tablekey[STRING];
};

struct tablerec {
    struct tableinforec tablearray[MAX_TABLE_SIZE];
    unsigned table_size;
};
```

The structure **hashinfo** defines each element of the hash table:

```
struct hashinfo {
    char hashkey[STRING];
    struct hashinfo *nexthashptr;
};
```

The searching routines for Turbo C are covered next.

heuristic_search()   Performs a heuristic search on an unordered array. You can search for a particular occurrence of a string. The function returns the position of the search string in the array or –1 if no match is found.

Syntax:
```
int heuristic_search(char a[][STRING], unsigned numdata,
                     char* search_str, unsigned occurrence,
                     unsigned *actualoccur);
```

Parameters:

a[ ][ ]	the array of strings being searched and whose elements are most likely to be moved.
numdata	the number of elements of array a[ ][ ] being searched.
search_str	the search string.
occurrence	the number of the occurrence of the search string.
*actualoccur	the pointer to the number of times the search string has been actually encountered.

Performs a binary search on an array sorted in an ascending order. The **binary_search()**
function returns the position of the search string in the array or –1 if no
match is found.

Syntax:
```
int binary_search(char a[][STRING], unsigned numdata,
                  char* search_str);
```

Parameters:

a[ ][ ]   the array of strings being searched.
numdata   the number of elements of array **a[ ][ ]** being searched.
search_str the search string.

Initializes the indexed search table. This function must be called before   **init_index_search()**
index_search() is used.

Syntax:
```
void init_index_search(char a[][STRING], unsigned numdata,
              struct tablerec *table, enum boolean *done);
```

Parameters:

a[ ][ ]   the array of sorted strings whose indexed search table is
              being built.
numdata   the number of elements of array **a[ ][ ]** used in the index table.
*table   the index table structure.
*done   a pointer to a boolean flag used to signal whether the table
              was initialized successfully. A TRUE indicates **success**, a
              FALSE signals failure.

Performs an indexed search. The function returns the position of the search   **index_search()**
string in the array or –1 if no match is found.

Syntax:
```
int index_search(char a[][STRING], unsigned numdata,
                  struct tablerec *table, char* search_str);
```

Parameters:

a[ ][ ]   the array of strings being searched.
numdata   the number of elements of array **a[ ][ ]** being searched.
table   the indexed search table.
search_str the search string.

hash0()   Obtains a hash address from a string of any size.

Syntax:
```
unsigned hash0(char *strng);
```

Parameter:
strng   the string being mapped onto a hash address.

init_hash_table()   Initializes a hash table.

Syntax:
```
void init_hash_table(struct hashinfo*
                    hashtable[MAX_HASH_TABLE_SIZE]);
```

Parameter:
hashtable   the initialized hash table.

insert_hash_table() Inserts an element in the hash table.

Syntax:
```
void insert_hash_table(struct hashinfo*
                    hashtable[MAX_HASH_TABLE_SIZE],
                    char* item);
```

Parameters:
hashtable   the hash table.
item   an inserted string.

search_hash_table() Searches the hash table for a string.

Syntax:
```
void search_hash_table(struct hashinfo*
                    hashtable[MAX_HASH_TABLE_SIZE], char*
                    search_str, struct hashinfo *ptr);
```

Parameters:
hashtable   the hash table.
search_str   the search string.
*ptr   the pointer to the hash table matching the search string. A
                 NULL value indicates that no match occurred.

Turbo Pascal

The Turbo Pascal search routines are provided in Listing 2.3. They are encapsulated in the **SEARCH** library unit that uses the **SORT** unit presented in Section 1. The **SortType** data type is imported from the unit **SORT**. Consequently, changes in the definition of **SortType** in unit **SORT** also affects future compilations with the unit **SEARCH**.

The **MAX_TABLE_SIZE** and **MAX_HASH_TABLE_SIZE** constants define the maximum index table size and the maximum hash table size, respectively. You can alter these values to fine tune the search operations for strings using hash tables or a larger or smaller index.

The indexed search table requires the following three data types:

```
TableInfoRec = RECORD
    TableIndex  : WORD;
    TableKey    : SortType;
END;
TableArrayType = ARRAY [1..MAX_TABLE_SIZE] OF TableInfoRec;
TableRec = RECORD
    TableArray : TableArrayType;
    Table_Size : WORD;
END;
```

Here are the pointer, record, and array used to implement the hash table:

```
HashPtr = ^HashInfo;
HashInfo  = RECORD
    HashKey : SortType;
    NextHashPtr : HashPtr;
END;
HashArray = ARRAY [0..MAX_HASH_TABLE_SIZE] OF HashPtr;
```

Performs a heuristic search on an unordered array. You can search for a particular occurrence of the desired string. The function returns the position of the search string in the array or −1 if no match is found.

Heuristic_Search

Syntax:
```
FUNCTION Heuristic_Search(VAR A: SortArray; NumData : WORD;
                          Search_Str : SortType;
                          Occurrence : WORD;
                          VAR ActualOccur : WORD) : WORD;
```

Parameters:

A	the array of strings being searched and whose elements are most likely to be moved.
NumData	the number of elements of array **A** being searched.
Search_Str	the search string.
Occurrence	the specified occurrence of the search string.
ActualOccur	the pointer to the number of times the search string has been actually encountered.

Binary_Search   Performs a binary search on an array sorted in ascending order. The function returns the position of the search string in the array or 0 if no match is found.

Syntax:
```
FUNCTION Binary_Search(VAR A : SortArray; NumData : WORD;
                       Search_Str : SortType) : WORD;
```

Parameters:

A	the array of string being searched.
NumData	the number of elements of array **A** being searched.
Search_Str	the search string.

Init_Index_Search   Initializes the indexed search table.

Syntax:
```
PROCEDURE Init_Index_Search(VAR A : SortArray; NumData : WORD;
                            VAR Table : TableRec;
                            VAR Done : BOOLEAN);
```

Parameters:

A	the array of sorted strings whose indexed search table is being built.
NumData	the number of elements of array **A** used to build the index table.
Table	the index table record.
Done	a pointer to a boolean flag used to signal whether the table was initialized successfully. A TRUE indicates success, a FALSE signals failure.

Index_Search   Performs an indexed search. The function returns the position of the search string in the array or 0 if no match is found.

Syntax:
```
FUNCTION Index_Search(VAR A : SortArray; NumData : WORD;
                      VAR Table : TableRec;
                      Search_Str : SortType) : WORD;
```

Parameters:

A	the array of strings being searched.
NumData	the number of elements of array **A** being searched.
Table	the indexed search table.
Search_Str	the search string.

Obtains a hash address from a string of any size. **Hash0**

Syntax:
```
FUNCTION Hash0(Strng : SortType) : WORD;
```

Parameter:

Strng   the string being mapped onto a hash address.

Initializes a hash table. **Init_Hash_Table**

Syntax:
```
PROCEDURE Init_Hash_Table(VAR HashTable : HashArray);
```

Parameter:

HashTable   the initialized hash table.

Inserts an element in the hash table. **Insert_Hash_Table**

Syntax:
```
PROCEDURE Insert_Hash_Table(VAR HashTable : HashArray;
                            Item : SortType);
```

Parameters:

HashTable	the hash table.
Item	the inserted string.

Searches the hash table for a string. **Search_Hash_Table**

Syntax:

```
PROCEDURE Search_Hash_Table(VAR HashTable : HashArray;
                            Search_Str : SortType;
                            VAR Ptr : HashPtr);
```

Parameters:

HashTable   the hash table.
Search_Str   the search string.
Ptr   the pointer to the hash table matching the search string. A
                  NIL value indicates that no matching occurred.

• Listing 2.1. Turbo BASIC source code for the search routines

```
SUBHeuristic.Search(A$(1),NumData%,Search.Str$,Occurrence%,ActualOccur%,Result%)
' Performs heuristic search in a sorted array. The parameters
' specify both the sought data and the specific occurrence
' number. The function returns the index of the located
' element. If the latter is not the first one in the array, it
' swaps one element toward the front.
LOCAL i%, j%
ActualOccur% = 0 ' initialize count for number of matches
Result% = 0
i% = 1
DO WHILE (i% <= NumData%) AND (ActualOccur% < Occurrence%) 'begin
   IF A$(i%) = Search.Str$ THEN INCR ActualOccur%
   INCR i%
LOOP
DECR i%
' swaps indices
IF ActualOccur% = Occurrence% THEN
   IF i% > 1 THEN
      SWAP A$(i%),A$(i%-1)
      Result% = i%-1
   ELSE
      Result% = 1
   END IF
END IF
END SUB ' Heuristic.Search

SUB Binary.Search(A$(1), NumData%, Search.Str$, Result%)
' performs binary searching on a sorted array
```

```
LOCAL low%, high%, median%
' sets lower and upper search limits
low% = 1
high% = NumData%
DO
    median% = (low% + high%) \ 2
    IF Search.Str$ < A$(median%) THEN
        high% = median% - 1
    ELSE
        low% = median% + 1
    END IF
LOOP UNTIL (Search.Str$ = A$(median%)) OR (low% > high%)
IF Search.Str$ = A$(median%) THEN Result% = median% ELSE Result% = 0
END SUB ' Binary.Search


SUB Init.Index.Search(A$(1), NumData%, Table.Key$(1), _
                      Table.Index%(1), Table.Size%, Done%)
' initializes a table for indexed searching
LOCAL i%, skip%, tbl.size%
tbl.size% = 0 ' initializes local table size
skip% = NumData% \ UBound(Table.Key$(1))
IF skip% > 0 THEN
    i% = 1
    DO
        INCR tbl.size%
        Table.Index%(tbl.size%) = i%
        Table.Key$(tbl.size%) = A$(i%)
        INCR i%, skip%
    LOOP UNTIL (i% >= NumData%) OR (tbl.size% = Table.Size%)
    IF tbl.size% < Table.Size% THEN Table.Size% = tbl.size%
    Done% = 1
ELSE
    Done% = 0
END IF
END SUB ' Init.Index.Search


SUB Index.Search(A$(1),NumData%,Table.Key$(1),Table.Index%(1),_
                 Table.Size%, Search.Str$, Result%)
' Performs indexed searching. The parameter Result%
' returns the index of the matching array member.
```

```
' A zero is returned if no match is found.
LOCAL i%, j%, first%, last%, found.entry%, no.match%
Result% = 0 ' initializes with a not-found value
' performs a quick check to see if sought element is in the
' range of values stored in the array "A"
IF (Search.Str$ >= A$(1)) AND (Search.Str$ <= A$(NumData%)) THEN
    i% = 1
    found.entry% = 0 ' initialize search flag
    no.match% = 1
    DO
        IF Search.Str$ > Table.Key$(i%) THEN
            INCR i%
        ELSE
            found.entry% = 1
        END IF
    LOOP UNTIL (i% > Table.Size%) OR (found.entry% <> 0)
    IF found.entry% <> 0 THEN
        first% = Table.Index%(i%-1)
        IF i% < Table.Size% THEN
            last%  = Table.Index%(i%)
        ELSE
            last%  =  NumData%
        END IF
    ELSE
        first% = Table.Index%(i%-1)
        last% = NumData%
    END IF
    i% = first%
    DO WHILE (i% <= last%) AND (no.match% <> 0)
        IF Search.Str$ <> A$(i%) THEN INCR i% ELSE no.match% = 0
    LOOP
    IF no.match% = 0 THEN Result% = i%
END IF
END SUB ' Index.Search

DEF FNHash0%(Strng$,Hash.Table.Size%)
' performs the hash function
LOCAL i%, hash%
hash% = ASC(MID$(Strng$,1,1))
FOR i% = 2 TO LEN(Strng$)
```

```
    hash% = ((hash% * 64) MOD 13 + ASC(MID$(Strng$,i%,1)))_
               MOD Hash.Table.Size% + 1
NEXT i%
FNHash0% = hash%
END DEF ' Hash0%


SUB Init.Hash.Table(HashTable$(1), Hash.Table.Size%)
' initializes hash table
LOCAL i%
FOR i% = 1 TO Hash.Table.Size%
    HashTable$(i%) = ","
NEXT i%
END SUB ' Init.Hash.Table


SUB Insert.Hash.Table(HashTable$(1), Item$)
' Builds a hash table by inserting a single datum.
' This routine should be called a number of times to
' build a complete hash table.
LOCAL hash.address%
hash.address% = FNHash0%(Item$,UBound(HashTable$(1)))
HashTable$(hash.address%) = HashTable$(hash.address%) + Item$ + ","
END SUB ' Insert.Hash.Table


Search.Hash.Table(HashTable$(1), Search.Str$, Ptr%, Hash.Address%)
' Searches hash table for a specific string. The Hash.Address%
' returns the array index where the search string MIGHT be found.
' The Ptr% parameter returns the character index to the
' matching string, or zero if the search string is not found.

Hash.Address% = FNHash0%(Search.Str$,UBound(HashTable$(1)))
Ptr% = INSTR(HashTable$(Hash.Address%), ","+Search.Str$+"," )
END SUB ' Search.Hash.Table
```

• Listing 2.2. Turbo C source code for the search routines

```c
#include <string.h>
#include <stdlib.h>
#define STRING 81
#define MAX_TABLE_SIZE 10
```

```
#define MAX_HASH_TABLE_SIZE 100
enum boolean { FALSE, TRUE };

struct tableinforec {
   unsigned tableindex;
   char tablekey[STRING];
};
struct tablerec {
   struct tableinforec tablearray[MAX_TABLE_SIZE];
   unsigned table_size;
};
struct hashinfo {
   char hashkey[STRING];
   struct hashinfo *nexthashptr;
};


int heuristic_search(char a[][STRING], unsigned numdata, char* search_str,
                     unsigned occurrence, unsigned *actualoccur);
int binary_search(char a[][STRING], unsigned numdata, char* search_str);
void init_index_search(char a[][STRING], unsigned numdata,
                     struct tablerec *table, enum boolean *done);
int index_search(char a[][STRING], unsigned numdata,
                struct tablerec *table, char* search_str);
unsigned hash0(char *strng);
void init_hash_table(struct hashinfo *hashtable[MAX_HASH_TABLE_SIZE]);
void insert_hash_table(struct hashinfo* hashtable[MAX_HASH_TABLE_SIZE],
                     char* item);
void search_hash_table(struct hashinfo* hashtable[MAX_HASH_TABLE_SIZE],
                     char* search_str, struct hashinfo **ptr);


int heuristic_search(char a[][STRING], unsigned numdata, char* search_str,
                     unsigned occurrence, unsigned *actualoccur)
/* performs heuristic search in a sorted array */
{
   unsigned i, result;
   char tempo[STRING];

   *actualoccur = 0; /* initialize count for number of matches */
   result = -1;
   i = 0;
```

```
    while (i < numdata && *actualoccur < occurrence) {
        if (strcmp(a[i],search_str) == 0)
            (*actualoccur)++;
        i++;
    } /* while */
    i--;
    /* swap indices */
    if (*actualoccur == occurrence)
        if (i > 0)   {
            strcpy(tempo,a[i]);
            strcpy(a[i],a[i-1]);
            strcpy(a[i-1],tempo);
            result = i;
        }
        else result = 0;
        return result; /* return function result */
}


int binary_search(char a[][STRING], unsigned numdata, char* search_str)
/* performs binary searching on a sorted array */
{
    unsigned low, high, median;

    /* set lower and upper search limits */
    low = 0;
    high = numdata-1;
    do {
        median = (low + high) / 2;
        if (strcmp(search_str,a[median]) < 0)
            high = median - 1;
        else
            low = median + 1;
    } while (!(strcmp(search_str,a[median]) == 0 || low > high));
    if (strcmp(search_str,a[median]) == 0)
        return median;
    else
        return -1;
}
```

```
void init_index_search(char a[][STRING], unsigned numdata,
                       struct tablerec *table, enum boolean *done)
/* initializes a table for indexed searching */
{
    unsigned i, skip;

    table->table_size = 0; /* initialize table size */
    skip = numdata / MAX_TABLE_SIZE;
    if (skip > 0) {
        i = 0;
        do {
            table->tablearray[table->table_size].tableindex = i;
            strcpy(table->tablearray[table->table_size].tablekey,a[i]);
            i += skip;
            table->table_size++;
        } while (!(i >= numdata || table->table_size == MAX_TABLE_SIZE));
        *done = TRUE;
    }
    else
        *done = FALSE;
}


int index_search(char a[][STRING], unsigned numdata,
                 struct tablerec *table, char* search_str)
/* performs indexed searching */
{
    unsigned i, first, last, location;
    enum boolean found_entry, no_match;

    location = -1; /* initialize with a NOT-found value */
    /* perform a quick check to see if sought element is in the
       range of values stored in the array "a" */
    if (strcmp(search_str,a[0]) >= 0 && strcmp(search_str,a[numdata]) <= 0)
      {
        i = 0;
        found_entry = FALSE; /* initialize search flag */
        no_match = TRUE;
        do {
            if (strcmp(search_str,table->tablearray[i].tablekey) > 0)
            i++;
```

```
            else
                found_entry = TRUE;
        } while (i < table->table_size && found_entry == FALSE);
        if (i == 0) return i;    /* element is first in list */
        if (found_entry == TRUE) {
            first = table->tablearray[i-1].tableindex;
            if (i < table->table_size)
                last = table->tablearray[i].tableindex;
            else
                last = numdata;
        }
        else {
            first = table->tablearray[i-1].tableindex;
            last  = numdata;
        } /* if */
        i = first;
        while (i <= last && no_match == TRUE)
            if (strcmp(search_str, a[i]) != 0)
                i++;
            else
                no_match = FALSE;
            if (no_match == FALSE) location = i;
    } /* if */
    return location;
}


unsigned hash0(char *strng)
/* hash function */
{
    unsigned i, hash;

    hash = strng[0];
    for (i = 1; i < strlen(strng); i++)
        hash = ((hash * 64) % 13 + strng[i]) % MAX_HASH_TABLE_SIZE;
    return hash;
}


void init_hash_table(struct hashinfo *hashtable[MAX_HASH_TABLE_SIZE])
/* initializes a hash table */
{
```

```
    unsigned i;

    for (i = 0 ; i < MAX_HASH_TABLE_SIZE; i++) {
        hashtable[i]->hashkey[0] = '\0';
        hashtable[i] = NULL;
    }
}


void insert_hash_table(struct hashinfo* hashtable[MAX_HASH_TABLE_SIZE],
                       char* item)
/* builds a hash table by inserting a single element */
{
    unsigned hash_address;
    struct hashinfo *ptr;

    hash_address = hash0(item);
    ptr = (struct hashinfo*) malloc(sizeof(struct hashinfo));
    strcpy(ptr->hashkey,item);
    ptr->nexthashptr = hashtable[hash_address];
    hashtable[hash_address] = ptr;
}


void search_hash_table(struct hashinfo* hashtable[MAX_HASH_TABLE_SIZE],
                       char* search_str, struct hashinfo **ptr)
/* searches hash table for a specific string */
{
    enum boolean not_found = TRUE;
    unsigned hash_address;

    hash_address = hash0(search_str);
    *ptr = hashtable[hash_address];
    while (not_found == TRUE) {
        if (*ptr == NULL)
            not_found = FALSE;
        else if (strcmp((*ptr)->hashkey, search_str) == 0)
            not_found = FALSE;
        else
            *ptr = (*ptr)->nexthashptr;
    }
}
```

• Listing 2.3. Turbo Pascal source code for the search routines

```pascal
UNIT Search;
Uses Sort;

CONST MAX_TABLE_SIZE = 10;
   MAX_HASH_TABLE_SIZE = 100;

TYPE TableInfoRec = RECORD
        TableIndex   : WORD;
        TableKey     : SortType;
     END;
     TableArrayType = ARRAY [1..MAX_TABLE_SIZE] OF TableInfoRec;
     TableRec = RECORD
        TableArray : TableArrayType;
        Table_Size : WORD;
     END;
     HashPtr = ^HashInfo;
     HashInfo  = RECORD
        HashKey : SortType;
        NextHashPtr : HashPtr;
     END;
     HashArray = ARRAY [0..MAX_HASH_TABLE_SIZE] OF HashPtr;

FUNCTION Heuristic_Search(VAR A          : SortArray; { in/out  }
                              NumData     : WORD;      { input   }
                              Search_Str  : SortType;  { input   }
                              Occurrence  : WORD;      { input   }
                          VAR ActualOccur : WORD       { output  }) : WORD;

{ Performs heuristic search in a sorted array. The parameters specify
  both the sought data and the specific occurrence number. The function
  returns the index of the located element. If the latter is not the
  first one in the array, it swaps one element toward the front. }

FUNCTION Binary_Search(VAR A          : SortArray; { input   }
                           NumData     : WORD;      { input   }
                           Search_Str  : SortType   { input   }) : WORD;
{ performs binary searching on a sorted array }
```

```
PROCEDURE Init_Index_Search(VAR A        : SortArray; { input   }
                                NumData : WORD;      { input   }
                            VAR Table   : TableRec;  { output  }
                            VAR Done    : BOOLEAN    { output  });
{ initializes a table for indexed searching }


FUNCTION Index_Search(VAR A              : SortArray; { input   }
                          NumData        : WORD;      { input   }
                      VAR Table          : TableRec;  { input   }
                          Search_Str     : SortType   { input   } ) : WORD;
{ Performs indexed searching. The parameter 'Location'
  returns the index of the matching array member.
  A zero is returned if no match is found. }


FUNCTION Hash0(Strng : SortType { input  }) : WORD;
{ hash function }


PROCEDURE Init_Hash_Table(VAR HashTable : HashArray { output });
{ initializes a hash table }


PROCEDURE Insert_Hash_Table(VAR HashTable : HashArray; { in/out }
                                Item      : SortType   { input  });
{ Builds a hash table by inserting a single datum.
  This routine should be called a number of times to build
  a complete hash table. }


PROCEDURE Search_Hash_Table(VAR HashTable    : HashArray; { input   }
                                Search_Str   : SortType;  { input   }
                            VAR Ptr          : HashPtr    { output  });
{ Searches hash table for a specific string. The Ptr
  parameter returns the pointer to the matching record. }


{*******************************************************************}
FUNCTION Heuristic_Search(VAR A          :   SortArray; { in/out }
                              NumData     :   WORD;      { input   }
                              Search_Str  :   SortType;  { input   }
                              Occurrence  :   WORD;      { input   }
                          VAR ActualOccur:   WORD       { output }): WORD;

VAR i, j, result : WORD;
   tempo : SortType;
```

```
BEGIN
    ActualOccur := 0; { initialize count for number of matches }
    result := 0;
    i := 1;
    WHILE (i <= NumData) AND (ActualOccur < Occurrence) DO BEGIN
        IF A[i] = Search_Str THEN
            INC(ActualOccur);
        INC(i);
    END; { WHILE }
    DEC(i);
    { swaps indices }
    IF ActualOccur = Occurrence THEN
        IF i > 1 THEN BEGIN
            tempo := A[i];
            A[i] := A[i-1];
            A[i-1] := tempo;
            result := i
        END
        ELSE result := 1;
    Heuristic_Search := result { return function result }
END; { Heuristic_Search }

FUNCTION Binary_Search(VAR A            : SortArray; { input   }
                           NumData      : WORD;      { input   }
                           Search_Str   : SortType   { input   })
                                                     : WORD;


VAR low, high, median, result : WORD;


BEGIN
    { sets lower and upper search limits }
    low := 1;
    high := NumData;
    REPEAT
        median := (low + high) div 2;
        IF Search_Str < A[median] THEN
            high := median - 1
        ELSE
            low := median + 1;
    UNTIL (Search_Str = A[median]) OR (low > high);
```

```
      IF Search_Str = A[median] THEN result := median
      ELSE result := 0;
      Binary_Search := result { return function result }
END; { Binary_Search }


PROCEDURE Init_Index_Search(VAR A       : SortArray; { input  }
                                NumData : WORD;       { input  }
                            VAR Table   : TableRec;   { output }
                            VAR Done    : BOOLEAN     { output });


VAR i, skip : WORD;


BEGIN
    Table.Table_Size := 0; { initializes table size }
    skip := NumData div MAX_TABLE_SIZE;
    IF skip > 0 THEN
       WITH Table DO BEGIN
          i := 1;
          REPEAT
             INC(Table_Size);
             TableArray[Table_Size].TableIndex := i;
             TableArray[Table_Size].TableKey    := A[i];
             INC(i, skip);
          UNTIL (i >= NumData) OR (Table_Size = MAX_TABLE_SIZE);
          Done := TRUE;
       END { WITH Table }
    ELSE Done := FALSE;
END; { Init_Index_Search }


FUNCTION Index_Search(VAR A         : SortArray; { input  }
                          NumData    : WORD;       { input  }
                      VAR Table      : TableRec;   { input  }
                          Search_Str : SortType    { input  }) : WORD;


VAR i, j, first, last, location  : WORD;
    found_entry, no_match : BOOLEAN;


BEGIN
    location := 0; { initialize with a not-found value }
    WITH Table DO  BEGIN
```

```
    { performs a quick check to see if sought element is in the
      range of values stored in the array 'A' }
    IF (Search_Str >= A[1]) AND (Search_Str <= A[NumData]) THEN BEGIN
        i := 1;
        found_entry := FALSE; { initialize search flag }
        no_match := TRUE;
        REPEAT
            IF Search_Str > TableArray[i].TableKey THEN INC(i)
            ELSE found_entry := TRUE;
        UNTIL (i > Table_Size) OR found_entry;
        IF i = 1 THEN location := 1;
        IF found_entry THEN BEGIN
            first := TableArray[i-1].TableIndex;
            IF i < Table_Size THEN
                last   := TableArray[i].TableIndex
            ELSE
                last :=   NumData;
        END
        ELSE BEGIN
            first := TableArray[i-1].TableIndex;
            last   := NumData
        END; { IF }
        i := first;
        WHILE (i <= last) AND no_match DO
            IF Search_Str <> A[i] THEN
                INC(i)
            ELSE
                no_match := FALSE;
        IF NOT no_match THEN location := i;
    END; { IF }
  END; { WITH }
  Index_Search := location { return function value }
END; { Index_Search }

FUNCTION Hash0(Strng : SortType { input   }) : WORD;
VAR i, hash : WORD;

BEGIN
    hash := Ord(Strng[1]);
```

```
    FOR i := 2 TO Length(Strng) DO
        hash := ((hash * 64) MOD 13 + Ord(Strng[i])) MOD
MAX_HASH_TABLE_SIZE;
    Hash0 := hash;
END; { Hash0 }


PROCEDURE Init_Hash_Table(VAR HashTable : HashArray { output });
VAR i : WORD;


BEGIN
    FOR i := 1 TO MAX_HASH_TABLE_SIZE DO
        HashTable[i] := NIL;
END; { Init_Hash_Table }


PROCEDURE Insert_Hash_Table(VAR HashTable : HashArray; { in/out }
                                Item      : SortType   { input  });


VAR hash_address : WORD;
    ptr : HashPtr;


BEGIN
    hash_address := Hash0(Item);
    NEW(ptr);
    ptr^.HashKey := Item;
    ptr^.NextHashPtr := HashTable[hash_address];
    HashTable[hash_address] := ptr
END; { Insert_Hash_Table }


PROCEDURE Search_Hash_Table(VAR HashTable  : HashArray; { input  }
                                Search_Str  : SortType;  { input  }
                            VAR Ptr         : HashPtr    { output });


VAR not_found : BOOLEAN;
    hash_address : WORD;


BEGIN
    hash_address := Hash0(Search_Str);
    Ptr := HashTable[hash_address];
    not_found := TRUE;
    WHILE not_found DO
```

```
        IF Ptr = NIL THEN not_found := FALSE
        ELSE IF Ptr^.HashKey = Search_Str THEN not_found := FALSE
        ELSE Ptr := Ptr^.NextHashPtr;
END; { Search_Hash_Table }
END.
```

Mathematical Algorithms

3

Introduction

Because mathematics plays an important role in computer programs, we'll need adequate tools for solving mathematics-related problems. To help you develop a useful mathematics toolset, we'll present a variety of algorithms for solving both arithmetic and numerical analysis problems. Of course, entire books have been written on the subject of mathematical algorithms, so we have elected to present a subset of popular and useful algorithms from the following categories.

- Simple and transcendental functions
- Numerical analysis methods
- Matrix operations

The algorithms presented are implemented in each language as a standalone library that you can combine with your own applications. In cases where the algorithms presented are already implemented in some of the languages, we skip these implementations.

Simple and Transcendental Functions

The Turbo languages provide a full set of useful math functions that enable you to perform all of the fundamental math operations—trigonometric, exponential, square root, absolute value, and logarithmic. We can, however, add a few functions to enhance the built-in libraries, including:

- a simple power function (for C, Pascal, and Prolog).
- inverse sine and cosine functions.
- factorial and Gamma functions.
- hyperbolic functions and their inverses.

The names of these functions are listed in Table 3.1.

The Power Functions

The power functions, which compute the value

Result = x^n

Table 3.1. Mathematical functions

BASIC	C	Pascal	Prolog
—	sqr()	—	sqr
—	power()	Power	power
—	rpower()	RPower	rpower
FNArcsin#	arcsin()	Arcsin	arcsin
FNArccos#	arccos()	Arccos	arccos
FNFactorial#	factorial()	Factorial	factorial
FNStirling.Factorial#	stirling()	Stirling	stirling
FNGamma#	gamma()	Gamma	gamma
FNSinh#	sinh()	Sinh	sinh
FNCosh#	cosh()	Cosh	cosh
FNTanh#	tanh()	Tanh	tanh
FNArcSinh#	arcsinh()	ArcSinh	arcsinh
FNArcCosh#	arccosh()	ArcCosh	arccosh
FNArcTanh#	arctanh()	ArcTanh	arctanh

are presented in two versions. The first version (**power**) handles integer exponents, and the second version (**rpower**) handles real exponents. The integer version uses recursion to perform the power function. The basic strategy used is similar to the divide-and-conquer technique in Section 1. After an exponent is passed to the power function, the function divides the exponent in half and calls itself with the new value. This process continues until the exponent cannot be divided as a whole number. Let's look at an example to see how this algorithm works.

Assume we want to calculate

2^4

which is equivalent to

2 * 2 * 2 * 2

The calls to the **power** function would be:

```
        ┌── exponent
Power(2,4) ◄── initial call
```

Power(2,3) ◄——— recursive call
Power(2,2) ◄——— recursive call
Power(2,1) ◄——— recursive call

Here **power** calls itself recursively until the exponent argument is less than or equal to 1. Because the value 1 cannot be divided anymore, the recursion stops. The result is then determined by returning the following computed value from each level of the recursion:

SQR(<*return value from previous recursion*>) * Base

where **SQR** performs the square function. The recursion then unwinds and the above equation computes a new value at each level in the recursion.

The version of **power** that handles real-type exponents calculates the power using the following equation:

power = exp(exponent * ln(base))

In this case, recursion is not required, because the calculation is performed in a single step. Notice that this equation uses both the built-in **exp** function, which calculates an exponential e to the xth power, and the natural logarithmic function, **ln**. The actual equation calculated is:

$$power = e^{exponent\ *\ \ln(base)}$$

Inverse Sine and Cosine Functions

The Turbo languages provide a set of functions to perform trigonometric operations, and we can use these functions to implement inverse sine and cosine functions. Both of these functions are calculated with the following equations:

$arcsin(x) = \arctan(x\ /\ sqrt(1 - x^2))$
$arccos(x) = \arctan(1\ /\ sqrt(1 - x^2))$

Because each Turbo language provides an **arctan** and **sqrt** (square root) function, both inverse trigonometric functions are easy to write.

The Factorial and Gamma Functions

The factorial algorithm is a popular one that finds its way into most programming books. We've included it here for the sake of completeness. This algorithm can easily be implemented with or without recursion. We'll implement it in Turbo BASIC, C, and Pascal without using recursion. The Turbo Prolog version, on the other hand, uses recursion.

Actually, the factorial functions presented come in two versions. The first version computes the factorial of an integer value and the second version can handle real values.

The heart of the integer version, which uses a simple **FOR** loop, is simply:

```
FOR i := 1 TO N DO
    product := product *i;
factorial := product;
```

The second version, which handles real values, employs Stirling's approximation as shown:

$x! = $ sqrt$(2 * Pi * x) * $ exp$(x) * x^\wedge x * cf$

where *cf* is the correction factor, given by:

$cf = 1 + 1/(12 * x) + 1/(288 * x^\wedge 2) - 139/(51840 * x^\wedge 3) - 571/(2488320 * x^\wedge 4)$

Once we have the factorial function, we can easily implement the Gamma function. It is defined as

$(x - 1)!$

For its implementation, we'll use the Stirling approximation version of the factorial function.

Hyperbolic Functions

Our toolset of mathematical functions also includes six hyperbolic functions. The three fundamental functions are **sinh**, **cosh**, and **tanh**. Here are the equations for these functions:

sinh(x) = (exp(x) − exp(−x)) / 2
cosh(x) = (exp(x) + exp(−x)) / 2
tanh(x) = (exp(x) − exp(−x)) / (exp(x) + exp(−x))

The inverse hyperbolic functions, on the other hand, are defined by the following equations:

arcsinh(x) = ln(x + sqrt(x^2 + 1))
arccosh(x) = ln(x + sqrt(x^2 −1)) for x >= 1
arctanh(x) = ln((1 + x) / (1 − x)) /2 for | x | < 1

Numerical Analysis Algorithms

The second class of algorithms presented is used for numerical analysis methods. The field of numerical analysis is concerned with solving complex mathematical problems such as random number generation, solving simultaneous equations, integration, and data fitting. Because of the complexity of many of the numerical analysis algorithms, we don't present all of the analysis topics. However, we will cover some of the more important areas, including

- solving for the root of a single nonlinear function.
- solving for the minimum/maximum point of a function.
- interpolation.
- integration.

Solving for Functions

The algorithms presented in this section work with nonlinear functions. By *nonlinear function*, we mean a function that when plotted, generates a curved area. Our first algorithm solves a nonlinear function by finding the root of the function. The technique used is called the *Newton-Raphson method*. Essentially, the algorithm seeks to find the value of x for a nonlinear function at the point where:

$f(x) = 0$

The Newton-Raphson method supplies a guess for the root and refines it repeatedly using

improved guess, $x = x - f(x) / f'(x)$

where $f'(x)$ is the derivative of $f(x)$ with respect to x (that is, $df(x)/dx$). The derivative of the function can be approximated using

$$f'(x) = (f(x + h) - f(x)) / h$$

where h is an increment calculated as

$h = 0.01 \quad$ for $|x| <= 1$
$\quad = 0.01 * x$ for $|x| > 1$

Thus Newton's original algorithm is approximated with

improved guess, $x = x - diff$
$diff = h * f(x) / (f(x + h) - f(x))$

The absolute value of the improvement in the guess, *diff*, is compared with a root tolerance value. A good value for the tolerance falls in the ranges of 1.0E – 6 to 1.0E – 10. If absolute *diff* is less than or equal to the preset tolerance, the iteration stops. Another safety factor can be introduced in the implementation: checking divergence. In some cases, the Newton-Raphson method causes the guess for the root to oscillate in values, never fulfilling the tolerance criteria. Thus, it is good practice to impose a ceiling on the number of iterations allowed. A good general value is 30. In addition, keep in mind that the tolerance value should be in the range indicated above. Values that are large (such as 0.1) generally yield inaccurate answers. By contrast, values that are too small impose a high accuracy demand on the solution. This demand may not be met by the system's numeric accuracy, giving you the impression that the solution diverged when it is actually good for most practical purposes!

Minimum/Maximum Point of a Function

We can use Newton's method to determine the minimum or maximum point of a function. The difference is that we seek to find the value of x for:

$$f'(x) = 0$$

instead of $f(x) = 0$. The technique is essentially the same as solving for the root of a function. To test whether the solution points to a maximum or minimum, we select neighboring points and compare their function values with the function value at the solution as shown:

if $(f(x + h) - 2 * f(x) + f(x - h)) > 0$ then solution is at a minimum, else solution is at a maximum

where h is an increment calculated as:

$$h = 0.01 \quad \text{for } |x| <= 1$$
$$= 0.01 * x \text{ for } |x| > 1$$

Interpolation

Interpolation involves finding a polynomial given a set of X and Y points. The numerical interpolation employs the Lagrangian method. This method uses arrays of X and Y that are of arbitrary distances to interpolate the value of x on y. The interpolation algorithm is:

$$y = Y(1) * P(1) + Y(2) + P(2) + ... + Y(n) * P(n)$$

where,

$$P(i) = Y(i) * \text{Product of } [(X(i) - x)]/[(X(i) - X(j)] \text{ for } j = 1.., n \text{ and}$$
$$j <> i$$

Integration

Integration is a very important field of mathematical analysis and many different approaches have been developed by mathematicians over the years for integrating nonlinear functions. Most of the methods fall under two categories: *symbolic integration* and *numerical integration*. Symbolic integration methods use symbols to manipulate a function so that it can be represented in a form that makes it easy to solve. Unfortunately, symbolic integration algorithms are difficult to implement in computer languages because of the complexity and the large number of symbolic integration rules. In this section, we'll concentrate on presenting numerical integration techniques.

If you've taken a college math course, you're probably already familiar with the basic concept behind numerical integration. We can easily compute the value of an integral by determining the area of the curve produced by its function. Remember that when we plot the x and y values that are the solutions to a function, we obtain some type of curve.

The easiest technique for determining the approximate area under a curve is to use the *rectangle method*. This method partitions the area under the curve into a set of rectangles. We can then sum the areas of the rectangles to compute the area of the curve. Figure 3.1 presents an example of this method. Here we are performing the following integration:

$$\int f(x)dx$$

The area of a rectangle is simply its height times its width, so this integral can be expressed as:

height(yi) * width

where the term yi represents the height of each rectangle. In this case we can assume that the width of each rectangle (dx) is the same. This integral is equivalent to summing the parts (each rectangle):

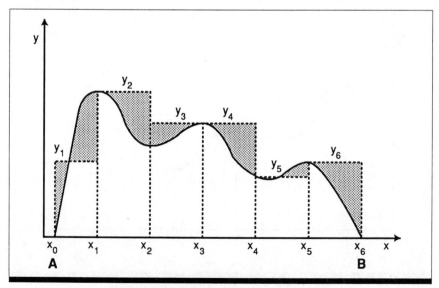

Figure 3.1. Integration using rectangles

$$\sum_{1<=i<=n} w * y(i)$$

where n is the number of rectangles.

The drawback with this method is that we lose some accuracy; parts of the rectangles extend outside the curve, and other parts don't quite fit. This is shown with the shaded areas in Figure 3.1.

A second method of integration that has been developed by mathematicians is the *trapezoid method*, which is a slight variation of the rectangle method. The concept behind this method as shown in Figure 3.2 consists of partitioning the region under a curve into a set of trapezoids instead of rectangles. To compute the area under the curve with this method, the following calculation is made:

$$\sum_{1<=i<=n} \frac{w * y(i) + y(i+1)}{2}$$

The area of a trapezoid is the width times one-half the sum of the height of each leg. Therefore, to compute the area of each trapezoid, we must use two points or solutions of the equation. In some cases, the trapezoid produces better results than the rectangle method; however, it is not as accurate for all cases. As you can see in Figure 3.2, all of the trapezoids

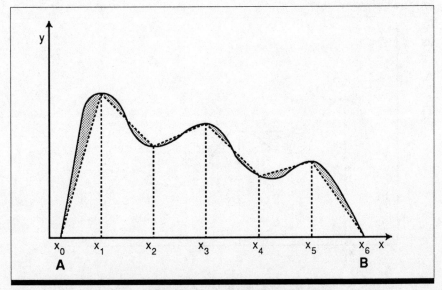

Figure 3.2. Integration using trapezoids

extend outside the curve; therefore, the area approximated with this method is actually greater than the true area.

The Simpson Method of Integration

Now that you have seen both the rectangle and trapezoid methods of integration, we're ready to examine a useful technique for determining the area under a curve. The technique is called the *Simpson method*, which is a hybrid of both the rectangle and trapezoid methods. With the Simpson method, the calculation for the rectangle method is combined with the calculation for the trapezoid method to reduce the margin of error produced independently by each method. How is this done? The basic algorithm consists of using two parts of the rectangle method and one part of the trapezoid method. That is, the following equation is used:

$$\sum_{1 <= i <= n} w * y(i) + 1/3 \quad \sum_{1 <= i <= n} \frac{w * y(i) + y(i+1)}{2} * 2$$

To calculate the area for one partition, the equation can be represented as

Area = Delta_X / 3 * [$Y(1)$ + 4 * $Y(2)$ + $Y(3)$]

where the term *Delta_X* represents the width and $Y(1)$, $Y(2)$, and $Y(3)$ are the three points or solutions to the equation. If we want to calculate the area, using a set of n points, the equation would be

Area = Delta_X / 3 * [$Y(1)$ + 4 * $Y(2)$ + 2 * $Y(3)$ + ... + 4 * $Y(n-1)$ + $Y(n)$]

The major requirement is that the number of points used, n, must be odd.

Implementation of Simpson's Method

The numerical integration algorithm that we've implemented in the Turbo languages uses the Simpson method. It calculates the area under the curve $Y(x)$ in the range of [A, B]. Fortunately this integration method is actually quite straightforward to implement. To use this method, two conditions are required. First, the values of the integrated points $Y(1)$, $Y(2)$, ..., $Y(N)$ must be taken at equal intervals (*X* values). This interval is called the *Delta_X*. Second, an odd number of *Y* points are required.

Our implementation calculates the basic equation presented in the previous section.

Area = Delta_X / 3 * [$Y(1) + 4 * Y(2) + 2 * Y(3) + ... + 4 * Y(n-1) + Y(n)$]

To compute this approximate area, our routine requires you to pass an array of *Y* points and the *Delta_X* value as arguments. A simple while loop is used to sum up the even and odd points that are stored in the variables *sum_even* and *sum_odd*. Once the even and odd sums are computed, the following statement is used to calculate the area under the curve:

```
SimpsonArea := DeltaX/3.0 * (Y[1] + 4*sum_even + 2*sum_odd
               + Y[NData]);
```

An example of how this calculation is used on a set of points is shown in Figure 3.3.

Matrix Operations

The last mathematical algorithms presented in this section are designed to process matrices. The matrix operations supported are

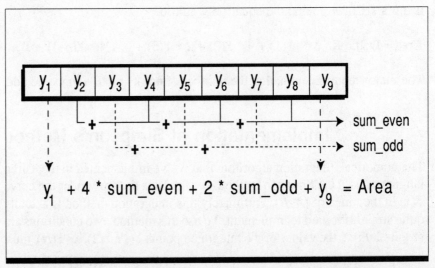

Figure 3.3. Computing the area using Simpson's method

- Matrix addition
- Matrix multiplication
- Matrix inversion

A *matrix* is essentially a two-dimensional representation of a set of numbers, as shown:

```
20  -3  45  67  100  0
 9   7  -2   2    3  9
12   7   1   1   -2  4
```

Such matrices are useful for many types of applications, including computer graphics and programs for solving linear equations.

Matrix Addition

Matrix addition is a fairly straightforward operation. Here we are showing how two matrices are summed:

```
5   7  8     4 -2  3     9  5  11
2  -2  4     3  9  4     5  7   8
1   1  1     8 -1  2     9  0   3
```

The algorithm adds a value in a given position in the first matrix to the value in the corresponding position of the second matrix to obtain the sum for the third matrix. This algorithm is illustrated with the following pseudocode, which adds the matrices A and B to give matrix C:

```
for row = first_row to last_row
    for col = first_col to last_col
        C[row,col] = A[row,col] + B[row,col]
```

Matrix Multiplication

Matrix multiplication is a bit more involved than matrix addition. In multiplying two matrices, say A and B, the following rules must be satisfied:

1. The number of columns in A must equal the number of rows in B.

2. The number of rows in A must equal the number of rows in C.
3. The number of columns in B must equal the number of columns in C.

The following example illustrates how two matrices are multiplied:

```
5   7   8      4  –2   3        105   45   59
2  –2   4      3   9   4         34  –26    6
1   1   1      8  –1   2         15    6    9
```

For example, to compute the value 105, which is in the first row and first column of matrix C, the following calculation is made:

5*4 + 7*3 + 8*8 = 105

As shown, each row,column value (i,j) in the product matrix C is produced by taking the dot product of the elements in row i of matrix A with the elements in column j of matrix B. Here is the pseudocode for the matrix multiplication of A and B to produce matrix C:

```
for row = first_row of A to last_row of A
    for col = first_col of B to last_col of B
        C[row,col] = 0
        for i = first_col of A to last_col of A
            C[row,col] = C[row,col] + A[row,i] * B[i,col]
```

Matrix Inversion

The matrix inversion algorithm provided in the listings employs a pivoting technique. This guards against serious numeric roundoff error due to having matrix elements that are considerably larger in magnitude than others. Rather than presenting pseudocode that practically duplicates the listings, we would like to emphasize the main steps employed by the inversion algorithm. They are

1. Search for the pivot elements.
2. Interchange the rows to place the pivot element on the diagonal.
3. Divide the pivot row by the pivot element.
4. Interchange columns.

Implementation of
Mathematical Algorithms

The routines provided for each of the Turbo languages are covered next.

Turbo BASIC

The implementation of the Turbo BASIC mathematical algorithms is presented in Listing 3.1. In this section we include a short description of each routine provided in the listing.

The simple and transcendental functions require only one argument. Therefore, the parameter description has been omitted.

Returns the inverse sine value in radians. **FNArcsin#**

Syntax:
```
DEF FNArcsin#(X#)
```

Returns the inverse cosine value in radians. **FNArccos#**

Syntax:
```
DEF FNArccos#(X#)
```

Returns the factorial (as a double-precision floating-point number). The **FNFactorial#**
function returns 1 for arguments equal to or less than 0.

Syntax:
```
DEF FNFactorial#(N%)
```

Returns the factorial (as a double-precision floating-point number) for a **FNStirling.Factorial#**
real number argument, using Stirling's approximation. The function returns
1 for arguments equal to or less than 0.

Syntax:
```
DEF FNStirling.Factorial#(X#)
```

Returns the gamma function for a real-number argument. The function **FNGamma#**
returns 1 for arguments equal to or less than 0.

Syntax:
```
DEF FNGamma#(X#)
```

FNSinh#   Calculates the hyperbolic sine.

Syntax:
```
DEF FNSinh#(X#)
```

FNCosh#   Calculates the hyperbolic cosine.

Syntax:
```
DEF FNCosh#(X#)
```

FNTanh#   Calculates the hyperbolic tangent.

Syntax:
```
DEF FNTanh#(X#)
```

FNArcSinh#   Calculates the inverse hyperbolic sine.

Syntax:
```
DEF FNArcSinh#(X#)
```

FNArcCosh#   Calculates the inverse hyperbolic cosine. If the argument **X#** is less than
                          1.0, the function returns 0 as a numeric-coded error, because no real value
                          of **X#** yields 0.

Syntax:
```
DEF FNArcCosh#(X#)
```

FNArcTanh#   Calculates the inverse hyperbolic tangent. If the argument **X#** is less than
                          1.0, the function returns 2 as a numeric-coded error, because no real value
                          of **X#** yields 2.

Syntax:
```
DEF FNArcTanh#(X#)
```

FNUserFunc#   Returns the value of a single-argument, user-defined function. This func-
                          tion is used by subroutines **Root** and **Optimum**.

Syntax:
```
DEF FNUserFunc#(X#)
```

Calculates the root of the user-defined function. The initial guess, root **Root**
tolerance, and maximum number of iterations are specified.

Syntax:
```
SUB Root(Guess#, Tolerance#, Max.Iter%, Diverge%)
```

Parameters:

Guess#   the initial guess for the root that is refined by the
                  subroutine.

Tolerance#   the tolerance (that is, accuracy) for the root.

Max.Iter%   the maximum number of iterations.

Diverge%   a flag that indicates whether the solution diverges.
                  0 –> solution converges and the answer is satisfactory.
                  1 –> solution diverges, because the maximum number of
                        iterations has been exceeded.

Calculates the point where the user-defined function reaches a minimum **Optimum**
or a maximum. The initial guess, tolerance, and maximum number of
iterations are specified.

Syntax:
```
SUB Optimum(Guess#, Tolerance#, Max.Iter%, Diverge%)
```

Parameters:

Guess#   the initial guess for the optimum that is refined by the
                  subroutine.

Tolerance#   the tolerance (that is, accuracy) for the optimum value.

Max.Iter%   the maximum number of iterations.

Diverge%   a flag that indicates whether the solution diverges.
                  0 –> solution converges and the answer is satisfactory.
                  1 –> solution diverges, because the maximum number of
                        iterations has been exceeded.

Interpolates the value of **Xint#** using the paired array of data **X#()** and **Y#()**. **YInterp**
OPTION BASE 1 is assumed to be in effect when you use this subroutine.

Syntax:
```
SUB YInterp(Y#(1), X#(1), NData%, Xint#, Yint#)
```

Parameters:

Y#()	the array of Y's.
X#()	the arrays of X's.
NData%	the number of points in arrays **Y#()** and **X#()** involved in the interpolation. There must be at least 2.
Xint#	the value of the interpolated X.
Yint#	the value of the interpolated Y.

SimpsonArea   Calculates the area under the curve (that is, the integral) using Simpson's rule. A 0 is returned if **NData%** is even.

Syntax:
```
SUB SimpsonArea(Y#(1), DeltaX#, NData%, Area#)
```

Parameters:

Y#()	the array of Y's taken for equidistant X's.
DeltaX#	the uniform space between the equidistant X's.
NData%	the number of elements in array **Y#()** used in the integration. This value must be an odd number.
Area#	the area under the curve.

Add.Matrix   Adds matrices **A#(,)** and **B#(,)** to yield matrix **C#(,)**. The three matrices must have the same dimensions. It is assumed that each matrix is entirely occupied with meaningful data.

Syntax:
```
SUB Add.Matrix(C#(2), A#(2), B#(2), OK%)
```

Parameters:

C#(,)	the resulting matrix.
A#(,), B#(,)	the added matrices.
OK%	the flag to signal the success of the matrix addition. 0 –> matrices were not added. 1 –> matrices were added.

Mult.Matrix   Multiplies matrices **A#(,)** and **B#(,)** to yield matrix **C#(,)**. The three matrices must satisfy the following conditions:

columns in A = rows in B
columns in C = rows in A
rows in C   = columns in B

It is assumed that each matrix is entirely occupied with meaningful data.

Syntax:
```
SUB Mult.Matrix(C#(2), A#(2), B#(2), OK%)
```

Parameters:

C#(,)   the resulting matrix.
A#(,), B#(,)   the added matrices.
OK%   the flag to signal the success of the matrix multiplication.
                0 –> matrices were not multiplied.
                1 –> matrices were multiplied.

Inverts a square matrix **A#(,)** in place. The determinant is also calculated. **Invert.Matrix**

Syntax:
```
SUB Invert.Matrix(A#(2), Det#, OK%)
```

Parameters:

A#(,)   the inverted square matrix.
Det#   the determinant of the inverted matrix.
OK%   the flag to signal the success of the matrix inversion.
        0 –> matrix was not inverted, because it is not a square matrix.
        1 –> matrix was inverted.

Turbo C

Listing 3.2 shows the header file for the Turbo C math routines. The header file contains a number of declared constants and data types used by the C functions. The following constants are declared:

```
#define MAX_ROW 10
#define MAX_COL 10
#define MAX_ARRAY 10
```

The **MAX_ROW** and **MAX_COL** macros define the size of the matrix fields in the **matrix_struct** structure shown. The **MAX_ARRAY** defines the size of the arrays used in the interpolation and numeric integration functions.

The **matrix_struct** structure shown is used to declare matrices. Two fields keep track of the number of columns and rows in the matrix that contain meaningful data.

```
struct matrix_struct {
    double mat[MAX_ROW][MAX_COL];
    unsigned short rows;
    unsigned short cols;
};


typedef struct matrix_struct matrix;
```

The **vector_struct** structure shown is used to declare vectors. A field tracks the number of vector elements that contain meaningful data.

```
struct vector_struct {
    double elm[MAX_COL];
    unsigned short numelm;
};


typedef struct vector_struct vector;
```

The simple array **wordarray** shown here is declared for use with the **decomp()** and **solve()** routines:

```
typedef unsigned wordarray[MAX_COL];
```

The simple array **dataarray** is declared for use with the routines for numerical integration and interpolation.

```
typedef double dataarray[MAX_ARRAY];
```

The enumerated type **boolean_enum** is declared to implement booleans in the C math functions.

```
enum boolean_enum { FALSE, TRUE };
typedef enum boolean_enum boolean;
```

The Turbo C math routines are described next. Because the simple and transcendental functions require only a single argument, the parameters sections for these functions have been omitted.

Calculates a square of a double number.   **sqr()**

Syntax:
```
double sqr(double x);
```

Recursive function that raises a real number to an integer power.   **power()**

Syntax:
```
double power(double base, int exponent);
```

Function that raises a real number to a real power. If the base is 0 or negative,   **rpower()**
the function returns a 0.

Syntax:
```
double rpower(double base, double exponent);
```

Returns the inverse sine value in radians.   **arcsin()**

Syntax:
```
double arcsin(double x);
```

Returns the inverse cosine value in radians.   **arccos()**

Syntax:
```
double arccos(double x);
```

Returns the factorial (as a floating-point number). The function returns 1   **factorial()**
for arguments equal to or less than 0.

Syntax:
```
double factorial(unsigned short n);
```

Returns the factorial (as a floating-point number) for a real-number argu-   **stirling_factorial()**
ment, using Stirling's approximation. The function returns 1 for arguments
equal to or less than 0.

Syntax:
```
double stirling_factorial(double x);
```

gamma()

Returns the gamma function for a real-number argument. The function returns 1 for arguments equal to or less than 1.

Syntax:
```
double gamma(double x);
```

sinh()

Calculates the hyperbolic sine. This function is also prototyped in **math.h**.

Syntax:
```
double sinh(double x);
```

cosh()

Calculates the hyperbolic cosine. This function is also prototyped in **math.h**.

Syntax:
```
double cosh(double x);
```

tanh()

Calculates the hyperbolic tangent. This function is also prototyped in **math.h**.

Syntax:
```
double tanh(double x);
```

arcsinh()

Calculates the inverse hyperbolic sine.

Syntax:
```
double arcsinh(double x);
```

arccosh()

Calculates the inverse hyperbolic cosine. If the argument x is less than 1.0, the function returns 0 as a numeric-coded error, because no real value of x yields 0.

Syntax:
```
double arccosh(double x);
```

arctanh()

Calculates the inverse hyperbolic tangent. If x is less than 1.0, the function returns 2 as a numeric-coded error—no real value of x yields 2.

Syntax:
```
double arctanh(double x);
```

Returns the value of a single-argument, user-defined function. This function is used by functions **root**() and **optimum**().

userfunc()

Syntax:
```
double userfunc(double x);
```

Calculates the root of the user-defined function. The initial guess, root tolerance, and maximum number of iterations are specified. The function returns the root value.

root()

Syntax:
```
double root(double guess, double tolerance,
            unsigned short max_iter, boolean *diverge);
```

Parameters:

guess	the initial guess for the root.
tolerance	the tolerance (that is, accuracy) for the root.
max_iter	the maximum number of iterations.
diverge	a pointer that indicates whether the solution diverges.

FALSE–> solution converges and the answer is satisfactory.
TRUE –> solution diverges, because the maximum number
of iterations has been exceeded.

Calculates the point where the user-defined function reaches a minimum or a maximum. The initial guess, tolerance, and maximum number of iterations are specified.

optimum()

Syntax:
```
double optimum(double guess, double tolerance,
               unsigned short max_iter, boolean *diverge);
```

Parameters:

guess	the initial guess for the optimum that is refined by the function.
tolerance	the tolerance (that is, accuracy) for the optimum value.
max_iter	the maximum number of iterations.

diverge   a pointer that indicates whether the solution diverges.
FALSE –> solution converges and the answer is satisfactory.
TRUE –> solution diverges, because the maximum number
of iterations has been exceeded.

yinterp()

Interpolates the value of **Xint** using the paired array of data **x**[ ] and **y**[ ].
The function returns the interpolated value of **Y**.

Syntax:
```
double yinterp(dataarray y, dataarray x, unsigned ndata,
               double xint);
```

Parameters:
y[ ]   the array of y's.
x[ ]   the arrays of x's.
ndata   the number of points in arrays **y**[ ] and **x**[ ] involved in the interpolation. There must be at least 2.
xint   the value of the interpolated **x**.

simpsonarea()

Calculates the area under the curve (that is, the integral) using Simpson's
rule. The function returns the calculated area or 0 if **ndata** is even.

Syntax:
```
double simpsonarea(dataarray y, double deltax, unsigned ndata);
```

Parameters:
y[ ]   the array of y's taken for equidistant x's.
deltax   the uniform space between the equidistant x's.
ndata   the number of elements in array **y**[ ] used in the integration. The
value must be an odd number.

add_matrix()

Adds matrices **a**[ ][ ] and **b**[ ][ ] to yield matrix **c**[ ][ ]. The three matrices
must have the same dimensions. The function returns a logical value to
signal the success of the matrix addition.

Syntax:
```
boolean add_matrix(matrix *c, matrix *a, matrix *b);
```

Parameters:
c[ ][ ]   a pointer to the resulting matrix.
a[ ][ ], **b**[ ][ ]   the pointers to the added matrices.

Multiplies matrices **a**[ ][ ] and **b**[ ][ ] to yield matrix **c**[ ][ ]. The three   **mult_matrix()**
matrices must satisfy the following conditions:

columns in A = rows in B
columns in C = rows in A
rows in C   = columns in B

The function returns a logical value to signal the success of the matrix
multiplication.

Syntax:
```
boolean mult_matrix(matrix *c, matrix *a, matrix *b);
```

Parameters:
c[ ][ ]   the pointer to the resulting matrix.
a[ ][ ], **b**[ ][ ]   the pointers to the multiplied matrices.

Inverts a square matrix **a**[ ][ ] in place. The determinant is also calculated.   **invert_matrix()**
The function returns a logical value to signal the success of the matrix
inversion.

Syntax:
```
boolean invert_matrix(matrix *a, double *det);
```

Parameters:
a[ ][ ]   the inverted square matrix.
det   the pointer to the determinant of the inverted matrix.

Turbo Pascal

Listing 3.3 shows the library unit for the Turbo Pascal math routines. It
contains a number of declared constants and data types used by the Pascal
routines. The following constants are declared:

```
CONST MAX_ROW = 10;
   MAX_COL = 10;
   MAX_ARRAY = 10;
```

The **MAX_ROW** and **MAX_COL** constants define the size of the matrix
fields in the **Matrix** record shown. The **MAX_ARRAY** defines the size

of the arrays used in the interpolation and numeric integration functions. The **Matrix** record shown is used to declare matrices. Two fields are used to keep track of the number of columns and rows in the matrix that contain meaningful data.

```
TYPE Matrix = RECORD
        Mat : ARRAY [1..MAX_ROW,1..MAX_COL] OF REAL;
        Rows, Cols : BYTE;
      END;
```

The **Vector** record shown is used to declare vectors. A field tracks the number of vector elements that contain meaningful data.

```
Vector = RECORD
    Elm : ARRAY [1..MAX_COL] OF REAL;
    NumElm : BYTE;
END;
```

The simple array **WordArray** is declared for use with the **Decomp()** and **Solve()** routines.

```
WordArray = ARRAY [1..MAX_COL] OF WORD;
```

The simple array **DataArray** is declared for use with the routines for numerical integration and interpolation.

```
DataArray = ARRAY [1..MAX_ARRAY] OF REAL;
```

The Turbo Pascal math routines are covered next.

Power   Raises a real number to an integer power.

Syntax:
```
FUNCTION Power(Base : REAL; Exponent : INTEGER) : REAL;
```

RPower   Raises a real number to a real power. If the base is 0 or negative, the function returns a 0.

Syntax:
```
FUNCTION RPower(Base, Exponent : REAL) : REAL;
```

Returns the inverse sine value in radians.   **Arcsin**

Syntax:
```
FUNCTION Arcsin(X : REAL) : REAL;
```

                                                                              Arccos

Returns the inverse cosine value in radians.

Syntax:
```
FUNCTION Arccos(X : REAL) : REAL;
```

Returns the factorial (as a floating-point number). The function returns 1   **Factorial**
for arguments equal to or less than 0.

Syntax:
```
FUNCTION Factorial(N : BYTE) : REAL;
```

Returns the factorial (as a floating-point number) for a real-number argu-   **Stirling_Factorial**
ment, using Stirling's approximation. The function returns 1 for arguments
equal to or less than 0.

Syntax:
```
FUNCTION Stirling_Factorial(X : REAL) : REAL;
```

Returns the gamma function for a real-number argument. The function   **Gamma**
returns 1 for arguments equal to or less than 1.

Syntax:
```
FUNCTION Gamma(X : REAL) : REAL;
```

Calculates the hyperbolic sine.   **Sinh**

Syntax:
```
FUNCTION Sinh(X : REAL) : REAL;
```

Calculates the hyperbolic cosine.   **Cosh**

Syntax:
```
FUNCTION Cosh(X : REAL) : REAL;
```

Tanh   Calculates the hyperbolic tangent.

Syntax:
```
FUNCTION Tanh(X : REAL) : REAL;
```

ArcSinh   Calculates the inverse hyperbolic sine.

Syntax:
```
FUNCTION ArcSinh(X : REAL) : REAL;
```

ArcCosh   Calculates the inverse hyperbolic cosine. If the argument **X** is less than 1.0, the function returns 0 as a numeric-coded error, because no real value of **X** yields 0.

Syntax:
```
FUNCTION ArcCosh(X : REAL) : REAL;
```

ArcTanh   Calculates the inverse hyperbolic tangent. If the argument **X** is less than 1.0, the function returns 2 as a numeric-coded error, because no real value of **X** yields 2.

Syntax:
```
FUNCTION ArcTanh(X : REAL) : REAL;
```

UserFunc   Returns the value of a single-argument, user-defined function. This function is used by functions **Root** and **Optimum**.

Syntax:
```
FUNCTION UserFunc(X : REAL) : REAL;
```

Root   Calculates the root of the user-defined function. The initial guess, root tolerance, and maximum number of iterations are specified. The function returns the root value.

Syntax:
```
FUNCTION Root(Guess, Tolerance : REAL; Max_Iter : BYTE;
              VAR Diverge : BOOLEAN) : REAL;
```

Parameters:
Guess   the initial guess for the root.
Tolerance   the tolerance (that is, accuracy) for the root.

Max_Iter   the maximum number of iterations.

Diverge   a flag that indicates whether the solution diverges.

FALSE –> solution converges and answer is satisfactory.

TRUE –> solution diverges, because the maximum number of iterations has been exceeded.

Calculates the point where the user-defined function reaches a minimum or a maximum. The initial guess, tolerance, and maximum number of iterations are specified.   **Optimum**

Syntax:

```
FUNCTION Optimum(Guess, Tolerance : REAL; Max_Iter : BYTE;
            VAR Diverge : BOCLEAN) : REAL;
```

Parameters:

Guess   the initial guess for the optimum that is, refined by the subroutine.

Tolerance   the tolerance (that is, accuracy) for the optimum value.

Max_Iter   the maximum number of iterations.

Diverge   a flag that indicates whether the solution diverges.

FALSE –> solution converges and answer is satisfactory.

TRUE –> solution diverges, because the maximum number of iterations has been exceeded.

Interpolates the value of **Xint** using the paired array of data **X[ ]** and **Y[ ]**. The function returns the interpolated value of **Y**.   **YInterp**

Syntax:

```
FUNCTION YInterp(VAR Y, X : DataArray; NData : WORD;
            Xint : REAL) : REAL;
```

Parameters:

Y[ ]   the array of Y's.

X[ ]   the arrays of X's.

NData   the number of points in arrays **Y[ ]** and **X[ ]** involved in the interpolation. There must be at least 2.

Xint   the value of the interpolated **X**.

Calculates the area under the curve (that is, the integral) using Simpson's rule. The function returns the area under the curve. A 0 is returned if **NData** is even.   **SimpsonArea**

Syntax:

```
FUNCTION SimpsonArea(VAR Y : DataArray; DeltaX : REAL;
                     NData : WORD) : REAL;
```

Parameters:

Y[ ] the array of Y's taken for equidistant X's.

DeltaX the uniform space between the equidistant X's.

NData the number of elements in array **Y[ ]** used in the integration. The value must be an odd number.

Add_Matrix Adds matrices **A[,]** and **B[,]** to yield matrix **C[,]**. The three matrices must have the same dimensions. The function returns a logical value to signal the success of the matrix addition.

Syntax:

```
FUNCTION Add_Matrix(VAR C, A, B : Matrix) : BOOLEAN;
```

Parameters:

C[,] the resulting matrix.

A[,], B[,] the added matrices.

Mult_Matrix Multiplies matrices **A[,]** and **B[,]** to produce matrix **C[,]**. The three matrices must satisfy the following conditions:

columns in A = rows in B
columns in C = rows in A
rows in C   = columns in B

The function returns a logical value to signal the success of the matrix multiplication.

Syntax:

```
FUNCTION Mult_Matrix(VAR C, A, B : Matrix) : BOOLEAN;
```

Parameters:

C[,] the resulting matrix.

A[,], B[,] the multiplied matrices.

Invert_Matrix Inverts a square matrix **A[,]** in place. The determinant is also calculated. The function returns a logical value to signal the success of the matrix inversion.

Syntax:
```
FUNCTION Invert_Matrix(VAR A : Matrix; VAR Det : REAL) : BOOLEAN;
```

Parameters:
A[,]   the inverted square matrix.
Det   the determinant of the inverted matrix.

Turbo Prolog

Listing 3.4 presents the implementations of the math algorithms in Turbo Prolog. Note that only one constant is required:

```
constants:
   pi = 355 / 113
```

The Turbo Prolog math predicates are described next.

Calculates the square of a real number.   **sqr**

Syntax:
```
sqr(X, Result)      (i,o)
   (real, real)
```

Parameters:
X   the real number to be squared.
Result   the number squared.

Raises a real number to an integer power.   **power**

Syntax:
```
power(Base, Exponent, Result)      (i,i,o)
     (real, integer, real)
```

Parameters:
Base   the base number.
Exponent   the integer exponent.
Result   the returned value.

Raises a real number to an real power. If the base is 0 or negative, the   **rpower**
predicate returns a 0.

Syntax:
```
rpower(Base, Exponent, Result)      (i,i,o)
      (real, real, real)
```

Parameters:
Base   the base number.
Exponent   the real exponent.
Result   the returned value.

arcsin   Returns the inverse sine value in radians.

Syntax:
```
arcsin(X, Result)      (i,o)
      (real, real)
```

Parameters:
X   the sine value.
Result   the inverse sine result.

arccos   Returns the inverse cosine value in radians.

Syntax:
```
arccos(X, Result)      (i,o)
      (real, real)
```

Parameters:
X   the cosine value.
Result   the inverse cosine result.

factorial   Returns the factorial (as a real number).

Syntax:
```
factorial(X, Result)      (i,o)
          (integer, real)
```

Parameters:
X   the positive integer whose factorial is calculated.
Result   the computed factorial.

Returns the factorial (as a real number) for a real-number argument, using **stirling_factorial** Stirling's approximation. The predicate returns 1 for arguments equal to or less than 0.

Syntax:
```
stirling_factorial(X, Result)      (i,o)
                 (real, real)
```

Parameters:
X   the positive number whose factorial is calculated.
Result   the factorial computed as an approximation.

Returns the gamma function for a real-number argument. The predicate **gamma** returns 1 for arguments equal to or less than 1.

Syntax:
```
gamma(X, Result)      (i,o)
     (real, real)
```

Parameters:
X   the positive number used as an argument.
Result   the gamma calculation result.

Calculates the hyperbolic sine.   **sinh**

Syntax:
```
sinh(X, Result)      (i,o)
    (real, real)
```

Parameters:
X   the argument for the hyperbolic sine predicate.
Result   the computed hyperbolic sine.

Calculates the hyperbolic cosine.   **cosh**

Syntax:
```
cosh(X, Result)      (i,o)
    (real, real)
```

Parameters:
X   the argument for the hyperbolic cosine predicate.
Result   the computed hyperbolic cosine.

tanh   Calculates the hyperbolic tangent.

Syntax:
```
tanh(X, Result)      (i,o)
    (real, real)
```

Parameters:
X   the argument for the hyperbolic tangent predicate.
Result   the computed hyperbolic tangent.

arcsinh   Calculates the inverse hyperbolic sine.

Syntax:
```
arcsinh(X, Result)      (i,o)
      (real, real)
```

Parameters:
X   the argument for the inverse hyperbolic sine predicate.
Result   the computed inverse hyperbolic sine.

arccosh   Calculates the inverse hyperbolic cosine. If the argument **x** is less than 1.0, the predicate returns 0 as a numeric-coded error, because no real value of **x** yields 0.

Syntax:
```
arccosh(X, Result)      (i,o)
      (real, real)
```

Parameters:
X   the argument for the inverse hyperbolic cosine predicate.
Result   the computed inverse hyperbolic cosine.

arctanh   Calculates the inverse hyperbolic tangent. If the argument **x** is less than 1.0, the predicate returns 2 as a numeric-coded error, because no real value of **x** yields 2.

Syntax:
```
arctanh(X, Result)        (i,o)
        (real, real)
```

Parameters:

X   the argument for the inverse hyperbolic tangent predicate.

Result   the computed inverse hyperbolic tangent.

• Listing 3.1. Turbo BASIC math routines

```
OPTION BASE 1
DEFDBL A-Z


DEF FNArcsin#(X#) = ATN(X# / SQR(1 - X#*X#)) ' inverse sine function

DEF FNArccos#(X#) = ATN(1 / SQR(1 - X#*X#))  ' inverse cosine function

DEF FNFactorial#(N%)
' calculates the factorial of an integer using a loop
product# = 1
IF N% > 1 THEN
   FOR i% = 1 TO N%
       product# = product# * i%
   NEXT i%
END IF
FNFactorial# = product#
END DEF ' FNFactorial#

DEF FNStirling.Factorial#(X#)
' calculates factorial for integer or fractional argument using
' Stirling's approximation with correction factor
IF X# > 0 THEN
   FNStirling.Factorial# = SQR(2 * 4 * ATN(1) * X#) *    _
                      EXP(X# * LOG(X#) - X#) *            _
                      (1 + 1 / (12 * X#) +                _
                      1 / (288 * X#^2) +                  _
                      139 / (51840 * X#^3) +              _
                      571 / (2488320 * X#^4))
ELSE
```

```
    FNStirling.Factorial# = 1
END IF
END DEF ' FNStirling.Factorial#


DEF FNGamma#(X#) = FNStirling.Factorial#(X# - 1)
' calculates Gamma function for integer and fractional values


DEF FNSinh#(X#) = (EXP(X#) - EXP(-X#)) / 2.0 ' hyperbolic sine function


DEF FNCosh#(X#) = (EXP(X#) + EXP(-X#)) / 2.0 ' hyperbolic cosine function


DEF FNTanh#(X#)
' calculates hyperbolic tangent function
Y# = EXP(X#)
FNTanh# = (Y# - 1/Y#) / (Y# + 1/Y#)
END DEF ' Tanh


DEF FNArcSinh#(X#) = LOG(X# + SQR(X#^2 + 1))
' calculates inverse hyperbolic sine function


DEF FNArcCosh#(X#)
' calculates inverse hyperbolic cosine function
IF X# >= 1.0 THEN
    FNArcCosh# = LOG(X# + SQR(X#^2 - 1))
ELSE
    FNArcCosh# = 0.0 ' error code, because there is no
    ' real x to make the arccosh value 0
END IF
END DEF ' FNArcCosh#


DEF FNArcTanh#(X#)
' calculates inverse hyperbolic tangent function
IF ABS(X#) < 1.0 THEN
    FNArcTanh# = LOG((1+X#)/(1-X#)) / 2.0
ELSE
    FNArcTanh# = 2.0 ' error code, because arctanh(x) <> 2 for all x
END IF
END DEF ' FNArcTanh#


DEF FNUserFunc#(X#)
' user-defined function
```

```
FNUserFunc# = EXP(X#) - 3 * X# * X#
END DEF ' FNUserFunc#


SUB Root(Guess#, Tolerance#, Max.Iter%, Diverge%)
' finds the root of a function using Newton's method
LOCAL incrm#, diff#, h#, fx#, iter%
incrm# = 0.01
iter% = 0 ' initialize iteration counter
Diverge% = 0
DO ' start root-refining loop
   IF ABS(Guess#) > 1.0 THEN h# = incrm# * Guess# ELSE h# = incrm#
   fx# = FNUserFunc#(Guess#)
   diff# = h# * fx# / (FNUserFunc#(Guess#+h#) - fx#)
   Guess# = Guess# - diff#
   INCR iter%
   IF iter% > Max.Iter% THEN Diverge% = 1
LOOP UNTIL (ABS(diff#) <= Tolerance#) OR (Diverge% <> 0)
END SUB ' Root


SUB Optimum(Guess#, Tolerance#, Max.Iter%, Diverge%)
' finds the optimum point of a function using Newton's method
LOCAL incrm#, diff#, h#, fx#, fp#, fm#, iter%
incrm# = 0.01
iter% = 0 ' initialize iteration counter
Diverge% = 0
DO ' start root-refining loop
   IF ABS(Guess#) > 1.0 THEN h# = incrm# * Guess# ELSE h# = incrm#
   fx# = FNUserFunc#(Guess#)
   fp# = FNUserFunc#(Guess# + h#)
   fm# = FNUserFunc#(Guess# - h#)
   diff# = h# / 2.0 * (fp# - fm#) / (fp# - 2 * fx# + fm#)
   Guess# = Guess# - diff#
   INCR iter%
   IF iter% > Max.Iter% THEN Diverge% = 1
LOOP UNTIL (ABS(diff#) <= Tolerance#) OR (Diverge% <> 0)
END SUB ' Optimum


SUB YInterp(Y#(1), X#(1), NData%, Xint#, Yint#)
' Performs Lagrangian interpolation. The numeric arrays
' need not be sorted.
```

```
LOCAL i%, j%, product#
Yint# = 0.0
FOR i% = 1 TO NData%
   product# = 1.0
   FOR j% = 1 TO NData%
      IF i% <> j% THEN _
         product# = product# * (X#(j%) - XInt#) / (X#(j%) - X#(i%))
   NEXT j%
   Yint# = Yint# + Y#(i%) * product#
NEXT i%
END SUB ' YInterp


SUB SimpsonArea(Y#(1), DeltaX#, NData%, Area#)
' uses Simpson rule to perform numerical integration
LOCAL i%, sum.odd#, sum.even#
IF ((NData% MOD 2) = 0) OR (NData% < 3) THEN
   Area# = 0.0
   EXIT SUB
END IF
sum.odd# = -Y#(NData%)
sum.even# = 0.0
FOR i% = 2 TO NData%-1 STEP 2
   sum.even# = sum.even# + Y#(i%)
   sum.odd# = sum.odd# + Y#(i%+1)
NEXT i%
Area# = DeltaX# / 3.0 * (Y#(1) + 4*sum.even# + 2*sum.odd#  + Y#(NData%))
END SUB ' SimpsonArea


SUB Add.Matrix(C#(2), A#(2), B#(2), OK%)
' adds matrices A and B to give matrix C
LOCAL i%, j%
' are matrices A, B, and C of the same size?
IF (UBound(A#(1)) <> UBound(B#(1))) OR _
   (UBound(A#(2)) <> UBound(B#(2))) OR _
   (UBound(A#(1)) <> UBound(C#(1))) OR _
   (UBound(A#(2)) <> UBound(C#(2))) THEN
   OK% = 0
   EXIT SUB
END IF
```

```
FOR i% = 1 TO  UBound(A#(1))
    FOR j% = 1 TO  UBound(A#(2))
        C#(i%,j%)  = A#(i%,j%)  + B#(i%,j%)
    NEXT j%
NEXT i%
OK% = 1
END SUB ' Add.Matrix


SUB Mult.Matrix(C#(2),  A#(2),  B#(2),  OK%)
' multiplies matrices A and B to give matrix C
LOCAL i%,  j%,  k%
IF  (UBound(A#(2))  <>  UBound(B#(1)))  OR _
    (UBound(A#(1))  <>  UBound(C#(1)))  OR _
    (UBound(B#(2))  <>  UBound(C#(2)))  THEN
    OK% = 0
        EXIT SUB
END IF
FOR i% = 1  TO  UBound(A#(1))
    FOR j% = 1  TO  UBound(B#(2))
        C#(i%,j%)  = 0.0
        FOR k% = 1  TO  UBound(A#(1))
            C#(i%,j%)  = C#(i%,j%)  + A#(i%,k%)  * B#(k%,j%)
        NEXT k%
    NEXT j%
NEXT i%
OK% = 1
END SUB ' Mult.Matrix


SUB Invert.Matrix(A#(2),  Det#,  OK%)
' inverts matrix and returns the determinant
LOCAL i%,  j%,  k%,  m%,  n%,  row%,  col%,  num.rows%
LOCAL tempo#,  big#,  pvt#
LOCAL pvt.ind#()
LOCAL index%()
DIM pvt.ind#(Ubound(A#(2))),  index%(Ubound(A#(2)),2)
IF  (UBound(A#(1))  <>  UBound(A#(2)))  THEN
    Det# = 0.0
    OK% = 0
    ERASE pvt.ind#,  index%
    EXIT SUB
```

```
END IF
Det# = 1.0
num.rows% = UBound(A#(1))
FOR i% = 1 TO num.rows%
    pvt.ind#(i%) = 0
    FOR i% = 1 TO num.rows%
        big# = 0.0 ' initialize pivot element
        FOR j% = 1 TO num.rows%
            IF pvt.ind#(j%) <> 1 THEN
                FOR k% = 1 TO num.rows%
                    IF ABS(big#) < ABS(A#(j%,k%)) THEN
                        row% = j%
                        col% = k%
                        big# = A#(j%,k%)
                    END IF
                NEXT k%
            END IF
        NEXT j%
    NEXT i%
    INCR pvt.ind#(col%)
    ' swaps rows and places pivot in diagonal element
    IF row% <> col% THEN
        Det# = -Det# ' change sign
        FOR m% = 1 TO num.rows%
            tempo# = A#(row%,m%)
            A#(row%,m%) = A#(col%,m%)
            A#(col%,m%) = tempo#
        NEXT m%
    END IF
    index%(i%,1) = row%
    index%(i%,2) = col%
    pvt# = A#(col%,col%)
    Det# = Det# * pvt#
    ' divides pivot row% by pivot element
    A#(col%,col%) = 1.0
    FOR m% = 1 TO num.rows%
        A#(col%,m%) = A#(col%,m%) / pvt#
    NEXT m%
    ' reduces nonpivot rows
```

```
     FOR n% = 1 TO num.rows%
        IF n% <> col% THEN
            tempo# = A#(n%,col%)
            A#(n%,col%) = 0.0
            FOR m% = 1 TO num.rows%
                A#(n%,m%) = A#(n%,m%) - A#(col%,m%) * tempo#
            NEXT m%
        END IF
     NEXT n%
NEXT i%
' interchanges columns
FOR i% = 1 TO num.rows%
    m% = num.rows% + 1 - i%
    IF index%(m%,1) <> index%(m%,2) THEN
        row% = index%(m%,1)
        col% = index%(m%,2)
        FOR k% = 1 TO num.rows%
            tempo# = A#(k%,row%)
            A#(k%,row%) = A#(k%,col%)
            A#(k%,col%) = tempo#
        NEXT k%
    END IF
NEXT i%
ERASE pvt.ind#, index% ' erase local arrays
OK% = 1
END SUB ' Invert.Matrix
```

• Listing 3.2. Turbo C math routines

```c
#include <math.h>
#define MAX_ROW 10
#define MAX_COL 10
#define MAX_ARRAY 10

struct matrix_struct {
    double mat[MAX_ROW][MAX_COL];
    unsigned short rows;
    unsigned short cols;
};
```

```
typedef struct matrix_struct matrix;
struct vector_struct {
    double elm[MAX_COL];
    unsigned short numelm;
};
typedef struct vector_struct vector;
typedef unsigned wordarray[MAX_COL];
typedef double  dataarray[MAX_ARRAY];
enum boolean_enum { FALSE, TRUE };
typedef enum boolean_enum boolean;


double sqr(double x);
double power(double base, int exponent);
double rpower(double base, double exponent);
double arcsin(double x);
double arccos(double x);
double factorial(unsigned short n);
double stirling_factorial(double x);
double gamma(double x);
double sinh(double x);
double cosh(double x);
double tanh(double x);
double arcsinh(double x);
double arccosh(double x);
double arctanh(double x);
double userfunc(double x);
double root(double guess, double tolerance,
            unsigned short max_iter, boolean *diverge);
double optimum(double guess, double tolerance,
               unsigned short max_iter, boolean *diverge);
double yinterp(dataarray y, dataarray x,
               unsigned ndata, double xint);
double simpsonarea(dataarray y, double deltax,
                   unsigned ndata);
boolean add_matrix(matrix *c, matrix *a, matrix *b);
boolean mult_matrix(matrix *c, matrix *a, matrix *b);
boolean invert_matrix(matrix *a, double *det);

/* Turbo C math functions */

double sqr(double x) { return x * x; }
```

```
double power(double base, int exponent)
/* raises a floating-point number to an integer power
   using a recursive power function */
{
    if (exponent < 0)  return 1.0/power(base,-exponent);
    else if (exponent == 0)   return 1.0;
    else if (exponent == 1)   return base;
    else if ((exponent % 2) == 0)
        return sqr(power(base, exponent / 2));
    else
        return sqr(power(base, exponent / 2)) * base;
}


double rpower(double base, double exponent)
/* raises a floating-point number to another using
   a nonrecursive power function */
{
    if (base <= 0.0) return 0.0;
    else return exp(exponent * log(base));
}


double arcsin(double x)
/* calculates inverse sine function */
{
    return atan(x / sqrt(1 - x*x));
}


double arccos(double x)
/* calculates inverse cosine function */
{
    return atan(1 / sqrt(1 - x*x));
}


double factorial(unsigned short n)
/* calculates the factorial of an integer using a loop */
{
    unsigned short i;
    double product;

    product = 1;
```

```
    if (n > 1)
        for (i = 1; i <= n; i++)
            product = product * (double) i;
    return product;
}


double stirling_factorial(double x)
/* calulates factorial for integer or fractional argument using
   Stirling's approximation with correction factor */
{
    double pi = 355.0/ 113.0;

    if (x > 0.0)
        return sqrt(2 * pi * x) * exp(x * log(x) - x) *
        /* correction factor */
        (1.0 + 1 / (12.0 * x) +
        1 / (288.0 * x*x) -
        139.0 / (51840.0 * x*x*x) -
        571.0 / (2488320.0 * power(x,4)));
    else
        return 0.0;
}


double gamma(double x)
/* Calculates Gamma function for integer and fractional values.
   Uses Stirling's formula, and thus works better with larger numbers. */
{
    return stirling_factorial(x - 1.0);
}


double sinh(double x)
/* calculates hyperbolic sine function */
{
    return (exp(x) - exp(-x)) / 2.0;
}


double cosh(double x)
/* calculates hyperbolic cosine function */
{
    return (exp(x) + exp(-x)) / 2.0;
}
```

```
double tanh(double x)
/* calculates hyperbolic tangent function */
{
    double y;

    y = exp(x);
    return  (y - 1/y) / (y + 1/y);
}


double arcsinh(double x)
/* calculates inverse hyperbolic sine function */
{
    return log(x + sqrt(x*x + 1));
}


double arccosh(double x)
/* calculates inverse hyperbolic cosine function */
{
    if (x >= 1.0)
        return log(x + sqrt(x*x - 1));
    else
        return 0.0; /* error code, because there is no
                       real x to make the arccosh value 0 */
}


double arctanh(double x)
/* calculates inverse hyperbolic tangent function */
{
    if (fabs(x) < 1.0)
        return log((1+x)/(1-x)) / 2.0;
    else
        return 2.0; /* error code, because arctanh(x) != 2 for all x */
}


double userfunc(double x)
{
    return exp(x) - 3 * x * x;
}


double root(double guess, double tolerance, unsigned short max_iter,
            boolean *diverge)
```

```
/* finds the root of a function using Newton's method */
{
    const double incrm = 0.01;
    double diff, h, userfuncx;
    unsigned short iter;

    iter = 0; /* initializes iteration counter */
    *diverge = FALSE;
    do { /* start root-refining loop */
        if (fabs(guess) > 1.0)  h = incrm * guess; else h = incrm;
        userfuncx = userfunc(guess);
        diff = h * incrm * userfuncx /(userfunc(guess+h) - userfuncx);
        guess = guess - diff;
        iter++;
        if (iter > max_iter) *diverge = TRUE;
    } while (fabs(diff) > tolerance && *diverge == FALSE);
    return guess;
}


double optimum(double guess, double tolerance, unsigned short max_iter,
               boolean *diverge)
/* finds the min/max of a function using Newton's method */
{
    const incrm = 0.01;
    double diff, h, fx, fm, fp;
    unsigned short iter;

    iter = 0; /* initializes iteration counter */
    *diverge = FALSE;
    do {/* start root-refining loop */
        if (fabs(guess) > 1.0)  h = incrm * guess; else h = incrm;
        fx = userfunc(guess);
        fp = userfunc(guess + h);
        fm = userfunc(guess - h);
        diff = h / 2.0 * (fp - fm) / (fp - 2 * fx + fm);
        guess = guess - diff;
        iter++;
    if (iter > max_iter) *diverge = TRUE;
    } while (fabs(diff) > tolerance && *diverge == FALSE);
    return guess;
}
```

```
double yinterp(dataarray y, dataarray x, unsigned ndata, double xint)
/* Performs lagrangian interpolation. The numeric arrays
   need not be sorted. */
{
    unsigned i, j;
    double yint, product;

    if (ndata > MAX_ARRAY) ndata = MAX_ARRAY;
    if (ndata < 2) ndata = 2;
    yint = 0.0;
    for (i = 0; i < ndata; i++)  {
        product = 1.0;
        for (j = 0; j < ndata; j++)
            if (i != j)
                product = product * (x[j] - xint) / (x[j] - x[i]);
        yint = yint + y[i] * product;
    }
    return yint; /* return function value */
}


double simpsonarea(dataarray y, double deltax, unsigned ndata)
/* uses Simpson's rule to perform numerical integration */
{
    double sum_odd, sum_even;
    unsigned i, n;

    if ((ndata % 2) == 0 || ndata < 3) return 0.0;
    if (ndata > MAX_ARRAY) ndata = MAX_ARRAY;
    n = ndata - 1;
    sum_odd = -y[n];
    sum_even = 0.0;
    i = 1;
    while (i < n)   {
        sum_even = sum_even + y[i];
        sum_odd = sum_odd + y[i+1];
        i += 2;
    }
    return deltax / 3.0 * (y[0] + 4 * sum_even + 2 * sum_odd  + y[n]);
}
```

```
boolean add_matrix(matrix *c, matrix *a, matrix *b)
/* adds matrices a and b to give matrix c */
{
    unsigned short i, j;

    /* are matrices a and b of the same effective size? */
    if (a->rows != b->rows || a->cols != b->cols)  return FALSE;
    c->rows = a->rows;
    c->cols = a->cols;
    for (i = 0; i < a->rows; i++)
        for (j = 0; j < a->cols; j++)
            c->mat[i][j] = a->mat[i][j] + b->mat[i][j];
    return TRUE;
}


boolean mult_matrix(matrix *c, matrix *a, matrix *b)
/* multiplies matrices a and b to give matrix c */
{
    unsigned short i, j, k;

    if (a->cols != b->rows) return FALSE;
    c->rows = a->rows;
    c->cols = b->cols;
    for (i = 0; i < a->rows; i++)
        for (j = 0; j < b->cols; j++) {
            c->mat[i][j] = 0.0;
            for (k = 0; j < a->cols; j++)
                c->mat[i][j] = c->mat[i][j] + a->mat[i][k] * b->mat[k][j];
        }
    return TRUE;
}


boolean invert_matrix(matrix *a, double *det)
/* inverts matrix and returns the determinant */
{
    unsigned short i, j, k, m, n, row, col;
    double tempo, big, pvt;
    unsigned short pvt_ind[MAX_COL];
    unsigned short index[MAX_COL][2];
```

```
if (a->cols != a->rows)   {
    *det = 0.0;
    return FALSE;
}
*det = 1.0;
for (i = 0;  i < a->cols;  i++)
    pvt_ind[i] = a->rows+1;
for (i = 0;  i < a->cols;  i++)   {
    big = 0.0; /* initialize pivot element */
    for (j = 0;  j < a->cols;  j++)   {
        if (pvt_ind[j] != 0)
        for (k = 0;  k < a->cols;  k++)   {
            if (fabs(big) < fabs(a->mat[j][k]))   {
                row = j;
                col = k;
                big = a->mat[j][k];
            }
        }
    }
    pvt_ind[col]++;
    /* swaps rows and places pivot in diagonal element */
    if (row != col)   {
        *det = -*det; /* change sign */
        for (m = 0;  m < a->cols;  m++)   {
            tempo = a->mat[row][m];
            a->mat[row][m] = a->mat[col][m];
            a->mat[col][m] = tempo;
        }
    }
    index[i][0] = row;
    index[i][1] = col;
    pvt = a->mat[col][col];
    *det *= pvt;
    /* divides pivot row by pivot element */
    a->mat[col][col] = 1.0;
    for (m = 0;  m < a->cols;  m++)
        a->mat[col][m] /=  pvt;
    /* reduces nonpivot rows */
    for (n = 0;  n < a->cols;  n++)
    if (n != col)   {
```

```
            tempo = a->mat[n][col];
            a->mat[n][col] = 0.0;
            for (m = 0; m < a->cols; m++)
                a->mat[n][m] -= a->mat[col][m] * tempo;
        }
    }
    /* interchanges columns */
    for (i = 0; i < a->cols; i++)  {
        m = a->cols - i;
        if (index[m][0] != index[m][1])  {
            row = index[m][0];
            col = index[m][1];
            for (k = 0; k < a->cols; k++)  {
                tempo = a->mat[k][row];
                a->mat[k][row] = a->mat[k][col];
                a->mat[k][col] = tempo;
            }
        }
    }
    return  TRUE;
}
```

• Listing 3.3. Turbo Pascal math routines

```
Unit Math;

CONST MAX_ROW = 10;
    MAX_COL = 10;
    MAX_ARRAY = 20;

TYPE Matrix = RECORD
        Mat : ARRAY [1..MAX_ROW,1..MAX_COL] OF REAL;
        Rows, Cols : BYTE;
    END;
    Vector = RECORD
        Elm : ARRAY [1..MAX_COL] OF REAL;
        NumElm : BYTE;
    END;
    WordArray = ARRAY [1..MAX_COL] OF WORD;
    DataArray = ARRAY [1..MAX_ARRAY] OF REAL;
```

```
FUNCTION Power(Base     : REAL;    { input   }
               Exponent : INTEGER { input   }) : REAL;
{ raises a floating-point number to an integer power
  using a recursive power function }

FUNCTION RPower(Base,             { input   }
                Exponent : REAL { input   }) : REAL;
{ raises a floating-point number to another using a
  nonrecursive power function }

FUNCTION Arcsin(X : REAL) : REAL;
{ calculates inverse sine function }

FUNCTION Arccos(X : REAL) : REAL;
{ calculates inverse cosine function }

FUNCTION Factorial(N : BYTE) : REAL;
{ calculates the factorial of an integer using a loop }

FUNCTION Stirling_Factorial(X : REAL) : REAL;
{ calculates factorial for integer or fractional argument using
  Stirling's approximation with correction factor }

FUNCTION Gamma(X : REAL) : REAL;
{ Calculates Gamma function for integer and fractional values.
  Uses Stirling's formula, and thus works better with larger numbers. }

FUNCTION Sinh(X : REAL) : REAL;
{ calculates hyperbolic sine function }

FUNCTION Cosh(X : REAL) : REAL;
{ calculates hyperbolic cosine function }

FUNCTION Tanh(X : REAL) : REAL;
{ calculates hyperbolic tangent function }

FUNCTION ArcSinh(X : REAL) : REAL;
{ calculates inverse hyperbolic sine function }

FUNCTION ArcCosh(X : REAL) : REAL;
{ calculates inverse hyperpolic cosine function }
```

```
FUNCTION ArcTanh(X : REAL) : REAL;
{ calculates inverse hyperbolic tangent function }

FUNCTION UserFunc(X : REAL) : REAL;

FUNCTION Root(    Guess,                 { input  }
                  Tolerance : REAL;      { input  }
                  Max_Iter  : BYTE;      { input  }
              VAR Diverge   : BOOLEAN  { output }) : REAL;
{ finds the root of a function using Newton's method }

FUNCTION Optimum(    Guess,                 { input  }
                     Tolerance : REAL;      { input  }
                     Max_Iter  : BYTE;      { input  }
                 VAR Diverge   : BOOLEAN  { output }) : REAL;
{ finds the min/max of a function using Newton's method }

FUNCTION YInterp(VAR Y,                    { input  }
                     X     : DataArray; { input  }
                     NData : WORD;      { input  }
                     Xint  : REAL       { input  }) : REAL;
{ Performs Lagrangian interpolation. The numeric arrays need
  not be sorted. }

FUNCTION SimpsonArea(VAR Y      : DataArray; { input  }
                         DeltaX : REAL;      { input  }
                         NData  : WORD       { input  }) : REAL;
{ uses Simpson's rule to perform numerical integration }

FUNCTION Add_Matrix(VAR C,             { output }
                        A,             { input  }
                        B : Matrix  { input  }) : BOOLEAN;
{ adds matrices A and B to give matrix C }

FUNCTION Mult_Matrix(VAR C,             { output }
                         A,             { input  }
                         B : Matrix { input  }) : BOOLEAN;
{ multiplies matrices A and B to give matrix C }
```

```
FUNCTION Invert_Matrix(VAR A      : Matrix;      { input  }
                       VAR Det  : REAL         { output }) : BOOLEAN;
{ inverts matrix and returns the determinant }


{*****************************************************************}


FUNCTION Power(Base     : REAL;     { input  }
               Exponent : INTEGER { input  }) : REAL;
{ raises a floating-point number to an integer power
  using a recursive power function }
BEGIN
   IF Exponent < 0 THEN Power := 1.0/Power(Base,-Exponent)
   ELSE IF Exponent = 0 THEN Power := 1.0
   ELSE IF Exponent = 1 THEN Power := Base
   ELSE IF (Exponent mod 2) = 0 THEN
      Power := SQR(Power(Base, Exponent DIV 2))
   ELSE
      Power := SQR(Power(Base, Exponent DIV 2)) * Base;
END; { Power }


FUNCTION RPower(Base,              { input  }
                Exponent : REAL { input  }) : REAL;
{ raises a floating-point number to another using a
  nonrecursive power function }
BEGIN
   IF Base <= 0.0 THEN RPower := 0.0
   ELSE RPower := EXP(Exponent * Ln(Base))
END;


FUNCTION Arcsin(X : REAL) : REAL;
{ calculates inverse sine function }
BEGIN
   Arcsin := ARCTAN(X / SQRT(1 - X*X))
END; { Arcsin }


FUNCTION Arccos(X : REAL) : REAL;
{ calculates inverse cosine function }
BEGIN
   Arccos := ARCTAN(1 / SQRT(1 - X*X))
END; { Arccos }
```

```
FUNCTION Factorial(N : BYTE) : REAL;
{ calculates the factorial of an integer using a loop }
VAR i : BYTE;
    product : REAL;
BEGIN
    product := 1;
    IF N > 1 THEN
       FOR i := 1 TO N DO
           product := product * i;
    Factorial := product;
END; { Factorial }


FUNCTION Stirling_Factorial(X : REAL) : REAL;
{ calculates factorial for integer or fractional argument using
  Stirling's approximation with correction factor }
BEGIN
    IF X > 0.0 THEN
       Stirling_Factorial := SQRT(2 * Pi * X) * EXP(X * Ln(X) - X) *
                           { correction factor }
                           (1.0 + 1 / (12.0 * X) +
                           1 / (288.0 * X*X) -
                           139.0 / (51840.0 * X*X*X) -
                           571.0 / (2488320.0 * Power(x,4)))
    ELSE
       Stirling_Factorial := 1.0;
END; { Stirling_Factorial }


FUNCTION Gamma(X : REAL) : REAL;
{ Calculates Gamma function for integer and fractional values.
  Uses Stirling's formula, and thus works better with larger numbers.}
BEGIN
    Gamma := Stirling_Factorial(X - 1.0)
END; { Gamma }


FUNCTION Sinh(X : REAL) : REAL;
{ calculates hyperbolic sine function }
BEGIN
    Sinh := (EXP(X) - EXP(-X)) / 2.0
END; { Sinh }
```

```
FUNCTION Cosh(X : REAL) : REAL;
{ calculates hyperbolic cosine function }
BEGIN
    Cosh := (EXP(X) + EXP(-X)) / 2.0
END; { Cosh }


FUNCTION Tanh(X : REAL) : REAL;
{ calculates hyperbolic tangent function }
VAR Y : REAL;
BEGIN
    Y := EXP(X);
    Tanh := (Y - 1/Y) / (Y + 1/Y)
END; { Tanh }


FUNCTION ArcSinh(X : REAL) : REAL;
{ calculates inverse hyperbolic sine function }
BEGIN
    ArcSinh := Ln(X + SQRT(X*X + 1))
END; { ArcSinh }


FUNCTION ArcCosh(X : REAL) : REAL;
{ calculates inverse hyperbolic cosine function }
BEGIN
    IF X >= 1.0 THEN
        ArcCosh := Ln(X + SQRT(X*X - 1))
    ELSE
        ArcCosh := 0.0; { error code, because there is no
    real x to make the arccosh value 0 }
END; { ArcCosh }


FUNCTION ArcTanh(X : REAL) : REAL;
{ calculates inverse hyperbolic tangent function }

BEGIN
    IF ABS(X) < 1.0 THEN
        ArcTanh := Ln((1+X)/(1-X)) / 2.0
    ELSE
        ArcTanh := 2.0; { error code, because arctanh(x) <> 2 for all x }
END; { ArcTanh }
```

```
FUNCTION UserFunc(X : REAL) : REAL;
BEGIN
    UserFunc := EXP(X) - 3 * X * X;
END; { UserFunc }


FUNCTION Root(    Guess,                    { input  }
                  Tolerance :   REAL;       { input  }
                  Max_Iter  :   BYTE;       { input  }
            VAR Diverge   :    BOOLEAN    { output }) : REAL;
{ finds the root of a function using Newton's method }
CONST INCRM = 0.01;
VAR diff, h, UserFuncX : REAL;
    iter : BYTE;


BEGIN
    iter := 0; { initializes iteration counter }
    Diverge := FALSE;
    REPEAT { start root-refining loop }
       IF ABS(Guess) > 1.0 THEN h := INCRM * Guess ELSE h := INCRM;
       UserFuncX := UserFunc(Guess);
       diff := h * UserFuncX / (UserFunc(Guess+h) - UserFuncX);
       Guess := Guess - diff;
       INC(iter);
       IF iter > Max_Iter THEN Diverge := TRUE;
    UNTIL (ABS(diff) <= Tolerance) OR Diverge;
    Root := Guess;
END; { Root }

FUNCTION Optimum(    Guess,                    { input  }
                     Tolerance : REAL;         { input  }
                     Max_Iter  : BYTE;         { input  }
               VAR Diverge   : BOOLEAN    { output }) : REAL;
{ finds the min/max of a function using Newton's method }
CONST INCRM = 0.01;
VAR diff, h, FX, FM, FP : REAL;
    iter : BYTE;


BEGIN
    iter := 0; { initializes iteration counter }
    Diverge := FALSE;
```

```
    REPEAT { start root-refining loop }
        IF ABS(Guess) > 1.0 THEN h := INCRM * Guess ELSE h := INCRM;
        FX := UserFunc(Guess);
        FP := UserFunc(Guess + h);
        FM := UserFunc(Guess - h);
        diff := h / 2.0 * (FP - FM) / (FP - 2 * FX + FM);
        Guess := Guess - diff;
        INC(iter);
        IF iter > Max_Iter THEN Diverge := TRUE;
    UNTIL (ABS(diff) <= Tolerance) OR Diverge;
    Optimum := Guess;
END; { Optimum }


FUNCTION YInterp(VAR Y,                     { input   }
                     X    : DataArray; { input   }
                     NData : WORD;          { input   }
                     Xint : REAL            { input   }) : REAL;
{ Performs Lagrangian interpolation.
  The numeric arrays need not be sorted. }


VAR i, j : WORD;
    yint, product : REAL;
BEGIN
    IF NData > MAX_ARRAY THEN NData := MAX_ARRAY;
    IF NData < 2 THEN NData := 2;
    yint := 0.0;
    FOR i := 1 TO NData DO BEGIN
        product := 1.0;
        FOR j := 1 TO NData DO
            IF i <> j THEN
                product := product * (X[j] - XInt) / (X[j] - X[i]);
        yint := Yint + Y[i] * product;
    END;
    Yinterp := yint; { returns function value }
END;


FUNCTION SimpsonArea(VAR Y       : DataArray; { input   }
                         DeltaX  : REAL;        { input   }
                         NData   : WORD         { input   }) : REAL;
{ uses Simpson's rule to perform numerical integration }
```

```
VAR sum_odd, sum_even : REAL;
    i : WORD;
BEGIN
    IF ((NData MOD 2) = 0) OR (NData < 3) THEN BEGIN
        SimpsonArea := 0.0;
        EXIT;
    END;
    IF NData > MAX_ARRAY THEN NData := MAX_ARRAY;
    sum_odd := -Y[NData];
    sum_even := 0.0;
    i := 2;
    WHILE i < NData DO BEGIN
        sum_even := sum_even + Y[i];
        sum_odd := sum_odd + Y[i+1];
        INC(i,2);
    END;
    SimpsonArea := DeltaX / 3.0 * (Y[1] + 4 * sum_even +
                                      2 * sum_odd  + Y[NData]);
END; { SimpsonArea }


FUNCTION Add_Matrix(VAR C,              { output }
                        A,              { input  }
                        B :  Matrix     { input  }) : BOOLEAN;
{ adds matrices A and B to give matrix C }
VAR i, j : BYTE;

BEGIN
    { are matrices A and B of the same effective size? }
    IF (A.Rows <> B.Rows) OR (A.Cols <> B.Cols) THEN BEGIN
        Add_Matrix := FALSE;
        EXIT;
    END;
    C.Rows := A.Rows;
    C.Cols := A.Cols;
    FOR i := 1 TO A.Rows DO
        FOR j := 1 TO A.Cols DO
            C.Mat[i,j] := A.Mat[i,j] + B.Mat[i,j];
    Add_Matrix := TRUE;
END; { Add_Matrix }
```

```
FUNCTION Mult_Matrix(VAR C,              { output }
                         A,              { input  }
                         B : Matrix    { input  }) : BOOLEAN;
{ multiplies matrices A and B to give matrix C }


VAR i, j, k : BYTE;
BEGIN
    IF (A.Cols <> B.Rows) THEN BEGIN
        Mult_Matrix := FALSE;
        EXIT;
    END;
    C.Rows := A.Rows;
    C.Cols := B.Cols;
    FOR i := 1 TO A.Rows DO
        FOR j := 1 TO B.Cols DO BEGIN
            C.Mat[i,j] := 0.0;
            FOR k := 1 TO A.Cols DO
                C.Mat[i,j] := C.Mat[i,j] + A.Mat[i,k] * B.Mat[k,j];
        END;
    Mult_Matrix := TRUE;
END;


FUNCTION Invert_Matrix(VAR A     : Matrix; { input  }
                       VAR Det   : REAL    { output }) : BOOLEAN;
{ inverts matrix and returns the determinant }
VAR i, j, k, m, n, row, col : BYTE;
    tempo, big, pvt : REAL;
    pvt_ind : ARRAY [1..MAX_COL] OF BYTE;
    index : ARRAY [1..MAX_COL,1..2] OF BYTE;


BEGIN
    IF A.Cols <> A.Rows THEN BEGIN
        Det := 0.0;
        Invert_Matrix := FALSE;
        EXIT;
    END;
    Det := 1.0;
    FOR i := 1 TO A.Cols DO
        pvt_ind[i] := 0;
    FOR i := 1 TO A.Cols DO BEGIN
```

```
big := 0.0; { initializes pivot element }
FOR j := 1 TO A.Cols DO BEGIN
    IF pvt_ind[j] <> 1 THEN
        FOR k := 1 TO A.Cols DO BEGIN
            IF ABS(big) < ABS(A.Mat[j,k]) THEN BEGIN
                row := j;
                col := k;
                big := A.Mat[j,k];
            END;
        END;
    END;
END;
INC(pvt_ind[col]);
{ swaps rows and places pivot in diagonal element }
IF row <> col THEN BEGIN
    Det := -Det; { change sign }
    FOR m := 1 TO A.Cols DO BEGIN
        tempo := A.Mat[row,m];
        A.Mat[row,m] := A.Mat[col,m];
        A.Mat[col,m] := tempo;
    END;
END;
index[i,1] := row;
index[i,2] := col;
pvt := A.Mat[col,col];
Det := Det * pvt;
{ divides pivot row by pivot element }
A.Mat[col,col] := 1.0;
FOR m := 1 TO A.Cols DO
    A.Mat[col,m] := A.Mat[col,m] / pvt;
{ reduces nonpivot rows }
FOR n := 1 TO A.Cols DO
    IF n <> col THEN BEGIN
        tempo := A.Mat[n,col];
        A.Mat[n,col] := 0.0;
        FOR m := 1 TO A.Cols DO
        A.Mat[n,m] := A.Mat[n,m] - A.Mat[col,m] * tempo;
    END;
END;
{ interchanges columns }
FOR i := 1 TO A.Cols DO BEGIN
```

```
      m := A.Cols + 1 - i;
      IF index[m,1] <> index[m,2] THEN BEGIN
         row := index[m,1];
         col := index[m,2];
         FOR k := 1 TO A.Cols DO BEGIN
            tempo := A.Mat[k,row];
            A.Mat[k,row] := A.Mat[k,col];
            A.Mat[k,col] := tempo;
         END;
      END;
   END;
   Invert_Matrix := TRUE;
END; { Invert_Matrix }
```

• Listing 3.4. Turbo Prolog math routines

```
constants
   pi = 355 / 113

predicates
   sqr(real, real)
   power(real, integer, real)
   rpower(real, real, real)
   arcsin(real, real)
   arccos(real, real)
   factorial(integer, real)
   factorial(integer, real, integer, real)
   stirling_fact(real, real)
   gamma(real, real)
   sinh(real, real)
   cosh(real, real)
   tanh(real, real)
   arcsinh(real, real)
   arccosh(real, real)
   arctanh(real, real)

clauses

   sqr(Num, Result) :- Result = Num * Num.
```

```
power(Base, Exponent, Result) :-      % exponent is < 1
    Exponent < 1,
    X = -Exponent,
    power(Base, X, NewResult), !,
    Result = 1 / NewResult.
power(_, 0, 1) :- !.                  % exponent is 0, return 1
power(Base, 1, Base) :- !.            % exponent is 1, return base
power(Base, Exponent, Result) :-      % exponent mod 2 = 0
    0 = Exponent mod 2,
    X = Exponent / 2,
    power(Base, X, NewResult), !,
    sqr(NewResult, Result).
power(Base, Exponent, Result) :-
    X = Exponent div 2,
    power(Base, X, NewResult), !,
    sqr(NewResult, R),
    Result = R * Base.

rpower(0, _, 0).    % return 0 if base is 0
rpower(Base, Exponent, Result) :-
    Result = exp(Exponent * ln(Base)).

arcsin(Num, Result) :-
    Result = arctan(Num / sqrt(1 - Num * Num)).

arccos(Num, Result) :-
    Result = arctan(1 / sqrt(1 -  Num * Num)).

factorial(Num, Result) :-
    factorial(Num, Result, 1, 1).
factorial(Num, Result, Num, Result) :- !.
factorial(Num, Result, LC, R) :-
    Next = LC + 1,
    NewR = R * Next,
    factorial(Num, Result, Next, NewR).

stirling_fact(Num, 0) :- Num <= 0, !.
stirling_fact(Num, Result) :-
    power(Num, 4, Res1),
    V4 = 571 / (2488320 * Res1),
```

```
      V3 = 139 / (51840 * Num*Num*Num),
      V2 = 1 / (288 * Num*Num),
      V1 = 1 + 1/ (12 * Num),
      V = V1 + V2 - V3 - V4,
      X2 = exp(Num * ln(Num) - Num),
      X1 = sqrt(2 * pi * Num),
      Result = X1 * X2 * V.

gamma( Num, Result) :-
   X = Num-1,
   stirling_fact(X, Result).


sinh(Num, Result) :-
   Result = (exp(Num) - exp(-Num)) / 2.

cosh(Num, Result) :-
   Result = (exp(Num) + exp(-Num)) / 2.

tanh(Num, Result) :-
   Y = exp(Num),
   Result = (Y - 1/Y) / (Y + 1/Y).

arcsinh(Num, Result) :-
   Result = ln(Num + sqrt(Num*Num + 1)).

arccosh(Num, Result) :-    % return error code
   Num < 1,
   Result = 0.
arccosh(Num, Result) :-
   Result = ln(Num + sqrt(Num*Num - 1)).

arctanh(Num, Result) :-    % return error code
   Num >= 1,
   Result = 2.
arctanh(Num, Result) :-
   Result = log((1 + Num) / (1-Num)) / 2.
```

String Processing with Word Strings

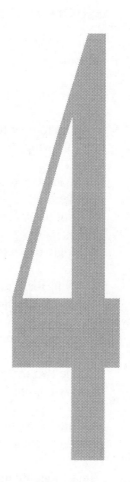

Introduction

Strings are important data types that are used in most programs for representing text. In this section, we present algorithms for processing strings composed of words; in the following section, we'll examine strings composed of tokens.

Representing Word Strings

Strings represented with words use the space character as the delimiter. As an example, the string:

"one two three four"

contains four words. For the algorithms that we'll develop for word strings, the following three rules apply:

1. At least one space character is required to separate one word from another.
2 Multiple space characters are allowed and have the same effect as single spaces.
3. Single or multiple leading and trailing spaces are allowed.

Applying these rules, you should be able to detect that each of the following strings are the same:

"one   two three   four"
"one two three four"
"   one two three four   "
"one two three four   "

A string consisting of only spaces contains no words. The other side of the coin is a string with no spaces, such as

"thisstringcontainsnospaces"

This string is said to contain a single word. Note that by definition, nonalphanumeric characters, such as the comma and the colon, count as part of a word. For example, in the string "one, two, three"

the three words in this string are: "one," "two," and "three".

The string processing tools in this section perform the following eight operations:

1. Trim leading and trailing spaces.
2. Replace a sequence of spaces with a single space.
3. Count the words in a string.
4. Determine the position of a word in a string.
5. Obtain a word by specifying its position.
6. Insert a word after a specified word or at the beginning of the string.
7. Delete one or more words using word position and word count.
8. Translate words by replacing them with other words.

These routines manipulate strings using word indices and word counts, instead of the character indices and character counts typically used to process strings stored as arrays.

The String Processing Algorithms

The most important algorithm for manipulating words in a string is the one that parses words. This algorithm must scan a string and detect the start and end of a word as shown in Figure 4.1.

We'll use the terms *head interface* and *tail interface* to indicate the string location where a word begins and ends, respectively. In its basic form, our word-scanning method must also detect whether a string contains leading and/or trailing spaces. This means that we must process two types of head interfaces: one, at the beginning of the string (when no leading spaces exist) and the other between a space and a nonspace character. This problem is illustrated in Figure 4.2.

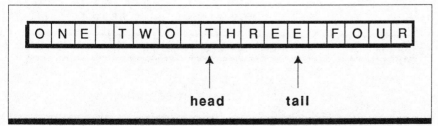

Figure 4.1. The starting and ending positions of a word

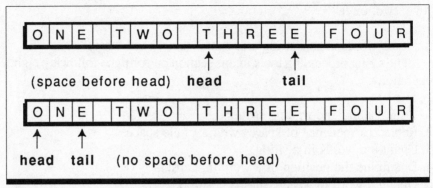

Figure 4.2. Two types of head interfaces

There are also two types of tail interfaces that we must process: one for the last character of a word that is also the last string character, and the other for a nonspace character followed by a space. Figure 4.3 illustrates both types.

Our algorithm can be simplified using a simple trick: add one space to the head and tail of the string. This means that before we attempt to process the words in a string, such as

"fire earth air water"

the two spaces are added to give us

" fire earth air water "

This method ensures that every word in the string begins and ends with at least one space. Consequently, this representation reduces the number of

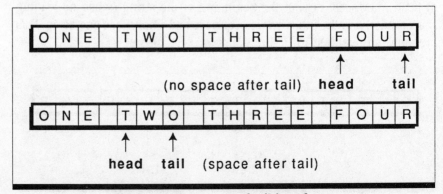

Figure 4.3. Two types of tail interfaces

head and tail interfaces to one for each side of a word. The head interface is now consistently between a space and a nonspace character. The end of a word is marked by the first space character that is encountered during scanning of the string characters.

Trimming and Compressing Spaces

The first two string processing operations implemented in our string processing library remove extra spaces from a string. The first, **Trim_Spaces**, removes all leading and trailing spaces from a string; the second routine, **Compress_Spaces**, replaces all multiple occurrences of space characters in a string with a single space character. For example, the string

"one   two   three   four"

after being compressed looks like

"one two three four"

Both of these string processing operations are easy to implement in the Turbo languages. To remove leading and trailing spaces in Turbo BASIC, C, and Pascal we use loops to check the beginning and end of each string array and remove space characters until a nonspace character is found. As an example, the following loop illustrates how leading spaces are removed in Turbo Pascal:

```
WHILE (strlen > 0) AND (Strng[1] = ' ') DO BEGIN
    Delete(Strng,1,1);
    DEC(strlen);
END;
```

In Turbo Prolog, strings are trimmed with the built-in **frontstr** and **frontchar** predicates. Our algorithm uses recursion to process both the right and left sides of a string. The recursion continues to examine each character in the string until a nonspace character is encountered.

The string compression algorithm is similar to the trimming algorithm except that in this case we use a loop to search and replace every occurrence of two space characters with a single space.

Counting Words in a String

By employing the trick of adding the leading and trailing spaces to a string, the work of counting the number of words is reduced to counting the number of times a space character is followed by a nonspace character. Internally, leading and trailing spaces do not affect the word count. In Turbo BASIC, C, and Pascal, the spaces are counted with the **Found_Space** routine. The general statement that performs the counting operation is demonstrated here in Turbo Pascal:

```
Found_Space := (Strng[Index-1] = ' ') AND
               (Strng[Index] <> ' ');
```

This routine is called by the **Count_Words** function, which uses a loop to check each character in the string. Remember that strings are represented in BASIC, C, and Pascal as arrays. Therefore, we can easily access the elements of the string using array indices.

Our technique for processing strings in Turbo Prolog is different than for the other languages, because Turbo Prolog provides a string data type. To determine the number of words in a string, the **count_words** predicate is called. This predicate adds a trailing space to the string and calls **wordcount**, which counts words using recursion. The predicate continues to call itself as it reduces the string by one word each time until the end of the string is reached. As the recursion unwinds, the word count is calculated using a simple counter:

```
Count = Oldcount + 1
```

Finding a Word

The method for finding a specific word is also simplified, because the word might be surrounded by at least one space on each side. Consequently, the search string is padded with a leading and trailing space before the substring search is carried out. You do not have to worry about the cases when the desired word is the first or last one—if the original string is free of leading and trailing spaces.

Inserting, Deleting, and Extracting Words

The string insertion, extraction, and deletion operations also benefit from the space-padding trick. With the insertion and deletion operations, the original string is altered by adding or removing a word. The word extraction operation returns the word stored in a given position of a string.

Inserting a word in a string is relatively straightforward. To insert a word, we must consider three possibilities.

1. Inserting the word at the beginning of the string
2. Inserting the word in the middle of the string
3. Inserting the word at the end of the string

If the word is inserted at the beginning or end of the string, the insertion is performed with string concatenation. In Turbo BASIC and Turbo Pascal, the concatenation is performed with the + operator. To concatenate strings in Turbo C, the **strcat()** function is used, and in Turbo Prolog, the **concat** predicate is used.

To insert a word in the middle of the string, the string must first be divided into two substrings. The first or left substring contains the words up to the position where the new string is to be inserted and the second or right substring contains the remaining words. For example, if we wanted to insert a word after the fourth word in the following string:

"Mark Alice Tom Gary Steve David Linda"

the two substrings would be

"Mark Alice Tom Gary" " Steve David Linda"

    ↑   ↑

  Left substring   Right substring

Once this division is made, the new word can be inserted by first appending it to the left substring and then joining the left with the right substring.

In Turbo BASIC, strings are divided into left and right substrings with the **LEFT$** and **RIGHT$** functions. For Turbo Pascal, we've included two functions called **LeftStr** and **CountMidStr** to extract the left and right components of a string. Strings are divided in Turbo C and Prolog with the **strcat()** function and **concat** predicate, respectively.

The procedure for deleting a word in a string is similar to that of inserting a word; however, with the delete operation we can remove more than one word from a string. Again we have three possibilities to consider.

1. Deleting a word(s) at the beginning of the string
2. Deleting a word(s) in the middle of the string
3. Deleting a word(s) at the end of the string

To delete words in a string, our algorithm requires two pointers or indexes to keep track of the starting and stopping words for deletion. Let's consider an example to illustrate how the algorithm works. Assume we have the following string and we want to remove words two through five:

"Mark Alice Tom Gary Steve David Linda"

The first step consists of locating the first word to delete and assigning a pointer or index to it, as shown:

"Mark Alice Tom Gary Steve David Linda"

ptr

Next, we locate the position of the first word that follows the last word to be deleted—in this case word six, as shown:

"Mark Alice Tom Gary Steve David Linda"

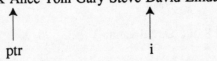

ptr   i

Now all we have to do is remove the characters between **ptr** and **i** and join the left and right parts of the string. In Turbo BASIC, the **LEFT$** and **MID$** functions are used to join the strings and in Turbo Pascal the **LeftStr** and **PosMidStr** functions are used. In Turbo C, strings are joined by inserting a string terminator character (**\0**) at position **ptr** and the first string is concatenated with the string starting at position **i** by calling **strcat()**. In Turbo Prolog, a predicate called **skipstr** is used to skip over the words to be deleted (this produces the second string), and the built-in **frontstr** predicate is then called to create the first string. The two strings are then joined with **concat**.

The final string operation included in this category, which we call string extraction, returns the string located at a specified position. To perform this operation, all we need to do is locate the start of the desired word and then step through the string until a space character is found. As for the delete operation, two pointers are used: one to reference the beginning of the word and the other to reference the end position.

Translating Strings

The last string processing operation translates a string by replacing all occurrences of a specified word in a string with another word. For example, given the string:

"Mark Alice Gloria Tom Gary Steve Gloria Linda"

we could translate the string by replacing the word Gloria with the word David. In this case the new string is:

"Mark Alice David Tom Gary Steve David Linda"

Notice that two replacements were made. The translation is performed by using three of the string processing operations discussed previously: **WordPos** to locate the position of a word, **DeleteWord** to remove a word, and **InsertWord** to insert the new word.

String Processing Algorithms

The code for the word-based string processing algorithms is presented in Listings 4.1 to 4.4. We've included a short discussion of some of the important implementation details for each language as well as a description of each string processing routine. We'll also include a short discussion on the general principles of how strings are represented and processed.

Turbo BASIC

Listing 4.1 includes the implementation of the string processing algorithms in Turbo BASIC. The code is written as a standalone library that you can use in your programs.

In general, strings are easy to represent and process in Turbo BASIC. A string can be directly assigned to a string variable, as shown in this example:

```
Newstr$ = "New string"
```

The only requirement is that the names of all string variables and functions that return string results must end with the $ character. Because Turbo BASIC directly supports string data types and provides functions and operators for processing strings, we do not need arrays to implement our string processing algorithms. Table 4.1 lists the built-in functions and operators used by our string processing routines.

Table 4.1. Turbo BASIC built-in string processing tools

Function or Operator	Description
MID$	Returns the middle characters
LEFT$	Returns leftmost n characters
LEN	Returns string length
+	String concatenation operator

The following text describes each of the Turbo BASIC string processing functions and subroutines. In addition to these routines, one local function called **FNFound.Space** is used to search for a word boundary in a string (a space character followed by a nonspace character). This function is called by most of the string processing routines.

FNTrim.Spaces$ Trims the leading and trailing spaces of a string.

Syntax:
```
DEF FNTrim.Spaces$(LString$)
```

Parameter:
LString$ the string whose copy is trimmed of leading and trailing spaces.

Compress.Spaces   Removes leading and trailing spaces and converts any sequence of spaces into a single space.

Syntax:
```
SUB Compress.Spaces(Words$)
```

Parameter:

Words$ the string to be compressed.

Returns the number of space-delimited words in a string.   **FNCount.Words%**

Syntax:
```
DEF FNCount.Words%(Words$)
```

Parameter:

Words$ the string whose words are counted.

Finds the word position in a string.   **FNWordPos%**

Syntax:
```
DEF FNWordPos%(WordStr$, Words$, WordIndex%)
```

Parameters:

WordStr$ the key search word.
Words$ the string that contains words.
WordIndex%   the word number where the search begins.

Inserts a word in a word-based string.   **InsertWord**

Syntax:
```
SUB InsertWord(WordStr$, Words$, AfterWord%)
```

Parameters:

WordStr$ the inserted word.
Words$ the string where the new word is inserted.
AfterWord%   the word index after which the new word is inserted. A
                    zero value indicates that the new word is inserted as the
                    new first word in the string.

Extracts a specific word from a string.   **GetWord**

Syntax:
```
SUB GetWord(Words$, WordSought$, WordIndex%)
```

Parameters:

Words$ the source string that contains the desired word.
WordSought$**   the word extracted from the string **Words$.
WordIndex%   the index for the desired word. If this index exceeds the number of words, a null string is returned.

DeleteWord

Deletes one or more words from a string.

Syntax:
```
SUB DeleteWord(Words$, WordIndex%, WordCount%)
```

Parameters:

Words$ the string whose words are deleted.
WordIndex%   the first word to delete. If this index is greater than the number of words, the **Words$** string is not changed.
WordCount%   the maximum number of deleted words. If it exceeds the available number of words, the difference is ignored.

TranslateWord

Translates specified words in a string by replacing all occurrences with another word. You can specify the maximum number of translations and the number of leading words to skip. You can limit translation to selected words.

Syntax:
```
SUB TranslateWord(FindWord$, ReplaceWord$, Words$, _
                  WordIndex%, Frequency%)
```

Parameters:

FindWord$ the specified word pattern.
ReplaceWord$ the replacement word pattern.
Words$ the strings whose words are translated.
WordIndex%   the index for the first word that can be affected by the translation.
Frequency%   the maximum number of translations to perform.

Turbo C

Listing 4.2 includes the implementation of the string processing algorithms in Turbo C. To compile the functions, the header files **stdio.h**, **stdlib.h**, and **string.h** must be included.

Strings are represented differently in Turbo C than in Turbo BASIC and Pascal. Turbo C does not provide a built-in string data type; however, strings can be represented and processed with arrays and pointers. Figure 4.4 illustrates how a string is represented in Turbo C. Notice that the null terminator, \0, is placed at the end of the string. All of the built-in C string processing functions use this terminator to detect the end of a string.

Although we can't cover all of the details of string processing in this book, here are some important points to keep in mind when working with the implementations of the string processing algorithms included in this section and in Section 5.

1. A string cannot be directly assigned to a variable. To store a string in a variable, memory must be allocated and a function such as **strcpy**() should be called.
2. Turbo C does not provide a string concatenation operator. To join strings, the **strcat**() function is used.
3. Whenever a string is no longer needed, its memory space allocated with **malloc**() or **calloc**() should be deallocated by calling the **free**() function.

Table 4.2 lists the built-in functions used by our string processing routines.

Table 4.2. Turbo C built-in string processing functions

Function	Description
strstr()	Returns position of a substring
strcpy()	Copies a string
strlen()	Returns string length
strcat()	String concatenation function
strdup()	Returns a duplicate copy of a string

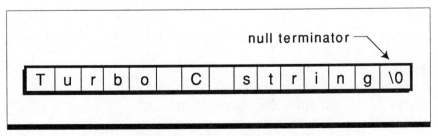

Figure 4.4. String Representation in Turbo C

The following text describes each of the Turbo C string processing functions. In addition to these routines, one local function called **found_space()** is used to search for a word boundary in a string (a space character followed by a nonspace character). This function is called by most of the string processing routines.

trim_spaces()   Trims the leading and trailing spaces of a string.

Syntax:
```
char *trim_spaces(char *strng);
```

Parameter:
strng   the string whose copy is trimmed of leading and trailing spaces.

compress_spaces()   Removes leading and trailing spaces and converts any sequence of space into a single space.

Syntax:
```
char *compress_spaces(char *strng);
```

Parameter:
strng   the string to compress.

count_words()   Returns the number of space-delimited words in a string.

Syntax:
```
int count_words(char *words);
```

Parameter:
words   the string whose words are counted.

wordpos()   Finds the word position in a string.

Syntax:
```
int wordpos(char *wordstr, char *words, int wordindex);
```

Parameters:
wordstr   the key search word.
words   the string that contains words.
wordindex   the word number where the search begins.

Inserts a word in a word-based string.   **insertword()**

Syntax:
```
char *insertword(char *wordstr, char *words, int afterword);
```

Parameters:

wordstr   the inserted word.

words   the string in which the new word is inserted.

afterword   the word index after which the new word is inserted. A zero
                value indicates that the new word becomes the new first
                word in the string.

Extracts a specific word from a string.   **getword()**

Syntax:
```
char *getword(char *words, int wordindex);
```

Parameters:

words   the source string that contains the desired word.

wordindex   the index for the desired word. If this index exceeds the
                number of available words, a null string is returned.

Deletes one or more words from a string.   **deleteword()**

Syntax:
```
char *deleteword(char *words, int wordindex, int wordcount);
```

Parameters:

words   the string whose words are deleted.

wordindex   the first word to be deleted.

wordcount   the maximum number of deleted words. If it exceeds the
                available number of words, the difference is ignored.

Translates specified words in a string by replacing all occurrences with   **translateword()**
another word. You can specify the maximum number of translations and
the number of leading words to skip. You can limit translation to selected
words.

Syntax:
```
char *translateword(char *findword, char *replaceword,
                char *words, int wordindex, int frequency);
```

Parameters:

findword	the specified word pattern.
replaceword	the replacement word pattern.
words	the strings whose words are translated.
wordindex	the index for the first word that can be affected by the translation.
frequency	the maximum number of translations to perform.

Turbo Pascal

Listing 4.3 shows the source code for the implementation of the string processing algorithms in Turbo Pascal for strings represented as words. The library unit shown also defines and exports the string identifier type **STRING255**.

String processing in Turbo Pascal is similar to string processing in Turbo BASIC, because Pascal also provides a built-in string data type. A string can be directly assigned to a string variable, as shown in this example:

```
Newstr := 'New string';
```

Notice that single quotes (' ') are used as string delimiters in Turbo Pascal. Because strings can be processed with both built-in string functions and array processing techniques, we'll use both methods in our algorithms. Table 4.3 lists the built-in functions and operators used by our string processing routines.

Table 4.3. Turbo Pascal built-in string processing tools

Function or Operator	Description
Pos	Returns position of a substring
Copy	Copies a string
Length	Returns string length
Delete	Deletes characters from a string
+	String concatenation operator

The following text describes each of the Turbo Pascal string processing functions and procedures. In addition to these routines, one local function called **Found_Space** is used to search for a word boundary in a string (a space character followed by a nonspace character). This function is called by most of the string processing routines. Our routines also make calls to the local functions listed in Table 4.4.

Table 4.4. Turbo Pascal local string processing functions

Function or Operator	Description
IPos	Determines position of a substring in a string using an offset
LeftStr	Returns leftmost n characters
PosMidStr	Returns middle characters using a range
CountMidStr	Returns middle characters using a count

Trims the leading and trailing spaces of a string.   **Trim_Spaces**

Syntax:
```
FUNCTION Trim_Spaces(Strng : STRING255) : STRING255;
```

Parameter:
Strng   the string whose copy is trimmed of leading and trailing spaces.

Removes leading and trailing spaces and converts any sequence of spaces   **Compress_Spaces**
into a single space.

Syntax:
```
PROCEDURE Compress_Spaces(VAR Words : STRING255);
```

Parameter:
Words   the string to compress.

Returns the number of space-delimited words in a string.   **Count_Words**

Syntax:
```
FUNCTION Count_Words(Words : STRING255) : BYTE;
```

Parameter:
Words   the string whose words are counted.

Finds the position of a word in a string.   **WordPos**

Syntax:
```
FUNCTION WordPos(WordStr, Words : STRING255;
                 WordIndex : BYTE) : BYTE;
```

Parameters:

WordStr the key search word.

Words the string that contains words.

WordIndex the word number where the search begins.

InsertWord Inserts a word in a word-based string.

Syntax:
```
PROCEDURE InsertWord(WordStr : STRING255; VAR Words :
                     STRING255; AfterWord : BYTE);
```

Parameters:

WordStr the inserted word.

Words the string in which the new word is inserted.

AfterWord the word index after which the new word is inserted. A zero value indicates that the new word is inserted as the first word in the string.

GetWord Extracts a specific word from a string.

Syntax:
```
PROCEDURE GetWord(Words : STRING255; VAR WordSought :
                  STRING255; WordIndex : BYTE);
```

Parameters:

Words the source string that contains the desired word.

WordSought the word extracted from the string **Words**.

WordIndex the index for the desired word. If this index exceeds the number of available words, a null string is returned.

DeleteWord Deletes one or more words from a string.

Syntax:
```
PROCEDURE DeleteWord(VAR Words : STRING255; WordIndex,
                     WordCount : BYTE);
```

Parameters:

Words	the string whose words are deleted.
WordIndex	the first word to be deleted. If this index is greater than the number of available words, the **Words$** string is not changed.
WordCount	the maximum number of deleted words. If it exceeds the available number of words, the difference is ignored.

Translates specified words in a string by replacing all occurrences with another word. You can specify the maximum number of translations and the number of leading words to skip. You can limit translation to selected words.

TranslateWord

Syntax:
```
PROCEDURE TranslateWord(FindWord, ReplaceWord : STRING255;
                        VAR Words : STRING255; WordIndex,
                        Frequency : BYTE);
```

Parameters:

FindWord	the specified word pattern.
ReplaceWord	the replacement word pattern.
Words	the strings whose words are translated.
WordIndex	the index for the first word that can be affected by the translation.
Frequency	the maximum number of translations to perform.

Turbo Prolog

Listing 4.4 includes the implementation of the string processing algorithms in Turbo Prolog. Because include files are not required, the code can be compiled and run as listed.

Turbo Prolog provides a built-in string data type; thus, strings are relatively easy to process. The Prolog implementations of the string processing algorithms resemble the BASIC and Pascal implementations; however, recursion is used in place of loop structures. Strings are delimited with double quotes (""). Table 4.5 lists the built-in predicates used by our string processing routines.

The following text describes each of the Turbo Prolog string processing predicates.

Table 4.5. Turbo Prolog built-in string processing predicates

Predicate	Description
frontchar	Returns the first character in a string
frontstr	Divides a string into two strings
str_len	Returns the string length
concat	String concatenation predicate

trim_spaces   Trims the leading and trailing spaces of a string.

Syntax:
```
trim_spaces(Str, Result)       (i,o)
            (string, string)
```

Parameters:
Str   the string whose copy is trimmed of leading and trailing spaces.
Result   the string with leading and trailing spaces removed.

compress_spaces   Removes leading and trailing spaces and converts any sequence of space into a single space.

Syntax:
```
compress_spaces(Str, Result)       (i,o)
                (string, string)
```

Parameters:
Str   the string to compress.
Result   the string with extra spaces removed.

count_words   Returns the number of space-delimited words in a string.

Syntax:
```
count_words(Str, Count)       (i,o)
            (string, integer)
```

Parameters:
Str   the string whose words are counted.
Count   the number of words in the string.

Finds the word position in a string. **wordpos**

Syntax:
```
wordpos(Wordstr, Str, Index, Pos)     (i,i,i,o)
        (string, string, integer, integer)
```

Parameters:

Wordstr   the key search word.
Str   the string that contains words.
Index   the word number where the search begins.
Pos   the position of the found word. If the word is not found, 0 is returned.

Inserts a word in a word-based string. **insertword**

Syntax:
```
insertword(Word, Str, Pos, Resultstr)     (i,i,i,o)
        (string, string, integer, string)
```

Parameters:

Word   the inserted word.
Str   the string in which the new word is inserted.
Pos   the word index after which the new word is inserted. A zero value indicates that the new word is inserted as the first word in the string.
Resultstr   the returned string with the inserted word.

Extracts a specific word from a string. **getword**

Syntax:
```
getword(Str, Trgword, Index)     (i,o,i)
        (string, string, integer)
```

Parameters:

Str   the source string that contains the desired word.
Trgword   the found string.
Index   the index for the desired word.

Deletes one or more words from a string. **deleteword**

Syntax:

```
deleteword(Str, Pos, Wordcount, Result)     (i,i,i,o)
           (string, integer, integer, string)
```

Parameters:

Str   the string whose words are deleted.
Pos   the first word to be deleted.
Wordcount the maximum number of deleted words. If it exceeds the
               available number of words, the difference is ignored.
Result   the string with the words removed.

translateword   Translates specified words in a string by replacing all occurrences with
                    another word. You can specify the maximum number of translations and
                    the number of leading words to skip. You can limit translation to selected
                    words.

Syntax:

```
translateword(Findword, Replword, Str, Index, Freq, Result)
              (string, string, string, integer, integer, string)
              (i,i,i,i,i,o)
```

Parameters:

Findword   the specified word pattern.
Replword   the replacement word pattern.
Str   the strings whose words are translated.
Index   the index for the first word that can be affected by the
               translation.
Freq   the maximum number of translations to perform.
Result   the translated string.

• Listing 4.1. Turbo BASIC word string library

```
%TRUE = 1
%FALSE = 0


DEF FNTrim.Spaces$(LString$)
' trims leading and trailing spaces from a string
LOCAL i%, strlen%
```

```
strlen% = LEN(LString$)
IF strlen% = 0 THEN
   FNTrim.Spaces$ = ""
   EXIT DEF
END IF
DO WHILE (strlen% > 0) AND (MID$(LString$,1,1) = " ")
   LString$ = MID$(LString$,2)
   DECR strlen%
LOOP
IF strlen% > 0 THEN
   DO WHILE (strlen% > 0) AND (MID$(LString$,strlen%,1) = " ")
      LString$ = LEFT$(LString$,strlen%-1)
      DECR strlen%
   LOOP
END IF
FNTrim.Spaces$ = LString$ ' return function value
END DEF ' FNTrim.Spaces$

SUB Compress.Spaces(Words$)
' reduces sequence of spaces into a single space and trims leading and
' trailing spaces
LOCAL strlen%, i%
strlen% = LEN(Words$)
IF strlen% = 0 THEN EXIT SUB
Words$ = FNTrim.Spaces$(Words$)
strlen% = LEN(Words$)
i% = 1
DO WHILE (i% < strlen%)
   IF (MID$(Words$,i%,1) = " ") AND (MID$(Words$,i%+1,1) = " ") THEN
      IF (i%+1) < strlen% THEN
         Words$ = LEFT$(Words$,i%) + MID$(Words$,i%+2)
      ELSE
         Words$ = LEFT$(Words$,i%)
      END IF
      DECR strlen%
   ELSE
      INCR i%
   END IF
LOOP
END SUB ' Compress.Spaces
```

```
DEF FNFound.Space%(LString$, Index%)
' detects the boundary between a space and a nonspace character
IF Index% > 1 THEN
    FNFound.Space% = ABS((MID$(LString$,Index%-1,1) = " ") AND_
                         (MID$(LString$,Index%,1) <> " "))
ELSE
    FNFound.Space% = %FALSE
END IF
END DEF ' FNFound.Space%


DEF FNCount.Words%(Words$)
LOCAL i%, count%, strlen%
IF Words$ = "" THEN
    FNCount.Words% = 0
    EXIT DEF
END IF
Words$ = " " + Words$ + " "
strlen% = LEN(Words$)
count% = 0 ' initialize word count%
FOR i% = 2 TO strlen%
    IF FNFound.Space%(Words$, i%) = %TRUE THEN INCR count%
NEXT i%
FNCount.Words% = count% ' return function value
END DEF ' FNCount.Words%


DEF FNWordPos%(WordStr$, Words$, WordIndex%)
LOCAL i%, n%, strlen%, count%, ptr%
IF (WordStr$ = "") OR (Words$ = "") THEN
    FNWordPos% = 0
    EXIT DEF
END IF
IF (INSTR(Words$, WordStr$) = 0) THEN
    ' sought word is not a string at all
    FNWordPos% = 0
    EXIT DEF
END IF
IF WordIndex% < 1 THEN WordIndex% = 1
' search for the WordIndex%'th word
Words$ = " " + Words$ + " "
WordStr$ = " " + WordStr$ + " "
```

```
strlen% = LEN(Words$)
n% = WordIndex%
i% = 2
' try to locate the WordIndex%'th word
DO WHILE (i% <= strlen%) AND (n% > 0)
    IF FNFound.Space%(Words$, i%) = %TRUE THEN DECR n%
    IF n% > 0 THEN INCR i%
LOOP
IF i% > strlen% THEN   ' WordIndex% is too high
    FNWordPos% = 0
    EXIT DEF
END IF
DECR i%
ptr% = INSTR(i%, Words$, WordStr$)
IF ptr% > 0 THEN
    INCR ptr% ' add one for leading space
    INCR i%
    count% = 0
    DO WHILE (i% <= ptr%)
        IF FNFound.Space%(Words$, i%) = %TRUE THEN
            INCR count%
        INCR i%
    LOOP
    FNWordPos% = count% + WordIndex% - 1
ELSE
    FNWordPos% = 0
END IF
END DEF ' FNWordPos%


SUB InsertWord(WordStr$, Words$, AfterWord%)
LOCAL i%, n%, strlen%
IF AfterWord% = 0 THEN ' concatenate to the left
    Words$ = WordStr$ + " " + Words$
    EXIT SUB
END IF
' search for the (AfterWord%+1)'th word
Words$ = " " + Words$ + " "
strlen% = LEN(Words$)
n% = AfterWord%+1
i% = 2
```

```
' try to locate the AfterWord%'th word
DO WHILE (i% <= strlen%) AND (n% > 0)
    IF FNFound.Space%(Words$, i%) = %TRUE THEN DECR n%
    IF n% > 0 THEN INCR i%
LOOP
IF i% > strlen% THEN  ' append new word
    Words$ = Words$ + WordStr$
ELSE
    DECR i%
    Words$ = LEFT$(Words$, i%) + WordStr$ + MID$(Words$, i%)
END IF
' remove leading and trailing blanks
Words$ = FNTrim.Spaces$(Words$)
END SUB' InsertWord


SUB GetWord(Words$, WordSought$, WordIndex%)
LOCAL i%, n%, strlen%, ptr%
IF WordIndex% < 1 THEN WordIndex% = 1
Words$ = " " + Words$ + " "
n% = WordIndex%
strlen% = LEN(Words$)
i% = 2
' try to locate the WordIndex%'th word
DO WHILE (i% <= strlen%) AND (n% > 0)
    IF FNFound.Space%(Words$, i%) = %TRUE THEN DECR n%
    IF n% > 0 THEN INCR i%
LOOP
IF i% > strlen% THEN
    WordSought$ = ""
ELSE
    ptr% = i% ' index the first character of the word and find the tail of
              ' the word, because a trailing space is always present in the
              ' main string
    DO WHILE (i% <= strlen%) AND (MID$(Words$,i%,1) <> " ")
       INCR i%
    LOOP
    DECR i%
    WordSought$ = MID$(Words$,ptr%,i%-ptr%+1)
END IF
' remove leading and trailing blanks
```

```
Words$ = FNTrim.Spaces$(Words$)
END SUB ' GetWord

SUB DeleteWord(Words$, WordIndex%, WordCount%)
LOCAL i%, strlen%, n%, ptr%
IF WordIndex% < 0 THEN WordIndex% = 1
IF WordCount% < 1 THEN WordCount% = 1
Words$ = " " + Words$ + " "
n% = WordIndex%
strlen% = LEN(Words$)
i% = 2
' try to locate the WordIndex%'th word
DO WHILE (i% <= strlen%) AND (n% > 0)
    IF FNFound.Space%(Words$, i%) = %TRUE THEN DECR n%
    IF n% > 0 THEN INCR i%
LOOP
IF i% <= strlen% THEN
    ptr% = i%-1  ' index space before the word
    n% = WordCount%
    DO WHILE (i% <= strlen%) AND (n% > 0)
       IF FNFound.Space%(Words$, i%) = %TRUE THEN DECR n%
       IF n% > 0 THEN INCR i%
    LOOP
    IF i% > strlen% THEN  ' WordCount too high, ignore extra
       Words$ = LEFT$(Words$,ptr%-1)
    ELSE
       ' scan to tail of last deleted word
       DO WHILE (i% < strlen%) AND (MID$(Words$,i%,1) <> " ")
          INCR i%
       LOOP
       IF ptr% > 1 THEN
           Words$ = LEFT$(Words$,ptr%-1) + MID$(Words$,i%)
       ELSE
           Words$ = MID$(Words$,i%)
        END IF
     END IF
END IF
' remove leading and trailing blanks
Words$ = FNTrim.Spaces$(Words$)
END SUB ' DeleteWord
```

```
SUB TranslateWord(FindWord$, ReplaceWord$, Words$, WordIndex%, Frequency%)
LOCAL index%
IF (FindWord$ = "") OR  (Words$ = "") THEN EXIT SUB
IF WordIndex% < 1 THEN WordIndex% = 1
IF Frequency% < 1 THEN Frequency% = 1
' get first location of first occurrence of FindWord$
index% = FNWordPos%(FindWord$, Words$, WordIndex%)
' translation loop
DO WHILE (index% > 0) AND (Frequency% > 0)
    DECR Frequency%
    ' remove found word
    CALL DeleteWord(Words$, index%, 1)
    IF ReplaceWord$ <> "" THEN_  ' replace with non-null word
        CALL InsertWord(ReplaceWord$, Words$, index% - 1)
    ' get index% for the next word
    IF Frequency% > 0 THEN_
        index% = FNWordPos%(FindWord$, Words$, index% + 1)
LOOP
END SUB ' TranslateWord
```

• Listing 4.2. Turbo C word string library

```
#include <stdio.h>
#include <string.h>
#include <stdlib.h>
#include <alloc.h>

/* The only routine that allocates memory for a returned string is
   getword(). All of the other routines return pointers. */

/* internal function */
int found_space(char *strng, int index);

/* main functions */
char *trim_spaces(char *strng);
char *compress_spaces(char *strng);
int count_words(char *words);
int wordpos(char *wordstr, char *words, int wordindex);
```

```c
char *insertword(char *wordstr, char *words, int afterword);
char *getword(char *words, int wordindex);
char *deleteword(char *words, int wordindex, int wordcount);
char *translateword(char *findword, char *replaceword, char *words, int
        wordindex, int frequency);

char *trim_spaces(char *strng)
/* Trims leading and trailing spaces from a string. This function does not
    allocate memory for the returned string.*/
{
    int strlength;

    strlength = strlen(strng);
    if (strlength == 0)  return NULL;  /* do nothing */
    /* check for leading spaces */
    while ((strlength > 0) && (strng[0] == ' ')) {
        strng++;
        --strlength;
    }
    if (strlength > 0) {  /* check for trailing spaces */
        while ((strlength > 0) && (strng[strlength-1] == ' ')) {
            strng[strlength-1] = '\0';   /* replace space with null char */
            --strlength;
        }
    }
    return strng; /* return pointer to trimmed string */
}

char *compress_spaces(char *strng)
/* Compresses sequence of spaces into a single space and removes leading
    and trailing spaces. Memory is not allocated for a new string. */
{
    int i, j, strlength;
    char *tempstr, *ptr, *tptr;

    strlength = strlen(strng);
    if (strlength == 0)  return NULL;
    /* remove leading and trailing spaces */
    ptr = trim_spaces(strng); /* memory is allocated */
    strlength = strlen(ptr);  /* get length of trimmed string */
```

```
    tempstr = malloc(strlength + 1);
    tptr = tempstr;
    i = 0;
    j = 0;
    while (i < strlength) {
        if ((ptr[i] == ' ') && (ptr[i+1] == ' '))    /* skip space */
            i++;
        else {
            tempstr[j] = ptr[i];   /* copy each character */
            i++;
            j++;
        }
    }
    tempstr[j] = '\0'; /* add null terminator */
    strcpy(strng, tempstr);
    free(tptr);   /* remove temp storage */
    return strng;
}


int found_space(char *strng, int index)
/* determines whether index points to a word boundary position */
{
    if (index > 0)
        return((strng[index-1] == ' ') && (strng[index] != ' '));
    else return 0;   /* space not found */
}


int count_words(char *words)
/* counts the number of words in a string */
{
    int i,count,strlength;
    char *tempstr;

    if (words[0] == '\0') return 0; /* string is empty */
    strlength = strlen(words) + 2;
    /* add spaces before and after the string */
    tempstr =  malloc(strlength + 1);
    strcpy(tempstr, " ");
    strcat(tempstr, words);
    strcat(tempstr, " ");
```

```
    count = 0;    /* initialize word count */
    /* count words by looking for spaces */
    for (i = 1; i <strlength; i++)
        if (found_space(tempstr, i)) count++;
    free(tempstr);
    return count;
}


int wordpos(char *wordstr, char *words, int wordindex)
/* determines position of a word in a string of words */
{
    int i,n,count,strlength;
    char *tempstr1, *tempstr2, *ptr, *tptr;

    if ((wordstr[0] == '\0') || (words[0] == '\0')) return 0;
    if (strstr(words, wordstr) == NULL) return 0;
    if (wordindex < 1) wordindex = 1;

    /* search for the wordindex'th word */
    strlength = strlen(words) + 2;
    /* add leading and trailing spaces */
    tempstr1 = malloc(strlength + 1);
    strcpy(tempstr1, " ");
    strcat(tempstr1, words);
    strcat(tempstr1, " ");
    tempstr2 = malloc(strlen(wordstr) + 3);
    /* add leading and trailing spaces */
    strcpy(tempstr2, " ");
    strcat(tempstr2, wordstr);
    strcat(tempstr2, " ");
    n = wordindex;
    i = 1;
    tptr = tempstr1;
    /* locate the wordindex'th word */
    while ((i < strlength) && (n > 0)) {
        if (found_space(tempstr1,i)) n--;
        if (n > 0) i++;
    }
    if (i > strlength) {
        free(tptr);
```

```
        free(tempstr2);
        return 0; /* wordindex is too high */
    }
    i--;
    /* find position of search string in word string */
    tempstr1 = tempstr1 + i;
    ptr = strstr(tempstr1, tempstr2);
    if (ptr != NULL) {
        count = 0;   /* initialize word count */
        while (ptr != tempstr1) {    /* determine word number */
            if (found_space(tempstr1, 1)) count++;
            tempstr1++;
        }
        count = count + wordindex;
    }
    else count = 0; /* not found */
    free(tptr);   /* free memory for temp strings */
    free(tempstr2);
    return count;
}


char *insertword(char *wordstr, char *words, int afterword)
/* Inserts a word in a string of words. This function does not allocate
   memory for the string returned. */
{
    int i,n,strlength;
    char *tempstr, *ptr, *tptr;

    if (afterword == 0) { /* concatenate to the left */
        tempstr = malloc(strlen(wordstr) + strlen(words) + 3);
        strcpy(tempstr, wordstr);
        strcat(tempstr, " ");
        strcat(tempstr, words);
        strcpy(words, tempstr);
        free(tempstr);
        return words;
    }
    strlength = strlen(words) + 2;
    tempstr =  malloc(strlen(wordstr) + strlen(words) + 5);
    /* add leading and trailing spaces */
```

```
        strcpy(tempstr, " ");
        strcat(tempstr, words);
        strcat(tempstr, " ");
        tptr = tempstr;
        n = afterword + 1;
        i = 1;
        /* find location to insert new word */
        while ((i < strlength) && (n > 0))    {
            if (found_space(tempstr,i)) n--;
            if (n > 0) i++;
        }
        if (i > strlength) strcat(tempstr,wordstr);
        else {
            tempstr[i] = '\0';
            strcat(tempstr, wordstr);
            words = words + i-2;
            strcat(tempstr, words);
        }
        ptr = trim_spaces(tempstr);
        strcpy(words, ptr);
        free(tptr);
        return words;
}


char *getword(char *words, int wordindex)
/* Returns a word from a string of words. Memory is allocated for the
    string returned. */
{
    int i,n,strlength,ptr;
    char *tempstr;

    if (wordindex < 1) wordindex = 1;
    strlength = strlen(words) + 2;
    tempstr = malloc(strlength + 1);
    strcpy(tempstr, " ");  /* append spaces */
    strcat(tempstr, words);
    strcat(tempstr, " ");
    n = wordindex;
    i = 1;
    /* find location to insert new word */
```

```
    while ((i < strlength) && (n > 0)) {
        if (found_space(tempstr,i)) n--;
        if (n > 0) i++;
    }
    if (i > strlength) {
        free(tempstr);
        return NULL;
    }
    else {
        ptr = i;
        while ((i < strlength) && (tempstr[i] != ' '))
            i++;
        tempstr = tempstr + ptr;
        tempstr[i - ptr] = '\0';
        return tempstr;
    }
}


char *deleteword(char *words, int wordindex, int wordcount)
/* Deletes a word from a word string. Memory is not allocated for the
   string returned. */
{
    int i,n,strlength, ptr;
    char *tempstr, *p1, *tptr, *sptr;

    if (wordindex < 0) wordindex = 1;
    if (wordcount < 1 ) wordcount = 1;
    strlength = strlen(words) + 2;
    tempstr = malloc(strlength + 1);
    strcpy(tempstr, " ");
    strcat(tempstr, words);
    strcat(tempstr, " ");
    tptr = tempstr;
    n = wordindex;
    i = 1;
    /* try to locate the wordindex'th word */
    while ((i < strlength) && (n > 0)) {
        if (found_space(tempstr,i)) n--;
        if (n > 0) i++;
    }
```

```
       if (i > strlength) {
          free(tptr);
          return words;
       }
       else {
          ptr = i-1;   /* index space before word */
          n = wordcount;
          while ((i < strlength) && (n > 0))  {
             if (found_space(tempstr,i)) n--;
             if (n > 0) i++;
          }
          if (i >= strlength)
             tempstr[ptr] = '\0';
          else {
             while ((i < strlength) && (words[i] != ' '))
                i++;
             if (ptr > 1)  {
                tempstr[ptr] = '\0';
                if (i < strlength-1) {
                   p1 = &tempstr[i+1];
                   strcat(tempstr, p1);
                }
             }
             else tempstr = tempstr + i+1;
          }
       }
       sptr = trim_spaces(tempstr);
       strcpy(words, sptr);
       free(tptr);
       return words;
}


char *translateword(char *findword, char *replaceword, char *words,
                    int wordindex, int frequency)
/* Tranlates a string by replacing a word in the string with another.
   Memory is not allocated for the string returned. */
{
    int index;

    if ((findword[0] == '\0') || (words[0] == '\0')) return NULL;
```

```
    if (wordindex < 1) wordindex = 1;
    if (frequency < 1) frequency = 1;
    /* get first location of first occurrence of findword */
    index = wordpos(findword, words, wordindex);
    while ((index > 0) && (frequency > 0)) {
        frequency--;
        words = deleteword(words, index,1);
        if (words == NULL) return NULL;
        if (replaceword[0] != '\0')
            words = insertword(replaceword, words, index - 1);
        if (frequency > 0)
            index = wordpos(findword, words, index + 1);
    }
    return words;
}
```

• Listing 4.3. Turbo Pascal word string library

```
UNIT WordStr1;

TYPE STRING255 = STRING[255];

FUNCTION Trim_Spaces(Strng : STRING255) : STRING255;
{ trims leading and trailing spaces from a string }

PROCEDURE Compress_Spaces(VAR Words : STRING255);
{ reduces sequence of spaces into a single space and trims leading and
  trailing spaces }

FUNCTION Count_Words(Words : STRING255) : BYTE;
{ counts the number of space-delimited words in string Words }

FUNCTION WordPos(WordStr, Words : STRING255; WordIndex : BYTE) : BYTE;
{ returns the position of WordStr in Words, starting at the WordIndex'th
  word }

PROCEDURE InsertWord(WordStr  : STRING255; VAR Words : STRING255;
                     AfterWord : BYTE);
{ inserts WordStr in Words after word number AfterWord }
```

```
PROCEDURE GetWord(Words : STRING255; VAR WordSought : STRING255;
                  WordIndex : BYTE);
{ returns the word at word-based position WordIndex }

PROCEDURE DeleteWord(VAR Words : STRING255; WordIndex, Wordcount : BYTE);
{ deletes Wordcount words in Words, starting with word number WordIndex }

PROCEDURE TranslateWord(FindWord, ReplaceWord : STRING255;
                        VAR Words : STRING255; WordIndex, Frequency : BYTE);
{ replaces word FindWord with ReplaceWord in Words }

{*************************************************************************}
FUNCTION IPos(SubStr,                       { input }
              Strng       : STRING255; { input }
              StartIndex  : BYTE         { input }) : BYTE;
{ simulates BASIC's INSTR function with an offset }
VAR strpos : BYTE;

BEGIN
    {- - - - - - - -  Argument checking  - - - - - - - -}
    IF (Strng = '') OR (SubStr = '') THEN BEGIN
        IPos := 0;
        EXIT;
    END; { IF }

    {- - - - - - Main body of the procedure - - - - - - -}
    strpos := 0; { initialize with default function value }
    IF (StartIndex > 0) AND (StartIndex <= Length(Strng)) THEN BEGIN
        { clip leading part of the string Strng? }
        IF StartIndex > 1 THEN Delete(Strng, 1, StartIndex);
        strpos := POS(SubStr, Strng);
        IF (strpos > 0) AND (StartIndex > 1) THEN
            INC(strpos, StartIndex);
    END; { IF }
    IPos := strpos { return function value }
END; { IPos }


FUNCTION LeftStr(Strng      : STRING255;   { in/out }
                 NumChars  : BYTE         { input }) : STRING255;
{ simulates BASIC's LEFT$ function }
```

```
BEGIN
    LeftStr := COPY(Strng, 1, NumChars);
END; { LeftStr }


FUNCTION PosMidStr(Strng : STRING255;    { input }
                   First,                { input }
                   Last  : BYTE          { input }) : STRING255;
{ simulates True BASIC's string extraction by indices }


BEGIN
    {- - - - - - - - Argument checking  - - - - - - - -}
    IF (Strng = '') OR (Last < First) THEN BEGIN   { bad arguments }
        PosMidStr := '';
        EXIT
    END; { IF }
    { return function value }
    PosMidStr := COPY(Strng, First, Last - First + 1)
END; { PosMidStr }


FUNCTION CountMidStr(Strng : STRING255;      { input }
                     First,                  { input }
                     Count : BYTE            { input }) : STRING255;
{ simulates MS-BASIC's MID$ function }


BEGIN
    CountMidStr := COPY(Strng, First, Count)
END; { CountMidStr }


FUNCTION Trim_Spaces(Strng : STRING255 { input }) : STRING255;
{ trims leading and trailing spaces from a string }
VAR i, strlen : BYTE;


BEGIN
    strlen := Length(Strng);
    IF strlen = 0 THEN BEGIN
        Trim_Spaces := '';
        EXIT
    END;
    WHILE (strlen > 0) AND (Strng[1] = ' ') DO BEGIN
        Delete(Strng,1,1);
        DEC(strlen);
```

```
        END;
    IF strlen > 0 THEN
        WHILE (strlen > 0) AND (Strng[strlen] = ' ') DO BEGIN
            Delete(Strng,strlen,1);
            DEC(strlen);
        END;
    Trim_Spaces := Strng   { return function value }
END; { Trim_Spaces }


PROCEDURE Compress_Spaces(VAR Words : STRING255 { in/out });
{ reduces sequence of spaces into a single space and trims leading and
  trailing spaces }


VAR strlen, i : BYTE;


BEGIN
    strlen := Length(Words);
    IF strlen = 0 THEN EXIT;
    Words := Trim_Spaces(Words);
    strlen := Length(Words);
    i := 1;
    WHILE (i < strlen) DO BEGIN
        IF (Words[i] = ' ') AND (Words[i+1] = ' ') THEN BEGIN
            Delete(Words,i,1);
            DEC(strlen);
        END
        ELSE
            INC(i);
    END;
END; { Compress_Spaces }


FUNCTION Found_Space(Strng : STRING255; { input }
                     Index : BYTE       { input }) : BOOLEAN;
{ detects the boundary between a space and a nonspace character }


BEGIN
    IF Index > 1 THEN
        Found_Space := (Strng[Index-1] = ' ') AND (Strng[Index] <> ' ')
    ELSE
        Found_Space := FALSE;
END; { Found_Space }
```

```
FUNCTION Count_Words(Words : STRING255 { input }) : BYTE;
{ counts the number of space-delimited words in string Words }

VAR i, count, strlen : BYTE;

BEGIN
    IF Words = '' THEN BEGIN
       Count_Words := 0;
       EXIT
    END;
    Words := ' ' + Words + ' ';
    strlen := Length(Words);
    count := 0; { initialize word count }
    FOR i := 2 TO strlen DO
       IF Found_Space(Words, i) THEN INC(count);
    Count_Words := count   { return function value }
END; { Count_Words }


FUNCTION WordPos( WordStr,                 { input }
                  Words      : STRING255; { input }
                  WordIndex  : BYTE        { input }) : BYTE;
{ returns the position of WordStr in Words, starting at the WordIndex'th
  word }

VAR i, n, strlen, count, ptr : BYTE;

BEGIN
    IF (WordStr = '') OR (Words = '') THEN BEGIN
       WordPos := 0;
       EXIT
    END; { IF }
    IF (Pos(WordStr, Words) = 0) THEN BEGIN
       { sought word is not a string at all }
       WordPos := 0;
       EXIT
    END; { IF }
    IF WordIndex < 1 THEN WordIndex := 1;
    { search for the WordIndex'th word }
    Words := ' ' + Words + ' ';
    WordStr := ' ' + WordStr + ' ';
```

```
   strlen := Length(Words);
   n := WordIndex;
   i := 2;
   { try to locate the WordIndex'th word }
   WHILE (i <= strlen) AND (n > 0) DO BEGIN
      IF Found_Space(Words, i) THEN DEC(n);
      IF n > 0 THEN INC(i);
   END; { WHILE }
   IF i > strlen THEN BEGIN { WordIndex is too high }
      WordPos := 0;
      EXIT;
   END; { IF }
   DEC(i);
   ptr := IPos(WordStr, Words, i);
   IF ptr > 0 THEN BEGIN
      INC(ptr); { add one for leading space }
      INC(i);
      count := 0;
      WHILE (i <= ptr) DO BEGIN
         IF Found_Space(Words, i) THEN INC(count);
         INC(i);
      END; { WHILE }
      WordPos := count + WordIndex - 1;
   END
   ELSE
      WordPos := 0;
END; { WordPos }

PROCEDURE InsertWord( WordStr    : STRING255;   { input  }
                      VAR Words  : STRING255;   { in/out }
                      AfterWord  : BYTE         { input });
{ inserts WordStr in Words after word number AfterWord }

VAR i, n, strlen : BYTE;

BEGIN
   IF AfterWord = 0 THEN { concatenate to the left }
      Words := WordStr + ' ' + Words;
      EXIT;
   END;
```

```
   { search for the (AfterWord+1)'th word }
   Words := ' ' + Words + ' ';
   strlen := Length(Words);
   n := AfterWord+1;
   i := 2;
   { try to locate the AfterWord'th word }
   WHILE (i <= strlen) AND (n > 0) DO BEGIN
      IF Found_Space(Words, i) THEN DEC(n);
      IF n > 0 THEN INC(i);
   END; { WHILE }
   IF i > strlen THEN { append new word }
      Words := Words + WordStr
   ELSE BEGIN
      DEC(i);
      Words := LeftStr(Words, i) + WordStr + CountMidStr(Words, i, strlen);
   END;
   { remove leading and trailing blanks }
   Words := Trim_Spaces(Words);
END; { InsertWord }


PROCEDURE GetWord( Words           : STRING255;   { input }
                   VAR WordSought  : STRING255;   { output }
                   WordIndex       : BYTE         { input });
{ returns the word at word-based position WordIndex }


VAR i, n, strlen, ptr : BYTE;


BEGIN
   IF WordIndex < 1 THEN WordIndex := 1;
   Words := ' ' + Words + ' ';
   n := WordIndex;
   strlen := Length(Words);
   i := 2;
   { try to locate the WordIndex'th word }
   WHILE (i <= strlen) AND (n > 0) DO BEGIN
      IF Found_Space(Words, i) THEN DEC(n);
      IF n > 0 THEN INC(i);
   END; { WHILE }
   IF i > strlen THEN BEGIN
      WordSought := '';
```

```
        EXIT;
    END
    ELSE BEGIN
        ptr := i; { index the first character of the word }
        { find the tail of the word, because a trailing space is always
            present in the main string }
        WHILE (i <= strlen) AND (Words[i] <> ' ') DO INC(i);
        DEC(i);
        WordSought := PosMidStr(Words,ptr,i);
    END; { IF }
END; { GetWord }


PROCEDURE DeleteWord(VAR Words   : STRING255; { in/out }
                         WordIndex,                { input }
                         WordCount  : BYTE           { input });
{ deletes WordCount words in Words, starting with word number WordIndex }

VAR i, strlen, n, ptr : BYTE;


BEGIN
    IF WordIndex < 0 THEN WordIndex := 1;
    IF WordCount < 1 THEN WordCount := 1;
    Words := ' ' + Words + ' ';
    n := WordIndex;
    strlen := Length(Words);
    i := 2;
    { try to locate the WordIndex'th word }
    WHILE (i <= strlen) AND (n > 0) DO BEGIN
        IF Found_Space(Words, i) THEN DEC(n);
        IF n > 0 THEN INC(i);
    END; { WHILE }
    IF i > strlen THEN
        EXIT
    ELSE BEGIN
        ptr := i-1; { index space before the word }
        n := WordCount;
        WHILE (i <= strlen) AND (n > 0) DO BEGIN
            IF Found_Space(Words, i) THEN DEC(n);
            IF n > 0 THEN INC(i);
        END; { WHILE }
```

```
      IF i > strlen THEN { WordCount too high, ignore difference }
          Words := LeftStr(Words,ptr-1)
      ELSE BEGIN
          { scan to tail of last deleted word }
          WHILE (i < strlen) AND (Words[i] <> ' ') DO INC(i);
          IF ptr > 1 THEN
              Words := LeftStr(Words,ptr-1) + PosMidStr(Words,i,strlen)
          ELSE
              Words := PosMidStr(Words,i,strlen);
      END; { IF }
   END; { IF }
   { remove leading and trailing blanks }
   Words := Trim_Spaces(Words);
END; { DeleteWord }


PROCEDURE TranslateWord( FindWord, ReplaceWord   : STRING255; { input  }
                         VAR Words               : STRING255; { in/out }
                         WordIndex, Frequency    : BYTE;      { input })
{ replaces word FindWord with ReplaceWord in Words }


VAR index : BYTE;


BEGIN
   IF (FindWord = '') OR  (Words = '') THEN EXIT;
   IF WordIndex < 1 THEN WordIndex := 1;
   IF Frequency < 1 THEN Frequency := 1;
   { get first location of first occurrence of FindWord }
   index := WordPos(FindWord, Words, WordIndex);
   { translation loop }
   WHILE (index > 0) AND (Frequency > 0) DO BEGIN
      DEC(Frequency);
      { remove found word }
      DeleteWord(Words, index, 1);
      IF ReplaceWord <> '' THEN { replace with non-null word }
          InsertWord(ReplaceWord, Words, index - 1);
      { get index for the next word }
      IF Frequency > 0 THEN
          index := WordPos(FindWord, Words, index + 1);
   END; { WHILE }
END; { TranslateWord }
END.
```

Listing 4.4. Turbo Prolog word string library

```
predicates
    trim_spaces(string, string)
    trimleft(string, string, char)
    trimright(string, string, char)
    compress_spaces(string, string)
    spacex(string, string, integer)
    strclean(string, string)
    count_words(string, integer)
    wordcount(string, integer)
    wordpos(string, string, integer, integer)
    getword(string, string, integer)
    skipstr(string, string, integer)
    insertword(string, string, integer, string)
    deleteword(string, integer, integer, string)
    translateword(string, string, string, integer, integer, string)
    replacestr(integer, string, string, string, integer, string)
    strsfind(string, string, integer)
    matchs(string, string, integer, integer)

clauses

/***************************    trim_spaces    ***************************/
    trim_spaces(Str, Result) :-
        trimleft(Str, Newstr, ' '),
        trimright(Newstr, Result, ' ').

    trimleft(Str, Newstr, Ch) :-            % trim spaces from left side
        Ch <> ' ',
        frontchar(Newstr, Ch, Str), !.

    trimleft(Str, Newstr, ' ') :-
        frontchar(Str, Fc, Rest),           % test each character
        trimleft(Rest, Newstr, Fc), !.

    trimright(Str, Newstr, Ch) :-           % trim spaces from right side
        Ch <> ' ',
        str_char(St2, Ch),                  % append last nonspace char
        concat(Str, St2, Newstr), !.
```

```
    trimright(Str, Newstr, ' ') :-
        str_len(Str, Len),
        L = Len-1,
        frontstr(L, Str, First, Rest),
        frontchar(Rest, Fc, _),
        trimright(First, Newstr, Fc), !.

/************************   compress_spaces   **************************/
    compress_spaces(Str, Result) :-
        trim_spaces(Str, S1),
        str_len(S1, Len),
        spacex(S1, Result, Len).          % remove middle spaces

    spacex(Str, Newstr, 0) :- Newstr = Str, !.

    spacex(Str, Newstr, Len) :-
        strclean(Str, S2),               % eliminate extra space
        L = Len - 1,
        spacex(S2, Newstr, L), !.

    strclean(Str, Trgstr) :-
        strsfind(Str, "  ", Pos),        % look for 2 spaces
        P = Pos - 1,
        frontstr(P, Str, First, Rest),
        frontstr(1, Rest, _, S2),
        concat(First, S2, Trgstr).

    strclean(Str, Str).                  % only a single space

/***************************   count_words   **************************/
    count_words(Str, Count) :-
        concat(Str, " ", Trgstr),        % add trailing space
        wordcount(Trgstr, Count).

    wordcount("", 0).                    % terminate word count

    wordcount(Str, Count) :- !,
        strsfind(Str, " ", Pos),         % look for a word delimiter
        frontstr(Pos, Str, _, Newstr),   % remove word
        wordcount(Newstr, Oldcount),     % count with new string
        Count = Oldcount + 1.
```

```
/***************************    wordpos     ***************************/
    wordpos(Wordstr, Str, Index, Pos) :-
        count_words(Str, C1),              % determine number of words
        I = Index - 1,
        concat(Str, " ", Trgstr),          % add trailing space
        skipstr(Trgstr, Newstr, I),        % skip to index position
        strsfind(Newstr, Wordstr, P),
        frontstr(P, Newstr, _, Newstr2),
        trim_spaces(Newstr2, S2),
        count_words(S2, C2),
        Pos = (C1-C2) + 1, !.              % calculate position


    wordpos(_, _, _, 0).


/***************************    getword     ***************************/
    getword(Str, Trgword, Index) :-
        concat(Str, " ", Trgstr),          % add trailing space
        I = Index - 1,
        skipstr(Trgstr, Newstr, I),        % skip to index position
        strsfind(Newstr, " ", Pos),        % locate word
        P = Pos - 1,
        frontstr(P, Newstr, Trgword, _).


/***************************    insertword     ***************************/
    insertword(Word, Str, 0, Resultstr) :-  % insert at beginning
        concat(Word, " ", Nw),
        concat(Nw, Str, Resultstr).


    insertword(Word, Str, Pos, Resultstr) :- % insert in middle
        str_len(Str, L1),
        concat(Str, " ", Trgstr),
        skipstr(Trgstr, Newstr, Pos),
        str_len(Newstr, L2),
        concat(" ", Word, W1),             % add trailing and leading
        concat(W1, " ", W2),               % spaces
        concat(W2, Newstr, W3),
        L3 = (L1 - L2),
        frontstr(L3, Str, First, _),
        concat(First, W3, R),
        trim_spaces(R, Resultstr).
```

```
/****************************** deleteword ******************************/
   deleteword(Str, Pos, Wordcount, Resultstr) :-
       str_len(Str, L1),
       concat(Str, " ", Trgstr),              % add trailing space
       P = Pos - 1,
       skipstr(Trgstr, Newstr, P),            % skip past offset
       str_len(Newstr, L2),
       Wc = Wordcount - 1,
       skipstr(Newstr, Nstr2, Wc),            % find position of word
       strsfind(Nstr2, " ", P2),              % find end of word
       frontstr(P2, Nstr2, _, Rest),          % remove word
       L3 = (L1 - L2) + 1,
       frontstr(L3, Str, First, _),
       concat(First, Rest, R),                % join strings
       trim_spaces(R, Resultstr).

/************************** translateword **************************/
   translateword(Findword, Replword, Str, Index, Freq, Resultstr) :-
       wordpos(Findword, Str, Index, Pos),    % locate search string
       replacestr(Pos, Findword, Replword, Str, Freq, Resultstr).

   replacestr(_, _, _, Str, 0, Newstr) :-     % terminate replacement
       Str = Newstr, !.

   replacestr(0, _, _, Str, _, Newstr) :-     % terminate replacement
       Str = Newstr, !.

   replacestr(Pos, Fword, Rword, Str, Freq, Newstr) :-
       F1 = Freq - 1,
       deleteword(Str, Pos, 1, Str2),         % remove word
       P = Pos - 1,
       insertword(Rword, Str2, P, Str3),      % replace with new string
       P2 = Pos + 1,
       wordpos(Fword, Str3, P2, P3),          % get position of next word
       replacestr(P3, Fword, Rword, Str3, F1, Newstr), !.

/********************** support predicates **********************/
   strsfind(Srcstr, Substr, Pos):-            % locate a substring
       str_len(Srcstr, Size),                 % get length of string
       str_len(Substr, Ssize),                % get length of substring
```

```
      matchs(Srcstr, Substr, Ssize, Sub1), !,    % check match
      Pos = Size - (Ssize + Sub1) + 1.           % update position


matchs(Str1, _, _, _):-                          % fail on null string
   Str1 = "", fail.


matchs(Str1, Str2, Size, Sub1):-
   frontstr(Size, Str1, First, Rest),            % extract substring
   First = Str2,                                 % substring matches
   str_len(Rest, Sub1).                          % get length of rest of
                                                 % string

matchs(Str1, Str2, Size, Sub1):-
   frontchar(Str1, _, Rest),
   matchs(Rest, Str2, Size, Sub1).


skipstr(Trgstr, Newstr, 0) :- Newstr = Trgstr, !.


skipstr(Str, Newstr, Count) :-                   % skip to index position
   strsfind(Str, " ", Pos),
   frontstr(Pos, Str, _, S2),
   C = Count - 1,
   skipstr(S2, Newstr, C), !.
```

String Processing with Token Strings

Introduction

In Section 4 we presented algorithms for processing strings represented with words and items. This section examines a more general type of string called *token strings*. The token strings are similar to the other types of strings we introduced; however, they provide a greater degree of flexibility because different delimiter types can be used in a string.

We begin this section by looking at how token strings are represented. Then we present implementations for a set of string processing operations for each of the Turbo languages.

Representing Strings with Tokens

Tokens are items delimited from one another by one or more token-delimiter characters. Unlike the word and item strings in Section 4, the token-delimiter characters are not predefined. Instead, they are user-supplied in the form of a string that contains the set of token-delimiter characters. Consequently, the string processing routines that we present here require that the token-delimiter characters be passed as a string parameter. Let's explore an example. Given the following strings:

"one%two three#four&five#six@seven"
"one@@two@@three"

we can process them using the following delimiter string:

"%#@ &"

For example, to count the number of tokens in the token string, we would search for any of the delimiter characters listed in the delimiter string.

The token strings that we'll represent follow rules similar to the word strings discussed in Section 4.

1. One or more token-delimiter characters separate a token from another.
2. A sequence of multiple token-delimiter characters has the same effect as any single token-delimiter character.
3. Single or multiple leading and trailing token-delimiter characters are allowed.

Using these rules, a string may contain token-delimiter characters only and consequently contain no tokens. By contrast, a string that does not contain any token-delimiter characters consists of only one token. Token strings can represent more sophisticated expressions, such as mathematical expressions. The string processing tools in this section perform the following three operations.

1. Count tokens in a string
2. Determine the position of a token in a string
3. Obtain a token by specifying its position

Counting Tokens

The same technique for counting words and items in a string is used to count tokens. Again we can simplify the algorithm using a variation of the string padding method introduced in Section 4. Here, the first character in the token-delimiter string is used to pad a token string at both ends. For example, given the following token and delimiter strings:

"one%two three#four&five#six@seven"
"%#@ &"

after padding would be represented as:

"%one%two three#four&five#six@seven%"

Notice that the character % is used as the padding character. Keep in mind that we must still test for the two extreme cases in which the token string contains only token-delimiter characters or does not contain any delimiters. Otherwise, the number of tokens equals the number of occurrences of a token-delimiter character followed by a nondelimiter character.

The general routine used to detect a token boundary in a string is a function called **Found_Token**. This function is also used by the other token processing operations to locate token boundaries in a string. Shown here in Turbo Pascal, **Found_Token** is the main statement that detects a token boundary:

```
Found_Token := (POS(Strng[Index-1], DelimStr) > 0) AND
               (POS(Strng[Index], DelimStr) = )
```

Essentially, this scanning operation is similar to the one we used to detect a word boundary in a string. With this function, we can easily count the number of tokens in a string using a simple loop, as shown:

```
For i := 1 TO strlen DO
    IF Found_Token(Tokens, DelimStr, i) THEN INC (count);
```

where the variable **i** serves as a character index for the token string and **count** stores the token count total. The counting technique shown here is also used in Turbo BASIC and Turbo C.

In Turbo Prolog, the recursive predicate **tokencheck** is used to scan for token boundaries. This predicate uses the built-in predicate **frontstr** to remove one character at a time from the delimiter string so that the token string can be searched. The token count is also performed with recursion. Each time a token boundary is detected, the token is removed from the token string. This process continues until the token string contains no more tokens. When the string is reduced to the null string, the recursion terminates and the token count is computed as the recursion unwinds.

Locating and Extracting Tokens

The algorithms for extracting a token and determining the position of a token are slightly more complex than the word or item string versions. The additional complexity is introduced because a token can be delimited by various characters on either end. Therefore, a more elaborate text scanning algorithm is required.

The algorithm for finding the position of a token is essentially a two-step process. First, the starting character position of the search token found in the token string is located. Once this position is known, the following loop structure is used to determine the token position of the found token:

```
WHILE (i <= ptr) DO BEGIN
    IF Found_Token(Tokens, DelimStr, i) THEN INC(count);
        INC(i);
END;
```

The variable **i** is used to keep track of the token number, and the variable **ptr** contains the starting character position of the token.

To extract a token, a repeating loop statement is used until the starting index of the token is detected. The basic loop is shown here in Turbo Pascal.

```
n := TokenIndex;
i := 2;
{ try to locate the token }
WHILE (i <= strlen) AND (n > 0) DO BEGIN
    IF Found_Token(Tokens, DelimStr, i) THEN DEC(n);
    IF n > 0 THEN INC(i);
END; { WHILE }
```

When the loop terminates, the variable **i** stores the character index where the token starts. Once we have this index, we simply scan the string starting at this position until a delimiter character is detected.

Adding Other Token Processing Operations

In our token processing implementations, we've only included routines for counting, locating, and extracting tokens. Other useful operations such as token insertion, deletion, and translation can be supported; however, they are complicated by the possible presence of sequences of meaningful token-delimiter characters. For example, consider the following mathematical expression:

```
futureVal = presentVal * (1 + interest)^timePeriods
```

In this case, let's assume that the tokens consist of alphanumeric characters and all of the other characters are treated as token-delimiters. The task of inserting new tokens introduces the problem of inserting the right sequence of token delimiters. Deleting tokens poses the reverse problem — what do you do with the sequence of remaining token delimiter characters? These operations and the translation of tokens are perhaps best handled by character-manipulation routines that provide you with a high level of control over what goes in and out of a string during the manipulation of tokens.

Implementations of Token String Processing Algorithms

The implementations of the token string processing operations are presented in Listings 5.1, 5.2, 5.3, and 5.4. We've included a short description of each token processing routine in each of the Turbo languages. If you need more information about how strings are represented in each language, review Section 4.

Turbo BASIC

Listing 5.1 shows the Turbo BASIC tokens library. The constants **%TRUE** and **%FALSE** are also defined. Descriptions of the nonlocal routines of the library are presented next.

FNCount.Tokens%   Returns the number of tokens in a string.

Syntax:
```
DEF FNCount.Tokens%(Tokens$, DelimStr$)
```

Parameters:

Tokens$ the string whose tokens are counted.
DelimStr$ the string of delimiter characters.

FNTokenPos%   Finds the token position in a string.

Syntax:
```
DEF FNTokenPos%(TokenStr$, Tokens$, DelimStr$, TokenIndex%)
```

Parameters:

TokenStr$ the key search token.
Tokens$ the string that contains tokens.
DelimStr$ the string of delimiter characters.
TokenIndex%   the token number where the search begins.

GetToken   Extracts a specific token from a string.

Syntax:
```
SUB GetToken(Tokens$, DelimStr$, TokenSought$, TokenIndex%)
```

Parameters:

Tokens$ the source string that contains the desired token.
DelimStr$ the string of delimiter characters.
TokenSought$**   the token extracted from the string **Tokens$.
TokenIndex%   the index for the desired token. If this index exceeds the number of available tokens, a null string is returned.

Turbo C

Listing 5.2 presents the Turbo C tokens library. The include files **stdio.h** and **string.h** are required to compile the routines described next.

Returns the number of tokens in a string.

count_tokens()

Syntax:
```
int count_tokens(char *tokens, char *delimstr);
```

Parameters:
tokens   the string whose tokens are counted.
delimstr   the string containing the delimiter characters.

Finds the position of a token in a string.

tokenpos()

Syntax:
```
int tokenpos(char *tokenstr, char *tokens, char *delimstr,
             int tokenindex);
```

Parameters:
tokenstr   the key search token.
tokens   the string that contains tokens.
delimstr   the string containing the delimiter characters.
tokenindex   the token number where the search begins.

Extracts a specified token from a string.

gettoken()

Syntax:
```
char *gettoken(char *tokens, char *delimstr, int tokenindex);
```

Parameters:
tokens   the source string that contains the desired token.
delimstr   the string containing the delimiter characters.
tokenindex   the index for the desired token. If this index exceeds the number of available tokens, a null string is returned.

Turbo Pascal

Listing 5.3 shows the source code for the Turbo Pascal tokens library unit. The unit also defines and exports the string identifier type **STRING255**. The exported library routines are presented next.

Count_Tokens

Returns the number of tokens in a string.

Syntax:
```
FUNCTION Count_Tokens(Tokens : STRING255;
                      DelimStr : STRING255) : BYTE;
```

Parameters:

Tokens   the string whose tokens are counted.
DelimStr   the string of delimiter characters.

TokenPos

Finds the token position in a string.

Syntax:
```
FUNCTION TokenPos(TokenStr, Tokens, DelimStr : STRING255;
                  TokenIndex : BYTE) : BYTE;
```

Parameters:

TokenStr   the key search token.
Tokens   the string that contains tokens.
DelimStr   the string of delimiter characters.
TokenIndex the token number where the search begins.

GetToken

Extracts a specific token from a string.

Syntax:
```
PROCEDURE GetToken( Tokens, DelimStr  : STRING255;
                VAR TokenSought        : STRING255;
                    TokenIndex         : BYTE);
```

Parameters:

Tokens   the source string that contains the desired token.
DelimStr   the string of delimiter characters.
TokenSought the token extracted from the string **Tokens**.
TokenIndex   the index for the desired token. If this index exceeds the number of available tokens, a null string is returned.

Turbo Prolog

Listing 5.4 shows the source code for the Turbo Prolog token processing predicates. The description of each main routine is included next.

Returns the number of tokens in a string.   **count_tokens**

Syntax:
```
count_tokens(Str, Delimstr, Count)       (i,i,o)
            (string, string, integer)
```

Parameters:
Str   the string whose tokens are counted.
Delimstr   the string containing the delimiter characters.
Count   the number of tokens in the string.

Finds the position of a token in a string.   **tokenpos**

Syntax:
```
tokenpos(Tokenstr, Str, Delimstr, Index, Pos) (i,i,i,i,o)
         (string, string, string, integer, integer)
```

Parameters:
Tokenstr   the key search token.
Str   the string that contains tokens.
Delimstr   the string containing the delimiter characters.
Index   the token number where the search begins.
Pos   the position of the found token.

Extracts a specified token from a string.   **gettoken**

Syntax:
```
gettoken(Str, Delimstr, Trgword, Index)       (i,i,o,i)
         (string, string, string, integer)
```

Parameters:
Str   the source string that contains the desired token.
Delimstr   the string containing the delimiter characters.
Trgword   the token extracted from the token string.
Index   the index for the desired token.

• Listing 5.1. Turbo Basic token string library

```
%TRUE = 1
%FALSE = 0


DEF FNFound.Token%(LString$, DelimStr$, Index%)
' detects the boundary between a token character and a nontoken character
IF Index% > 1 THEN
    FNFound.Token% = ABS((INSTR(DelimStr$, MID$(LString$,Index%-1,1)) > 0)_
        AND (INSTR(DelimStr$, MID$(LString$,Index%,1)) = 0))
    ELSE
        FNFound.Token% = %FALSE
END IF
END DEF ' FNFound.Token%


DEF FNCount.Tokens%(Tokens$, DelimStr$)
LOCAL i%, count%, strlen%, all.tokens%, no.tokens%, is.token%
IF Tokens$ = "" THEN
    FNCount.Tokens% = 0
    EXIT DEF
END IF
IF DelimStr$ = "" THEN DelimStr$ = " "
Tokens$ = LEFT$(DelimStr$,1) + Tokens$
strlen% = LEN(Tokens$)
' verify whether string contains characters that are all tokens or characters
' that are nontokens
all.tokens% = %TRUE
no.tokens% = %TRUE
i% = 1
DO WHILE (i% <= strlen%) AND ((all.tokens% = %TRUE) OR (no.tokens% = %TRUE))
    IF INSTR(DelimStr$,MID$(Tokens$,i%,1)) > 0 THEN
        is.token% = %TRUE
    ELSE
        is.token% = %FALSE
    END IF
    no.tokens% = ABS((is.token% = %FALSE) AND (no.tokens% = %TRUE))
    all.tokens% = ABS((is.token% = %TRUE) AND (all.tokens% = %TRUE))
    INCR i%
LOOP
```

```
IF (all.tokens% = %TRUE) OR (no.tokens% = %TRUE) THEN
    IF no.tokens% = %TRUE THEN_
        FNCount.Tokens% = 1 ' one token in entire string
    IF all.tokens% = %TRUE THEN_
        FNCount.Tokens% = 0 ' only token chars in string
    EXIT DEF
END IF
count% = 0 ' initialize token count%
FOR i% = 1 TO strlen%
    IF FNFound.Token%(Tokens$, DelimStr$, i%) = %TRUE THEN INCR count%
NEXT i%
FNCount.Tokens% = count% ' return function value
END DEF ' FNCount.Tokens%


DEF FNTokenPos%(TokenStr$, Tokens$, DelimStr$, TokenIndex%)
LOCAL i%, n%, strlen%, count%, ptr%, ch$
IF (TokenStr$ = "") OR (Tokens$ = "") THEN
    FNTokenPos% = 0
    EXIT DEF
END IF
IF (INSTR(Tokens$, TokenStr$) = 0) THEN
    ' sought token is not in string at all
    FNTokenPos% = 0
    EXIT DEF
END IF
IF TokenIndex < 1 THEN TokenIndex = 1
IF DelimStr$ = "" THEN DelimStr$ = " "
ch$ = LEFT$(DelimStr$,1)
' search for the TokenIndex'th token
Tokens$ = ch$ + Tokens$ + ch$
strlen% = LEN(Tokens$)
n% = TokenIndex
i% = 2
' try to locate the TokenIndex'th token
DO WHILE (i% <= strlen%) AND (n% > 0)
    IF FNFound.Token%(Tokens$, DelimStr$, i%) = %TRUE THEN DECR n%
    IF n% > 0 THEN INCR i%
LOOP
IF i% > strlen% THEN ' TokenIndex is too high
    FNTokenPos% = 0
```

```
    EXIT DEF
END IF
DECR i%
ptr% = INSTR(i%, Tokens$, TokenStr$)
IF ptr% > 0 THEN
    INCR ptr% ' add one for leading token
    INCR i%
    count% = 0
    DO WHILE (i% <= ptr%)
        IF FNFound.Token%(Tokens$, DelimStr$, i%) = %TRUE THEN INCR count%
        INCR i%
    LOOP
    FNTokenPos% = count% + TokenIndex - 1
ELSE
    FNTokenPos% = 0
END IF
END DEF ' FNTokenPos%


SUB GetToken(Tokens$, DelimStr$, TokenSought$, TokenIndex%)
LOCAL i%, n%, strlen%, ptr%, ch$
IF TokenIndex% < 1 THEN TokenIndex% = 1
IF DelimStr$ = "" THEN DelimStr$ = " "
ch$ = LEFT$(DelimStr$,1)
Tokens$ = ch$ + Tokens$ + ch$
n% = TokenIndex%
strlen% = LEN(Tokens$)
i% = 1
' try to locate the TokenIndex%'th token
DO WHILE (i% <= strlen%) AND (n% > 0)
    IF FNFound.Token%(Tokens$, DelimStr$, i%) = %TRUE THEN DECR n%
    IF n% > 0 THEN INCR i%
LOOP
IF i% > strlen% THEN
    TokenSought$ = ""
ELSE
    ptr% = i% ' index the first character of the token, find the tail of
             ' the token, because a trailing token character is always
             ' present in the main string
    DO WHILE (i% <= strlen%) AND (INSTR(DelimStr$,MID$(Tokens$,i%,1)) = 0)
        INCR i%
```

```
    LOOP
    DECR i%
    TokenSought$ = MID$(Tokens$,ptr%,i%-ptr%+1)
END IF
END SUB ' GetToken
```

Listing 5.2. Turbo C token string library

```c
#include <stdio.h>
#include <string.h>
#include <stdlib.h>
#include <alloc.h>

int found_token(char *strng, char *delimstr, int index);

/* main functions */
int count_tokens(char *tokens, char *delimstr);
int tokenpos(char *tokenstr, char *tokens, char *delimstr, int tokenindex);
char *gettoken(char *tokens, char *delimstr, int tokenindex);

int found_token(char *strng, char *delimstr, int index)
 /* detects the boundary between a token character and a nontoken character */
{
    if (index > 0)
        return (((strchr(delimstr, strng[index-1])) != NULL) &&
            ((strchr(delimstr, strng[index])) == NULL));
    else return 0;
}

int count_tokens(char *tokens, char *delimstr)
 /* counts the number of tokens in a string */
{
    int i, count, strlength;
    int all_tokens, no_tokens, is_token;
    char *tempstr;

    if (tokens[0] == '\0') return 0;
    if (delimstr[0] == '\0') strcpy(delimstr, " ");
    tempstr = malloc(strlen(tokens) + 2);
```

```
    tempstr[0] = delimstr[0];
    tempstr[1] = '\0';
    strcat(tempstr, tokens);
    strlength = strlen(tempstr);
    all_tokens = 1;
    no_tokens = 1;
    i = 0;
    while ((i < strlength) && (all_tokens || no_tokens)) {
        is_token = ((strchr(delimstr, tempstr[i]) != NULL));
        no_tokens = ((!is_token) && no_tokens);
        all_tokens = (is_token && all_tokens);
        i++;
    }
    if (all_tokens || no_tokens) {
        free(tempstr);
        if (no_tokens) return 1;
        if (all_tokens) return 0;
    }
    count = 0;
    for (i = 0; i < strlength; i++)
        if (found_token(tempstr, delimstr, i))
     count++;
    free(tempstr);
    return count;
}


int tokenpos(char *tokenstr, char *tokens, char *delimstr, int tokenindex)
/* returns the position of a token */
{
    int i, n, strlength, count;
    char ch, *tempstr, *ptr, *tptr;

    if ((tokenstr[0] == '\0') || (tokens[0] == '\0')) return 0;
    if (strstr(tokens, tokenstr) == NULL) return 0;
    if (tokenindex < 1) tokenindex = 1;
    if (delimstr[0] == '\0') strcpy(delimstr, " ");
    ch = delimstr[0];
    tempstr = malloc(strlen(tokens) + 3);
    tptr = tempstr;
    tempstr[0] = ch;
```

```
    tempstr[1] = '\0';
    strcat(tempstr, tokens);
    strlength = strlen(tempstr);
    tempstr[strlength] = ch;
    tempstr[++strlength] = '\0';
    n = tokenindex;
    i = 1;
    while ((i < strlength) &&   (n > 0)) {
        if (found_token(tempstr, delimstr, i)) n--;
        if (n > 0) i++;
    }
    if (i >= strlength) {
        free(tptr);
        return 0;
    }
    i--;
    /* find position of token string in string */
    tempstr = tempstr + i;
    ptr = strstr(tempstr, tokenstr);
    if (ptr != NULL) {
        count = 0;   /* initialize word count */
        while (ptr != tempstr) {  /* determine token number */
          if (found_token(tempstr, delimstr, 1)) count++;
          tempstr++;
        }
      count = count + tokenindex - 1;
    }
    else count = 0; /* not found */
    free(tptr);  /* free memory for temp string */
    return count;
}

char *gettoken(char *tokens, char *delimstr, int tokenindex)
/* returns a token from a string of tokens */
{
    int i,n,strlength,ptr;
    char ch, *tempstr;

    if (tokenindex < 1) tokenindex = 1;
    if (delimstr[0] == '\0') strcpy(delimstr, " ");
```

```
ch = delimstr[0];
tempstr = malloc(strlen(tokens) + 3);
tempstr[0] = ch;
tempstr[1] = '\0';
strcat(tempstr, tokens);
strlength = strlen(tempstr);
tempstr[strlength] = ch;
tempstr[++strlength] = '\0';
n = tokenindex;
i = 1;
/* find location to insert new token */
while ((i < strlength) && (n > 0))   {
    if (found_token(tempstr,delimstr,i)) n--;
    if (n > 0) i++;
}
if (i >= strlength) {
  free(tempstr);
  return NULL;
}
else {
    ptr = i;
    while ((i < strlength) && (strchr(delimstr, tempstr[i]) == NULL))
        i++;
    tempstr = tempstr + ptr;
    tempstr[i - ptr] = '\0';
    return tempstr;
}
}
```

Listing 5.3. Turbo Pascal token string library

```
UNIT TokenStr1;

TYPE STRING255 = STRING[255];

FUNCTION Count_Tokens(Tokens, DelimStr : STRING255) : BYTE;
{ counts the number of space-delimited tokens in string Tokens }

FUNCTION TokenPos(TokenStr, Tokens, DelimStr : STRING255;
                  TokenIndex : BYTE) : BYTE;
```

```
{ returns the position of TokenStr in Tokens, starting at the TokenIndex'th
  token }

PROCEDURE GetToken(Tokens, DelimStr : STRING255; VAR TokenSought : STRING255;
                   TokenIndex : BYTE);
{ returns the token at token-based position TokenIndex }


{**************************************************************************}


FUNCTION IPos(SubStr,                      { input }
              Strng      : STRING255; { input }
              StartIndex : BYTE       { input }) : BYTE;
{ simulates BASIC's INSTR function with an offset }


VAR strpos : BYTE;

BEGIN
   {- - - - - - - -  Argument checking  - - - - - - - - -}
   IF (Strng = '') OR (SubStr = '') THEN BEGIN
      IPos := 0;
      EXIT;
   END; { IF }
   {- - - - - - - Main body of the procedure - - - - - - -}
   strpos := 0; { initialize with default function value }
   IF (StartIndex > 0) AND (StartIndex <= Length(Strng)) THEN BEGIN
      { clip leading part of the string Strng? }
      IF StartIndex > 1 THEN Delete(Strng, 1, StartIndex);
      strpos := POS(SubStr, Strng);
      IF (strpos > 0) AND (StartIndex > 1) THEN
         INC(strpos, StartIndex);
   END; { IF }
   IPos := strpos { return function value }
END; { IPos }


FUNCTION LeftStr( Strng    : STRING255; { in/out }
                 NumChars : BYTE        { input }) : STRING255;
{ simulates BASIC's LEFT$ function }
BEGIN
   LeftStr := COPY(Strng, 1, NumChars);
END; { LeftStr }
```

```
FUNCTION PosMidStr(Strng  : STRING255;   { input }
                   First,                 { input }
                   Last   : BYTE         { input }) : STRING255;
{ simulates True BASIC's string extraction by indices }

BEGIN
   {- - - - - - - - Argument checking - - - - - - - -}
   IF (Strng = '') OR (Last < First) THEN BEGIN { bad arguments }
      PosMidStr := '';
      EXIT
   END; { IF }
   { return function value }
   PosMidStr := COPY(Strng, First, Last - First + 1)
END; { PosMidStr }


FUNCTION CountMidStr(Strng  : STRING255;  { input }
                     First,               { input }
                     Count  : BYTE        { input }) : STRING255;
{ simulates MS-BASIC's MID$ function }


BEGIN
   CountMidStr := COPY(Strng, First, Count)
END; { CountMidStr }


FUNCTION Found_Token(Strng,                { input }
                     DelimStr : STRING255; { input }
                     Index    : BYTE       { input }) : BOOLEAN;
{ detects the boundary between a token character and a nontoken character }


BEGIN
   IF Index > 1 THEN
      Found_Token := (POS(Strng[Index-1], DelimStr) > 0) AND
                     (POS(Strng[Index], DelimStr) = 0)
   ELSE
      Found_Token := FALSE;
END; { Found_Token }


FUNCTION Count_Tokens(Tokens,              { input }
                      DelimStr : STRING255 { input }) : BYTE;
{ counts the number of space-delimited tokens in string Tokens }
```

```
VAR i, count, strlen : BYTE;
    all_tokens, no_tokens, is_token : BOOLEAN;
BEGIN
    IF Tokens = '' THEN BEGIN
        Count_Tokens := 0;
        EXIT
    END;
    IF DelimStr = '' THEN DelimStr := ' ';
    Tokens := DelimStr[1] + Tokens;
    strlen := Length(Tokens);
    { verify whether string contains characters that are all tokens or
      characters that are nontokens }
    all_tokens := TRUE;
    no_tokens := TRUE;
    i := 1;
    WHILE (i <= strlen) AND (all_tokens OR no_tokens) DO BEGIN
        is_token := Pos(Tokens[i], DelimStr) > 0;
        no_tokens := (NOT is_token) AND no_tokens;
        all_tokens := is_token AND all_tokens;
        INC(i)
    END; { WHILE }
    IF all_tokens OR no_tokens THEN BEGIN
        IF no_tokens THEN Count_Tokens := 1;  { one token in entire string }
        IF all_tokens THEN Count_Tokens := 0; { only token chars in string }
        EXIT
    END;
    count := 0; { initialize token count }
    FOR i := 1 TO strlen DO
        IF Found_Token(Tokens, DelimStr, i) THEN INC(count);
    Count_Tokens := count { return function value }
END; { Count_Tokens }

FUNCTION TokenPos( TokenStr,                  { input }
                   Tokens,                    { input }
                   DelimStr   : STRING255; { input }
                   TokenIndex : BYTE        { input }) : BYTE;
{ returns the position of TokenStr in Tokens, starting at the TokenIndex'th
  token }

VAR i, n, strlen, count, ptr : BYTE;
    ch : CHAR;
```

```
BEGIN
    IF (TokenStr = '') OR (Tokens = '') THEN BEGIN
        TokenPos := 0;
        EXIT
    END; { IF }
    IF (Pos(TokenStr, Tokens) = 0) THEN BEGIN
        { sought token is not in string at all }
        TokenPos := 0;
        EXIT
    END; { IF }
    IF TokenIndex < 1 THEN TokenIndex := 1;
    IF DelimStr = '' THEN DelimStr := ' ';
    ch := DelimStr[1];
    { search for the TokenIndex'th token }
    Tokens := ch + Tokens + ch;
    strlen := Length(Tokens);
    n := TokenIndex;
    i := 2;
    { try to locate the TokenIndex'th token }
    WHILE (i <= strlen) AND (n > 0) DO BEGIN
        IF Found_Token(Tokens, DelimStr, i) THEN DEC(n);
        IF n > 0 THEN INC(i);
    END; { WHILE }
    IF i > strlen THEN BEGIN { TokenIndex is too high }
        TokenPos := 0;
        EXIT;
    END;
    DEC(i);
    ptr := IPos(TokenStr, Tokens, i);
    IF ptr > 0 THEN BEGIN
        INC(ptr); { add one for leading token }
        INC(i);
        count := 0;
        WHILE (i <= ptr) DO BEGIN
            IF Found_Token(Tokens, DelimStr, i) THEN INC(count);
            INC(i);
        END; { WHILE }
        TokenPos := count + TokenIndex - 1;
    END
    ELSE
```

```
        TokenPos := 0;
END; { TokenPos }


PROCEDURE GetToken(Tokens, DelimStr : STRING255; { input  }
               VAR TokenSought      : STRING255; { output }
                   TokenIndex       : BYTE       { input });
{ returns the token at token-based position TokenIndex }

VAR i, n, strlen, ptr : BYTE;
    ch : CHAR;


BEGIN
    IF TokenIndex < 1 THEN TokenIndex := 1;
    IF DelimStr = '' THEN DelimStr := ' ';
    ch := DelimStr[1];
    Tokens := ch + Tokens + ch;
    n := TokenIndex;
    strlen := Length(Tokens);
    i := 1;
    { try to locate the TokenIndex'th token }
    WHILE (i <= strlen) AND (n > 0) DO BEGIN
        IF Found_Token(Tokens, DelimStr, i) THEN DEC(n);
        IF n > 0 THEN INC(i);
    END; { WHILE }
    IF i > strlen THEN BEGIN
        TokenSought := '';
        EXIT;
    END
    ELSE BEGIN
        ptr := i; { index the first character of the token }
        { find the tail of the token, because a trailing token character is
          always present in the main string }
        WHILE (i <= strlen) AND (Pos(Tokens[i],DelimStr) = 0) DO
            INC(i);
        DEC(i);
        TokenSought := PosMidStr(Tokens,ptr,i);
    END; { IF }
END; { GetToken }
END.
```

• Listing 5.4. Turbo Prolog token string library

```
predicates
    count_tokens(string, string, integer)
    tokencount(string, string, integer)
    tokenpos(string, string, string, integer, integer)
    gettoken(string, string, string, integer)
    skipstr(string, string, string, integer)
    tokencheck(string, string, integer)
    strsfind(string, string, integer)
    matchs(string, string, integer, integer)

clauses
/*************************  count_tokens  *****************************/
    count_tokens(Str, Delimstr, Count) :-
        frontstr(1, Delimstr, F, _),
        concat(Str, F, Trgstr),                  % add trailing space
        tokencount(Trgstr, Delimstr, Count), !.
    tokencount("", _, 0).                        % terminate token count
    tokencount(Str, Delimstr, Count) :- !,
        tokencheck(Str, Delimstr, Pos),          % look for a word delimiter
        frontstr(Pos, Str, _, Newstr),           % remove word
        tokencount(Newstr, Delimstr, Oldcount),  % count with new string
        Count = Oldcount + 1.
    tokencheck(Str, Delimstr, Pos) :-            % locate a token character
        frontstr(1, Delimstr, _, Rest),
        tokencheck(Str, Rest, Pos).
    tokencheck(Str, Delimstr, Pos) :-            % locate a token character
        frontstr(1, Delimstr, First, _),
        strsfind(Str, First, Pos).

/*****************************  tokenpos  *****************************/
    tokenpos(Tokenstr, Str, Delimstr, Index, Pos) :-
        count_tokens(Str, Delimstr, C1),         % determine # of tokens
        I = Index - 1,
        frontstr(1, Delimstr, F, _),
        concat(Str, F, Trgstr),                  % add trailing delimiter
        skipstr(Trgstr, Delimstr, Newstr, I),    % skip to index position
        strsfind(Newstr, Tokenstr, P),
        P2 = P - 1,
```

```
        frontstr(P2, Newstr, _, Newstr2),
        str_len(Newstr2, Len),
        L = Len - 1,
        frontstr(L, Newstr2, S2, _),                % remove trailing delimiter
        count_tokens(S2, Delimstr, C2),
        Pos = (C1-C2) + 1, !.                       % calculate position
    tokenpos(_, _, _, _, 0).


/***************************** gettoken *****************************/
    gettoken(Str, Delimstr, Trgword, Index) :-
        frontstr(1, Delimstr, F, _),
        concat(Str, F, Trgstr),                     % add trailing delimiter
        I = Index - 1,
        skipstr(Trgstr, Delimstr, Newstr, I), !,    % skip to index position
        tokencheck(Newstr, Delimstr, Pos),
        strsfind(Newstr, " ", Pos),                 % locate word
        P = Pos - 1,
        frontstr(P, Newstr, Trgword, _), !.


/************************ support predicates ************************/
    strsfind(Srcstr, Substr, Pos):-                 % locate a substring
    str_len(Srcstr, Size),                          % get length of string
        str_len(Substr, Ssize),                     % get length of substring
        matchs(Srcstr, Substr, Ssize, Sub1), !,     % check match
        Pos = Size - (Ssize + Sub1) + 1.            % update position
    matchs(Str1, _, _, _):-                         % fail on null string
        Str1 = "", fail.
    matchs(Str1, Str2, Size, Sub1):-
        frontstr(Size, Str1, First, Rest),          % extract substring
        First = Str2,                               % substring matches
        str_len(Rest, Sub1).                        % get length of rest of string
    matchs(Str1, Str2, Size, Sub1):-
        frontchar(Str1, _, Rest),
        matchs(Rest, Str2, Size, Sub1).
    skipstr(Trgstr, _, Newstr, 0) :- Newstr = Trgstr, !.
    skipstr(Str, Delimstr, Newstr, Count) :-        % skip to index position
        % strsfind(Str, " ", Pos),
        tokencheck(Str, Delimstr, Pos),
        frontstr(Pos, Str, _, S2),
        C = Count - 1,
        skipstr(S2, Delimstr, Newstr, C), !.
```

List Processing with Singly Linked Lists

Introduction

In the previous two sections we showed how to represent lists of data as word and token strings. We can also represent lists using array structures, pointers, and dynamic memory allocation techniques.

This section presents list processing algorithms and data structures for working with a popular list structure called the *singly linked list*. We'll explore different methods for representing singly linked lists from the use of arrays in Turbo BASIC to the use of pointers and structures in Turbo C. The list tools that we present in each of the Turbo languages provide all of the basic operations you'll need to use singly linked lists in your own applications.

Overview of the Singly Linked List

Borrowing from Pascal and C terminology, *lists* are linear structures made up of a sequence of linked nodes. (Keep in mind that because Turbo Prolog provides its own built-in list types, it is not necessary to use singly linked lists.) Each node is connected, at most, with two other nodes. The beginning of the list is called the *head* and the end of the list is called the *tail*. Both the head and the tail link up with only one other node. There are basically two types of lists: singly linked and doubly linked. *Circular lists* are a variation of the general linked lists, and they can be implemented as singly linked or doubly linked lists. In this section we concentrate on singly linked lists; Section 7 presents doubly linked lists and circular lists.

Singly linked lists are characterized by the fact that one link or pointer is used to connect any two nodes, as shown in Figure 6.1. Consequently, node traversal in a singly linked list is unidirectional, proceeding from the head to the tail of the list. To return to a node, you must store a reference to the node you want to return to, or you must restart traversing the list from its head node. Needless to say, this traversal method is inefficient.

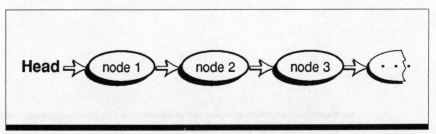

Figure 6.1. Connecting list nodes with links

Singly linked lists come in two flavors: unordered and ordered. With unordered lists, new nodes are added to the tail of the list. Thus, a list is always constructed in a simple chronological order. A data key is not required to maintain the nodes in any order. By contrast, with ordered lists, new nodes are inserted such that an ascending (or descending) order is always maintained—a new node may become the new head or tail, or it can be inserted somewhere in the middle of the list—between two nonterminal nodes. The difference between unordered and ordered lists becomes evident in search operations. The worst case scenario of searching for a nonexistent element means that an entire unordered list is searched. This is compared with a more efficient search in an ordered list where searching starts at the head and stops at a node beyond which the element searched for cannot be found.

Representing Singly Linked Lists

Singly linked lists are implemented in Pascal and C with records or structures, dynamic memory allocation techniques, and pointers. To illustrate how a list is represented, let's examine the data structure used in Turbo Pascal. The basic list node is implemented as a record as shown:

```
{ basic node element }
ListInfoRec = RECORD
    ListKey : ListKeyStr
    { other fields here }
END;


{ singly linked list data types }
SListPtr = ^SListRec;
{ basic list node }
SListRec = RECORD
    ListInfo    : ListInfoRec;
    NextListPtr : SListPtr
END;
```

Our list node consists of a record that contains a node link pointer called **NextListPtr** and a record called **ListInfoRec** used to store the data for each node. The main advantage of the representation that we've chosen is that the type of data stored in each node can be easily modified by changing the **ListInfoRec** record.

In Turbo BASIC, where dynamic allocation is not supported, arrays are used instead to represent the singly linked list. Lists in BASIC can be implemented with or without the use of pseudopointer (or index) arrays. In our implementation of the Turbo BASIC routines we'll use both methods. We'll present a complete discussion of how arrays are used when we cover the Turbo BASIC implementation.

List Processing Operations

The major list processing operations include list insertion, deletion, and search. Algorithms vary depending on the type of lists used. We present the algorithms for ordered and unordered singly linked lists. The first type of singly linked list that we'll examine is the unordered list.

List Insertion with Unordered Lists

Inserting an element in a singly linked list is simple. Here are the general rules that we follow.

1. Allocate memory for the new list node. Exit if a memory allocation problem occurs.
2. Set the link pointer of the new node to nil.
3. If the head of the list is null, the head pointer is set to the new node.
4. Set the tail pointer to the new node.

The last step is required to keep the tail pointer current.

Searching an Unordered List

The second important operation we'll need is one for searching for a list element. Because we're discussing unordered lists, it is necessary to start at the head of the list and examine each list member until we find the element we are searching for or until we reach the end of the list. Here is the general algorithm used.

1. Set the match pointer to nil.
2. Set a search pointer to the head of the list.

3. Set a last pointer to nil.

4. While the search pointer is not nil and the match pointer is nil, use the following rule:

> if the current node matches the element searched for
>   set the match pointer to the current node
> else
>   set the last pointer to the search pointer
>   set the search pointer to the next node
> end if

5. The match pointer indicates the success or failure of the search operation. A nil value signals that the element searched for was not found.

Deleting a List Element from an Unordered List

Our final operation consists of deleting an element from a list. This operation is slightly more complex than the other two operations we've presented, because we must reassign link pointers whenever an element is removed from a list. Of course, the worst case occurs when we attempt to remove an element that is not the head or tail. We'll illustrate this problem with a quick example. Figure 6.2 shows a linked list with three elements. If we remove the middle element, Tom, we must "patch up" the list by reassigning the link pointer in element Bob to element Carol, as shown in Figure 6.3.

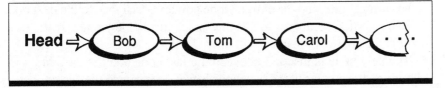

Figure 6.2. List with three elements

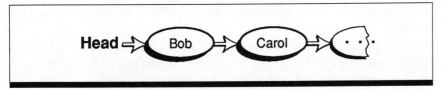

Figure 6.3. List with middle element removed

Here is a summary of the steps that are used in the deletion algorithm.

1. Search for the matching element in the list. Obtain the match pointer and the last node pointer.
2. If the match pointer is nil, stop.
3. If the match pointer is the list-head pointer, set the new head pointer to be the pointer accessed by the match pointer. Resume at step 6.
4. Set the last node pointer to access the same node accessed by the match pointer.
5. If the match pointer is accessed by the list tail, set the new tail pointer to access the node of the "last node pointer."
6. Reclaim the space for the deleted node area.

List Insertion with Ordered Lists

In an ordered list, we can't just insert a new element at the end of the list like we did with the unordered list. To insert the element, we must first find its proper insert position by searching through the list. The steps required for the algorithm are as follows:

1. Set the search flag to false, set the current node pointer to access the head of the list, and set the last node pointer to nil.
2. Search for the proper location to insert the new node. A **While** loop is used to check if the current node pointer is nil (the end of the list is encountered). The loop tests whether the proper location is found. If so, the search flag is set to true. Otherwise, the last node pointer is set to point at the current node, and the current node pointer is assigned to the next one.
3. The insertion continues to allocate space for the new node. If the new node is the first one, resume with step 7.
4. The new node is inserted between the last node and the current node. Therefore, the pointer of the new node is made to point to the current node.
5. If the pointer to the current node is nil, the new node is the new tail of the list. Therefore the tail pointer is updated accordingly. In addition, the last node pointer is made to access the new node. The insertion is accomplished.
6. If the pointer to the current node is not nil, the new node may be inserted within the list, or as the new head of the list. If the last node pointer is nil, the new node is the new head of the list. Otherwise, the last node pointer is given access to the new node. The insertion is accomplished.

7. The new node is the head and tail of the new linked list. The pointer of the new node is set to nil. The insertion is accomplished.

Searching an Ordered List

This algorithm requires that the element searched for is in the range between the head and tail of the list. The steps used are

1. The search pointer is assigned a starting node, usually the head of the list. Pointers to other nodes can be used to bypass a leading portion of the list. In addition, a search pointer is set to nil, and a search flag is also set to false.
2. The search examines the list until either the search pointer is nil (the end has been reached) or the search flag is true.
3. With every node visited, the node's key data is compared with the search value using this rule:

> if the search value is equal to or greater than the node's key data
> then
> > the search flag is set to true in order to halt further node traversal.
> > if the compared data match
> > then
> > > the search pointer is copied to the match pointer
> else
> > the search pointer is copied onto the last node pointer
> > the search pointer accesses the next node
> end if

4. The search pointer reflects the outcome of the search. A nil value indicates that the search item is not in the list.

Deleting a List Element from an Ordered List

The deletion operation is essentially the same as the one used for deleting an element from an unsorted list. The only difference is that the search routine used to locate the position of the element assumes that the list is in a sorted order. The following steps are used to delete an element:

1. Search for the node containing the information marked for deletion.

2. If the match pointer is nil, the information is not in the list and the deletion process ends.

3. If the match pointer is the list-head pointer, set the new head pointer to be the pointer accessed by the match pointer. Resume at step 6.

4. Set the last node pointer to access the same node accessed by the match pointer.

5. If the match pointer is accessed by the list tail, set the new tail pointer to access the node of the "last node pointer."

6. Reclaim the space for the deleted node area.

Implementation of the List Processing Algorithms

The code for the list processing routines is included in Listing 6.1 through Listing 6.6. We'll start with a discussion of the Turbo BASIC implementation, then we'll work our way through all of the other languages.

Turbo BASIC

To implement the various types of linked lists, arrays provide the best data structure for Turbo BASIC. Arrays are useful because their elements are easy to access, whereas the nodes in a linked list normally must be traversed in sequence. On the other hand, the array size must be declared at the beginning of a program, whereas lists can grow or shrink during program execution.

Lists of simple data types can be implemented in BASIC using one of two schemes. The first and simpler one uses a single array manipulated to behave like a list. In this simple form, pointers are not required; array elements can be randomly accessed. Such a scheme enables you to implement singly linked and even doubly linked lists. However, this scheme with its simplicity and low data overhead has its price, namely, speed. Deleting any list node, except the tail, requires that array elements be copied to recover the space left out by the deleted node. In addition, the insertion of new nodes in ordered lists requires, in most cases, moving the existing array elements to make room for the new node. For small lists, the time spent moving array elements may not be significant—in fact it may be worthwhile, because you also save data overhead. If the lists are large, on the other hand, this technique might be too inefficient.

The Turbo BASIC Simple Array Representation

The unordered list routines that use the simple array representation are presented in Listing 6.1 and the ordered array routines are presented in Listing 6.2. In the unordered list routines, the array **UAList$()** and scalar **List.Size%** are the parameters required for each routine. Because of the simple array representation, the routines are easy to follow. To insert a new node, the incoming data is stored in the first available array location. When you search for an item in the list, you sequentially visit the array elements until the search element is found. In the deletion routine, array elements are moved whenever the deleted node is not the tail of the list.

For the ordered list routines, the array **OAList$()** and scalar **List.Size%** are the parameters that appear in every routine and again, **OPTION BASE 1** is required. To insert a new node, the node's insertion position must first be located with a search, and the array elements must then be moved over one position after the element is inserted, unless the new node is also the new tail. The search operation takes advantage of the fact that the nodes are in a sorted order and consequently terminates beyond a cutoff point, as described earlier. The node deletion algorithm uses this efficient search, and moves array elements, except when the tail is deleted.

The Turbo BASIC routines for unordered and ordered lists follow next.

Initializes the unordered list.   **Initialize.UAList**

Syntax:
```
SUB Initialize.UAList(UAList$(1), List.Size%)
```

Parameters:
UAList$()   the array of list nodes.
List.Size%   the list size.

Inserts a new node in the unordered list. If the array is full, the node is not   **Insert.UAList**
inserted.

Syntax:
```
SUB Insert.UAList(UAList$(1), List.Size%, Item$)
```

Parameters:
UAList$()   the array of list nodes.
List.Size%   the list size.
Item$ the new list node.

Search.UAList   Searches the unordered list for **Item$**, starting at node **Head%**. The location of the matching node is reported by **Index%**. If no match occurs, **Index%** returns a value of 0.

Syntax:
```
SUB Search.UAList(Head%, UAList$(1), List.Size%, Item$,
                    Index%)
```

Parameters:

Head%	the head of the list (or trailing sublist).
UAList$()	the array of list nodes.
List.Size%	the list size.
Item$	the desired list node.
Index%	the index of the array containing the desired data.

Delete.UAList   Removes the **Item$** from the unordered list. The outcome of the deletion operation is reported by the **Done%** parameter. A **%TRUE** value indicates that the **Item$** was found in the list and removed.

Syntax:
```
SUB Delete.UAList(Head%, UAList$(1), List.Size%, Item$, Done%)
```

Parameters:

Head%	the head of the list (or trailing sublist).
UAList$()	the array of list nodes.
List.Size%	the list size.
Item$	the desired list node.
Done%	the flag that returns the outcome of the deletion operation.

Initialize.OAList   Initializes the ordered list.

Syntax:
```
SUB Initialize.OAList(OAList$(1), List.Size%)
```

Parameters:

OAList$()	the array of list nodes.
List.Size%	the list size.

Insert.OAList   Inserts a new node in the ordered list. If the array is full, the node is not inserted.

Syntax:
```
SUB Insert.OAList(OAList$(1), List.Size%, Item$)
```

Parameters:

OAList$()   the array of list nodes.
List.Size%   the list size.
Item$ the new list node.

Searches the ordered list for **Item$**, starting at node **Head%**. The location   **Search.OAList**
of the matching node is reported by **Index%**. If no match occurs, **Index%**
returns a value of 0.

Syntax:
```
SUB Search.OAList(Head%, OAList$(1), List.Size%, Item$,
                  Index%)
```

Parameters:

Head%   the head of the list (or trailing sublist).
OAList$()   the array of list nodes.
List.Size%   the list size.
Item$ the desired list node.
Index%   the index of the array containing the desired data.

Removes the **Item$** from the ordered list. The success of the deletion   **Delete.OAList**
operation is reported by the **Done%** parameter. A **%TRUE** value indicates
that the **Item$** was found in the list and removed.

Syntax:
```
SUB Delete.OAList(Head%, OAList$(1), List.Size%, Item$,
                  Done%)
```

Parameters:

Head%   the head of the list (or trailing sublist).
OAList$()   the array of list nodes.
List.Size%   the list size.
Item$ the desired list node.
Done%   the flag that returns the outcome of the deletion operation.

Summary of the Simple Array Scheme

The advantage of the simple array scheme is that you can access the list nodes in the same sequence as the array elements. Thus, the first node is stored in the first array element, the second node in the second array element, and so on. Using the ordered list, you actually have a sorted array at all times.

Representing a List with Pseudopointers

The second scheme for implementing a list using arrays incorporates an array of indexes to function as pointers. This means that the operation of accessing a list node is determined by the array of pointers and not with the array indexes. To support this method, we'll need to use two arrays. The first array stores the data keys, and the second array stores the set of pointers (array indexes) that are used to reference the list elements stored in the first array. This technique greatly simplifies the list processing operations, because the array of list nodes does not have to be rearranged every time an element is inserted or deleted. For example, the head of the list might end up in the third array element; however, because the pointer to the head is maintained in the second array, we can still keep track of the location of the list head without having to move it.

The deletion operation introduces another requirement for our pseudo-pointer method: the ability to maintain the location of deleted elements. In this scheme, array elements are not moved to reclaim the vacant space left by a deleted node. Consequently, repeated deletions create "holes" in the array. Rather than use an array of integers to keep track of these deleted nodes, a string that maps vacant and occupied array elements is incorporated. This string is called the **Map$** parameter, and it is passed to most of the list processing routines. The index of each character serves as a vacancy status flag for the array of nodes. The **Map$** parameter is initialized with spaces. To locate the first vacant array element, the index of the first space character in **Map$** is sought. This location is then changed to a nonspace character (we are using the + symbol) to indicate that the array element is not occupied. By contrast, when a node is deleted, the character at the index of **Map$** that matches the array index is assigned a space character. This signals that the particular array element is once more vacant.

The essential parameters of our singly linked unordered list processing routines are an array of strings (that maintains lists of strings), **USList$()**; an array of indices or pointers, **USPtr%()**; and the scalars **Head%**, **Tail%**, **Map$**, and **List.Size%**. The **Head%** and **Tail%** parameters maintain the location of the head and tail nodes in the list. Listing 6.3 contains the Turbo BASIC routines that implement an unordered linked list using the index scheme. The routines that implement the list manipulation closely follow the general algorithms described earlier in this chapter.

The Turbo BASIC routines for the unordered singly linked lists are covered next.

Initializes the unordered singly linked list. **Initialize.USList**

Syntax:
```
SUB Initialize.USList(USList$(1), USPtr%(1), Head%, Tail%,
                      Map$, List.Size%)
```

Parameters:

USList$()	the array of singly linked list nodes.
USPtr%()	the array of single links.
Head%	the index to the list head.
Tail%	the index to the list tail.
Map$	the map of vacant **USList$** array elements.
List.Size%	the list size, set to zero.

Inserts a new node in the singly linked unordered list. If the array is full, **Insert.USList** the node is not inserted.

Syntax:
```
SUB Insert.USList(USList$(1), USPtr%(1), Map$,   Head%,
                  Tail%, List.Size%, Item$)
```

Parameters:

USList$()	the array of singly linked list nodes.
USPtr%()	the array of single links.
Map$	the map of vacant **USList$** array elements.
Head%	the index to the list head.
Tail%	the index to the list tail.
List.Size%	the list size.
Item$	the new list node, inserted as the new list tail.

Search.USList   Searches the unordered singly linked list for a node that matches the **Item$** parameter. The **Index%** parameter returns the location of the matching array. The **LastIndex%** parameter returns the location of the node that links with the matching node.

Syntax:
```
SUB Search.USList(USList$(1), USPtr%(1), Head%, List.Size%,
                  Item$, Index%, LastIndex%)
```

Parameters:

USList$()	the array of singly linked list nodes.
USPtr%()	the array of single links.
Head%	the index to the list head.
List.Size%	the list size.
Item$	the desired list node.
Index%	the index to the array containing the matching list node. If no match occurs, **Index%** returns **%NIL**.
LastIndex%	the index of the node that points to the matching node. If the head node matches **Item$**, **LastIndex%** returns **%NIL**.

Delete.USList   Deletes a list node matching the **Item$** parameter. The deletion success is reported by the **Done%** parameter. A value of **%TRUE** is assigned to **Done%** when the node has been deleted; otherwise, **%FALSE** is returned by **Done%**.

Syntax:
```
SUB Delete.USList(USList$(1), USPtr%(1), Map$, Head%,
                  Tail%, List.Size%, Item$, Done%)
```

Parameters:

USList$()	the array of singly linked list nodes.
USPtr%()	the array of single links.
Map$	the map of vacant **USList$** array elements.
Head%	the index to the list head.
Tail%	the index to the list tail.
List.Size%	the list size.
Item$	the desired list node.
Done%	the flag that returns the outcome of the node deletion.

Turbo C

The Turbo C functions for the singly linked list processing routines are shown in Listing 6.4. The code requires the two include files **stdio.h** and **string.h**. The singly linked data structure is represented with the following C structure:

```
typedef struct slistmem *slistptr;
    struct listinforec {
    char listkey[40];
};

/* singly linked list structure */
struct slistmem {
    struct listinforec listinfo;
    slistptr nextlistptr;
};
```

The node structure called **slistmem** contains two components: **listinfo**, which is itself a structure; and **nextlistptr**, which serves as the node link. The **listinfo** component stores the data for each list node. Keep in mind that this component can be altered so that other types of data can be stored for each node's key. Additional fields can be included in **listinforec** so the C lists can handle more advanced data structures. When you examine the Turbo Pascal implementation, you'll see that we've used the same representation for the list node data structure.

In our data structure declaration, note also the use of the **typedef** statement for declaring the **slistptr** variable. The **typedef** statement defines **slistptr** to be a pointer data type to the structure **struct slistmem**. The **slistptr** type is used in each function to declare list pointer parameters.

In general, the implementation of the Turbo C singly linked list package is similar to the Turbo Pascal version. To use pointers in C, however, extra care must be taken. Probably the most confusing C pointer-related issue is determining how to pass a pointer parameter to a function so that it can be altered. For example, one of the list processing routines, **init_slist()**, initializes a list by setting the head pointer to **NULL**. Therefore, we must be able to pass a pointer that the function can alter so the new value assigned to the pointer is stored correctly. In Turbo Pascal this issue is resolved for us with **VAR** parameters. For instance, in the following Turbo Pascal declaration, the parameter **Head** is passed by reference or address and not by value. Because we are working here with the address of a pointer, we can easily alter its contents (the address that it references).

```
PROCEDURE Init_SList(VAR Head : SListPtr);
```

In Turbo C, we can produce the same results using the following declaration:

```
void init_slist(slistptr *head);
```

The ***** symbol indicates that the function is passed the address of the pointer argument **head** instead of its contents. Whenever we need to alter a list by inserting or deleting elements, we'll use this technique of passing pointer arguments.

The Turbo C functions for the unordered and ordered singly linked lists are presented next.

init_slist()   Initializes a new singly linked list. The list can be ordered or unordered.

Syntax:
```
void init_slist(slistptr *head);
```

Parameter:
*head   the pointer to the head of the new singly linked list.

clear_slist()   Clears the nodes of a singly linked list and restores its dynamically allocated space. The list can be ordered or unordered.

Syntax:
```
void clear_slist(slistptr *head);
```

Parameter:
*head   the pointer to the head of the deleted singly linked list.

search_slist()   Searches for the unordered list node that matches the ***search_key** parameter. The outcome of the search is reported by a 1 (element found) or 0 (element not found). The matching node is indicated by the pointer parameter, ***thisptr**, and the node pointing to it by the ***lastptr** parameter. Searching for a nonexistent element requires that the entire list be searched.

Syntax:
```
int search_slist(slistptr head, slistptr *thisptr,
                 slistptr*lastptr, char *search_key);
```

Parameters:

head	the head of the list (or trailing sublist).
***thisptr**	the pointer to the matching node. A **NULL** is returned if no match occurs.
***lastptr**	the pointer to the last node before the matching node.
***search_key**	the search key data.

Searches for the ordered list node that matches the ***search_key** parameter. **search_sorted_slist()**
The outcome of the search is reported by a 1 (element found) or 0 (element not found). The matching node is indicated by the pointer parameter, ***thisptr,** and the node pointing to it by the ***lastptr** parameter. Searching for a nonexistent element normally requires that part of the list be searched.

Syntax:
```
int search_sorted_slist(slistptr head, slistptr *thisptr,
                        slistptr *lastptr, char *search_key);
```

Parameters:

head	the head of the list (or trailing sublist).
***thisptr**	the pointer to the matching node. A **NULL** is returned if no match occurs.
***lastptr**	the pointer to the last node before the matching node.
***search_key**	the search key data.

Inserts a new node at the tail of the unordered singly linked list. **insert_slist()**

Syntax:
```
int insert_slist(slistptr *head, char *item);
```

Parameters:

***head**	the head of the unordered singly linked list.
***item**	the new node, inserted as the new list tail.

Inserts a new node in the ordered singly linked list. Depending on the key **insert_sorted_slist()**
value of the new node, it may be inserted as the new head, new tail, or nonterminal node.

Syntax:
```
int insert_sorted_slist(slistptr *head, char *item);
```

Parameters:
*head   the head of the ordered singly linked list.
*item   the new node.

delete_slist()   Deletes the unordered list node that matches the ***search_key** parameter. A 1 value is returned if the node searched for was found and deleted; otherwise, 0 is returned.

Syntax:
```
int delete_slist(slistptr *head, char *search_key);
```

Parameters:
*head   the head of the unordered singly linked list.
*search_key   the search key used to locate a node for deletion.

delete_sorted_slist()   Deletes the ordered list node that matches the ***search_key** parameter. A 1 value is returned if the node searched for was found and deleted; otherwise, 0 is returned.

Syntax:
```
int delete_sorted_slist(slistptr *head, char *search_key);
```

Parameters:
*head   the head of the ordered singly linked list.
*search_key   the search key used to locate a node for deletion.

slist_length()   Returns the number of nodes in an ordered or unordered singly linked list.

Syntax:
```
int slist_length(slistptr head);
```

Parameter:
head   the head of the singly linked list.

Turbo Pascal

The Turbo Pascal library unit for lists is shown in Listing 6.5. The library exports the following data types for the singly linked lists:

```
TYPE ListKeyStr = STRING[40];

{ record used by singly linked list }
ListInfoRec = RECORD
   ListKey : ListKeyStr
   { other fields here }
END;

{ singly linked lists data types }
SListPtr = ^SListRec;

SListRec = RECORD
   ListInfo     : ListInfoRec;
   NextListPtr  : SListPtr
END;
```

The above declarations illustrate that **STRING[40]** is used as the key field. It is incorporated as a field (actually, the only field) in the record type **ListInfoRec**. The **ListKey** field can be altered so that other types of data can be stored for each node's key. Additional fields can be included in the **ListInfoRec** to allow the Pascal lists to handle more advanced data structures. These additional fields, however, are not directly used to search a list or determine the order of a list.

The versatile advanced data structures, support for dynamic memory allocation, and access of dynamic memory using pointers are major factors that enable Pascal code to easily implement the list manipulation algorithms. In other words, the powerful constructs of the Pascal language help the programmer avoid the programming tricks necessary with Turbo BASIC.

The Turbo Pascal procedures for unordered and ordered singly linked lists are presented next.

Initializes a new singly linked list. The list can be ordered or unordered. **Init_SList**

Syntax:
```
PROCEDURE Init_SList(VAR Head : SListPtr);
```

Parameter:
Head   the pointer to the head of the new singly linked list.

Clear_SList   Clears the nodes of a singly linked list and restores its dynamically allocated space. The list can be ordered or unordered.

Syntax:
```
PROCEDURE Clear_SList(VAR Head : SListPtr);
```

Parameter:
Head   the pointer to the head of the deleted singly linked list.

Search_SList   Searches for the unordered list node that matches the **Search_Key** parameter. The outcome of the search is reported by a **TRUE** or **FALSE** value returned by the **Found** parameter. The matching node is indicated by the pointer parameter, **ThisPtr,** and the node pointing to it by the **LastPtr** parameter. Searching for a nonexistent element requires that the entire list be searched.

Syntax:
```
PROCEDURE Search_SList(VAR  Head, ThisPtr,
                            LastPtr    : SListPtr;
                            Search_Key : ListKeyStr;
                       VAR  Found      : BOOLEAN);
```

Parameters:
Head   the head of the list (or trailing sublist).
ThisPtr   the pointer to the matching node. A **NIL** is returned if no match occurs.
LastPtr   the pointer to the last node before the matching node.
Search_Key   the search key data.
Found   the flag that signals the success or failure of the search.

Search_Sorted_SList   Searches for the ordered list node that matches the **Search_Key** parameter. The outcome of the search is reported by a **TRUE** or **FALSE** value returned by the **Found** parameter. The matching node is indicated by the pointer parameter, **ThisPtr,** and the node pointing to it by the **LastPtr** parameter. Searching for a nonexistent element normally requires that part of the list be searched.

Syntax:
```
PROCEDURE Search_Sorted_SList(VAR Head, ThisPtr,
                                  LastPtr      :SListPtr;
                                  Search_Key   : ListKeyStr;
                              VAR Found        : BOOLEAN);
```

Parameters:

Head   the head of the list (or trailing sublist).
ThisPtr   the pointer to the matching node. A **NIL** is returned if no match occurs.
LastPtr   the pointer to the last node before the matching node.
Search_Key   the search key data.
Found   the flag that signals the success or failure of the search.

Inserts a new node at the tail of the unordered singly linked list.   **Insert_SList**

Syntax:
```
PROCEDURE Insert_SList(VAR Head : SListPtr;
                           Item : ListInfoRec);
```

Parameters:

Head   the head of the unordered singly linked list.
Item   the new node, inserted as the new list tail.

Inserts a new node in the ordered singly linked list. Depending on the key   **Insert_Sorted_SList**
value of the new node, it may be inserted as the new head, new tail, or
nonterminal node.

Syntax:
```
PROCEDURE Insert_Sorted_SList(VAR Head : SListPtr;
                                  Item : ListInfoRec);
```

Parameters:

Head   the head of the ordered singly linked list.
Item   the new node.

Deletes the unordered list node that matches the **Search_Key** parameter.   **Delete_SList**
The **Done** parameter returns the status of the deletion. A **TRUE** value
signals that the node searched for was found and deleted. A **FALSE** value
indicates that the node is not in the list.

Syntax:
```
PROCEDURE Delete_SList(VAR Head      : SListPtr;
                           Search_Key : ListKeyStr;
                       VAR Done       : BOOLEAN);
```

Parameters:

Head　　　　　the head of the unordered singly linked list.
Search_Key　　the search key used to locate a node for deletion.
Done　　　　　the flag that signals the status of the deletion.

Delete_Sorted_SList Deletes the ordered list node that matches the **Search_Key** parameter. The **Done** parameter returns the status of the deletion. A **TRUE** value signals that the node searched for was found and deleted. A **FALSE** value indicates that the node is not in the list.

Syntax:
```
PROCEDURE Delete_Sorted_SList(VAR Head      : SListPtr;
                                  Search_Key : ListKeyStr;
                              VAR Done       : BOOLEAN);
```

Parameters:

Head　　　　　the head of the ordered singly linked list.
Search_Key　　the search key used to locate a node for deletion.
Done　　　　　the flag that signals the status of the deletion.

SList_Length　Returns the number of nodes in an ordered or unordered singly linked list.

Syntax:
```
FUNCTION SList_Length(Head : SListPtr) : WORD;
```

Parameter:

Head　　the head of the singly linked list.

Turbo Prolog

When it comes to list processing, Turbo Prolog surpasses the other Turbo languages. To represent and process lists we don't have to worry about pointers, memory allocation, and linked list data structures, because Turbo Prolog provides a built-in list data type.

The basic list type in Turbo Prolog consists of two components, a *head* and a *tail*. The head is the first element and the tail is the list that is left after the first element is removed. The symbol | separates the head and the tail. If we have a list such as

[one, two, three, four]

and we match it with the terms

[Head | Tail]

the match produces

Head = one
Tail = [two, three, four]

The list processing routines implemented in Turbo Prolog and shown in Listing 6.6 rely heavily on recursion. The following domain type is used to represent our lists:

```
domain
    symlist = symbol*
```

You can, however, process other types of lists by adding additional domain types. The descriptions of the predicates for processing unordered and ordered lists are presented next.

Searches for a key in an unordered list. If the key is found, its position in the list is returned with the argument **Position**. If the key is not found, the predicate fails.   **search_list**

Syntax:
```
search_list(List, Key, Position)        (i,i,o)
           (symlist, symbol, integer)
```

Parameters:
List   the list to search.
Key   the search key data.
Position   the index position of the found key.

search_sorted_list   Searches for a key in an ordered list. If the key is found, its position in the list is returned with the argument **Position**. If the key is not found, the predicate fails.

Syntax:
```
search_sorted_list(List, Key, Position)      (i,i,o)
                   (symlist, symbol, integer)
```

Parameters:

List   the list to search.
Key   the search key data.
Position   the index position of the found key.

insert_list   Inserts a new node at the end of the unordered list.

Syntax:
```
insert_list(List, Item, NewList)      (i,i,o)
            (symlist, symbol, symlist)
```

Parameters:

List   the unordered list where the element is inserted.
Item   the new element, inserted at the end of the list.
NewList   the list containing the inserted element.

insert_sorted_list   Inserts a new element in an ordered list. Depending on the value of the new element, it may be inserted as the new head, new tail, or somewhere between the head and the tail.

Syntax:
```
insert_sorted_list(List, Item, NewList)      (i,i,o)
                   (symlist, symbol, symlist)
```

Parameters:

List   the ordered list where the element is inserted.
Item   the new element, inserted at the end of the list.
NewList   the list containing the inserted element.

delete_list   Deletes the element from an unordered list. If the element to be deleted is not found, the predicate fails.

Syntax:
```
delete_list(List, Item, NewList)       (i,i,o)
            (symlist, symbol, symlist)
```

Parameters:

List   the unordered list where the element is to be deleted.
Item   the element to be deleted.
NewList   the list returned.

Deletes an element from an ordered list. If the element to be deleted is not   **delete_sorted_list**
found, the predicate fails.

Syntax:
```
delete_sorted_list(List, Item, NewList)       (i,i,o)
                   (symlist, symbol, symlist)
```

Parameters:

List   the ordered list where the element is to be deleted.
Item   the element to be deleted.
NewList   the list returned.

Returns the number of elements in an ordered or unordered list.   **list_length**

Syntax:
```
list_length(List, Count)       (i,o)
            (symlist, integer)
```

Parameters:

List   the list to count.
Count the number of elements in the list.

**• Listing 6.1. Turbo BASIC routines for unordered lists using the simple
implementation scheme**

```
OPTION BASE 1 ' declaration in user's program

%TRUE = 1
%FALSE = 0
%NIL = 0
```

```
'--- Singly unordered array-based lists   ---

SUB Initialize.UAList(UAList$(1), List.Size%)
' initializes unordered list
LOCAL i%
FOR i% = LBound(UAList$(1)) TO UBound(UAList$(1))
    UAList$(i%) = ""
NEXT i%
List.Size% = 0
END SUB ' Initialize.UAList


SUB Insert.UAList(UAList$(1), List.Size%, Item$)
' inserts Item$ in list
IF List.Size% < UBound(UAList$(1)) THEN
    INCR List.Size%
    UAList$(List.Size%) = Item$
END IF
END SUB ' Insert.UAList


SUB Search.UAList(Head%, UAList$(1), List.Size%, Item$, Index%)
' Searches for Item$ in list UAList$() starting at the Head%.
' The location of the matching element is reported by Index%.
' If no matching occurs, Index% returns 0.
LOCAL i%
Index% = 0
IF Head% > List.Size% THEN EXIT SUB
i% = Head%
DO WHILE (i% <= List.Size%) AND (Index% = 0)
    IF UAList$(i%) = Item$ THEN Index% = i% ELSE INCR i%
LOOP
END SUB ' Search.UAList


SUB Delete.UAList(Head%, UAList$(1), List.Size%, Item$, Done%)
' Searches for Item$ in list UAList$() starting at the Head% to delete it.
' Done% is a flag that signals the deletion outcome.
LOCAL i%, index%
Done% = %FALSE
IF Head% > List.Size% THEN EXIT SUB
index% = 0
i% = Head%
```

```
DO WHILE (i% <= List.Size%) AND (index% = 0)
    IF UAList$(i%) = Item$ THEN index% = i% ELSE INCR i%
LOOP
IF index% > 0 THEN ' found element, delete it
    IF index% < List.Size% THEN
        FOR i% = index%+1 TO List.Size%
            UAList$(i%-1) = UAList$(i%)
        NEXT i%
    END IF
    DECR List.Size%
    Done% = %TRUE
END IF
END SUB ' Delete.UAList
```

• Listing 6.2. Turbo BASIC routines for ordered lists using the simple implementation scheme

---

```
OPTION BASE 1 ' declaration in user's program

%TRUE = 1
%FALSE = 0
%NIL = 0


'------ Singly linked ordered array-based lists ------

SUB Initialize.OAList(OAList$(1), List.Size%)
' initializes unordered list
LOCAL i%
FOR i% = LBound(OAList$(1)) TO UBound(OAList$(1))
    OAList$(i%) = ""
NEXT i%
List.Size% = 0
END SUB ' Initialize.OAList


SUB Insert.OAList(OAList$(1), List.Size%, Item$)
' inserts Item$ in list
LOCAL i%, j%, found%
IF List.Size% < UBound(OAList$(1)) THEN
    i% = 1
```

```
      found% = %FALSE
      DO WHILE (i% <= List.Size%) AND (found% = %FALSE)
          IF Item$ > OAList$(i%) THEN
              INCR i%
          ELSE
              found% = %TRUE
          END IF
      LOOP
      IF found% = %TRUE THEN
          FOR j% = List.Size% TO i% STEP -1
              OAList$(j%+1) = OAList$(j%)
          NEXT j%
          OAList$(i%) = Item$
      ELSE ' Item$ is inserted at the end of the array
          OAList$(List.Size%+1) = Item$
      END IF
      INCR List.Size%
  END IF
  END SUB ' Insert.OAList


  SUB Search.OAList(Head%, OAList$(1), List.Size%, Item$, Index%)
  ' Searches for Item$ in list OAList$() starting at the Head%.
  ' The location of the matching element is reported by Index%.
  ' If no matching occurs, Index% returns 0.
  LOCAL i%, found%
  Index% = 0
  IF Head% > List.Size% THEN EXIT SUB
  i% = Head%
  found% = %FALSE
  DO WHILE (i% <= List.Size%) AND (found% = %FALSE)
      IF OAList$(i%) >= Item$ THEN
          found% = %TRUE
          IF OAList$(i%) = Item$ THEN Index% = i% ELSE Index% = 0
      ELSE
          INCR i%
      END IF
  LOOP
  END SUB ' Search.OAList
```

```
SUB Delete.OAList(Head%, OAList$(1), List.Size%, Item$, Done%)
' Searches for Item$ in list OAList$() starting at the Head% to delete it.
' Done% is a flag that signals the deletion outcome.
LOCAL i%, found%, index%
Done% = %FALSE
IF Head% > List.Size% THEN EXIT SUB
index% = 0
i% = Head%
found% = %FALSE
DO WHILE (i% <= List.Size%) AND (found% = %FALSE)
    IF OAList$(i%) >= Item$ THEN
        found% = %TRUE
        IF OAList$(i%) = Item$ THEN Index% = i% ELSE Index% = 0
    ELSE
        INCR i%
    END IF
LOOP
IF index% > 0 THEN ' found element, delete it
    IF index% < List.Size% THEN
        FOR i% = index%+1 TO List.Size%
            OAList$(i%-1) = OAList$(i%)
        NEXT i%
    END IF
    DECR List.Size%
    Done% = %TRUE
END IF
END SUB ' Delete.OAList
```

• Listing 6.3. Turbo BASIC routines for unordered singly linked lists using the indexing scheme

---

```
$STACK 5000
OPTION BASE 1 ' user's program declarations

'---------- Included library starts here ------------
%TRUE = 1
%FALSE = 0
%NIL = 0
```

```
'---- Singly linked unordered array-based lists -----

SUB Initialize.USList(USList$(1), USPtr%(1), Head%, Tail%, Map$, List.Size%)
' initializes unordered list
LOCAL i%
FOR i% = LBound(USList$(1)) TO UBound(USList$(1))
    USList$(i%) = ""
NEXT i%
FOR i% = LBound(USPtr%(1)) TO UBound(USPtr%(1))
  USPtr%(i%) = %NIL
NEXT i%
Map$ = SPACE$(UBound(USList$(1)) - LBound(USList$(1)) + 1)
Head% = %NIL
Tail% = %NIL
List.Size% = 0
END SUB ' Initialize.USList


SUB Insert.USList(USList$(1), USPtr%(1), Map$, Head%, Tail%, List.Size%, Item$)
' inserts Item$ in the singly linked list
LOCAL index%
IF List.Size% < UBound(USList$(1)) THEN
    index% = INSTR(Map$, " ")
    USList$(index%) = Item$
    MID$(Map$,index%,1) = "+"
    USPtr%(index%) = %NIL
    IF List.Size% > 0 THEN
        USPtr%(Tail%) = index%
    ELSE
        Head% = index%
    END IF
    Tail% = index%
    INCR List.Size%
END IF
END SUB ' Insert.USList


SUB Search.USList(USList$(1), USPtr%(1), Head%, List.Size%, Item$,_
                  Index%, LastIndex%)
' Searches for Item$ in list USList$() starting at the Head%.
' The location of the matching element is reported by Index%.
' If no matching occurs, Index% returns %NIL.
```

```
LOCAL i%
Index% = %NIL
LastIndex% = %NIL
IF List.Size% > 0 THEN
    i% = Head%
    DO WHILE (i% <> %NIL) AND (Index% = %NIL)
        IF USList$(i%) = Item$ THEN
            Index% = i%
        ELSE
            LastIndex% = i%
            i% = USPtr%(i%)
        END IF
    LOOP
END IF
END SUB ' Search.USList


SUB Delete.USList(USList$(1), USPtr%(1), Map$, Head%, Tail%, List.Size%,_
                Item$, Done%)
' Searches for Item$ in list USList$() starting at the Head% to delete it.
' Done% is a flag that signals the deletion outcome.
LOCAL i%, index%, lastindex%
Done% = %FALSE
IF List.Size% < 1 THEN EXIT SUB
CALL Search.USList(USList$(), USPtr%(), Head%, List.Size%, Item$, Index%,_
                LastIndex%)
IF index% <> %NIL THEN ' found element, delete it
    USList$(index%) = ""
    IF index% <> Head% THEN ' is a nonhead element being removed?
        USPtr%(lastindex%) = USPtr%(index%)
    ELSE
        Head% = USPtr%(index%)
    END IF
    MID$(Map$,index%,1) = " " ' update deleted-elements map
    ' is the current tail being deleted?
    IF index% = Tail% THEN Tail% = lastindex%
    DECR List.Size%
    Done% = %TRUE
END IF
END SUB ' Delete.USList
```

• Listing 6.4. Turbo C singly linked list processing functions

```c
#include <stdio.h>
#include <stdlib.h>
#include <string.h>
#include <alloc.h>

typedef struct slistmem *slistptr;
struct listinforec {
    char listkey[40];
};
/* singly linked list structure */
struct slistmem {
    struct listinforec listinfo;
    slistptr nextlistptr;
};

/* function prototypes */
void init_slist(slistptr *head);
void clear_slist(slistptr *head);
int search_slist(slistptr head, slistptr *thisptr, slistptr *lastptr,
                 char *search_key);
int search_sorted_slist(slistptr head, slistptr *thisptr, slistptr *lastptr,
                        char *search_key);
int insert_slist(slistptr *head, char *item);
int insert_sorted_slist(slistptr *head, char *item);
int delete_slist(slistptr *head, char *search_key);
int delete_sorted_slist(slistptr *head, char *search_key);
int slist_length(slistptr head);

void init_slist(slistptr *head)
/* Initializes a new singly linked list. The list can be ordered or
   unordered. */
{
    *head = NULL;   /* initialize list */
}

void clear_slist(slistptr *head)
/* Clears the nodes of a singly linked list and restores its dynamically
   allocated space. The list can be ordered or unordered. */
```

```
{
    slistptr ptr;

    while (*head != NULL)  {
        ptr = *head;
        *head = (*head)->nextlistptr; /* go to next element */
        free(ptr);    /* remove each node */
    }
}


int search_slist(slistptr head, slistptr *thisptr, slistptr *lastptr,
                 char *search_key)
/* searches for the unordered list node that matches the *search_key
   parameter */
{
    int found;

    *lastptr = NULL;
    *thisptr = head;
    found = 0;
    while ((*thisptr != NULL) && !found) {
        if ((strcmp((*thisptr)->listinfo.listkey, search_key)) != 0) {
            *lastptr = *thisptr;
            *thisptr = (*thisptr)->nextlistptr;
        }
        else found = 1;
    }
    return found;
}


int search_sorted_slist(slistptr head, slistptr *thisptr, slistptr *lastptr,
                        char *search_key)
/* searches for the ordered list node that matches the *search_key
   parameter */
{
    int found;

    *lastptr = NULL;
    *thisptr = head;
    found = 0;
```

```
    while ((*thisptr != NULL) && !found) {
        if ((strcmp(search_key, (*thisptr)->listinfo.listkey)) > 0) {
            *lastptr = *thisptr;
            *thisptr = (*thisptr)->nextlistptr;
        }
        else found = 1;
    }
    if (found) found = (strcmp(search_key,
                        (*thisptr)->listinfo.listkey) == 0);
    return found;
}


int insert_slist(slistptr *head, char *item)
/* inserts a new node at the tail of the unordered singly linked list */
{
    slistptr thisptr, lastptr;

    lastptr = NULL;
    thisptr = *head;
    while (thisptr != NULL) { /* get to last element */
        lastptr = thisptr;
        thisptr = thisptr->nextlistptr;
    }
    thisptr = (slistptr) malloc(sizeof(struct slistmem));
    if (thisptr == NULL) return 0;  /* memory allocation error */
    thisptr->nextlistptr = NULL;
    lastptr->nextlistptr = thisptr;
    strcpy(thisptr->listinfo.listkey, item);
    if (*head == NULL) *head = thisptr; /* test for empty list */
    return 1;
}


int insert_sorted_slist(slistptr *head, char *item)
/* inserts a new node in the ordered singly linked list   */
{
    slistptr thisptr, lastptr, ptr;

    if ((search_sorted_slist(*head, &thisptr, &lastptr, item)) == 1)
        exit(1);
    if (lastptr == NULL) {/* insert item at beginning of list */
```

```
        ptr = (slistptr) malloc(sizeof(struct slistmem));
        if (ptr == NULL) return 0;   /* memory allocation error */
        ptr->nextlistptr = *head;
        strcpy(ptr->listinfo.listkey, item);
        *head = ptr;
    }
    else {
        ptr = (slistptr) malloc(sizeof(struct slistmem));
        if (ptr == NULL) return 0;   /* memory allocation error */
        ptr->nextlistptr = lastptr->nextlistptr;
        lastptr->nextlistptr = ptr;
        strcpy(ptr->listinfo.listkey, item);
    }
    return 1;
}


int delete_slist(slistptr *head, char *search_key)
/* deletes the unordered list node that matches the *search_key parameter */
{
    slistptr thisptr, lastptr;
    int done;

    done = search_slist(*head, &thisptr, &lastptr, search_key);
    if (done)
        if (lastptr == NULL) {
            lastptr = (*head)->nextlistptr;
            free(*head);
            *head = lastptr;
        }
        else {
            lastptr->nextlistptr = thisptr->nextlistptr;
            free(thisptr);
        }
    return done;
}


int delete_sorted_slist(slistptr *head, char *search_key)
/* deletes the ordered list node that matches the *search_key parameter */
{
    slistptr thisptr, lastptr;
    int done;
```

```
    done = search_sorted_slist(*head, &thisptr, &lastptr, search_key);
    if (done)
        if (lastptr == NULL) {
            lastptr = (*head)->nextlistptr;
            free(*head);
            *head = lastptr;
        }
        else {
            lastptr->nextlistptr = thisptr->nextlistptr;
            free(thisptr);
        }
    return done;
}


int slist_length(slistptr head)
/* returns the number of nodes in an ordered or unordered singly linked
   list */
{
    int count;

    count = 0;
    while (head != NULL) {
        count++;
        head = head->nextlistptr;
    }
    return count;
}
```

• Listing 6.5. Turbo Pascal list library unit

```
UNIT List;

CONST MAX_ARRAY_LIST = 100;

TYPE ListKeyStr = STRING[40];
    { record used by singly linked }
    ListInfoRec = RECORD
        ListKey : ListKeyStr
        { other fields here }
    END;
```

```
    SListPtr = ^SListRec;
    SListRec = RECORD
        ListInfo    : ListInfoRec;
        NextListPtr : SListPtr
    END;

    ListArrayType = ARRAY [1..MAX_ARRAY_LIST] OF ListInfoRec;

PROCEDURE Init_SList(VAR Head : SListPtr);
{ initializes the head of any new singly linked list }

PROCEDURE Clear_SList(VAR Head : SListPtr);
{ clears any existing singly linked list }

PROCEDURE Search_SList(VAR Head, ThisPtr, LastPtr : SListPtr;
                            Search_Key : ListKeyStr; VAR Found : BOOLEAN);
{ Searches for 'Search_Key' in the unordered list with 'Head' as the
  pointer to its head. The current and previous pointers are also returned
  in the argument list.}

PROCEDURE Search_Sorted_SList(VAR Head, ThisPtr, LastPtr : SListPtr;
                                Search_Key : ListKeyStr; VAR Found : BOOLEAN);
{ Searches for 'Search_Key' in the sorted list with 'Head' as the pointer
  to its head. The current and previous pointers are returned in the
  argument lists.}

PROCEDURE Insert_SList(VAR Head : SListPtr; Item : ListInfoRec);
{ performs simple list insertion }

PROCEDURE Insert_Sorted_SList(VAR Head : SListPtr; Item : ListInfoRec);
{ performs ordered list insertion }

PROCEDURE Delete_SList(VAR Head : SListPtr; Search_Key : ListKeyStr;
                        VAR Done : BOOLEAN);
{ Attempts to delete an item from an unordered list. The boolean parameter
  'Done' confirms the deletion process. }

PROCEDURE Delete_Sorted_SList(VAR Head : SListPtr; Search_Key : ListKeyStr;
                                VAR Done : BOOLEAN);
{ Attempts to delete an item from an ordered list. The boolean parameter
  'Done' confirms the deletion process. }
```

```
FUNCTION SList_Length(Head : SListPtr) : WORD;
{ returns the size of any singly linked list }


{*************************************************************************}


PROCEDURE Init_SList(VAR Head : SListPtr { output });
{ initializes the head of any new singly linked list }
BEGIN
   Head := NIL
END; { Init_SList }


PROCEDURE Clear_SList(VAR Head : SListPtr { in/out });
{ clears any existing singly linked list }


VAR Ptr : SListPtr;


BEGIN
   WHILE Head <> NIL DO  BEGIN
      Ptr := Head;
      Head := Head^.NextListPtr;
      Dispose(Ptr)
   END; { WHILE }
END; { Clear_SList }


PROCEDURE Search_SList(VAR Head,                     { input  }
                           ThisPtr,                  { output }
                           LastPtr   : SListPtr;     { output }
                           Search_Key : ListKeyStr;  { input  }
                       VAR Found      : BOOLEAN       { output });
{ Searches for 'Search_Key' in the unordered list with 'Head' as the
  pointer to its head. The current and previous pointers are also returned
  in the argument list. }


BEGIN
   LastPtr := NIL;
   ThisPtr := Head;
   Found := FALSE;
   WHILE (ThisPtr <> NIL) AND (NOT Found) DO
      IF Search_Key <> ThisPtr^.ListInfo.ListKey THEN BEGIN
         LastPtr := ThisPtr;
```

```
                ThisPtr := ThisPtr^.NextListPtr
        END
        ELSE Found := TRUE; { found sought element }
END; { Search_SList }

PROCEDURE Search_Sorted_SList(VAR  Head,              { input  }
                                   ThisPtr,           { output }
                                   LastPtr    : SListPtr; { output }
                                   Search_Key : ListKeyStr; { input  }
                              VAR  Found      : BOOLEAN    { output });
{ Searches for 'Search_Key' in the sorted list with 'Head' as the pointer
  to its head. The current and previous pointers are returned in the
  argument lists. }

BEGIN
    LastPtr := NIL;
    ThisPtr := Head;
    Found := FALSE;
    WHILE (ThisPtr <> NIL) AND (NOT Found) DO
        IF Search_Key > ThisPtr^.ListInfo.ListKey THEN BEGIN
            LastPtr := ThisPtr;
            ThisPtr := ThisPtr^.NextListPtr
        END
        ELSE Found := TRUE; { element might be in the list }
        { confirm suspected match }
        IF Found THEN Found := (Search_Key = ThisPtr^.ListInfo.ListKey);
END; { Search_Sorted_SList }

PROCEDURE Insert_SList(VAR Head : SListPtr;    { in/out }
                           Item : ListInfoRec { input });
{ performs simple list insertion }

VAR thisptr, lastptr, ptr : SListPtr;

BEGIN
    thisptr := Head;
    lastptr := NIL;
    { traverse to the end of the list }
    WHILE thisptr <> NIL DO BEGIN
        lastptr := thisptr;
```

```
        thisptr := thisptr^.NextListPtr
    END;
    NEW(thisptr);
    thisptr^.NextListPtr := NIL; { new node is the new list tail }
    { link back with the 'previous' node }
    lastptr^.NextListPtr := thisptr;
    thisptr^.ListInfo := Item; { assign key and other fields }
END; { Insert_SList }


PROCEDURE Insert_Sorted_SList(VAR Head    : SListPtr;    { in/out }
                                  Item    : ListInfoRec { input  });
{ performs ordered list insertion }


VAR thisptr, lastptr, ptr : SListPtr;
    match : BOOLEAN;


BEGIN
    Search_Sorted_SList(Head, thisptr, lastptr, Item.ListKey, match);
    { the line below may be commented out to enable multiple data items
      with the same key to be stored in the list }
    IF match THEN EXIT;
    IF lastptr = NIL THEN BEGIN { new item is the new list head }
        NEW(ptr);
        ptr^.NextListPtr := Head;
        ptr^.ListInfo := Item; { assign key and other fields }
        Head := ptr; { assign new pointer to the head of the list }
    END
    ELSE BEGIN { insert new item inside the list or at its tail }
        NEW(ptr);
        { link ahead with the 'current' node }
        ptr^.NextListPtr := lastptr^.NextListPtr;
        { link back with the 'previous' node }
        lastptr^.NextListPtr := ptr;
        ptr^.ListInfo := Item; { assign key and other fields }
    END;
END; { Insert_Sorted_SList }


PROCEDURE Delete_SList(VAR Head        : SListPtr;    { in/out }
                           Search_Key  : ListKeyStr;  { input  }
                       VAR Done        : BOOLEAN      { output });
```

```
{ Attempts to delete an item from an unordered list. The boolean parameter
  'Done' confirms the deletion process. }

VAR thisptr, lastptr : SListPtr;

BEGIN
    { search for item to delete }
    Search_SList(Head, thisptr, lastptr, Search_Key, Done);
    IF Done THEN { found item in list }
        IF lastptr = NIL THEN BEGIN { delete the list head }
            lastptr := Head^.NextListPtr;
            Dispose(Head);
            Head := lastptr;
        END
        ELSE BEGIN
            lastptr^.NextListPtr := thisptr^.NextListPtr;
            Dispose(thisptr);
        END;
END; { Delete_SList }


PROCEDURE Delete_Sorted_SList(VAR Head      : SListPtr;   { in/out }
                                  Search_Key : ListKeyStr; { input  }
                              VAR Done       : BOOLEAN     { output });
{ Attempts to delete an item from an ordered list. The boolean parameter
  'Done' confirms the deletion process. }
VAR thisptr, lastptr : SListPtr;

BEGIN
    { search for item to delete }
    Search_Sorted_SList(Head, thisptr, lastptr, Search_Key, Done);
    IF Done THEN { found item in list }
        IF lastptr = NIL THEN BEGIN { delete the list head }
            lastptr := Head^.NextListPtr;
            Dispose(Head);
            Head := lastptr;
        END
        ELSE BEGIN
            lastptr^.NextListPtr := thisptr^.NextListPtr;
            Dispose(thisptr);
        END;
END; { Delete_Sorted_SList }
```

```
FUNCTION SList_Length(Head : SListPtr { input }) : WORD;
{ returns the size of any singly linked list }

VAR count : WORD;

BEGIN
    count := 0; { initialize list size }
    WHILE Head <> NIL DO BEGIN
        INC(count);
        Head := Head^.NextListPtr;
    END;
    SList_Length := count { return function value }
END; { SList_Length }
```

• Listing 6.6. Turbo Prolog list processing predicates

```
% Turbo Prolog implementation of the list processing
% routines.

domains
    symlist = symbol*

predicates
    search_list(symlist, symbol, integer)
    search_sorted_list(symlist, symbol, integer)
    list_length(symlist, integer)
    insert_list(symlist, symbol, symlist)
    insert_sorted_list(symlist, symbol, symlist)
    delete_list(symlist, symbol, symlist)
    delete_sorted_list(symlist, symbol, symlist)

clauses
    search_list([Key |_], Key, 1).              % stop when key matches
head
    search_list([_ | Tail], Key, Position) :- !, % remove one element
        search_list(Tail, Key, CurPosition),
        Position = CurPosition + 1.

    search_sorted_list([First |_], Key, 1) :-    % stop key matches head
```

```
      Key <= First, !,
      Key = First.
search_sorted_list([_  | Tail], Key, Position) :- !,    % remove one element
      search_sorted_list(Tail, Key, CurPosition),
      Position = CurPosition + 1.


insert_list([], Item, [Item]).
insert_list([H | Tail1], Item, [H | Tail2]) :-
      insert_list(Tail1, Item, Tail2), !.


insert_sorted_list([E | Sortlst], H, [E | Lst2]) :-  % check order
      H > E, !,
      insert_sorted_list(Sortlst, H, Lst2).
insert_sorted_list(Sortlst, H, [H | Sortlst]).        % add element to head


delete_list([], _, []).                               % list is empty
delete_list([Item | Tail], Item, Tail) :- !.
delete_list([Head | Tail], Item, [Head | Tail2]) :- !,
      delete_list(Tail, Item, Tail2).


delete_sorted_list([], _, []).                        % list is empty
delete_sorted_list([First | Tail], Item, Tail) :-
      Item <= First,!,
      Item = First.
delete_sorted_list([Head | Tail], Item, [Head | Tail2]) :- !,
      delete_sorted_list(Tail, Item, Tail2).


list_length([], 0).                                   % list is empty
list_length([_  | Tail], Count) :- !,
      list_length(Tail, PrevCount),
      Count = PrevCount + 1.
```

List Processing with Doubly Linked and Circular Lists

Introduction

In this section we continue our discussion of list processing algorithms as we explore doubly linked lists and circular lists. Both of these structures are simple variations of the singly linked structures we presented in the previous section. These new structures, however, improve the performance of some of our list processing operations such as searching for list nodes.

We begin by presenting the basic structures used to represent doubly linked lists and circular lists. We then introduce a set of list processing tools in each language that are similar to ones in Section 6.

Overview of the Doubly Linked List

In a doubly linked list, two links are used to reference each node, as shown in Figure 7.1. Because two links are used, we can easily traverse the list in both directions, and we can change the traversal direction at any time. To move forward in the list, we follow the forward links; to move backward, we follow the backward links. The flexibility that the two links provide does unfortunately cost programs some additional processing overhead. For example, when a node is inserted or deleted, special care must be taken to make sure that both links are set to the proper nodes. Like singly linked lists, doubly linked lists may be ordered or unordered.

The Circular List

Circular lists are usually constructed using unordered lists (either singly or doubly linked). Because a circular list does not have any real ends, nodes

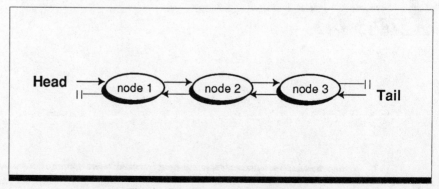

Figure 7.1. The doubly linked list

are accessed by starting any place in the list. This means that the free links at the ends of a circular list are connected, as shown in Figure 7.2.

In our implementations of the circular list, we use the singly linked structure introduced in Section 6 as the foundation. This means that we'll only be able to traverse the list in one direction. You can, however, easily modify the routines that we present for processing a circular list to support the doubly linked list structure.

Representing Doubly Linked Lists

Doubly linked lists are implemented in Turbo Pascal and Turbo C using records and structures, dynamic memory allocation techniques, and pointers. The basic data structure used is a slight modification of the singly linked structure. Following is the doubly linked list record structure implemented in Turbo Pascal.

```
DListPtr = ^DListRec;
DListRec = RECORD
    ListInfo    : ListInfoRec;
    NextListPtr,
    PrevListPtr : DListPtr
END;
```

Notice the pointer **PrevListPtr**; it enables us to move from one node to the previous node.

Turbo BASIC uses arrays for this purpose. For the doubly linked list implementation we'll use the pseudopointer technique only.

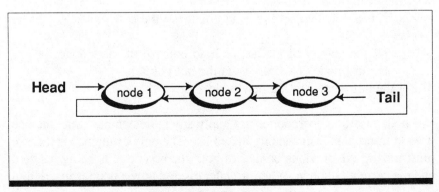

Figure 7.2. The circular list

Because lists are represented quite differently in Turbo Prolog, the doubly linked representation does not really apply and therefore we have omitted its implementation.

List Processing Operations

The basic doubly linked list operations are similar to the singly linked list operations; for this type of list we've included routines for list insertion, deletion, and searching. For the circular list, we've included a routine that illustrates how circular lists are searched. Keep in mind that the insertion and deletion operations for circular lists are the same as those used in singly linked lists.

Unordered Doubly Linked Lists

The first type of doubly linked list that we'll examine is the unordered list.

List Insertion

The following are general rules for inserting an element at the end of a doubly linked list:

1. Allocate memory for the new list node. Exit if memory allocation problem occurs.
2. Set the next-node pointer of the new node to nil.
3. Set the last-node pointer of the new node to access the old tail node.
4. If the head of the list is null then

> it is a new list; set the head pointer to the new node.

> else

>> set the pointer of the last node to point to the new node.

>> the last node is accessed via the tail pointer.

5. Set the tail pointer to the new node.

The node insertion operation is not really any more complex than the one used to insert a node in a singly linked list. The only difference is that we must link up the previous pointer of both the node that is being inserted and the current tail node. When we later discuss how a node is inserted in the middle of a list, you'll see that the previous node pointer requires some additional care.

Searching

Because we now have two links, we can search a list in two directions: forward and backward. Here are the rules used for the forward search:

1. Set a match pointer to nil.
2. Set a search pointer to the head of the list.
3. While the search pointer is not nil and the match pointer is nil
   if the current node matches the sought element

       set match pointer to current node

   else

       set search pointer to the next node

   end if
4. The match pointer indicates the success or failure of the search operation. A nil value signals that the sought element was not found.

The backward search is similar; however, this time we start with the tail of the list and use the previous pointers to traverse the list. The rules are

1. Set a match pointer to nil.
2. Set a search pointer to the tail of the list.
3. While the search pointer is not nil and the match pointer is nil
   if the current node matches the sought element

       set match pointer to current node

   else

       set search pointer to the previous node

   end if
4. The match pointer indicates the success or failure of the search operation. A nil value signals that the sought element was not found.

Deleting a List Element

Deleting an element from a doubly linked list is the most complex operation of the three operations we'll implement. Essentially, these variations occur:

1. Delete the first element.
2. Delete the last element.
3. Delete an element that is between the head and the tail.

The first two operations are relatively straightforward, because we don't need to reassign any previous link pointers. We simply remove the first or last element and set the head or tail pointer to reference the new head or tail of the list. By far, the most difficult operation is the last.

To delete an element from somewhere in the middle of the list, we reassign both the next link of the node that precedes the element being deleted and the previous link of the node that follows the element being deleted. Figure 7.3 illustrates how the links are reassigned. We've also included diagrams to illustrate how the head and tail nodes are deleted.

The following summarizes the steps used in the deletion algorithm:

1. Search for the matching element in the list. Obtain the match pointer.
2. If the match pointer is nil, stop.
3. If the match pointer is the list-head pointer, set the new head pointer to be the pointer accessed by the match pointer and set the last-node pointer of the new node to nil. Skip to step 6.
4. If the match pointer is accessed by the list-tail, set the new tail pointer to access the last-node pointer of the new node. Also set the next-node pointer of the new node to nil. Skip to step 6.

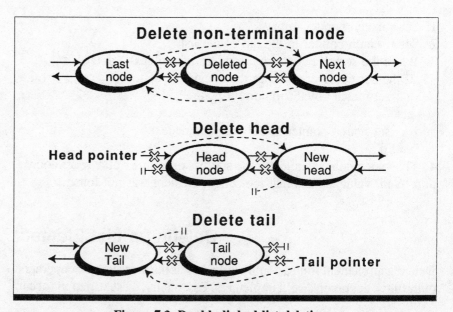

Figure 7.3. Doubly linked list deletions

5. Establish proper links between the new node and its two adjacent neighboring nodes.
6. Reclaim the space for the deleted node area.

Ordered Doubly Linked Lists

The second type of doubly linked list is the ordered list. Our implementations assume the sorted list is maintained in an ascending order.

List Insertion

To insert an element in a sorted list, we have more than one case to consider. (Remember that elements inserted in an unsorted list are inserted at the end of the list only.) The three variations are similar to the ones encountered in deleting an element from a list, as follows:

1. Insert element at the head.
2. Insert element at the tail.
3. Insert element somewhere between the head and tail.

   As can be expected, the most complex of these three operations is that of inserting an element between the head and the tail. Figure 7.4 illustrates how an element is inserted in each case. When the element is inserted between the head and the tail, notice that four link pointers must be set.
   The actual steps used in the algorithm are

1. Set the search flag to false; set the current node pointer to access the head of the list.
2. Search for the proper location to insert the new node. A **While** loop checks whether the current node pointer is nil (having reached the end of the list) and whether the search flag is still false. The loop tests whether the proper location has been found. If so, the search flag is set to true. Otherwise, the current node is set to point to the next one.
3. Insertion proceeds by allocating memory for the new node. If the new node is the first one, skip to step 7.
4. The new node is inserted between the last node and the current node. Therefore, the next-node pointer of the new node is set to point to the current node, and the last-node pointer is given access to the last node.

5. If the pointer to the current node is nil, the new node becomes the new tail of the list. Therefore, the tail pointer is updated accordingly. In addition, the last-node pointer of the new node is linked with the old tail, and the old tail is likewise linked with the new node. The insertion is completed.

6. If the pointer to the current node is not nil, the new node may be inserted within the list or as the new head of the list. If the last-node pointer is nil, the new node becomes the new head of the list. Otherwise, the pointers of the last and current node are linked with the new node. The insertion is completed.

7. The new node is the head and tail of the new linked list. The pointer of the new node is set to nil. The insertion is completed.

Searching

This algorithm makes use of the fact that the element searched for is in the range between the head and the tail. Therefore, only that range (which starts at the head of the list and until the search item equals or is greater than the key data of the node) is searched. The steps used are

1. The search pointer is assigned a starting node, usually the head of the list. Pointers to other nodes can be used to bypass a leading portion of the

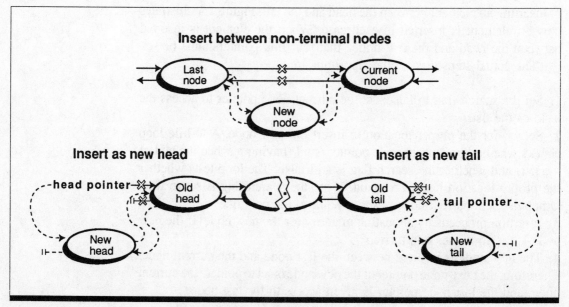

Figure 7.4. Doubly linked list insertions

list. In addition, a search pointer is set to nil, and a search flag is also set to false.

2. The search is conducted traversing the list until either the search pointer is nil (reaches the tail of the list) or the search flag is true.

3. With every node visited, the node's key data is compared with the search value.

> If the search value equals or is greater than the node's key data
> then
>> the search flag is set to true to halt further node traversal.
>> If the compared data matches
>> then
>>> the search pointer is copied to the match pointer.
> else
>> the search pointer is copied onto the last-node pointer
>> the search pointer accesses the next node
> end if

4. The search pointer reflects the outcome of the search. A nil value indicates that the sought item is not in the searched nodes.

Deleting a List Element

To delete an element from an ordered list, we follow the same basic steps as those used to delete an element from an unordered list. The only difference is that the search routine used to locate the element assumes the list is in a sorted order. Here is the algorithm.

1. Search for the node containing the information marked for deletion.
2. If the match pointer is nil, the information is not in the list and the deletion process ends.
3. If the match pointer is the list-head pointer, set the new head pointer to be the pointer accessed by the match pointer. Skip to step 6.
4. Set the last-node pointer to access the same node accessed by the match pointer.
5. If the match pointer is accessed by the list tail, set the new tail pointer to access the node of the "last-node pointer."
6. Reclaim the space for the deleted node area.

Implementation of the List Processing Algorithms

The code for the doubly linked and circular list processing routines is included in Listings 7.1 through 7.5.

Turbo BASIC

Like the singly linked list implementation, arrays serve as the basic list structure. We'll use the index scheme to implement a two-dimensional array of indices to play the role of pointers. The routines for the unordered and ordered doubly linked lists presented in Listings 7.1 and 7.2 are discussed next.

Initialize.UDList Initializes the unordered doubly linked list.

Syntax:
```
SUB Initialize.UDList(UDList$(1), UDPtr%(2),_
                    Head%, Tail%, Map$, List.Size%)
```

Parameters:

UDList$()	the array of list nodes.
UDPtr%()	the two-dimensional array of double links.
Head%	the index to the list head.
Tail%	the index to the list tail.
Map$	the map of vacant **UDList$()** array elements.
List.Size%	the list size, set to zero.

Insert.UDList Inserts a new node in the doubly linked unordered list. If the array is full, the element is not inserted.

Syntax:
```
SUB Insert.UDList(UDList$(1), UDPtr%(2), Map$,_
                    Head%, Tail%, List.Size%, Item$)
```

Parameters:

UDList$()	the array of list nodes.
UDPtr%()	the two-dimensional array of double links.

Map$** the map of vacant **UDList$() array elements.
Head% the index to the list head.
Tail% the index to the list tail.
List.Size% the list size.
Item$ the new node, inserted as the new list tail.

Searches for a list node that matches the **Item$** parameter. The search **Search.UDList**
proceeds in the direction from head to tail. The **Index%** parameter returns
the array index of the matching node. If a match is not found, a **%NIL** value
is returned.

Syntax:
```
SUB Search.UDList(UDList$(1), UDPtr%(2), Head%,_
                  List.Size%, Item$, Index%)
```

Parameters:
UDList$() the array of list nodes.
UDPtr%() the two-dimensional array of double links.
Head% the index to the list head.
List.Size% the list size.
Item$ the searched for node.
Index% the array index of the matching node. A **%NIL** is returned
     if a match is not found.

Searches for a list node that matches the **Item$** parameter. The search **BackSearch.UDList**
proceeds in the direction from tail to head. The **Index%** parameter returns
the array index of the matching node. If a match is not found, a **%NIL** value
is returned.

Syntax:
```
SUB BackSearch.UDList(UDList$(1), UDPtr%(2),_
                      Tail%, List.Size%, Item$, Index%)
```

Parameters:
UDList$() the array of list nodes.
UDPtr%() the two-dimensional array of double links.
Tail% the index to the list tail.
List.Size% the list size.
Item$ the searched for node.
Index% the array index of the matching node. A **%NIL** is returned
     if a match is not found.

Delete.UDList   Deletes the list node that matches the **Item$** parameter. The success or failure is reported by a **%TRUE** or **%FALSE** value assigned to the **Done%** parameter.

Syntax:
```
SUB Delete.UDList(UDList$(1), UDPtr%(2), Map$, Head%,_
                  Tail%, List.Size%, Item$, Done%)
```

Parameters:

UDList$()	the array of list nodes.
UDPtr%()	the two-dimensional array of double links.
Map$	the map of vacant **UDList$()** array elements.
Head%	the index to the list head.
Tail%	the index to the list tail.
List.Size%	the list size.
Item$	the node to delete.
Done%	the flag that signals the success or failure of the node deletion.

Initialize.ODList   Initializes the ordered doubly linked list.

Syntax:
```
SUB Initialize.ODList(ODList$(1), ODPtr%(2), Head%,_
                      Tail%, Map$, List.Size%)
```

Parameters:

ODList$()	the array of list nodes.
ODPtr%()	the two-dimensional array of double links.
Head%	the index to the list head.
Tail%	the index to the list tail.
Map$	the map of vacant **ODList$()** array elements.
List.Size%	the list size, set to zero.

Insert.ODList   Inserts a new node in the doubly linked ordered list. If the array is full, the node is not inserted.

Syntax:
```
SUB Insert.ODList(ODList$(1), ODPtr%(2), Map$, Head%,_
                  Tail%, List.Size%, Item$)
```

Parameters:

ODList$()	the array of list nodes.
ODPtr%()	the two-dimensional array of double links.
Map$	the map of vacant **ODList$()** array elements.
Head%	the index to the list head.
Tail%	the index to the list tail.
List.Size%	the list size.
Item$	the new node, inserted as the new list tail.

Searches the list for a node that matches the **Item$** parameter. The search proceeds in the direction from head to tail. The **Index%** parameter returns the array index of the matching node. If a match is not found, a **%NIL** value is returned.

Search.ODList

Syntax:
```
SUB Search.ODList(ODList$(1), ODPtr%(2), Head%,_
                  List.Size%, Item$, Index%)
```

Parameters:

ODList$()	the array of list nodes.
ODPtr%()	the two-dimensional array of double links.
Head%	the index to the list head.
List.Size%	the list size.
Item$	the searched for node.
Index%	the array index of the matching node. A **%NIL** is returned if the node is not found.

Searches a list for a node that matches the **Item$** parameter. The search proceeds in the direction from tail to head. The **Index%** parameter returns the array index of the matching node. If a match is not found, a **%NIL** value is returned.

BackSearch.ODList

Syntax:
```
SUB BackSearch.ODList(ODList$(1), ODPtr%(2), Tail%,_
                      List.Size%, Item$, Index%)
```

Parameters:

ODList$()	the array of list nodes.
ODPtr%()	the two-dimensional array of double links.
Tail%	the index to the list tail.

List.Size%	the list size.
Item$	the searched for node.
Index%	the array index of the matching node. A **%NIL** is returned if a match is not found.

Delete.ODList   Deletes the list node that matches the **Item$** parameter. The success or failure is reported by a **%TRUE** or **%FALSE** value assigned to the **Done%** parameter.

Syntax:
```
SUB Delete.ODList(ODList$(1), ODPtr%(2), Map$, Head%,_
                Tail%, List.Size%, Item$, Done%)
```

Parameters:

ODList$()	the array of list nodes.
ODPtr%()	the two-dimensional array of double links.
Map$	the map of vacant **ODList$()** array elements.
Head%	the index to the list head.
Tail%	the index to the list tail.
List.Size%	the list size.
Item$	the searched for node.
Done%	the flag that signals the success or failure of the node deletion.

Circular Lists

Circular lists in Turbo BASIC are also implemented using the array index scheme. Using unordered singly linked lists, circular lists are slightly different than the simple linear lists presented earlier. The difference becomes apparent as we look at the technique used to search each type of list. Let's first consider the main **WHILE** loop involved in the search process for the simple linear linked list:

```
DO WHILE (i% <> %NIL) AND (Index% = %NIL)
    IF USList$(i%) = Item$ THEN
        Index% = i%
    ELSE
        LastIndex% = i%
        i% = USPtr%(i%)
```

```
      END IF
LOOP
```

Compare this to the following loop used to search the circular list:

```
DO WHILE (count% <= List.Size%) AND (Index% = %NIL)
    IF CSList$(i%) = Item$ THEN
        Index% = i%
    ELSE
        LastIndex% = i%
        i% = CSPtr%(i%)
        IF i% = %NIL THEN i% = Head%
    END IF
LOOP
```

The linear list version scans every node until the tail is reached or a match is found. By contrast, the circular list counts the number of nodes visited and wraps around if necessary. The wrapping is performed by the nested **IF** in the **ELSE** clause, as shown:

```
IF i% = %NIL THEN i% = Head%
```

The routines for the unordered singly linked circular lists presented in Listing 7.3 are discussed next.

Initializes the unordered singly linked circular list.   **Initialize.CSList**

Syntax:
```
SUB Initialize.CSList(CSList$(1), CSPtr%(1), Head%,_
                    Tail%, Map$, List.Size%)
```

Parameters:

CSList$()	the array of singly linked circular list nodes.
CSPtr%()	the array of single links.
Head%	the index to the circular list head.
Tail%	the index to the circular list tail.
Map$	the map of vacant **CSList$()** array elements.
List.Size%	the circular list size, set to zero.

Inserts a new node in the singly linked unordered circular list. If the array   **Insert.CSList**
is full, the node is not inserted.

Syntax:
```
SUB Insert.CSList(CSList$(1), CSPtr%(1), Map$, Head%,_
                  Tail%, List.Size%, Item$)
```

Parameters:

CSList$()	the array of singly linked circular list nodes.
CSPtr%()	the array of single links.
Map$	the map of vacant **CSList$()** array elements.
Head%	the index to the circular list head.
Tail%	the index to the circular list tail.
List.Size%	the circular list size.
Item$	the new circular list node, inserted as the new list tail.

Search.CSList Searches the unordered singly linked circular list for a node that matches the **Item$** parameter. The **Index%** parameter returns the location of the matching array. The **LastIndex%** returns the location of the node that links with the matching node.

Syntax:
```
SUB Search.CSList(CSList$(1), CSPtr%(1), Head%,_
                  List.Size%, Item$, Index%, LastIndex%)
```

Parameters:

CSList$()	the array of singly linked circular list nodes.
CSPtr%()	the array of single links.
Head%	the index to the circular list head.
List.Size%	the circular list size.
Item$	the searched for circular list node.
Index%	the index to the array containing the matching list node. If no match occurs, **Index%** returns **%NIL**.
LastIndex%	the index of the node that points to the matching node. If the head node matches **Item$**, **LastIndex%** returns a **%NIL**.

Delete.CSList Deletes a list node matching the **Item$** parameter. The result of the operation is reported by the **Done%** parameter. A value of **%TRUE** is assigned to **Done%** when the node has been deleted; otherwise, **%FALSE** is returned by **Done%**.

Syntax:
```
SUB Delete.CSList(CSList$(1), CSPtr%(1), Map$, Head%,_
                Tail%, List.Size%, Item$, Done%)
```

Parameters:

CSList$()	the array of singly linked circular list nodes.
CSPtr%()	the array of single links.
Map$	the map of vacant **CSList$()** array elements.
Head%	the index to the circular list head.
Tail%	the index to the circular list tail.
List.Size%	the circular list size.
Item$	the node to delete.
Done%	the flag that signals the outcome of the node deletion.

Turbo C

The code for the Turbo C doubly linked and circular list processing routines is shown in Listing 7.4. Notice that a slight modification of the singly linked structure, **slistmem**, is used, which is called **dlistmem**, to represent each doubly linked list node. The circular list implementation uses the **slistmem** structure. We've only included one routine for processing circular lists: **search_circ_list()**. As its name implies, this function searches a circular list for a specified node. Other operations, such as list insertion and deletion, are accomplished using the same routines we presented in Section 6.

The following is a short description of each function implemented in this section.

Initializes a new doubly linked list. The list can be ordered or unordered.   **init_dlist()**

Syntax:
```
void init_dlist(dlistptr *head, dlistptr *tail);
```

Parameters:

*head   the pointer to the head of the new doubly linked list.
*tail   the pointer to the tail of the new doubly linked list.

Clears the nodes of a doubly linked list and restores its dynamically   **clear_dlist()**
allocated space. The list can be ordered or unordered.

Syntax:
```
void clear_dlist(dlistptr *head, *tail);
```

Parameters:
*head   the pointer to the head of the deleted doubly linked list.
*tail   the pointer to the tail of the new doubly linked list.

search_dlist()   Searches an unordered list for the node that matches **search_key**. The status of the search is returned by a 1 or 0 value. The matching node is indicated by the pointer parameter, **thisptr**.

Syntax:
```
int search_dlist(dlistptr head, dlistptr *thisptr;
                 char *search_key);
```

Parameters:
head   the head of the list.
*thisptr   the pointer to the matching node. A **NULL** is returned if the node is not found.
*search_key   the search key data.

search_sorted_dlist()   Searches an ordered list for the node that matches **search_key**. The status of the search is returned as a 1 or 0 value. The matching node is indicated by the pointer parameter, **thisptr**.

Syntax:
```
int search_sorted_dlist(dlistptr head, dlistptr *thisptr,
                        char *search_key);
```

Parameters:
head   the head of the list.
*thisptr   the pointer to the matching node. A **NULL** is returned if the node is not found.
*search_key   the search key data.

insert_dlist()   Inserts a new node at the tail of the unordered singly linked list.

Syntax:
```
int insert_dlist(dlistptr *tail, char *item);
```

Parameters:
*tail   the tail of the unordered doubly linked list.
*item   the new node, inserted as the new list tail.

Inserts a new node in the ordered doubly linked list. Depending on the key **insert_sorted_dlist**()
value of the new node, it may be inserted as the new head, new tail, or as
a nonterminal node.

Syntax:
```
int insert_sorted_dlist(dlistptr *head, dlistptr *tail,
                        char *item);
```

Parameters:
*head   the head of the ordered doubly linked list.
*tail   the tail of the ordered doubly linked list.
*item   the new node.

Deletes from an unordered list the node that matches **search_key**. The **delete_dlist**()
function returns the status of the deletion operation. A 1 value indicates
that the searched for node was found and deleted. A 0 value indicates that
the node is not in the list.

Syntax:
```
int delete_dlist(dlistptr *head, dlistptr *tail,
                 char *search_key);
```

Parameters:
*head   the head of the unordered doubly linked list.
*tail   the tail of the ordered doubly linked list.
*search_key   the search key used to locate a node for deletion.

Deletes from an ordered list the node that matches **search_key**. The **delete_sorted_dlist**()
function returns the status of the deletion operation. A 1 value indicates
that the searched for node was found and deleted. A 0 value indicates that
the node is not in the list.

Syntax:
```
int delete_sorted_dlist(dlistptr *head, dlistptr *tail,
                        char *search_key);
```

Parameters:

*head   the head of the ordered doubly linked list.
*tail   the tail of the ordered doubly linked list.
*search_key   the search key used to locate a node for deletion.

search_circlist()   Searches through an unordered singly linked list, treating it as a circular list. The search begins at the list element pointed to by **startptr**. The last and current list element pointers are returned, along with the results of the search.

Syntax:
```
int search_circlist(slistptr head, slistptr *startptr,
                    slistptr *thisptr, slistptr *lastptr,
                    char *search_key);
```

Parameters:

head   the head of the list.
*startptr   the pointer to the first node being searched.
*thisptr   the pointer to the matching node. A **NULL** is returned if the node is not found.
*lastptr   the pointer to the last node before the matching node.
*search_key   the search key data.

Turbo Pascal

The Turbo Pascal library unit for processing doubly linked and circular lists is shown in Listing 7.5. The library exports the following data types for both singly and doubly linked lists:

```
TYPE ListKeyStr = STRING[40];
    ListInfoRec = RECORD
        ListKey : ListKeyStr
        { other fields here }
END;

{ doubly linked lists data types }
DListPtr = ^DListRec;
    DListRec = RECORD
        ListInfo   : ListInfoRec;
```

```
     NextListPtr,
     PrevListPtr : DListPtr
  END;
```

As with the singly linked lists, the **STRING[40]** component is used as the key field.

The following includes a short description for each routine.

Initializes a new doubly linked list. The list can be ordered or unordered.   **Init_DList** ·

Syntax:
```
PROCEDURE Init_DList(VAR Head, Tail : DListPtr);
```

Parameters:
Head   the pointer to the head of the new doubly linked list.
Tail   the pointer to the tail of the new doubly linked list.

Clears the nodes of a doubly linked list and restores its dynamically   **Clear_DList**
allocated space. The list can be ordered or unordered.

Syntax:
```
PROCEDURE Clear_DList(VAR Head, Tail : DListPtr);
```

Parameters:
Head   the pointer to the head of the deleted doubly linked list.
Tail   the pointer to the tail of the new doubly linked list.

Searches an unordered list for the node that matches **Search_Key**. The   **Search_DList**
status of the search is reported by a **TRUE** or **FALSE** value returned by
the **Found** parameter. The matching node is indicated by the pointer
parameter, **ThisPtr**.

Syntax:
```
PROCEDURE Search_DList(VAR Head, ThisPtr : DListPtr;
                           Search_Key    : ListKeyStr;
                       VAR Found          : BOOLEAN);
```

Parameters:
Head   the head of the list (or trailing sublist).
ThisPtr   the pointer to the matching node. A **NIL** is returned if
                the node is not found.

Search_Key   the search key data.

Found   the flag indicating the results of the search.

Search_Sorted_DList Searches an ordered list for the node that matches **Search_Key**. The status of the search is reported by a **TRUE** or **FALSE** value returned by the **Found** parameter. The matching node is indicated by the pointer parameter, **ThisPtr**.

Syntax:

```
PROCEDURE Search_Sorted_DList(VAR Head, ThisPtr : DListPtr;
                                   Search_Key : ListKeyStr;
                              VAR Found       : BOOLEAN);
```

Parameters:

Head   the head of the list (or trailing sublist).

ThisPtr   the pointer to the matching node. A **NIL** is returned if the node is not found.

Search_Key   the search key data.

Found   the flag indicating the results of the search.

Insert_DList Inserts a new node at the tail of the unordered singly linked list.

Syntax:

```
PROCEDURE Insert_DList(VAR Tail : DListPtr;
                           Item : ListInfoRec);
```

Parameters:

Tail   the tail of the unordered doubly linked list.

Item   the new node, inserted as the new list tail.

Insert_Sorted_DList Inserts a new node in the ordered doubly linked list. Depending on the key value of the new node, it may be inserted as the new head, new tail, or as a nonterminal node.

Syntax:

```
PROCEDURE Insert_Sorted_DList(VAR Head, Tail : DListPtr;
                                  Item : ListInfoRec);
```

Parameters:

Head   the head of the ordered doubly linked list.

Tail   the tail of the ordered doubly linked list.
Item   the new node.

Deletes from an unordered list the node that matches **Search_Key**. The **Done** parameter returns the status of the deletion operation. A **TRUE** value indicates that the searched for node was found and deleted. A **FALSE** value indicates that the node is not in the list.   **Delete_DList**

Syntax:
```
PROCEDURE Delete_DList(VAR Head, Tail : DListPtr;
                           Search_Key : ListKeyStr;
                       VAR Done        : BOOLEAN);
```

Parameters:
Head   the head of the unordered doubly linked list.
Tail   the tail of the ordered doubly linked list.
Search_Key   the search key used to locate a node for deletion.
Done   a flag that signals the status of the deletion.

Deletes from an ordered list the node that matches **Search_Key**. The **Done** parameter returns the status of the deletion operation. A **TRUE** indicates that the searched for node was found and deleted. A **FALSE** value indicates that the node is not in the list.   **Delete_Sorted_DList**

Syntax:
```
PROCEDURE Delete_Sorted_DList(VAR  Head, Tail : DListPtr;
                                   Search_Key : ListKeyStr;
                              VAR  Done        : BOOLEAN);
```

Parameters:
Head   the head of the ordered doubly linked list.
Tail   the tail of the ordered doubly linked list.
Search_Key   the search key used to locate a node for deletion.
Done   the flag that signals the status of the deletion.

Searches through an unordered singly linked list, treating it as a circular list. The search begins at the list element pointed to by **StartPtr**. The last and current list element pointers are returned, along with a status flag.   **Search_CircList**

Syntax:

```
PROCEDURE Search_CircList(VAR Head, StartPtr, ThisPtr,
                             LastPtr    : SListPtr;
                             Search_Key : ListKeyStr;
                         VAR Found      : BOOLEAN);
```

Parameters:

Head	the head of the list.
StartPtr	the pointer to the first node being searched.
ThisPtr	the pointer to the matching node. A **NIL** is returned if the node is not found.
LastPtr	the pointer to the last node before the matching node.
Search_Key	the search key data.
Found	the flag that indicates the search outcome.

• Listing 7.1. Turbo BASIC routines for unordered doubly linked lists using the indexing scheme

---

```
'--------------- user's program declarations ----------------
$STACK 5000
OPTION BASE 1


'--------------- included library starts here ---------------
%TRUE = 1
%FALSE = 0
%NIL = 0
%NEXTNODE = 1
%LASTNODE = 2

SUB Initialize.UDList(UDList$(1), UDPtr%(2), Head%, Tail%, Map$, List.Size%)
' initializes unordered list
LOCAL i%
FOR i% = LBound(UDList$(1)) TO UBound(UDList$(1))
   UDList$(i%) = ""
NEXT i%
FOR i% = LBound(UDPtr%(1)) TO UBound(UDPtr%(1))
   UDPtr%(i%,%NEXTNODE) = %NIL
   UDPtr%(i%,%LASTNODE) = %NIL
NEXT i%
```

```
Map$ = SPACE$(UBound(UDList$(1)) - LBound(UDList$(1)) + 1)
Head% = %NIL
Tail% = %NIL
List.Size% = 0
END SUB ' Initialize.UDList


SUB Insert.UDList(UDList$(1), UDPtr%(2), Map$, Head%, Tail%,_
                  List.Size%, Item$)
' inserts Item$ in the singly linked list
LOCAL index%
IF List.Size% < UBound(UDList$(1)) THEN
    index% = INSTR(Map$, " ")
    UDList$(index%) = Item$
    MID$(Map$,index%,1) = "+"
    UDPtr%(index%,%NEXTNODE) = %NIL
    UDPtr%(index%,%LASTNODE) = Tail%
    IF List.Size% > 0 THEN
        UDPtr%(Tail%,%NEXTNODE) = index%
    ELSE
        Head% = index%
    END IF
    Tail% = index%
    INCR List.Size%
END IF
END SUB ' Insert.UDList


SUB Search.UDList(UDList$(1), UDPtr%(2), Head%, List.Size%, Item$, Index%)
' Searches for Item$ in list UDList$() starting at the Head%.
' The location of the matching element is reported by Index%.
' If no matching occurs, Index% returns %NIL.
LOCAL i%
Index% = %NIL
IF List.Size% > 0 THEN
    i% = Head%
    DO WHILE (i% <> %NIL) AND (Index% = %NIL)
        IF UDList$(i%) = Item$ THEN
            Index% = i%
        ELSE
            i% = UDPtr%(i%, %NEXTNODE)
        END IF
```

```
    LOOP
END IF
END SUB ' Search.UDList


SUB BackSearch.UDList(UDList$(1), UDPtr%(2), Tail%, List.Size%,_
                   Item$, Index%)
' Searches for Item$ in the list UDList$() starting at the tail end.
' The location of the matching element is reported by Index%.
' If no matching occurs, Index% returns %NIL.
LOCAL i%
Index% = %NIL
IF List.Size% > 0 THEN
    i% = Tail%
    DO WHILE (i% <> %NIL) AND (Index% = %NIL)
        IF UDList$(i%) = Item$ THEN
            Index% = i%
        ELSE
            i% = UDPtr%(i%, %LASTNODE)
        END IF
    LOOP
END IF
END SUB ' BackSearch.UDList


SUB Delete.UDList(UDList$(1), UDPtr%(2), Map$, Head%, Tail%, List.Size%,_
                 Item$, Done%)
' Searches for Item$ in list UDList$() starting at the Head% to delete it.
' Done% is a flag that signals the deletion outcome.
LOCAL i%, index%, lastindex%, nextindex%
Done% = %FALSE
IF List.Size% < 1 THEN EXIT SUB
CALL Search.UDList(UDList$(), UDPtr%(), Head%, List.Size%, Item$, index%)
IF index% <> %NIL THEN ' found element, delete it
    lastindex% = UDPtr%(index%, %LASTNODE)
    nextindex% = UDPtr%(index%, %NEXTNODE)
    UDList$(index%) = ""
    SELECT CASE index%
        CASE Head%
            Head% = UDPtr%(index%, %NEXTNODE)
            UDPtr%(nextindex%, %LASTNODE) = %NIL
        CASE Tail%
```

```
            Tail% = UDPtr%(index%, %LASTNODE)
            UDPtr%(lastindex%, %NEXTNODE) = %NIL
        CASE ELSE
            UDPtr%(lastindex%, %NEXTNODE) = UDPtr%(index%, %NEXTNODE)
            UDPtr%(nextindex%, %LASTNODE) = UDPtr%(index%, %LASTNODE)
    END SELECT
    MID$(Map$,index%,1) = " "  ' update deleted-elements map
    DECR List.Size%
    Done% = %TRUE
END IF
END SUB ' Delete.UDList
```

• Listing 7.2. Turbo BASIC routines for ordered doubly linked lists using the indexing scheme

---

```
'--------------- user's program declarations ---------------
$STACK 5000
OPTION BASE 1

'-------------- included library starts here ---------------
%TRUE = 1
%FALSE = 0
%NIL = 0
%NEXTNODE = 1
%LASTNODE = 2


SUB Initialize.ODList(ODList$(1), ODPtr%(2), Head%, Tail%, Map$, List.Size%)
' initializes unordered list
LOCAL i%
FOR i% = LBound(ODList$(1)) TO UBound(ODList$(1))
   ODList$(i%) = ""
NEXT i%
FOR i% = LBound(ODPtr%(1)) TO UBound(ODPtr%(1))
    ODPtr%(i%,%NEXTNODE) = %NIL
    ODPtr%(i%,%LASTNODE) = %NIL
NEXT i%
Map$ = SPACE$(UBound(ODList$(1)) - LBound(ODList$(1)) + 1)
Head% = %NIL
```

```
Tail% = %NIL
List.Size% = 0
END SUB ' Initialize.ODList


SUB Insert.ODList(ODList$(1), ODPtr%(2), Map$, Head%, Tail%,_
                  List.Size%, Item$)
' inserts Item$ in the singly linked list
LOCAL index%, ptr%, lastptr%, nextptr%, found%
IF List.Size% >= UBound(ODList$(1)) THEN EXIT SUB
found% = %FALSE
ptr% = Head%
DO WHILE (ptr% <> %NIL) AND (found% = %FALSE)
    IF ODList$(ptr%) >= Item$ THEN
        found% = %TRUE
    ELSE
        ptr% = ODPtr%(ptr%, %NEXTNODE)
    END IF
LOOP
IF List.Size% > 0 THEN
    index% = INSTR(Map$, " ")
    MID$(Map$,index%,1) = "+"
    ODList$(index%) = Item$
    ODPtr%(index%, %NEXTNODE) = ptr%
    IF ptr% <> %NIL THEN
        lastptr% = ODPtr%(ptr%, %LASTNODE)
        ODPtr%(index%, %LASTNODE) = lastptr%
        IF lastptr% <> %NIL THEN
            ODPtr%(lastptr%, %NEXTNODE) = index%
            ODPtr%(ptr%, %LASTNODE) = index%
        ELSE
            Head% = index%
            ODPtr%(ptr%, %LASTNODE) = index%
        END IF
    ELSE ' insert new tail
        ODPtr%(index%, %LASTNODE) = Tail%
        ODPtr%(Tail%, %NEXTNODE) = index%
        Tail% = index%
    END IF
ELSE ' the head of the new list
    Head% = 1
```

```
      Tail% = 1
      ODList$(1) = Item$
      MID$(Map$,1,1) = "+"
      ODPtr%(1, %NEXTNODE) = %NIL
      ODPtr%(1, %LASTNODE) = %NIL
END IF
INCR List.Size%
END SUB ' Insert.ODList


SUB Search.ODList(ODList$(1), ODPtr%(2), Head%, List.Size%, Item$, Index%)
' Searches for Item$ in list ODList$() starting at the Head%.
' The location of the matching element is reported by Index%.
' If no matching occurs, Index% returns %NIL.
LOCAL i%
Index% = %NIL
IF List.Size% > 0 THEN
    i% = Head%
    DO WHILE (i% <> %NIL) AND (Index% = %NIL)
        IF ODList$(i%) = Item$ THEN
            Index% = i%
        ELSE
            i% = ODPtr%(i%, %NEXTNODE)
        END IF
    LOOP
END IF
END SUB ' Search.ODList


SUB BackSearch.ODList(ODList$(1), ODPtr%(2), Tail%, List.Size%,_
                      Item$, Index%)
' Searches for Item$ in the list ODList$() starting at the tail end.
' The location of the matching element is reported by Index%.
' If no matching occurs, Index% returns %NIL.
LOCAL i%
Index% = %NIL
IF List.Size% > 0 THEN
    i% = Tail%
    DO WHILE (i% <> %NIL) AND (Index% = %NIL)
        IF ODList$(i%) = Item$ THEN
            Index% = i%
        ELSE
```

```
              i% = ODPtr%(i%, %LASTNODE)
         END IF
    LOOP
END IF
END SUB ' BackSearch.ODList


SUB Delete.ODList(ODList$(1), ODPtr%(2), Map$, Head%, Tail%, List.Size%,_
                 Item$, Done%)
' Searches for Item$ in list ODList$() starting at the Head% to delete it.
' Done% is a flag that signals the deletion outcome.
LOCAL i%, index%, lastindex%, nextindex%
Done% = %FALSE
IF List.Size% < 1 THEN EXIT SUB
CALL Search.ODList(ODList$(), ODPtr%(), Head%, List.Size%, Item$, index%)
IF index% <> %NIL THEN ' found element, delete it
    lastindex% = ODPtr%(index%, %LASTNODE)
    nextindex% = ODPtr%(index%, %NEXTNODE)
    ODList$(index%) = ""
    SELECT CASE index%
       CASE Head%
           Head% = ODPtr%(index%, %NEXTNODE)
           ODPtr%(nextindex%, %LASTNODE) = %NIL
       CASE Tail%
           Tail% = ODPtr%(index%, %LASTNODE)
           ODPtr%(lastindex%, %NEXTNODE) = %NIL
       CASE ELSE
           ODPtr%(lastindex%, %NEXTNODE) = ODPtr%(index%, %NEXTNODE)
           ODPtr%(nextindex%, %LASTNODE) = ODPtr%(index%, %LASTNODE)
    END SELECT
    MID$(Map$,index%,1) = " " ' update deleted-elements map
    DECR List.Size%
    Done% = %TRUE
END IF
END SUB ' Delete.ODList
```

• **Listing 7.3. Turbo BASIC routines for unordered circular lists using the indexing scheme**

```
'--------------- user's program declarations ---------------
OPTION BASE 1
```

```
'-------------- included library starts here --------------
%TRUE = 1
%FALSE = 0
%NIL = 0

SUB Initialize.CAList(CAList$(1), List.Size%)
' initializes unordered list
LOCAL i%
FOR i% = LBound(CAList$(1)) TO UBound(CAList$(1))
    CAList$(i%) = ""
NEXT i%
List.Size% = 0
END SUB ' Initialize.CAList


SUB Insert.CAList(CAList$(1), List.Size%, Item$)
' inserts Item$ in list
IF List.Size% < UBound(CAList$(1)) THEN
    INCR List.Size%
    CAList$(List.Size%) = Item$
END IF
END SUB ' Insert.CAList


SUB Search.CAList(Head%, CAList$(1), List.Size%, Item$, Index%)
' Searches for Item$ in the circular list CAList$() starting at the Head%.
' The search goes through the entire list, including wrapping around the
' array, if Head% is greater than 1. The location of the matching element
' is reported by Index%. If no matching occurs, Index% returns 0.
LOCAL i%, count%
Index% = 0
count% = 1
IF Head% > List.Size% THEN Head% = 1
i% = Head%
DO WHILE (count% <= List.Size%) AND (Index% = 0)
    IF CAList$(i%) = Item$ THEN
        Index% = i%
    ELSE
        i% = i% MOD List.Size% + 1
        INCR count%
    END IF
LOOP
END SUB ' Search.CAList
```

```
SUB Delete.CAList(Head%, CAList$(1), List.Size%, Item$, Done%)
' Searches for Item$ in circular list CAList$() starting at
' the Head% to delete it.
' Done% is a flag that signals the deletion outcome.
LOCAL i%, index%, count%
Done% = %FALSE
IF Head% > List.Size% THEN Head% = 1
count% = 1
index% = 0
i% = Head%
DO WHILE (count% <= List.Size%) AND (index% = 0)
   IF CAList$(i%) = Item$ THEN
       index% = i%
   ELSE
       INCR count%
       i% = i% MOD List.Size% + 1
   END IF
LOOP
IF index% > 0 THEN ' found element, delete it
   IF index% < List.Size% THEN
       FOR i% = index%+1 TO List.Size%
           CAList$(i%-1) = CAList$(i%)
       NEXT i%
   END IF
   DECR List.Size%
   Done% = %TRUE
END IF
END SUB ' Delete.CAList
```

• Listing 7.4. Turbo C doubly linked and circular list processing routines

```c
#include <stdlib.h>
#include <string.h>
#include <alloc.h>


typedef struct slistmem *slistptr;
typedef struct dlistmem *dlistptr;
struct listinforec {
   char listkey[40];
};
```

```
/* singly linked list structure */
struct slistmem {
    struct listinforec listinfo;
    slistptr nextlistptr;
};
/* doubly linked list structure */
struct dlistmem {
    struct listinforec listinfo;
    dlistptr nextlistptr;
    dlistptr prevlistptr;
};

/* function prototypes */
void init_dlist(dlistptr *head, dlistptr *tail);
void clear_dlist(dlistptr *head, dlistptr *tail);
int search_dlist(dlistptr head, dlistptr *thisptr, char *search_key);
int search_sorted_dlist(dlistptr head, dlistptr *thisptr, char *search_key);
int insert_dlist(dlistptr *tail, char *item);
int insert_sorted_dlist(dlistptr *head, dlistptr *tail, char *item);
int delete_dlist(dlistptr *head, dlistptr *tail, char *search_key);
int delete_sorted_dlist(dlistptr *head, dlistptr *tail, char *search_key);
int dlist_length(dlistptr head);
int search_circlist(slistptr head, slistptr *startptr, slistptr *thisptr,
                    slistptr *lastptr, char *search_key);

void init_dlist(dlistptr *head, dlistptr *tail)
/* initializes a doubly linked list */
{
    *head = NULL;    /* initializes list */
    *tail = NULL;
}

void clear_dlist(dlistptr *head, dlistptr *tail)
/* clears the nodes of a doubly linked list */
{
    dlistptr ptr;

    while (*head != NULL) {
        ptr = *head;
        *head = (*head)->nextlistptr;    /* go to next element */
```

```
        free(ptr);    /* remove each node */
    }
    *tail = NULL;
}


int search_dlist(dlistptr head, dlistptr *thisptr, char *search_key)
/* searches an unordered list for the node that matches search_key */
{
    int found;

    *thisptr = head;
    found = 0;

    while ((*thisptr != NULL) && !found) {
        if ((strcmp((*thisptr)->listinfo.listkey, search_key)) != 0) {
            *thisptr = (*thisptr)->nextlistptr;
        }
        else found = 1;
    }
    return found;
}


int search_sorted_dlist(dlistptr head, dlistptr *thisptr, char *search_key)
/* searches an ordered list for the node that matches search_key */
{
    int found;

    *thisptr = head;
    found = 0;

    while ((*thisptr != NULL) && !found) {
        if ((strcmp(search_key, (*thisptr)->listinfo.listkey)) > 0) {
            *thisptr = (*thisptr)->nextlistptr;
        }
        else found = 1;
    }
    if (found)
        found = (strcmp(search_key, (*thisptr)->listinfo.listkey) == 0);
    return found;
}
```

```
int insert_dlist(dlistptr *tail, char *item)
/* inserts a new node at the tail of the unordered singly linked list */
{
    dlistptr ptr;

    ptr = (dlistptr) malloc(sizeof(struct dlistmem));
    if (ptr == NULL) return 0;   /* memory allocation error */
    ptr->nextlistptr = NULL;
    ptr->prevlistptr = *tail;
    (*tail)->nextlistptr = ptr;
    strcpy(ptr->listinfo.listkey, item);
    (*tail) = ptr;
    return 1;
}


int insert_sorted_dlist(dlistptr *head, dlistptr *tail, char *item)
/* inserts a new node in the ordered doubly linked list */
{
    dlistptr thisptr, ptr;

    if ((search_sorted_dlist(*head, &thisptr, item)) == 1)
        exit(1);
    if (thisptr == NULL) {   /* insert item at end of list */
        ptr = (dlistptr) malloc(sizeof(struct dlistmem));
        if (ptr == NULL) return 0;       /* memory allocation error */
        ptr->nextlistptr = NULL;
        ptr->prevlistptr = *tail;
        (*tail)->nextlistptr = ptr;
        strcpy(ptr->listinfo.listkey, item);
        *tail = ptr;
        if (*head == NULL) *head = ptr;
    }
        /* insert at beginning of list */
    else if (thisptr->prevlistptr == NULL) {
        ptr = (dlistptr) malloc(sizeof(struct dlistmem));
        if (ptr == NULL) return 0;       /* memory allocation error */
        ptr->nextlistptr = *head;
        ptr->prevlistptr = NULL;
        (*head)->prevlistptr = ptr;
        strcpy(ptr->listinfo.listkey, item);
```

```
        *head = ptr;
    }
    else { /* insert somewhere in the middle */
        ptr = (dlistptr) malloc(sizeof(struct dlistmem));
        if (ptr == NULL) return 0;        /* memory allocation error */
        ptr->nextlistptr = thisptr;
        ptr->prevlistptr = thisptr->prevlistptr;
        thisptr->prevlistptr->nextlistptr = ptr;
        thisptr->prevlistptr = ptr;
        strcpy(ptr->listinfo.listkey, item);
    }
    return 1;
}


int delete_dlist(dlistptr *head, dlistptr *tail, char *search_key)
/* deletes from an unordered list the node that matches search_key */
{
    dlistptr thisptr, ptr;
    int done;

    done = search_dlist(*head, &thisptr, search_key);
    if (done)
        if (thisptr->nextlistptr == NULL) {
            /* delete last element */
            if (thisptr->prevlistptr != NULL) {
                ptr = thisptr->prevlistptr;
                ptr->nextlistptr = NULL;
            }
            else {
                ptr = NULL;
                *head = NULL;
            }
            free(*tail);
            *tail = ptr;
        }
        else if (thisptr->prevlistptr == NULL) {
            /* delete head */
            ptr = thisptr->nextlistptr;
            ptr->prevlistptr = NULL;
```

```
            free(*head);
            *head = ptr;
        }
        else {
            thisptr->prevlistptr->nextlistptr = thisptr->nextlistptr;
            thisptr->nextlistptr->prevlistptr = thisptr->prevlistptr;
            free(thisptr);
        }
    return done;
}


int delete_sorted_dlist(dlistptr *head, dlistptr *tail, char *search_key)
/* deletes from an ordered list the node that matches search_key */
{
    dlistptr thisptr, ptr;
    int done;

    done = search_sorted_dlist(*head, &thisptr, search_key);
    if (done)
        if (thisptr->nextlistptr == NULL)        {
            /* delete last element */
            ptr = thisptr->prevlistptr;
            ptr->nextlistptr = NULL;
            free(*tail);
            *tail = ptr;
        }
        else if (thisptr->prevlistptr == NULL) {
            /* delete head */
            ptr = thisptr->nextlistptr;
            ptr->prevlistptr = NULL;
            free(*head);
            *head = ptr;
        }
        else {
            thisptr->prevlistptr->nextlistptr = thisptr->nextlistptr;
            thisptr->nextlistptr->prevlistptr = thisptr->prevlistptr;
            free(thisptr);
        }
    return done;
}
```

```
int dlist_length(dlistptr head)
/* returns the length of a list */
{
    int count;

    count = 0;
    while (head != NULL)  {
        count++;
        head = head->nextlistptr;
    }
    return count;
}


int search_circlist(slistptr head, slistptr *startptr, slistptr *thisptr,
                    slistptr *lastptr, char *search_key)
/* searches through an unordered singly linked list */
{
    int found;

    if ((strcmp((*startptr)->listinfo.listkey, search_key)) == 0) {
        found = 1;
        *thisptr = (*startptr)->nextlistptr;
        *lastptr = *startptr;
    }
    else {
        *lastptr = *startptr;
        *thisptr = (*startptr)->nextlistptr;
        found = 0;
        while ((*thisptr != NULL) && !found)
            if ((strcmp((*thisptr)->listinfo.listkey, search_key)) != 0) {
                *lastptr = *thisptr;
                *thisptr = (*thisptr)->nextlistptr;
        if (*thisptr == NULL)   *thisptr = head;
    }
    else found = 1;
    if (found)   found = (strcmp(search_key,
        (*thisptr)->listinfo.listkey) == 0);
    }
    return found;
}
```

• Listing 7.5. Turbo Pascal list library unit

```pascal
UNIT DoubList;

CONST MAX_ARRAY_LIST = 100;
TYPE ListKeyStr = STRING[40];
   { record used by singly linked and doubly linked lists }
   ListInfoRec = RECORD
      ListKey : ListKeyStr
      { other fields here }
   END;


   { singly linked lists data types }
   SListPtr = ^SListRec;
   SListRec = RECORD
      ListInfo    : ListInfoRec;
      NextListPtr : SListPtr
   END;


   { doubly linked lists data types }
   DListPtr = ^DListRec;
   DListRec = RECORD
      ListInfo    : ListInfoRec;
      NextListPtr,
      PrevListPtr : DListPtr
   END;


   ListArrayType = ARRAY [1..MAX_ARRAY_LIST] OF ListInfoRec;

{========================= DOUBLY LINKED LISTS =========================}
PROCEDURE Init_DList(VAR Head, Tail : DListPtr { output });
{ initializes a doubly linked list }

PROCEDURE Clear_DList(VAR Head, Tail : DListPtr { in/out });
{ clears any existing singly linked list }

PROCEDURE Search_DList(VAR Head,                      { input  }
                           ThisPtr    : DListPtr;     { output }
                           Search_Key : ListKeyStr;   { input  }
                       VAR Found      : BOOLEAN       { output });
```

```
{ Searches for 'Search_Key' in the unordered list with 'Head' as the
  pointer to the head of the list. The current pointer is also returned in
  the argument lists. }

PROCEDURE Search_Sorted_DList(VAR Head,                      { input  }
                                  ThisPtr    : DListPtr;   { output }
                                  Search_Key : ListKeyStr; { input  }
                              VAR Found      : BOOLEAN      { output });
{ Searches for 'Search_Key' in the sorted list with 'Head' as the pointer
  to its head. The current pointer is returned in the argument list.}

PROCEDURE Insert_DList(VAR Head,                 { in/out }
                           Tail  : DListPtr;   { in/out }
                           Item  : ListInfoRec { input });
{ performs simple list insertion }

PROCEDURE Insert_Sorted_DList(VAR Head,                 { in/out }
                                  Tail : DListPtr;    { in/out }
                                  Item : ListInfoRec  { input });
{ performs ordered list insertion }

PROCEDURE Delete_DList(VAR Head,                       { in/out }
                           Tail       : DListPtr;    { in/out }
                           Search_Key : ListKeyStr;  { input  }
                       VAR Done       : BOOLEAN       { output });
{ Attempts to delete an item from an unordered list.
  The boolean parameter 'Done' confirms the deletion process.}

PROCEDURE Delete_Sorted_DList(VAR Head,                        { in/out }
                                  Tail       : DListPtr;     { in/out }
                                  Search_Key : ListKeyStr;   { input  }
                              VAR Done       : BOOLEAN        { output });
{ Attempts to delete an item from an ordered list.
  The boolean parameter 'Done' confirms the deletion process.}

PROCEDURE Search_CircList(VAR Head,                        { input  }
                              StartPtr,                    { input  }
                              ThisPtr,                     { output }
                              LastPtr    : SListPtr;     { output }
                              Search_Key : ListKeyStr;   { input  }
                          VAR Found      : BOOLEAN        { output });
```

```
                          Search_Key : ListKeyStr;  { input   }
                    VAR   Found      : BOOLEAN       { output });
{ Searches through an unordered singly linked list, treating it as a
  circular list. The search begins at the list element pointed to by
  StartPtr. The last and current list element pointers are returned along
  with a boolean search outcome. }


{***********************************************************************}
{========================= DOUBLY  LINKED  LISTS  =====================}
PROCEDURE Init_DList(VAR Head, Tail : DListPtr { output });
{ initializes a doubly linked list }
BEGIN
    Head := NIL;
      Tail := NIL;
END; { Init_DList }


PROCEDURE Clear_DList(VAR Head, Tail : DListPtr { in/out });
{ clears any existing singly linked list }
VAR ptr : DListPtr;


BEGIN
    WHILE Head <> NIL DO   BEGIN
       ptr := Head;
       Head := Head^.NextListPtr;
       Dispose(ptr)
    END; { WHILE }
    Tail := NIL; { reset tail pointer }
END; { Clear_DList }


PROCEDURE Search_DList(VAR Head,                      { input   }
                          ThisPtr    : DListPtr;   { output  }
                          Search_Key : ListKeyStr; { input   }
                    VAR   Found      : BOOLEAN       { output });
{  searches for 'Search_Key' in an unordered list }
BEGIN
    ThisPtr := Head;
    Found := FALSE;
    WHILE (ThisPtr <> NIL) AND (NOT Found) DO
       IF Search_Key <> ThisPtr^.ListInfo.ListKey THEN
           ThisPtr := ThisPtr^.NextListPtr
```

```
PROCEDURE Search_Sorted_DList(VAR Head,                        { input  }
                                  ThisPtr     : DListPtr;      { output }
                                  Search_Key  : ListKeyStr;    { input  }
                              VAR Found       : BOOLEAN        { output });
{ searches for Search_Key in a sorted list }
BEGIN
    ThisPtr := Head;
    Found := FALSE;
    WHILE (ThisPtr <> NIL) AND (NOT Found) DO
        IF Search_Key > ThisPtr^.ListInfo.ListKey THEN
            ThisPtr := ThisPtr^.NextListPtr
        ELSE
            Found := TRUE; { element might be in the list }
    { confirm suspected match }
    IF Found THEN Found := (Search_Key = ThisPtr^.ListInfo.ListKey);
END; { Search_Sorted_DList }


PROCEDURE Insert_DList(VAR Head,                  { in/out }
                           Tail  : DListPtr;      { in/out }
                           Item  : ListInfoRec    { input  });
{ performs simple list insertion }
VAR ptr : DListPtr;

BEGIN
    IF (Head = NIL) AND (Tail = NIL) THEN BEGIN
        { insert first item in the list }
        NEW(Head);
        Head^.NextListPtr := NIL;
        Head^.PrevListPtr := NIL;
        Tail := Head;
        Head^.ListInfo := Item;
    END

    ELSE BEGIN
        { new item inserted at the tail of the list }
        NEW(ptr);
        ptr^.NextListPtr := NIL;
        ptr^.PrevListPtr := Tail;
        Tail^.NextListPtr := ptr;
        ptr^.ListInfo := Item; { assign key and other fields }
```

```
        Tail := ptr; { reassign pointer to new tail }
    END;
END; { Insert_DList }


PROCEDURE Insert_Sorted_DList(VAR Head,              { in/out }
                                  Tail : DListPtr;   { in/out }
                                  Item : ListInfoRec { input });
{ performs ordered list insertion }
VAR thisptr, ptr : DListPtr;
    match : BOOLEAN;


BEGIN
    Search_Sorted_DList(Head, thisptr, Item.ListKey, match);
    { the line below may be commented out to enable multiple
      data items with the same key to be stored in the list }
    IF match THEN EXIT;
    IF thisptr = NIL THEN BEGIN
        { new item inserted at the tail of the list }
        NEW(ptr);
        ptr^.NextListPtr := NIL;
        ptr^.PrevListPtr := Tail;
        Tail^.NextListPtr := ptr;
        ptr^.ListInfo := Item; { assign key and other fields }
        Tail := ptr;
        IF Head = NIL THEN
            Head := ptr;
    END
    ELSE IF thisptr^.PrevListPtr = NIL THEN BEGIN
        { new item is the new list head }
        NEW(ptr);
        ptr^.NextListPtr := Head;
        ptr^.PrevListPtr := NIL;
        Head^.PrevListPtr := ptr;
        ptr^.ListInfo := Item; { assign key and other fields }
        Head := ptr; { assign new pointer to the head of the list }
    END
    ELSE BEGIN
        { insert new item inside the list or at its tail }
        NEW(ptr);
        { link ahead with the 'current' node }
```

```
        ptr^.NextListPtr := thisptr;
        { link back with the 'previous' node }
        ptr^.PrevListPtr := thisptr^.PrevListPtr;
        thisptr^.PrevListPtr^.NextListPtr := ptr;
        thisptr^.PrevListPtr := ptr;
        ptr^.ListInfo := Item; { assign key and other fields }
    END;
END; { Insert_Sorted_DList }


PROCEDURE Delete_DList(VAR Head,                        { in/out }
                           Tail      : DListPtr;        { in/out }
                           Search_Key : ListKeyStr;     { input  }
                       VAR Done      : BOOLEAN          { output });
{ attempts to delete an item from an unordered list }
VAR thisptr, ptr : DListPtr;


BEGIN
    { search for item to delete }
    Search_DList(Head, thisptr, Search_Key, Done);
    IF Done THEN { found item in list }
        IF thisptr^.NextListPtr = NIL THEN BEGIN
            { delete the last list member }
            ptr := thisptr^.PrevListPtr;
            ptr^.NextListPtr := NIL;
            Dispose(Tail);
            Tail := ptr; { link tail pointer with new last element }
        END
        ELSE IF thisptr^.PrevListPtr = NIL THEN BEGIN
            { delete the list head }
            ptr := thisptr^.NextListPtr;
            ptr^.PrevListPtr := NIL;
            Dispose(Head);
            Head := ptr; { link head with new first element }
        END
        ELSE BEGIN
            thisptr^.PrevListPtr^.NextListPtr := thisptr^.NextListPtr;
            thisptr^.NextListPtr^.PrevListPtr := thisptr^.PrevListPtr;
            Dispose(thisptr)
        END;
END; { Delete_DList }
```

```
PROCEDURE Delete_Sorted_DList(VAR  Head,                        { in/out }
                                   Tail       : DListPtr;       { in/out }
                                   Search_Key : ListKeyStr;     { input  }
                              VAR  Done       : BOOLEAN         { output });
{ attempts to delete an item from an ordered list }
VAR thisptr, ptr : DListPtr;

BEGIN
    { search for item to delete }
    Search_Sorted_DList(Head, thisptr, Search_Key, Done);
    IF Done THEN { found item in list }
        IF thisptr^.NextListPtr = NIL THEN BEGIN
            { delete the last list member }
            ptr := thisptr^.PrevListPtr;
            ptr^.NextListPtr := NIL;
            Dispose(Tail);
            Tail := ptr; { link tail pointer with new last element }
        END
        ELSE IF thisptr^.PrevListPtr = NIL THEN BEGIN
            { delete the list head }
            ptr := thisptr^.NextListPtr;
            ptr^.PrevListPtr := NIL;
            Dispose(Head);
            Head := ptr; { link head with new first element }
        END

        ELSE BEGIN
            thisptr^.PrevListPtr^.NextListPtr := thisptr^.NextListPtr;
            thisptr^.NextListPtr^.PrevListPtr := thisptr^.PrevListPtr;
            Dispose(thisptr)
        END;
END; { Delete_Sorted_DList }


{========================= CIRCULAR LISTS =========================}

PROCEDURE Search_CircList(VAR Head,                        { input  }
                              StartPtr,                    { input  }
                              ThisPtr,                     { output }
                              LastPtr    : SListPtr;       { output }
                              Search_Key : ListKeyStr;     { input  }
                         VAR  Found      : BOOLEAN         { output });
```

```
{ searches through an unordered singly linked list }
BEGIN
    IF Search_Key = StartPtr^.ListInfo.ListKey THEN BEGIN
        Found := TRUE;
        ThisPtr := StartPtr^.NextListPtr;
        LastPtr := StartPtr
    END
    ELSE BEGIN
        LastPtr := StartPtr;
        ThisPtr := StartPtr^.NextListPtr;
        Found := FALSE;
        WHILE (ThisPtr <> StartPtr) AND (NOT Found) DO
            IF Search_Key <> ThisPtr^.ListInfo.ListKey THEN BEGIN
                LastPtr := ThisPtr;
                ThisPtr := ThisPtr^.NextListPtr;
                IF ThisPtr = NIL THEN { reached the end of the list }
                    ThisPtr := Head; { reset to the head of the list }
            END
            ELSE Found := TRUE; { element might be in the list }
        { confirm suspected match }
    IF Found THEN
            Found := (Search_Key = ThisPtr^.ListInfo.ListKey);
    END; { IF }
END; { Search_CircList }
END.
```

Stacks and Queues

Introduction

In previous sections, you learned how to represent and process simple list structures by using singly linked and doubly linked lists. In this section, we present two new structures called *stacks* and *queues*, which are very simple yet extremely powerful data structures based on the basic linear list structure. Stacks, for example, are used by compiled programs to pass parameters of functions and procedures. Queues, on the other hand, often represent data that must be processed in chronological order.

We begin by examining the basic representation of both stacks and queues; then we present a set of routines in each of the Turbo languages for processing both of these structures. The Turbo C and Pascal algorithms we present are designed to work with array-based and linked list-based stacks and queues. The Turbo BASIC implementations support array-based stacks and queues only, and the Turbo Prolog implementations support built-in list data types.

Overview of Stacks and Queues

Stacks and queues store and retrieve data in a chronological manner. Data is placed in a stack or a queue and is removed using the order in which it was placed in the structure. How are stacks different from queues? The difference lies in the manner in which the data is ordered in each structure. A stack is a first-in last-out (FILO) structure. This means that the more recent elements are removed from the stack first. (When an element is removed, we say that it has been *popped*.) By contrast, a queue is a first-in first-out (FIFO) structure. With queues, the older queue elements leave the queue first. The keyboard type-ahead buffer in your PC is a good example of a queue.

Both structures require a storage space and the use of one or more pointers (or counters) to keep track of the transient information. The storage space can be an array or a linked list. For stacks, a stack height counter or a top-of-the-stack pointer keeps track of the size of the stack. Elements are pushed onto and popped off the top of the stack. Thus, the stack has one end of the storage space (the top of the stack) expanding and contracting—whereas the other end is fixed. For queues, we must keep track of the queue size, and use head and tail pointers to manage the structure. This is because both ends of the storage space of a queue are changing. As new elements are added, the tail of the queue expands. By contrast, when an element is removed from the queue, the head of the queue contracts toward the tail. Next we discuss in more detail how stacks and queues are represented.

Representing Stacks

Stacks can be represented with either simple arrays or linked lists that take advantage of dynamic memory allocation. Of course, both representations have their strengths and weaknesses. The linked list representation allows the stack space to easily grow and shrink because memory is allocated and deallocated for the stack as it is needed. This technique is illustrated in Figure 8.1. The *top of stack* pointer is used to both push and pop an element. Notice that element 4—which is the last element placed in the stack—is inserted at the beginning of the list and is therefore the first element removed. With this type of implementation we only need to traverse the list in one direction. Unfortunately, using linked lists complicates some additional stack manipulation tasks, such as rotating the stack and swapping the two topmost elements.

When an array structure is used to implement a stack, the size of the stack (array size) must be preset before the stack is used in a program. To access array-based stacks, we simply store the index position of the top of the stack, as shown in Figure 8.2. When an element is pushed, the stack

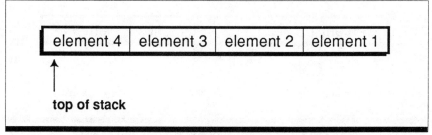

Figure 8.1. Representing a stack with a linked list

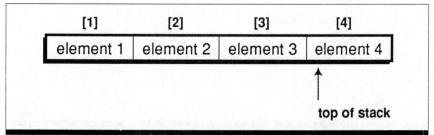

Figure 8.2. Representing a stack with an array

pointer is increased by 1; when an element is popped, the stack pointer is decreased by 1.

Representing Queues

Like stacks, queues can also be implemented with either arrays or linked lists. Queues implemented with linked lists are very similar to array-based stacks. Two pointers are required to keep track of the head and the tail of the queue. The basic technique is presented in Figure 8.3. Here an element is placed in the queue by inserting it at the location referenced by the *tail pointer*. An element is removed by taking the element referenced by the *head pointer*. After an element is removed, the head pointer is advanced to reference the next element in the queue.

When queues are implemented with arrays, the queue must be of a fixed size. An added twist to using arrays is the problem of handling the movement of the queue's head and tail that occurs after elements are inserted and removed. Let's examine this problem. Figure 8.4 represents a partially filled queue from which no elements have been removed.

As elements are removed from the queue, the leading array elements become vacant and the queue data is stored somewhere in the middle of the array, as shown in Figure 8.5.

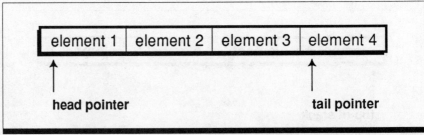

Figure 8.3. A queue represented as a linked list

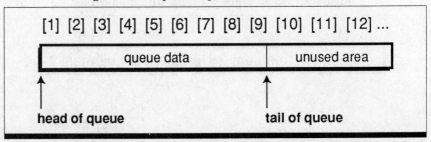

Figure 8.4. A partially filled queue

As new elements are added, the tail of the queue moves toward the back. If elements are simultaneously being removed, the head of the queue also moves toward the tail of the array. Eventually, the tail of the queue reaches the last array element. Wrapping the queue is required. Figure 8.6 shows a queue with its tail boundary wrapped around the front end of the array. The unused array elements are now sandwiched between the tail and head of the queue.

Implementations of Stack and Queue Processing Algorithms

Now that we've shown how stacks and queues can be represented, we'll develop a set of routines for processing these structures. Unlike linked lists, stacks and queues only require a few basic operations.

1. Initialize a stack or queue.
2. Insert an element.
3. Remove an element.

We next discuss how each of these operations are implemented in each Turbo language.

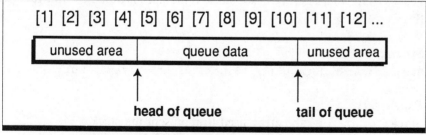

Figure 8.5. A queue after elements are removed

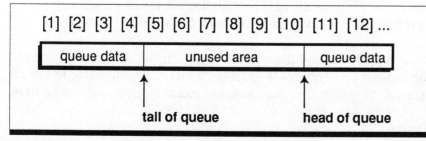

Figure 8.6. A queue with wrapping

Turbo BASIC

Stacks and queues are implemented with arrays only in Turbo BASIC. Listings 8.1 and 8.2 present the source code for the Turbo BASIC stack and queue routines, respectively. The routines are written to make use of the predefined **UBound** function that passes arrays of various sizes. The **OPTION BASE 1** setting is also used. Consequently, the BASIC routines themselves do not impose a limit on the size of the array used. The stack and queue structures implemented in these listings store strings. You can support other types of data by changing the array's explicit data type. For example, the subroutine **Push.ArStk** defined as

```
SUB Push.ArStk(Stack$(1), Stack.Height%, Item$, Full.Stack%)
```

can be altered to work with integers simply by changing the array **Stack$(1)** to **Stack%(1)**, and the parameter **Item$** to **Item%**. The result, illustrated by the following declaration part, is

```
SUB Push.ArStk(Stack%(1), Stack.Height%, Item%, Full.Stack%)
```

The Turbo BASIC stack and queue processing routines are described next.

Push.ArStk

Pushes **Item$** into an array-based stack. If the stack is full, the **Full.Stack%** flag is set to **%TRUE**.

Syntax:
```
SUB Push.ArStk(Stack$(1), Stack.Height%, Item$, Full.Stack%)
```

Parameters:

Stack$()	the array used to represent the stack.
Stack.Height%	the location of the top of the stack in the array.
Item$	the item pushed onto the top of the stack.
Full.Stack%	flag to report stack-full status.

Pop.ArStk

Returns (and removes) the topmost stack element. If the stack is empty, the boolean **Empty.Stack%** is set to **%TRUE**. Use this flag to test the status of the stack before you attempt to access the data in argument **Item**.

Syntax:
```
SUB Pop.ArStk(Stack$(1), Stack.Height%, Item$, Empty.Stack%)
```

Parameters:

Stack$()	the array used to represent a stack.
Stack.Height %	the location of the top of the stack in the array.
Item$	the item popped off the top of the stack.
Empty.Stack %	the flag to report stack-empty status.

Clears the stack.   **Clear.ArStk**

Syntax:
```
SUB Clear.ArStk(Stack$(1), Stack.Height%)
```

Parameters:

Stack$()	the array implementing a stack.
Stack.Height %	the location of the top of the stack in the array. Its value is set to zero.

Pushes **Item$** into an array-based queue. If the queue is full, the   **Push.ArQue**
Full.Queue % flag is set to **%TRUE**.

Syntax:
```
SUB Push.ArQue(Queue$(1), QSize%, HeadQ%, TailQ%,_
               Item$, Full.Queue%)
```

Parameters:

Queue$()	the array used to represent a queue.
QSize %	the size of the queue.
HeadQ %	the array index to the head of the queue.
TailQ %	the array index to the tail of the queue.
Item$	the item entering the tail of the queue.
Full.Queue %	the flag to report queue-full status.

Returns (and removes) the first queue element. If the queue is empty, the   **Pop.ArQue**
boolean **Empty.Queue %** is set to **%TRUE**. Use this flag to test the status
of the queue before you attempt to access the data in argument **Item**.

Syntax:
```
SUB Pop.ArQue(Queue$(1), QSize%, HeadQ%, TailQ%,_
              Item$, Empty.Queue%)
```

Parameters:

Queue$()	the array used to represent a queue.

QSize%	the size of the queue.
HeadQ%	the array index to the head of the queue.
TailQ%	the array index to the tail of the queue.
Item$	the item leaving the head of the queue.
Empty.Queue%	the flag to report queue-empty status.

Clear.ArQue Clears the queue.

Syntax:
```
SUB Clear.ArQue(Queue$(1), QSize%, HeadQ%, TailQ%)
```

Parameters:

Queue$()	the array used as a queue.
QSize%	the size of the queue, set to 0.
HeadQ%	the array index to the head of the queue, set to 1.
TailQ%	the array index to the tail of the queue, set to 0.

Turbo C

Stacks and queues are implemented with both arrays and linked lists in Turbo C. Listings 8.3 and 8.4 show the source code for the array-based implementation and the linked list-based implementation of stacks, respectively. The queue processing routines are presented in Listings 8.5 and 8.6.

In the array implementations of the stacks and queues, the following macros define the size of the stack and queue:

```
#define MAX_ARRAY_STACK 100
#define MAX_ARRAY_QUEUE 100
```

To change the size of either structure, you can alter the value of the appropriate macro. The following C structure is used to represent the array-based stack:

```
typedef struct stackstruct stackarrayrec;
struct stackstruct  {
    char member[MAX_ARRAY_STACK][STRING_SIZE];
    int height;
};
```

This structure is designed to represent stacks of strings. If you want to store other types of data in the stack, change the data type of the **member** component.

Listing 8.4 shows the source code for the linked list-based stack processing routines. The following structure is declared for representing the stack:

```
typedef struct stackstruct *stackptr;
struct stackstruct   {
    char stackdata[STRING_SIZE];
    stackptr nextptr;
};
```

This structure is also designed for stacks of strings. The functions for processing array-based and list-based stacks are presented next.

Pushes **item** into an array-based stack. If the stack is already full, a value of 1 is returned; otherwise, 0 is returned.

push_arstk()

Syntax:
```
int push_arstk(stackarrayrec *stack, char *item);
```

Parameters:
*stack　the structure used to represent the stack.
*item　the item pushed onto the top of the stack.

Returns (and removes) the topmost stack element. If the stack is empty, a value of 1 is returned; otherwise, 0 is returned.

pop_arstk()

Syntax:
```
int pop_arstk(stackarrayrec *stack, char *item);
```

Parameters:
*stack　the structure used to implement the stack.
*item　the item pushed onto the top of the stack.

Clears the stack.

clear_arstk()

Syntax:
```
void clear_arstk(stackarrayrec *stack);
```

Parameter:
*stack   the structure used to implement the stack.

push_lsstk()   Pushes **item** onto the list-based stack.

Syntax:
```
int push_lsstk(stackptr *top_of_stack, char *item);
```

Parameters:
*top_of_stack   the pointer to the top of the stack.
*item   item pushed onto the top of the stack.

pop_lsstk()   Returns (and removes) the topmost stack element. If the stack is empty, a value of 1 is returned; otherwise, 0 is returned.

Syntax:
```
int pop_lsstk(stackptr *top_of_stack, char *item);
```

Parameters:
*top_of_stack   the pointer to the top of the stack.
*item   item popped from the stack.

clear_lsstk()   Deletes the linked list of elements forming the stack. The dynamic memory space used by the list is deallocated.

Syntax:
```
void clear_lsstk(stackptr *top_of_stack);
```

Parameter:
*top_of_stack   the pointer to the top of the stack.

Queue Processing Routines

The queue processing routines are also presented in an array and a linked-list version. Listing 8.5 shows the source code for the array-based queue functions and Listing 8.6 presents the linked-list version.

In the array-based implementation, the following structure represents the queue:

```
typedef struct questruct quearrayrec;
struct questruct {
    char member[MAX_ARRAY_QUEUE][STRING_SIZE];
    int qsize, headq, tailq;
};
```

Notice that both a head and tail index (**headq** and **tailq**) are required to process the array-based queue. In addition, we need the component **qsize** to keep track of the number of elements stored in the queue at any given time. The data placed in the queue is stored in the **member** component.

The array-based and list-based queue processing routines are covered next.

Pushes **item** into an array-based queue. If the queue is already full, a value **push_arque()**
of 1 is returned; otherwise, 0 is returned.

Syntax:
```
int push_arque(quearrayrec *queue, char *item);
```

Parameters:
*queue   the structure implementing the array-based queue.
*item   the item placed at the tail of the queue.

Returns (and removes) the first queue element. If the queue is empty, a value **pop_arque()**
of 1 is returned; otherwise, 0 is returned.

Syntax:
```
int pop_arque(quearrayrec *queue, char *item);
```

Parameters:
*queue   the structure implementing the array-based queue.
*item   the item removed from the head of the queue.

Clears the queue and resets the head and tail queue indices.   **clear_arque()**

Syntax:
```
void clear_arque(quearrayrec *queue);
```

Parameter:
*queue   the structure implementing the array-based queue.

push_lsque()   Pushes **item** in list-based queue.

Syntax:
```
int push_lsque(queueptr *head_of_queue,
               queueptr *tail_of_queue, char *item);
```

Parameters:
*head_of_queue   the pointer to the head of the queue.
*tail_of_queue   the pointer to the tail of the queue.
*item   the item placed in the queue.

pop_lsque()   Returns (and removes) the first queue element. If the queue is empty, a value of 1 is returned; otherwise, 0 is returned.

Syntax:
```
int pop_lsque(queueptr *head_of_queue, char *item);
```

Parameters:
*head_of_queue   the pointer to the head of the queue.
*item   the item leaving the queue.

clear_lsque()   Deletes the linked list forming the queue.

Syntax:
```
void clear_lsque(queueptr *head_of_queue,
                 queueptr *tail_of_queue);
```

Parameters:
*head_of_queue   the pointer to the head of the queue, which is set to **NULL**.
*tail_of_queue   the pointer to the tail of the queue, which is set to **NULL**.

Turbo Pascal

Stacks and queues are implemented with both arrays and linked lists in Turbo Pascal. Listing 8.7 shows the source code for the array-based stack library unit in Turbo Pascal.

The library declares the following constant for the size of the array-based stack:

```
CONST MAX_ARRAY_STACK = 100; {size of array}
```

To change the size of the stack, you alter the value of the above constant. The following data types are also declared and exported by the library:

```
TYPE
    StackData = STRING[80];
    StackArray = ARRAY [1..MAX_ARRAY_STACK] OF StackData;
    StackArrayRec = RECORD
        Member : StackArray;
        Height : INTEGER;
    END;
```

These data types are written for stacks of strings. The **StackData** type can be changed to other simple types, such as integers or reals or even records. The routines themselves do not need to be altered to support other data types.

Listing 8.8 shows the source code for the linked list-based stack library unit in Turbo Pascal. The following data types are also declared and exported by the library:

```
TYPE
    StackData = STRING[80];
    StackPtr = ^StackRec;
    StackRec = RECORD
        StackData : StackData;
        NextPtr   : StackPtr
    END;
```

These data types are written for stacks of strings. The **StackData** type can be changed to other simple types or to records. Here is the description of each array-based and list-based stack processing routine.

Pushes **Item** into an array-based stack. If the stack is already full, the **Full_Stack** flag is set to **TRUE**.   **Push_ArStk**

Syntax:
```
PROCEDURE Push_ArStk(VAR Stack      : StackArrayRec;
                         Item       : StackData;
                     VAR Full_Stack : BOOLEAN);
```

Parameters:
Stack   the record used to represent the stack.
Item   the item pushed onto the top of the stack.
Full_Stack   the flag to report stack-full status.

Pop_ArStk

Returns (and removes) the topmost stack element. If the stack is empty, the boolean **Empty_Stack** is set to **TRUE**. Use this flag to test the status of the stack before you attempt to access the data in argument **Item**.

Syntax:
```
PROCEDURE Pop_ArStk(VAR Stack       :  StackArrayRec;
                    VAR Item        :  StackData;
                    VAR Empty_Stack :  BOOLEAN);
```

Parameters:
Stack   the record used to implement the stack.
Item   the item pushed onto the top of the stack.
Empty_Stack   the flag to report stack-empty status.

Clear_ArStk

Clears the stack.

Syntax:
```
PROCEDURE Clear_ArStk(VAR Stack : StackArrayRec);
```

Parameter:
Stack   the record implementing the stack.

Push_LsStk

Pushes **Item** onto the list-based stack.

Syntax:
```
PROCEDURE Push_LsStk(VAR Top_of_Stack : StackPtr;
                         Item          : StackData);
```

Parameters:
Top_of_Stack   the pointer to the top of the stack.
Item   item pushed onto the top of the stack.

Pop_LsStk

Returns (and removes) the topmost stack element. If the stack is empty, the boolean **Empty_Stack** is set to **TRUE**. Use this flag to test the status of the stack before you attempt to access the data in argument **Item**.

Syntax:
```
PROCEDURE Pop_LsStk(VAR Top_of_Stack   :   StackPtr;
                    VAR Item           :   StackData;
                    VAR Empty_Stack    :   BOOLEAN);
```

Parameters:

Top_of_Stack   the pointer to the top of the stack.
Item   the item popped out of the stack.
Empty_Stack   the flag that returns the stack-empty status.

Deletes the linked list of elements forming the stack. The dynamic memory   **Clear_LsStk**
space used by the list is freed.

Syntax:
```
PROCEDURE Clear_LsStk(VAR Top_of_Stack : StackPtr);
```

Parameter:
Top_of_Stack   the pointer to the top of the stack.

Queue Processing Routines

The queue processing routines are also presented in an array and a linked-list version. Listing 8.9 shows the source code for the array-based queue library unit, and Listing 8.10 presents the linked-list version.

In the array-based implementation, the following constant for the size of the array-based queue is defined:

```
CONST MAX_ARRAY_QUEUE = 100; { size of array }
```

You can change the size of the queue by altering this constant. In addition, the following data types are declared and exported by the library:

```
TYPE
    QueueData = STRING[80];
    QueueArray = ARRAY [1..MAX_ARRAY_QUEUE] OF QueueData;
    QueueArrayRec = RECORD
        Member : QueueArray;
        QSize,
        HeadQ,
        TailQ : INTEGER;
    END;
```

Notice that both a head and tail index (**HeadQ** and **TailQ**) are required to process the array-based queue. In addition, we need the component **QSize** to keep track of the number of elements stored in the queue at any given time. The data placed in the queue is stored in the **Member** component. We've declared this component as a record so that it can easily be altered to support other types of data besides strings.

Listing 8.10 shows the source code for the list-based queue library unit in Turbo Pascal. The following data types are also declared and exported by the library:

```
TYPE
    QueueData = STRING[80];
    QueuePtr  = ^QueueRec;
    QueueRec  = RECORD
        QueueData : QueueData
        NextPtr   : QueuePtr
    END;
```

The library routines are presented next.

Push_ArQue

Pushes **Item** into an array-based queue. If the queue is already full, the **Full_Queue** flag is set to **TRUE**.

Syntax:
```
PROCEDURE Push_ArQue(VAR Queue        :    QueueArrayRec;
                         Item         :    QueueData;
                     VAR Full_Queue   :    BOOLEAN);
```
Parameters:
Queue   the record structure implementing the array-based queue.
Item   the item entering the tail of the queue.
Full_Queue   the flag that returns the queue-full status.

Pop_ArQue

Returns (and removes) the first queue element. If the queue is empty, the boolean **Empty_Queue** is set to **TRUE**. Use this flag to test the status of the queue before you attempt to access the data in argument **Item**.

Syntax:
```
PROCEDURE Pop_ArQue(VAR Queue        :    QueueArrayRec;
                    VAR Item         :    QueueData;
                    VAR Empty_Queue  :    BOOLEAN);
```

Parameters:

Queue   the record structure implementing the array-based queue.

Item   the item leaving the head of the queue.

Empty_Queue   the flag that returns the queue-empty status.

Clears the queue and resets the head and tail queue indices.   **Clear_ArQue**

Syntax:
```
PROCEDURE Clear_ArQue(VAR Queue : QueueArrayRec);
```

Parameter:

Queue the record structure implementing the array-based queue.

Pushes **Item** in list-based queue.   **Push_LsQue**

Syntax:
```
PROCEDURE Push_LsQue(VAR Head_of_Queue,
                         Tail_Of_Queue : QueuePtr;
                         Item          : QueueData);
```

Parameters:

Head_of_Queue   the pointer to the head of the queue.

Tail_of_Queue   the pointer to the tail of the queue.

Item   the item entering the queue.

Returns (and removes) the first queue element. If the queue is empty, the   **Pop_LsQue**
boolean **Empty_Queue** is set to **TRUE**. Use this flag to test the status of
the queue before you attempt to access the data in argument **Item**.

Syntax:
```
PROCEDURE Pop_LsQue(VAR Head_of_Queue  :    QueuePtr;
                        VAR Item        :    QueueData;
                        VAR Empty_Queue :    BOOLEAN);
```

Parameters:

Head_of_Queue   the pointer to the head of the queue.

Item   the item leaving the queue.

Empty_Queue   the flag that returns the queue-empty status.

Clear_LsQue   Deletes the linked list forming the queue.

Syntax:
```
PROCEDURE Clear_LsQue(VAR Head_of_Queue,
                          Tail_of_Queue : QueuePtr);
```

Parameters:

Head_of_Queue   the pointer to the head of the queue, set to **NIL**.
Tail_of_Queue   the pointer to the tail of the queue, set to **NIL**.

Turbo Prolog

Stacks and queues are implemented using Turbo Prolog's built-in list structures. This means we don't have to worry about processing arrays or linked lists. The predicates for processing both stacks and queues are shown in Listing 8.11.

Both the stacks and queues are represented with lists of symbols. The domain type used is:

```
domains
    symlist = symbol*
```

You can, however, use other domain types such as integers, characters, or strings.

The predicates for processing list-based stacks and queues are presented next.

push_stk   Pushes **Item** into a list-based stack.

Syntax:
```
push_stk(Stack, Item, NewStack)        (i,i,o)
        (symlist, symbol, symlist)
```

Parameters:

Stack   the list used to represent the stack.
Item   the item pushed onto the top of the stack.
NewStack   the stack with the item inserted.

pop_stk   Returns (and removes) the topmost stack element.

Syntax:
```
pop_stk(Stack, Item, NewStack)        (i,o,o)
        (symlist, symbol, symlist)
```

Parameters:

Stack	the list used to implement the stack.
Item	the item popped from the top of the stack.
NewStack	the stack with the item removed.

Pushes **item** into a list-based queue.   **push_queue**

Syntax:
```
push_queue(Queue, Item, NewQueue)        (i,i,o)
          (symlist, symbol, symlist)
```

Parameters:

Queue	the list implementing the queue.
Item	the item entering the tail of the queue.
NewQueue	the queue with the item inserted.

Returns (and removes) the first queue element.   **pop_queue**

Syntax:
```
pop_queue(Queue, Item, NewQueue)        (i,o,o)
          (symlist, symbol, symlist)
```

Parameters:

Queue	the list implementing the queue.
Item	the item removed from the queue.
NewQueue	the queue with the item removed.

• Listing 8.1. Turbo BASIC source code for array-based stacks library

---

```
'------------- User's program declarations ------------
OPTION BASE 1


'------------- Included Library starts here ------------
%FALSE = 0
%TRUE = 1
```

```
SUB Push.ArStk(Stack$(1), Stack.Height%, Item$, Full.Stack%)
' Pushes Item$ into an array-based stack. If the stack is full, the
' Full.Stack% flag is set to %TRUE
IF Stack.Height% < UBound(Stack$(1))  THEN
    INCR Stack.Height%
    Stack$(Stack.Height%) = Item$
    Full.Stack% = %FALSE
ELSE
    Full.Stack% = %TRUE
END IF
END SUB ' Push.ArStk


SUB Pop.ArStk(Stack$(1), Stack.Height%, Item$, Empty.Stack%)
' Returns (and removes) the topmost stack element. If the
' stack is empty, the boolean Empty.Stack% is set to %TRUE.
' Use this flag to test the status of the stack before you
' attempt to access the data in argument Item.
IF Stack.Height% > 0 THEN
    Item$ = Stack$(Stack.Height%)
    DECR Stack.Height%
    Empty.Stack% = %FALSE
ELSE
    Empty.Stack% = %TRUE
END IF
END SUB ' Pop.ArStk


SUB Clear.ArStk(Stack$(1), Stack.Height%)
' clears the stack
LOCAL i%
FOR i% = LBound(Stack$(1)) TO UBound(Stack$(1))
    Stack$(i%) = ""
NEXT i%
Stack.Height% = 0
END SUB ' Clear.ArStk
```

• Listing 8.2. Turbo BASIC source code for array-based queues library

```
'---------- User's program declarations ----------
OPTION BASE 1
```

```
'---------- Included Library starts here ------------
%TRUE = 1
%FALSE = 0


SUB Push.ArQue(Queue$(1), QSize%, HeadQ%, TailQ%, Item$, Full.Queue%)
' Pushes Item$ into an array-based queue. If the queue is full, the
' Full.Queue% flag is set to %TRUE
IF QSize% < UBound(Queue$(1)) THEN
    INCR QSize%
    TailQ% = TailQ% MOD UBound(Queue$(1)) + 1
    Queue$(TailQ%) = Item$
    Full.Queue% = %FALSE
ELSE
    Full.Queue% = %TRUE
END IF
END SUB ' Push.ArQue


SUB Pop.ArQue(Queue$(1), QSize%, HeadQ%, TailQ%, Item$, Empty.Queue%)
' Returns (and removes) the first queue element. If the
' queue is empty, the boolean Empty.Queue% is set to %TRUE.
' Use this flag to test the status of the queue before you
' attempt to access the data in argument Item.
IF QSize% > 0 THEN
    Item$ = Queue$(QSize%)
    DECR QSize%
    HeadQ% = HeadQ% MOD UBound(Queue$(1)) + 1
    Empty.Queue% = %FALSE
ELSE
    Empty.Queue% = %TRUE
END IF
END SUB ' Pop.ArQue


SUB Clear.ArQue(Queue$(1), QSize%, HeadQ%, TailQ%)
' clears the queue
LOCAL i%
FOR i% = LBound(Queue$(1)) TO UBound(Queue$(1))
    Queue$(i%) = ""
NEXT i%
QSize% = 0
HeadQ% = 1
```

```
TailQ% = 0
END SUB ' Clear.ArQue
```

• Listing 8.3. Turbo C source code for array-based stacks library

```c
#include <string.h>
#define MAX_ARRAY_STACK 100
#define STRING_SIZE 80

typedef struct stackstruct stackarrayrec;
struct stackstruct  {
    char member[MAX_ARRAY_STACK][STRING_SIZE];
    int height;
};

int push_arstk(stackarrayrec *stack, char *item);
int pop_arstk(stackarrayrec *stack, char *item);
void clear_arstk(stackarrayrec *stack);

int push_arstk(stackarrayrec *stack, char *item)
/* Pushes item into an array-based stack. If the stack is
   full, a value of 1 is returned; otherwise, 0 is returned. */
{
    if ((*stack).height < MAX_ARRAY_STACK) {
        (*stack).height++;
        strcpy((*stack).member[(*stack).height], item);
        return 0; /* stack not full; item inserted */
    }
    return 1;   /* stack is full */
}

int pop_arstk(stackarrayrec *stack, char *item)
/* Removes (pops) the topmost stack element. If the stack is
   empty, a value of 1 is returned; otherwise, 0 is returned. */
{
    if ((*stack).height >= 0) {
        strcpy(item,(*stack).member[(*stack).height]);
        (*stack).height--;
        return 0;   /* stack not empty; item removed */
```

```
    }
    return 1;   /* stack is empty */
}


void clear_arstk(stackarrayrec *stack)
/* clears the array-based stack by initializing its height */
{
    (*stack).height = -1;
}
```

• Listing 8.4. Turbo C source code for linked list-based stacks library

```
#include <string.h>
#include <alloc.h>
#include <stdio.h>
#define STRING_SIZE 80

typedef struct stackstruct *stackptr;
struct stackstruct   {
    char stackdata[STRING_SIZE];
    stackptr nextptr;
};

int push_lsstk(stackptr *top_of_stack, char *item);
int pop_lsstk(stackptr *top_of_stack, char *item);
void clear_lsstk(stackptr *top_of_stack);

int push_lsstk(stackptr *top_of_stack, char *item)
/* Pushes item onto a list-based stack. If the element is
   inserted, a value of 0 is returned; otherwise, 1 is returned. */
{
    stackptr ptr;

    ptr = (stackptr) malloc(sizeof(struct stackstruct));
    if (ptr == NULL) return 1;   /* memory allocation problem */
    strcpy(ptr->stackdata, item);
    ptr->nextptr = *top_of_stack;
    *top_of_stack = ptr;
    return 0; /* element inserted */
}
```

```
int pop_lsstk(stackptr *top_of_stack, char *item)
/* Returns (pops) the topmost stack element. If the stack is empty, a
   value of 1 is returned; otherwise, 0 is returned. */
{
    stackptr ptr;

    if (*top_of_stack != NULL) {
        strcpy(item,(*top_of_stack)->stackdata);
        ptr = *top_of_stack;
        *top_of_stack = (*top_of_stack)->nextptr;
        free(ptr);
        return 0; /* stack not empty; item removed */
    }
    return 1;   /* stack is empty */
}


void clear_lsstk(stackptr *top_of_stack)
/* deletes the list of stack elements */
{
    char dummy;

    while (pop_lsstk(top_of_stack, &dummy) == 0);
}
```

• Listing 8.5. Turbo C source code for array-based queues library

```
#include <string.h>
#define STRING_SIZE 80
#define MAX_ARRAY_QUEUE 100

typedef struct questruct quearrayrec;
struct questruct {
    char member[MAX_ARRAY_QUEUE][STRING_SIZE];
    int qsize, headq, tailq;
};


int push_arque(quearrayrec *queue, char *item);
int pop_arque(quearrayrec *queue, char *item);
void clear_arque(quearrayrec *queue);
```

```
int push_arque(quearrayrec *queue, char *item)
/* Pushes item into an array-based queue. If the queue is
   full, a value of 1 is returned; otherwise, 0 is returned. */
{
    if ((*queue).qsize < MAX_ARRAY_QUEUE) {
        (*queue).qsize++;
        (*queue).tailq = ((*queue).tailq + 1) % MAX_ARRAY_QUEUE;
        strcpy((*queue).member[(*queue).tailq], item);
        return 0; /* queue not full; item inserted */
    }
    return 1; /* queue is full */
}


int pop_arque(quearrayrec *queue, char *item)
/* Returns (pops) the first queue element. If the queue is empty, a value
   of 1 is returned; otherwise, 0 is returned. */
{
    if ((*queue).qsize > 0) {
        strcpy(item,(*queue).member[(*queue).headq]);
        (*queue).qsize--;
        (*queue).headq = ((*queue).headq + 1) % MAX_ARRAY_QUEUE;
        return 0; /* queue not empty; item removed */
    }
    return 1; /* queue is empty */
}


void clear_arque(quearrayrec *queue)
/* clears the queue by initializing the head, tail, and
   size indexes */
{
    (*queue).qsize = 0;
    (*queue).headq = 0;
    (*queue).tailq = -1;
}
```

• Listing 8.6. Turbo C source code for linked list-based queues library

```
#include <stdio.h>
#include <alloc.h>
```

```
#include <string.h>
#define STRING_SIZE 80

typedef struct queuestruct *queueptr;
struct queuestruct  {
    char queuedata[STRING_SIZE];
    queueptr nextptr;
};


int push_lsque(queueptr *head_of_queue, queueptr *tail_of_queue, char *item);
int pop_lsque(queueptr *head_of_queue, char *item);
void clear_lsque(queueptr *head_of_stack, queueptr *tail_of_queue);


int push_lsque(queueptr *head_of_queue, queueptr *tail_of_queue, char *item)
/* Places item in the list-based queue. If the element is
    inserted, a value of 0 is returned; otherwise, 1 is returned. */
{
    queueptr ptr;

    ptr = (queueptr) malloc(sizeof(struct queuestruct));
    if (ptr == NULL) return 1;   /* memory allocation problem */
    strcpy(ptr->queuedata, item);
    if (*head_of_queue != NULL) {
        (*tail_of_queue)->nextptr = ptr;
        *tail_of_queue = ptr;
    }
    else {
        *head_of_queue = ptr;
        *tail_of_queue = ptr;
        ptr->nextptr = NULL;
    }
    return 0; /* element inserted */
}


int pop_lsque(queueptr *head_of_queue, char *item)
/* Returns (and removes) the first queue element. If the
    queue is empty, a value of 1 is returned; otherwise, 0 is
    returned. */
{
    queueptr ptr;
```

```
    if (*head_of_queue != NULL) {
        strcpy(item,(*head_of_queue)->queuedata);
        ptr = *head_of_queue;
        *head_of_queue = (*head_of_queue)->nextptr;
        free(ptr);
        return 0; /* queue not empty; item removed */
    }
    else return 1;  /* queue is empty */
}


void clear_lsque(queueptr *head_of_queue, queueptr *tail_of_queue)
/* deletes the list elements in the queue */
{
    char dummy;

    while (pop_lsque(head_of_queue, &dummy) == 0);
    *tail_of_queue = NULL;
}
```

• Listing 8.7. Turbo Pascal source code for array-based stack library unit

---

```
UNIT StackArr;

CONST MAX_ARRAY_STACK = 100; { size of array }
TYPE
    StackData = STRING[80];
    StackArray = ARRAY [1..MAX_ARRAY_STACK] OF StackData;
    StackArrayRec = RECORD
        Member : StackArray;
        Height : INTEGER;
    END;


PROCEDURE Push_ArStk(
                    VAR Stack      : StackArrayRec;   { in/out }
                        Item       : StackData;       { input  }
                    VAR Full_Stack : BOOLEAN          { output });
{ Pushes Item onto an array-based stack. If the stack is
  already full, the Full_Stack flag is set to TRUE. }
```

```
PROCEDURE Pop_ArStk(
                    VAR   Stack      : StackArrayRec;  { in/out }
                    VAR   Item       : StackData;      { output }
                    VAR   Empty_Stack : BOOLEAN        { output });
{ Returns (and removes) the topmost stack element. If the
  stack is empty, the boolean Empty_Stack is set to true.
  Use this flag to test the status of the stack before you
  attempt to access the data in argument Item. }

PROCEDURE Clear_ArStk(VAR Stack : StackArrayRec { in/out });
{ clears the stack }

{*******************************************************************}
PROCEDURE Push_ArStk(
                    VAR Stack      : StackArrayRec;  { in/out }
                        Item       : StackData;      { input  }
                    VAR Full_Stack : BOOLEAN         { output });
{ pushes Item onto an array-based stack }


BEGIN
   IF Stack.Height < MAX_ARRAY_STACK THEN BEGIN
      WITH Stack DO BEGIN
         INC(Height);
         Member[Height] := Item
      END;
      Full_Stack := FALSE;
   END
   ELSE Full_Stack := TRUE;
END; { Push_ArStk }


PROCEDURE Pop_ArStk(
                    VAR   Stack      : StackArrayRec;  { in/out }
                    VAR   Item       : StackData;      { output }
                    VAR   Empty_Stack : BOOLEAN        { output });
{ returns (and removes) the topmost stack element }


BEGIN
   IF Stack.Height > 0 THEN BEGIN
      WITH Stack DO BEGIN
         Item := Member[Height];
```

```
          DEC(Height);
      END;
      Empty_Stack := FALSE;
   END
   ELSE Empty_Stack := TRUE;
END; { Pop_ArStk }


PROCEDURE Clear_ArStk(VAR Stack : StackArrayRec { in/out });
{ clears the stack }


BEGIN
   Stack.Height := 0;
END; { Clear_ArStk }
END.
```

• Listing 8.8. Turbo Pascal source code for linked list-based stack library unit

```
UNIT StackLst;

TYPE
   StackData = STRING[80];
   StackPtr = ^StackRec;
   StackRec = RECORD
      StackData : StackData;
      NextPtr   : StackPtr
   END;


PROCEDURE Push_LsStk(VAR Top_of_Stack : StackPtr;  { in/out }
                         Item          : StackData { input });
{ pushes Item onto list-based stack }


PROCEDURE Pop_LsStk(VAR Top_of_Stack   : StackPtr;   { in/out }
                        VAR Item        : StackData;  { in/out }
                        VAR Empty_Stack : BOOLEAN     { output });
{ returns (and removes) the topmost stack element }


PROCEDURE Clear_LsStk(VAR Top_of_Stack : StackPtr { in/out });
{ deletes the list of elements forming the stack }
```

```
{**********************************************************************}
PROCEDURE Push_LsStk(VAR Top_of_Stack : StackPtr;   { in/out }
                         Item          : StackData { input });
{ pushes Item onto list-based stack }


VAR ptr : StackPtr;

BEGIN
   NEW(ptr);
   ptr^.StackData := Item;
   ptr^.NextPtr := Top_of_Stack;
   Top_of_Stack := ptr;   { point to new element as the top of the stack }
END; { Push_LsStk }

PROCEDURE Pop_LsStk(VAR Top_of_Stack  : StackPtr;    { in/out }
                        VAR Item          : StackData;   { in/out }
                        VAR Empty_Stack : BOOLEAN       { output });
{ returns (and removes) the topmost stack element }


VAR ptr : StackPtr;

BEGIN
   IF Top_of_Stack <> NIL THEN BEGIN
      Empty_Stack := FALSE;
      Item := Top_of_Stack^.StackData;
      ptr := Top_of_Stack;
      Top_of_Stack := Top_of_Stack^.NextPtr;
      Dispose(ptr)
   END
   ELSE Empty_Stack := TRUE;
END; { Pop_LsStk }

PROCEDURE Clear_LsStk(VAR Top_of_Stack : StackPtr { in/out });
{ deletes the list of elements forming the stack }


VAR done : BOOLEAN;
    dummy : StackData;

BEGIN
   REPEAT
```

```
        Pop_LsStk(Top_of_Stack, dummy, done);
    UNTIL done;
END; { Clear_LsStk }
END.
```

· Listing 8.9. Turbo Pascal source code for array-based queue library unit

```
UNIT QueArr;

CONST MAX_ARRAY_QUEUE = 100; { size of array }
TYPE
    QueueData = STRING[80];
    QueueArray = ARRAY [1..MAX_ARRAY_QUEUE] OF QueueData;
    QueueArrayRec = RECORD
        Member : QueueArray;
        QSize,
        HeadQ,
        TailQ : INTEGER;
    END;


PROCEDURE Push_ArQue(
                    VAR Queue      : QueueArrayRec;  { in/out }
                        Item       : QueueData;      { input  }
                    VAR Full_Queue : BOOLEAN         { output });
{ Pushes Item into an array-based queue. If the queue is
  already full, the Full_Queue flag is set to TRUE. }


PROCEDURE Pop_ArQue(
                    VAR  Queue       : QueueArrayRec; { in/out }
                    VAR  Item        : QueueData;     { output }
                    VAR  Empty_Queue : BOOLEAN        { output });
{ Returns (and removes) the first queue element. If the
  queue is empty, the boolean Empty_Queue is set to true.
  Use this flag to test the status of the queue before you
  attempt to access the data in argument Item. }


PROCEDURE Clear_ArQue(VAR Queue : QueueArrayRec { in/out });
{ clears the queue }
```

```
{*********************************************************************}
PROCEDURE Push_ArQue(
                    VAR Queue      : QueueArrayRec;   { in/out }
                        Item       : QueueData;       { input  }
                    VAR Full_Queue : BOOLEAN          { output });
{ Pushes Item into an array-based queue. If the queue is
  already full, the Full_Queue flag is set to TRUE. }

BEGIN
    IF Queue.QSize < MAX_ARRAY_QUEUE THEN BEGIN
        WITH Queue DO BEGIN
            INC(QSize);
            TailQ := TailQ MOD MAX_ARRAY_QUEUE + 1;
            Member[TailQ] := Item
        END;
        Full_Queue := FALSE;
    END
    ELSE Full_Queue := TRUE;
END; { Push_ArQue }


PROCEDURE Pop_ArQue(
                    VAR  Queue       : QueueArrayRec;   { in/out }
                    VAR  Item        : QueueData;        { output }
                    VAR  Empty_Queue : BOOLEAN           { output });
{ returns (and removes) the first queue element }

BEGIN
    IF Queue.QSize > 0 THEN BEGIN
        WITH Queue DO BEGIN
            Item := Member[HeadQ];
            DEC(QSize);
            HeadQ := HeadQ MOD MAX_ARRAY_QUEUE + 1;
        END;
        Empty_Queue := FALSE;
    END
    ELSE Empty_Queue := TRUE;
END; { Pop_ArQue }

PROCEDURE Clear_ArQue(VAR Queue : QueueArrayRec { in/out });
{ clears the queue }
```

```
BEGIN
    WITH Queue DO BEGIN
        QSize := 0;
        HeadQ := 1;
        TailQ := 0;
    END;
END; { Clear_ArQue }
END.
```

• Listing 8.10. Turbo Pascal source code for linked list-based queue library unit

```
UNIT QueLst;

TYPE
    QueueData = STRING[80];
    QueuePtr = ^QueueRec;
    QueueRec = RECORD
        QueueData : QueueData;
        NextPtr   : QueuePtr
    END;

PROCEDURE Push_LsQue(VAR Head_of_Queue,                    { in/out }
                         Tail_Of_Queue  : QueuePtr; { in/out }
                         Item           : QueueData { input  });
{ pushes Item into list-based queue }



PROCEDURE Pop_LsQue(VAR Head_of_Queue : QueuePtr; { in/out }
                    VAR Item          : QueueData; { in/out }
                    VAR Empty_Queue   : BOOLEAN    { output });
{ Returns (and removes) the first queue element. If the
  queue is empty, the boolean Empty_Queue is set to true.
  Use this flag to test the status of the queue before you
  attempt to access the data in argument Item. }

PROCEDURE Clear_LsQue(VAR Head_of_Queue,                    { in/out }
                          Tail_of_Queue  : QueuePtr { in/out });
{ deletes the list of elements forming the queue }
```

```
{*******************************************************************}
PROCEDURE Push_LsQue(VAR Head_of_Queue,                { in/out }
                         Tail_Of_Queue  : QueuePtr;     { in/out }
                         Item           : QueueData     { input });
{ pushes Item into list-based queue }


VAR ptr : QueuePtr;


BEGIN
   NEW(ptr);
   ptr^.QueueData := Item;
   IF Head_of_Queue <> NIL THEN BEGIN
      Tail_of_Queue^.NextPtr := ptr;
      Tail_of_Queue := ptr;
   END
   ELSE BEGIN
      Head_of_Queue := ptr;
      Tail_of_Queue := ptr;
      ptr^.NextPtr := NIL
   END;
END; { Push_LsQue }

PROCEDURE Pop_LsQue(VAR Head_of_Queue : QueuePtr;    { in/out }
                    VAR Item          : QueueData;   { in/out }
                    VAR Empty_Queue   : BOOLEAN      { output });
{ returns (and removes) the first queue element }


VAR ptr : QueuePtr;


BEGIN
   IF Head_of_Queue <> NIL THEN BEGIN
      Empty_Queue := FALSE;
      Item := Head_of_Queue^.QueueData;
      ptr := Head_of_Queue;
      Head_of_Queue := Head_of_Queue^.NextPtr;
      Dispose(ptr)
   END
   ELSE Empty_Queue := TRUE;
END; { Pop_LsQue }
```

```
PROCEDURE Clear_LsQue(VAR Head_of_Queue,                { in/out }
                          Tail_of_Queue  : QueuePtr { in/out });
{ deletes the list of elements forming the queue }

VAR done : BOOLEAN;
    dummy : QueueData;

BEGIN
    REPEAT
        Pop_LsQue(Head_of_Queue, dummy, done);
    UNTIL done;
    Tail_of_Queue := NIL;
END; { Clear_LsQue }
END.
```

• Listing 8.11. Turbo Prolog source code for linked list-based stacks and queues

```
% Turbo Prolog implementation of the stack and queue processing routines

domains
    symlist = symbol*

predicates
    push_stk(symlist, symbol, symlist)
    pop_stk(symlist, symbol, symlist)
    push_queue(symlist, symbol, symlist)
    pop_queue(symlist, symbol, symlist)

clauses
    push_stk([], Item, [Item]).
    push_stk([H | Tail1], Item, [H | Tail2]) :-
        push_stk(Tail1, Item, Tail2), !.

    pop_stk([H | T], H, []) :-
        T = [].
    pop_stk([H | T], Item, [H | T2]) :- !,
        pop_stk(T, Item, T2).

    push_queue([], Item, [Item]).
```

```
push_queue([H | Tail1], Item, [H | Tail2]) :-
    push_queue(Tail1, Item, Tail2), !.

pop_queue([H | T], H, T).
```

Binary Trees

Introduction

We designed all of the algorithms for processing the data structures throughout this book to work with simple variations of the linear list. In many cases, linear lists provide enough flexibility to efficiently represent the data that is required by our programs. Unfortunately, lists are inefficient data structures for storing data that must be searched—especially if the data set is large. We can, however, use a more powerful data structure called the *tree*, which is a derivation of a linked list.

In this section we present the algorithms for processing the most popular form of the tree data structure called the *binary tree*, and in Section 10 we introduce a more powerful extension of the binary tree called the *AVL tree*. We'll explain how binary trees are represented, and then we'll write a set of routines in each of the Turbo languages for creating and manipulating binary trees. We'll show you how binary trees can be represented with arrays (Turbo BASIC), linked lists (Turbo C and Pascal), and recursive domain types (Turbo Prolog). Because of the different implementations used to reflect the unique features of each Turbo language, this section provides you with a broad assortment of binary tree processing algorithms.

Overview of the Binary Tree

To start, examine how binary trees are different than the simple linked lists introduced in the previous two sections. If you remember from our discussions, a linked list is represented as a sequence of nodes linked by pointers, as shown in Figure 9.1. Remember that each node can only point to one other node. Binary trees are also composed of nodes; however, a node in a binary tree can be linked to more than one node. In fact, each node in

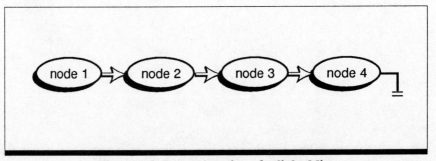

Figure 9.1. Representation of a linked list

a binary tree may serve as the start or what is called the *root* of an inner tree called a *subtree*.

We'll illustrate how trees work with an example. Figure 9.2 shows a tree with three nodes. Node A is called the *root* of the tree; it points to two other nodes, B and C. Both of these nodes serve as roots of subtrees. Node B is the left subtree of node A and node C is the right subtree of node A. In binary tree terminology, node B is called the *left child* of node A and node C is called the *right child* of node A. Because nodes B and C don't point to any other nodes, they are called *terminal nodes*. Figure 9.3 presents an expansion of the binary tree shown in Figure 9.2. In this figure, nodes B and C also serve as roots of subtrees.

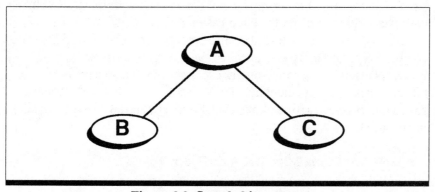

Figure 9.2. Sample binary tree

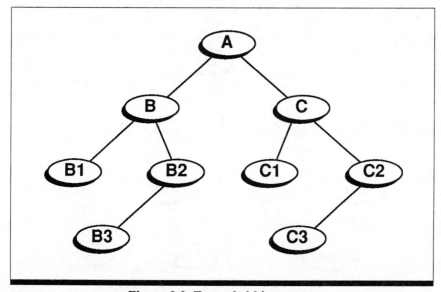

Figure 9.3. Expanded binary tree

The main thing you should realize from our description of binary trees is that they are natural recursive data structures. What is a recursive data structure? Essentially, it is a structure that is defined in terms of itself. (Binary trees are composed of left and right subtrees, which can themselves be composed of left and right subtrees, and so on.) Because of their recursive nature, binary trees are relatively easy to process. In fact, all of the main operations performed on binary trees, such as inserting and deleting elements, can be implemented as recursive procedures. When you attempt to represent binary trees in Turbo C and Pascal, you'll see that pointers must be used to simulate the recursive nature of a tree node structure. Pointers are required in these languages, because recursive data types are not supported. In Turbo Prolog, on the other hand, we can define true recursive data types, and therefore trees are easier to represent.

Binary trees often store data in some prearranged order. The most common type of binary tree is called the *sorted tree*. In such a tree, data is always inserted in a sorted order. The order of the nodes provides a very efficient structure for searching. To illustrate this point, we'll compare a sorted binary tree to a sorted linked list. First, let's start with a set of random names as shown:

Lori Zak Pete Gloria Mike Hal Alex Eileen Tom

Figures 9.4 and 9.5 show the linked list and sorted tree that represent these names. The tree is constructed by taking the first name, Lori, and making

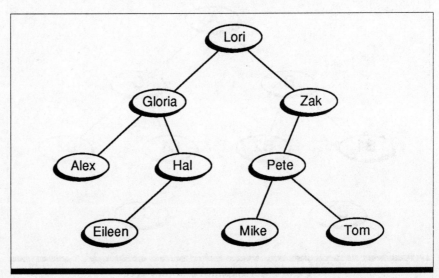

Figure 9.4. Linked list of names

it the root of the tree. We then take the second name, Zak, and insert it as the right child of Lori. The third name, Pete, is greater than the root Lori but less than the node Zak, so it becomes the left child of Zak. By this discussion you should see that the following two rules apply:

1. If a node is greater than a root node, insert it as a right child.
2. If a node is less than a root node, insert it as a left child.

Once the tree is represented, we use the same two rules to search it. But notice that in the worst case we only must examine four nodes. For instance, if we're searching for the node Tom, we would start with Lori, go right to Zak, left to Pete, and right to Tom. Now compare this to the linked list, where the worst case search (Zak) requires nine comparisons.

Representing Binary Trees

Binary trees are usually implemented with language-specific data structures such as Pascal records and C structures. In addition, pointers and dynamic memory allocation techniques are used to process trees. Trees can also be represented with simple arrays. In fact, we'll use arrays to represent binary trees in Turbo BASIC, because BASIC does not provide record structures or pointers. When we cover the Turbo BASIC implementation later in this section, we explain how binary trees are represented with arrays. For now, we'll concentrate on how trees are represented with dynamic structures.

The first step in representing a tree is coming up with a basic tree node. For each node, we need a component for storing the node's data and two pointers (one each to access the left and right child of the node). To illustrate

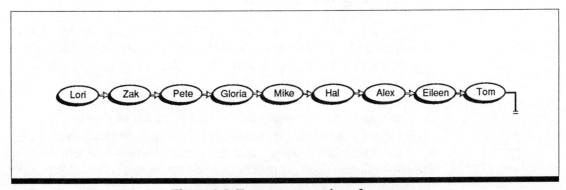

Figure 9.5. Tree representation of names

how a tree node can be represented, let's examine the record structure used in our Turbo Pascal implementation:

```
TreePtr = ^Binary_Tree_Rec;
   Binary_Tree_Rec = RECORD
      TreeData : TreeDataRec;
      Left, Right : TreePtr;
   END;
```

The component **TreeData** holds the node's data key, and the pointers **Left** and **Right** access the node's left and right subtrees. If a node does not have a left or right subtree, the appropriate subtree pointer is set to a null value. Each time a new node is added to a tree, memory is allocated for the node and linked in at its proper position.

Processing Binary Trees

As we've seen, the recursive nature of the binary tree structure lends itself to recursive operations. Our next goal is to explain how the following operations are performed with binary trees.

- Searching for a node
- Inserting a node
- Traversing a tree
- Deleting a node
- Removing a tree

Searching for a Node

The most important binary tree operation is perhaps the tree search operation. In fact, it is not only used to locate a given tree node but to insert a node and to delete a node as well. To search a binary tree, we start at the root node and follow these steps:

1. The search key is compared with the key of the root node.
2. If the keys are equal, the search stops with a successful find.
3. If the search key is greater than the root key, the search resumes with the right subtree. The right node is treated like the root node and you return to step 1. If the root has no right child node, the search halts.

4. If the search key is less than the root key, the search resumes with the left subtree. The left node is treated like the root node and you return to step 1. If the root has no left child node, the search halts.

We'll illustrate how the tree search algorithm works with a simple example. Figure 9.6 presents a tree that we'll search. If we wanted to search for the name Fran, the tree would be examined in the following manner.

1. Start with the root node:
   Fran < Jack
2. Go to the root's left subtree:
   Fran < George
3. Go to George's left subtree:
   Fran > Eileen
4. Go to Eileen's right subtree:
   Fran = Fran
5. Stop the search because the key is found.

Inserting a Node

The node insertion operation is an extension of the search operation just presented. Follow these steps to insert a node.

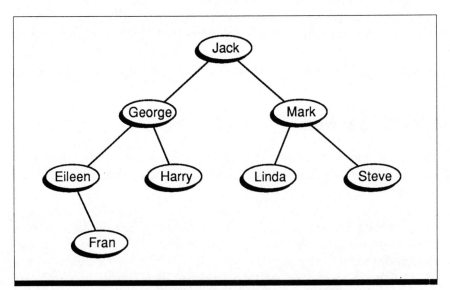

Figure 9.6. Tree used for search example

1. Allocate memory for a new node structure.
2. Search a tree to find the insertion position for the new node.
3. Link in the new node.

To search a tree for an insertion position, a design decision must be made regarding duplicate keys. If you want to allow for duplicate keys, modify the search steps we presented earlier by removing step 2 and making step 3 use the logical >= test. By contrast, if you do not allow duplicate keys, a successful search should result in exiting the insertion routine without adding a duplicate node.

Once the insertion position for the node is found, the node is linked into the tree by assigning it to either the right or left link of a current tree node. If the tree is empty, the new node becomes the root of the tree.

Tree Traversal

Traversing binary trees is accomplished in any one of three recursive methods: preorder, inorder, or postorder. With the *preorder traversal*, you visit and/or access a node, its left child node, and its right child node, in that order. Using the *inorder traversal*, you first visit the left child node, then the node itself, and finally the right child node. The inorder traversal enables you to access the node keys of the binary trees in ascending sorted order. The *postorder traversal* first visits the left child node, then the right child node, and finally the node itself. In implementing a routine to traverse a binary tree, we employ the inorder traversal. Converting the code to implement the other traversal modes is a simple matter of rearranging a few statements in the traversal routine.

Deleting a Node

Deleting a node from a binary tree is more elaborate than the insertion. Here are the following possible node deletion cases to consider. They are also shown in Figure 9.7.

1. Deleting a leaf node. This is the simplest case, because the removed node has no descendants. Removing the node from the binary tree is very straightforward.
2. Deleting a node with one empty subtree. This case occurs when the

deleted node has either a left or right subtree, but not both. The steps involve linking the root of the subtree with the parent node of the deleted node. 3. Deleting a node with nonempty subtrees. This case is handled by one of two methods that are mirror images of each other. The first technique promotes the left subtree and links the right subtree with a proper node in the promoted left subtree. The second performs essentially the same task, but switches the role of the left and right subtrees.

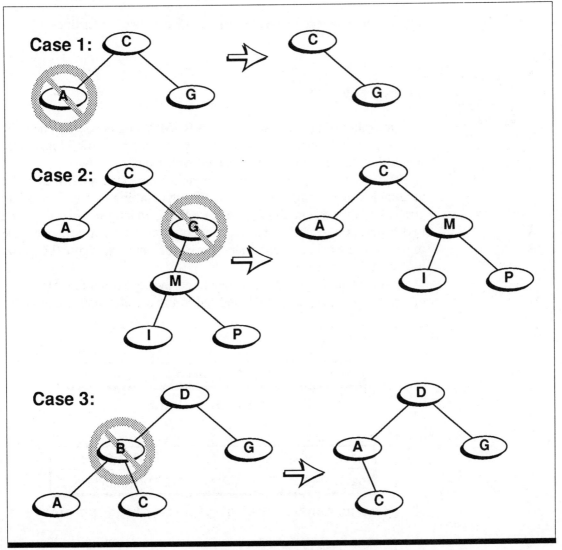

Figure 9.7. Node deletion cases

Removing a Tree

The last operation we'll cover is removing a binary tree. For this operation, we use the inorder traversal to visit each node. When a node is visited, its memory space is deallocated.

Implementations of the Binary Trees

The implementations of the binary trees are presented in Listings 9.1, 9.2, 9.3, and 9.4.

Turbo BASIC

Dynamic allocation is not supported in BASIC, so a binary tree must be implemented with arrays. Our goal here is to show you how a binary tree for storing strings can be implemented with simple arrays.

The basic principles for implementing a binary tree in BASIC are not as complex as you might think. The fundamental ingredients involve an array of strings to store the data for each node, which we'll call *keys*, and two paired arrays used as pseudopointers. The latter two arrays can be replaced by a single two-dimensional array or a matrix. Figure 9.8 shows the general storage scheme.

As elements are added to the binary tree, the keys are stored in the array of strings and new pointers are updated in the pseudopointers matrix. So

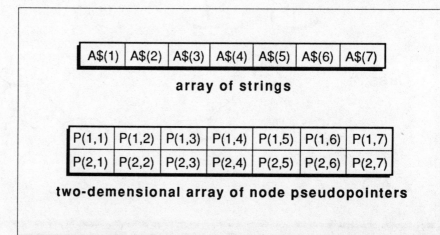

Figure 9.8. Storage scheme for binary trees in BASIC

far the arrays are easy to maintain until we attempt to delete a node and reuse its space. The complexity increases because any node can be deleted, which creates vacant elements scattered throughout the arrays.

The binary tree node deletion problem can be solved by forming a link of deleted nodes. At first, we are tempted to employ yet another array to track the chain of such deleted elements. This is avoided by using one of the two rows in the pseudopointers matrix. We arbitrarily choose the second row to form the index to the chain of deleted nodes.

The above strategy is further enhanced by considering all of the array-based nodes as initially deleted, except the root of the new tree. This simplifies the algorithm, which otherwise must make a distinction between deleted nodes and unused nodes. Avoiding this distinction also reduces the code overhead. Thus, initially we start with the root of the tree and a chain of deleted nodes in one perfect sequence. Before any tree node is deleted, the boundary between the occupied and vacant array elements is unique. That boundary is where the chain of deleted nodes begins, and the end of the array is where the chain terminates. Once node deletion occurs, the tail of the chain extends to the deleted elements in a (most likely) random sequence. The second row of the pseudopointers matrix keeps track of the chain of deleted elements throughout the insertions and deletions. However, two additional pseudopointers are needed to keep track of the head and tail of the chain for the deleted nodes. We use two scalar variables for that purpose.

Listing 9.1 contains the code for the Turbo BASIC binary tree processing routines. The library exports the following constants and declarations:

```
'OPTION BASE 1
$STACK 10000

' Define constants
%NIL = 0
%TRUE = 1
%FALSE = 0
%LEFT = 1
%RIGHT = 2
%CHAIN = 2
```

The **%LEFT** and **%RIGHT** constants are used to designate the left and right pseudopointer links. Using named constants makes the code more readable than using just numbers. In addition, the **%CHAIN** constant is used for two purposes. First, it indicates which row of the pseudopointers matrix is used to maintain the link of deleted nodes. Second, we use **%CHAIN** with the pseudopointers matrix whenever we want to indicate that a matrix element is used for the chain of deleted nodes, as opposed to maintaining the links between the tree nodes. The BASIC routines in the library are described next.

Init.BinTree

Initializes the arrays and indices used to implement the binary tree. This routine also inserts the root of the binary tree.

Syntax:
```
SUB Init.BinTree(Item$, Root%, Bin.Tree$(1), Ptr%(2),_
                 First%, Last%, Num.Nodes%)
```

Parameters:

Item$	the root of the new binary tree.
Root%	the root of the binary tree.
Bin.Tree$()	the array containing the string-typed keys of the tree.
Ptr%()	the matrix of pseudopointers.
First%	the first vacant array element.
Last%	the last vacant array element.
Num.Nodes%	the number of nodes in the binary tree.

Insert.BinTree

Inserts a new data item in a binary tree. This routine is implemented with recursion.

Syntax:
```
SUB Insert.BinTree(Item$, Root%, Bin.Tree$(1), Ptr%(2),_
                   First%, Last%, Num.Nodes%, OK%)
```

Parameters:

Item$	the item inserted in the binary tree.
Root%	the root of the binary tree.
Bin.Tree$()	the array of strings that store the key data of the binary tree.
Ptr%()	the matrix of pseudopointers.
First%	the first vacant array element.
Last%	the last vacant array element.

Num.Nodes%	the number of nodes in the binary tree.
OK%	a flag that indicates the status of the insertion operation.

Searches for a certain occurrence of a key in a binary tree. This assumes that the binary tree allows duplicate keys. If no match is found, the function returns a 0. If the key is encountered fewer times than desired, then the function's value reports that actual number. A successful search should return the same specified occurrence number via the parameter **Index%**.

Search.BinTree

Syntax:
```
SUB Search.BinTree(Item$, Occur%, Index%, Root%,_
                   Bin.Tree$(1), Ptr%(2), First%, Last%)
```

Parameters:

Item$	the item searched for in the binary tree.
Occur%	the occurrence of the sought item.
Index%	the array index of the matching element. A 0 indicates that the search failed.
Root%	the root of the binary tree.
Bin.Tree$()	the array of strings that store the key data of the binary tree.
Ptr%()	the matrix of pseudopointers.
First%	the first vacant array element.
Last%	the last vacant array element.

Visits the nodes of the binary trees and copies their data into an array. This operation supplies you with an ascending ordered array.

Get.Sorted.Array

Syntax:
```
SUB Get.Sorted.Array(Root%, Bin.Tree$(1), Ptr%(2),_
                     Tree.Ptr%(1))
```

Parameters:

Root%	the root of the binary tree.
Bin.Tree$()	the array of strings that store the binary tree's key data.
Ptr%()	the matrix of pseudopointers.
Tree.Ptr%()	the array of indices that store the ascending order of the tree nodes. The array is initialized with **%NIL** value.

Deletes a node specified by the supplied key and the occurrence number. If the specified key is found and the deletion is successful, the value of **Found%** matches that of **Occur%**.

Delete.Tree

Syntax:
```
SUB Delete.Tree(Item$, Occur%, Root%, Bin.Tree$(1),_
                Ptr%(2), First%, Last%, Num.Nodes%, Found%)
```

Parameters:

Item$	the item to be deleted from the binary tree.
Occur%	the occurrence of **Item$** to be deleted.
Root%	the root of the binary tree.
Bin.Tree$()	the array of strings storing the key data of the binary tree.
Ptr%()	the matrix of pseudopointers.
First%	the first vacant array element.
Last%	the last vacant array element.
Num.Nodes%	the number of nodes in the binary tree.
Found%	the number of times the **Item$** was found in the tree. If it is equal to **Occur%**, deletion has occurred.

Turbo C

Listing 9.2 contains the source code for the binary tree processing routines in Turbo C. The routines use the following data structure to represent a tree node:

```
/* basic tree node */
struct treestruct  {
   struct treedatarec treedata;
   treeptr left, right;
};
```

As shown, this structure contains three components: a structure to store the data for each node, a left node pointer, and a right node pointer. The data type of the node pointers is defined with the following **typedef** statement:

```
typedef struct treestruct *treeptr;
```

Another structure that is used is the **treedatarec,** as shown:

```
struct treedatarec {
   char key[STRING_SIZE];
   /*  put other fields here */
};
```

Because this structure is used to define the data type for the **treedata** component of the node structure, it determines how the key of the node is stored. To create your own custom version of the binary tree routines, you will probably want to add other fields to this structure.

The last definition you'll find in Listing 9.2 is for the **treerecarray** identifier, as shown:

```
typedef struct treedatarec treerecarray;
```

This data type is used to declare the array that is used to copy the visited tree nodes into an array. The resulting array contains data sorted, by the values of the node keys, in ascending order.

The main functions for processing binary trees in Turbo C are presented next.

Inserts a new node in a binary tree. This routine is implemented with recursion.

insert_binary()

Syntax:
```
int insert_bintree(treeptr *root, struct treedatarec item);
```

Parameters:
*root   the pointer to the root of the binary tree.
item   the item inserted in the binary tree.

Searches for a specified occurrence of a key in a binary tree. This assumes that the binary tree allows duplicate keys. If no match is found, the function returns a 0. If the key is encountered fewer times than desired, then the function's value reports that actual number. A successful search should return the same specified occurrence number.

search_bintree()

Syntax:
```
int search_bintree(treeptr root, struct treedatarec item,
                   int freq);
```

Parameters:
root   the pointer to the root of the binary tree.
item   the item searched for in the binary tree.
freq   the occurrence of the searched-for item.

sort_to_array()   Visits the nodes of the binary trees and copies them into an array. This operation supplies you with an ascending ordered array. This routine employs another local recursive procedure, called **traverse_tree**.

If there are more nodes in the binary tree than the storage capacity of the array, the surplus nodes are not included in the array. You can detect this when the returned value exceeds the value of the macro **MAX_TREE_NODES**.

Syntax:
```
int sort_to_array(treeptr root, treerecarray *sortx);
```

Parameters:
root   the pointer to the root of the binary tree.
*sortx   the array of nodes ordered in an ascending fashion.

delete_bintree()   Deletes a node specified by the supplied key and the occurrence number. The function returns a pointer to the new root of the tree. This function uses recursion to locate the node to delete.

Syntax:
```
treeptr delete_bintree(treeptr root, struct treedatarec item,
                       int freq);
```

Parameters:
root   the pointer to the root of the binary tree.
item   the item to be deleted from the binary tree.
freq   the occurrence of **item** to be deleted.

remove_tree()   Removes an entire binary tree and deallocates the memory space occupied by the tree nodes.

Syntax:
```
int remove_tree(treeptr *root);
```

Parameter:
*root   the pointer to the root of the binary tree.

Turbo Pascal

Listing 9.3 contains the library unit for the binary tree processing routines in Turbo Pascal. The library exports the following constants and data types:

```
CONST MAX_TREE_NODES = 100;
TYPE BinTreeStr = STRING[40];
    TreeDataRec = RECORD
        Key : BinTreeStr;
        { ***** put other fields here ***** }
    END;
    TreePtr = ^Binary_Tree_Rec;
    Binary_Tree_Rec = RECORD
        TreeData : TreeDataRec;
        Left, Right : TreePtr;
    END;
    TreeRecArray = ARRAY [1..MAX_TREE_NODES] OF TreeDataRec;
```

The most important structure is the record **Binary_Tree_Rec**. It defines the basic structure for the binary tree node. The **TreeDataRec** record is used to define at least the key of the node. To create your own custom version of the library, you can add other fields to this record.

The **TreeRecArray** copies the visited tree nodes into an array. The resulting array contains data sorted in ascending order by the values of the node key. The exported routines in the library are described next.

Inserts a new node in a binary tree. This routine is implemented with recursion. **Insert_Binary**

Syntax:
```
PROCEDURE Insert_BinTree(VAR Root : TreePtr; X : TreeDataRec);
```

Parameters:
Root   the root of the binary tree.
X   the item inserted in the binary tree.

Searches for a specified occurrence of a key in a binary tree. This assumes that the binary tree allows duplicate keys. If no match is found, the function returns a 0. If the key is encountered fewer times than desired, then the function's value reports that actual number. A successful search should return the same specified occurrence number. **Search_BinTree**

Syntax:
```
FUNCTION Search_BinTree(Root         : TreePtr;
                        X            : TreeDataRec;
                        Occurrence_Num : WORD) : WORD;
```

Parameters:

Root	the root of the binary tree.
X	the item searched for in the binary tree.
Occurrence_Num	the occurrence of the searched-for item.

Sort_to_Array

Visits the nodes of the binary trees and copies them into an array. This operation supplies you with an ascending ordered array. This routine employs another recursive procedure, called **traverse_tree**, that is not exported by the library. The procedure **Sort_to_Array** serves only to initialize the counter for the array size and launch the first call to the recursive **traverse_tree**.

If there are more nodes in the binary tree than the storage capacity of the array, the surplus nodes are not included in the array. You can detect this when the returned **Count** parameter exceeds the value of the constant **MAX_TREE_NODES**. The difference between **Count** and **MAX_TREE_NODES** gives you the number of surplus nodes.

Syntax:
```
PROCEDURE Sort_to_Array(    Root  : TreePtr;
                        VAR SortX : TreeRecArray;
                        VAR Count : WORD);
```

Parameters:

Root	the root of the binary tree.
SortX	the array of nodes ordered in an ascending fashion.
Count	the number of tree nodes in the array **SortItem**.

Delete_BinTree

Deletes a node specified by the supplied key and the occurrence number. The function returns **TRUE** if the supplied key is found and the deletion is successful; otherwise, a **FALSE** boolean value is obtained. This function uses function **find_node** to return the pointer to the search key.

Syntax:
```
FUNCTION Delete_BinTree(VAR Root  : TreePtr;
                            X     : TreeDataRec;
                            Occur : WORD) : BOOLEAN;
```

Parameters:

Root	the root of the binary tree.
X	the item to be deleted from the binary tree.
Occur	the occurrence of **Item** to be deleted.

Removes an entire binary tree and deallocates the memory space occupied by the tree nodes. The logical value returned by this function has no meaning to the calling program. Instead, it is used during the recursive function calls.

Syntax:

```
FUNCTION Remove_Tree(VAR Root : TreePtr) : BOOLEAN;
```

Parameter:

Root   the root of the binary tree.

Turbo Prolog

Because of Turbo Prolog's natural method of handling recursive predicates and recursive data types, binary trees are easy to represent and process. Like the list processing algorithms we presented in earlier chapters, the binary tree routines are much simpler than the Pascal and C versions, because we don't have to use pointers or memory allocation.

To understand how the binary tree processing predicates work, let's start with the basic tree structure. In Turbo Prolog, we define our tree using the following domain declaration:

```
domains
    bintreetype = tree(symbol, bintreetype, bintreetype); nil
```

This domain type called **bintreetype** states that our tree contains a functor called **tree**, and its arguments include a node declared as a symbol and a left subtree and a right subtree. Notice that **bintreetype** can be the functor **tree** or **nil**. The **nil** functor is required so that we can represent trees that don't have right or left child nodes.

The most interesting characteristic of this domain definition is that it is truly recursive. If you compare it to either of the tree structures used in the Turbo C or Pascal implementations, you'll see that the Prolog data structure is more efficient and natural. For instance, in the following C structure:

```
/* basic tree node */
struct treestruct {
    struct treedatarec treedata;
    treeptr left, right; };
```

notice that we must use a pointer to link a tree node to a right or left child node. In Turbo Prolog, the linking is done for us because of the true recursive nature of the data structure used.

To represent a tree, we simply nest the **tree** functors. For instance, the following statement defines a valid binary tree:

```
tree(Node_A,
    tree(Node_B, nil,
        tree(Node_D,nil,nil)),
    tree(Node_C,
        tree(Node_E,nil,nil), nil))
```

The tree defined by this statement is shown in Figure 9.9.

Listing 9.4 contains the source code for the binary tree processing routines in Turbo Prolog. Notice that we've also included a simple test driver predicate called **tree_driver** so that you can see how the binary tree predicates are called to process trees. The following descriptions of the binary tree predicates are included for a quick reference.

insert_bintree   Inserts a new node in a binary tree. This predicate is implemented with recursion.

Syntax:
```
insert_bintree(Item, OldTree, NewTree)      (i,i,o)
                (symbol, bintreetype, bintreetype)
```

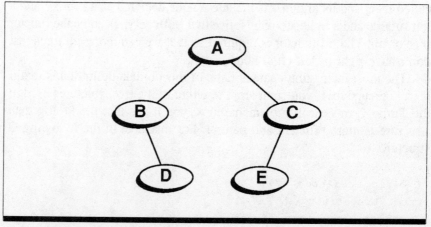

Figure 9.9. Tree representation of Turbo Prolog statement

Parameters:

Item   the item inserted in the binary tree.
OldTree   the tree where the item is inserted.
NewTree   the tree containing the new item.

Searches for a specified occurrence of a key in a binary tree. If no match   **search_bintree**
is found, the predicate fails; otherwise, it succeeds.

Syntax:
```
search_bintree(Item, BinTree)      (i,i)
                (symbol, bintreetype)
```

Parameters:

Item   the item searched for in the binary tree.
BinTree   the tree to search.

Deletes a specified node from a binary tree. This predicate uses recursion   **delete_bintree**
to locate the node to delete.

Syntax:
```
delete_bintree(Item, OldTree, NewTree)      (i,i,o)
                (symbol, bintreetype, bintreetype)
```

Parameters:

Item   the item to be deleted from the binary tree.
OldTree   the tree containing the item node to delete.
NewTree   the tree with the item node deleted.

Prints the nodes in a tree using inorder traversal.   **prttree**

Syntax:
```
prttree(BinTree)      (i)
        (bintreetype)
```

Parameter:

BinTree   the binary tree to display.

• Listing 9.1. Turbo BASIC source code for the binary tree library

---

```
'--------- user's program declarations --------
OPTION BASE 1
DEFINT A-Z
$STACK 10000

'----------- Library starts here -------------
' define constants
%NIL = 0
%TRUE = 1
%FALSE = 0
%LEFT = 1
%RIGHT = 2
%CHAIN = 2


SUB Init.BinTree(Item$, Root%, Bin.Tree$(1), Ptr%(2), First%, Last%,_
                 Num.Nodes%)
' initializes the binary tree
LOCAL I%, N%
Bin.Tree$(1) = Item$
Ptr%(%LEFT, 1) = %NIL
Ptr%(%RIGHT, 1) = %NIL
Num.Nodes% = 1
N% = UBound(Bin.Tree$(1))
' initialize right pointers to set chain of vacant elements
FOR I% = 2 TO N% - 1
    Ptr%(%CHAIN, I%) = I% + 1
NEXT I%
Ptr%(%CHAIN, N%) = %NIL
First% = 2   ' first available vacant array element
Last% = N%   ' last available vacant array element
Root% = 1
END SUB ' Init.BinTree


SUB Search.BinTree(Item$, Index%, Root%, Bin.Tree$(1), Ptr%(2), First%,_
                   Last%)
' searches for Item$ and returns Index% if found
Found% = %FALSE
Index% = Root%
```

```
DO WHILE (Index% <> %NIL) AND (Found% = %FALSE)
   IF Bin.Tree$(Index%) = Item$ THEN
      Found% = %TRUE
   ELSE
      IF Bin.Tree$(Index%) < Item$ THEN
         Index% = Ptr%(%RIGHT, Index%)
      ELSE
         Index% = Ptr%(%LEFT, Index%)
      END IF
   END IF
LOOP
END SUB ' Search.BinTree


SUB Insert.BinTree(Item$, Root%, Bin.Tree$(1), Ptr%(2), First%, Last%,_
                Num.Nodes%, OK%)
' inserts Item$ in the binary tree structure
LOCAL Index%, Found%, NextPtr%
IF First% = 0 THEN ' tree is full?
   OK% = %FALSE
   EXIT SUB
END IF
OK% = %TRUE
Index% = Root%
Found% = %FALSE
DO WHILE Found% <> %TRUE
   IF Bin.Tree$(Index%) < Item$ THEN
      IF Ptr%(%RIGHT, Index%) <> %NIL THEN
         Index% = Ptr%(%RIGHT, Index%)
      ELSE
         NextPtr% = Ptr%(%CHAIN, First%)
         Ptr%(%RIGHT, Index%) = First%
         Index% = First%
         First% = NextPtr%
         Found% = %TRUE
      END IF
   ELSE
      IF Ptr%(%LEFT, Index%) <> %NIL THEN
         Index% = Ptr%(%LEFT, Index%)
      ELSE
         NextPtr% = Ptr%(%CHAIN, First%)
```

```
            Ptr%(%LEFT, Index%) = First%
            Index% = First%
            First% = NextPtr%
            Found% = %TRUE
        END IF
    END IF
LOOP
Bin.Tree$(Index%) = Item$
Ptr%(%RIGHT, Index%) = %NIL
Ptr%(%LEFT, Index%) = %NIL
INCR Num.Nodes%
END SUB ' Insert.BinTree


SUB Delete.BinTree(Item$, Root%, Bin.Tree$(1), Ptr%(2), First%, Last%,_
                  Num.Nodes%, Found%)
' deletes Item$ in the binary tree structure
LOCAL Index%, LastIndex%, NextPtr%, Direction%
IF Num.Nodes% < 1 THEN
    Found% = %FALSE
    EXIT SUB
END IF
Index% = Root%
Found% = %FALSE
Direction% = %NIL
LastIndex% = %NIL
DO WHILE (Index% <> %NIL) AND (Found% = %FALSE)
    IF Bin.Tree$(Index%) = Item$ THEN
        Found% = %TRUE
    ELSE
        IF Bin.Tree$(Index%) < Item$ THEN
            LastIndex% = Index%
            Direction% = %RIGHT
            Index% = Ptr%(%RIGHT, Index%)
        ELSE
            LastIndex% = Index%
            Direction% = %LEFT
            Index% = Ptr%(%LEFT, Index%)
        END IF
    END IF
LOOP
```

```
IF Found% = %FALSE THEN EXIT SUB
' delete matching item
Bin.Tree$(Index%) = ""
IF Ptr%(%RIGHT, Index%) = %NIL THEN    ' reconnect left subtree
    IF LastIndex% <> %NIL THEN  ' delete nonroot node
        Ptr%(Direction%, LastIndex%) = Ptr%(%LEFT, Index%)
    ELSE  ' delete root
        Root% = Ptr%(%LEFT, Index%)
    END IF
    Ptr%(%LEFT, Index%) = %NIL
ELSEIF Ptr%(%LEFT, Index%) = %NIL THEN ' reconnect right subtree
    IF LastIndex% <> %NIL THEN  ' delete nonroot node
        Ptr%(Direction%, LastIndex%) = Ptr%(%RIGHT, Index%)
    ELSE  ' delete root
        Root% = Ptr%(%RIGHT, Index%)
    END IF
    Ptr%(%RIGHT, Index%) = %NIL
ELSE
    NextPtr% = Ptr%(%RIGHT, Index%)
    DO WHILE Ptr%(%LEFT, NextPtr%) <> %NIL
        NextPtr% = Ptr%(%LEFT, NextPtr%)
    LOOP
    Ptr%(%LEFT, NextPtr%) = Ptr%(%LEFT, Index%)
    IF LastIndex% <> %NIL THEN  ' delete a nonroot node
        Ptr%(Direction%, LastIndex%) = Ptr%(%RIGHT, Index%)
    ELSE  ' delete root
        Root% = Ptr%(%RIGHT, Index%)
    END IF
    Ptr%(%LEFT, Index%) = %NIL
    Ptr%(%RIGHT, Index%) = %NIL
END IF
Ptr%(%CHAIN, Last%) = Index%
Last% = Index%
DECR Num.Nodes%
END SUB ' Delete.BinTree

SUB Traverse.BinTree(Root%, Bin.Tree$(1), Ptr%(2), Tree.Ptr%(1),_
                     Node.Count%)
' traverses the binary tree using recursion
IF Root% <> %NIL THEN
```

```
      CALL Traverse.BinTree(Ptr%(%LEFT, Root%), Bin.Tree$(), Ptr%(),_
                      Tree.Ptr%(), Node.Count%)
      INCR Node.Count%
      Tree.Ptr%(Node.Count%) = Root%
      CALL Traverse.BinTree(Ptr%(%RIGHT, Root%), Bin.Tree$(), Ptr%(),_
                      Tree.Ptr%(), Node.Count%)
END IF
END SUB ' Traverse.BinTree

SUB Get.Sorted.Array(Root%, Bin.Tree$(1), Ptr%(2), Tree.Ptr%(1))
' obtains an array of pointers for the sorted list
LOCAL L%
FOR L% = 1 TO UBound(Tree.Ptr%(1))
   Tree.Ptr%(L%) = %NIL
NEXT L%
' start at the root of the tree and a zero node count
CALL Traverse.BinTree(Root%, Bin.Tree$(), Ptr%(), Tree.Ptr%(), 0)
END SUB ' Get.Sorted.Array
```

Listing 9.2. Turbo C source code for the binary tree library

```c
#include <stdio.h>
#include <alloc.h>
#include <string.h>
#define TRUE 1
#define FALSE 0
#define STRING_SIZE 40
#define MAX_TREE_NODES  100

typedef struct treestruct *treeptr;
struct treedatarec {
   char key[STRING_SIZE];
   /* put other fields here */
};

   /* basic tree node */
struct treestruct {
   struct treedatarec treedata;
   treeptr left, right;
};
```

```
typedef struct treedatarec treerecarray;

/* internal functions */
void traverse_tree(treeptr root, treerecarray *sortx, int *count);

/* main functions */
int insert_bintree(treeptr *root, struct treedatarec item);
int search_bintree(treeptr root, struct treedatarec item, int freq);
int sort_to_array(treeptr root, treerecarray *sortx);
treeptr delete_bintree(treeptr root, struct treedatarec item, int freq);
int remove_tree(treeptr *root);

int insert_bintree(treeptr *root, struct treedatarec item)
/* Inserts the data key item in a binary tree. If the key is
   inserted a 0 value is returned; otherwise 1 is returned. */
{
    int cmpresult;

    if (*root != NULL)  {
        cmpresult = strcmp(item.key,(*root)->treedata.key);
/* the following may be uncommented to enable this routine to avoid
   inserting duplicate keys
        if (cmpresult == 0) exit(1);
*/
        if (cmpresult > 0) /* insert in right subtree */
            insert_bintree(&(*root)->right, item);
        else  /* insert in left subtree */
            insert_bintree(&(*root)->left, item);
    }

    else { /* create new root */
        *root = (treeptr) malloc(sizeof(struct treestruct));
        if (*root == NULL) return 1;    /* memory allocation problem */
        (*root)->treedata = item; /* store node data */
        (*root)->left = NULL;
        (*root)->right = NULL;
    }
    return 0; /* element inserted */
}
```

```
int search_bintree(treeptr root, struct treedatarec item, int freq)
/* Searches for a specified number of a given key in a
   binary tree. The number of occurrences of the key are returned. */
{
    int count, cmpresult;

    count = 0;
        /* traverse the full tree */
    while ((root != NULL) && (count < freq)) {
        cmpresult = strcmp(item.key,root->treedata.key);
        if (cmpresult > 0)
            /* go to right subtree */
            root = root->right;
        else if (cmpresult < 0)
            /* go to left subtree */
            root = root->left;
        else {
            count++;  /* key found */
            root = root->left;
        }
    }
    return count;  /* number of keys found */
}

void traverse_tree(treeptr root, treerecarray *sortx, int *count)
/* Local function used to traverse a tree. This function is
   called by the sort_to_array function. */
{

    if (root != NULL) {
        traverse_tree(root->left, sortx, count);    /* visit left subtree */
        (*count)++;
        printf("\nCount is : %d", *count);
        if (*count <= MAX_TREE_NODES)
            strcpy(sortx[*count].key, root->treedata.key);
        traverse_tree(root->right, sortx, count);  /* visit right subtree */
        root = root->left;
    }
}
```

```
int sort_to_array(treeptr root, treerecarray *sortx)
/* traverses a tree and places the tree data in a sorted array */
{
    int count;

    if (root != NULL) {
        count = -1;
        traverse_tree(root, sortx, &count);
        return count;    /* number of nodes found */
    }
    return -1;
}


treeptr delete_bintree(treeptr root, struct treedatarec item, int freq)
/* deletes a node in the binary tree */
{
    treeptr t1,t12;
    int ch;

    if (root == NULL) return NULL;   /* element cannot be deleted */
    ch = strcmp(root->treedata.key, item.key); /* compare elements */
    if ((ch == 0) && (--freq == 0)) { /* element found */
        /* delete terminal node */
        if ((root->right == NULL) && (root->left == NULL)) {
            free(root);
            return NULL;
        }  /* delete node with right child only */
        else if (root->left == NULL) {
            t1 = root->right;      /* make right child new root */
            free(root);
            return t1;
        }  /* delete node with left child only */
        else if (root->right == NULL) {
            t1 = root->left;/* make left child new root */
            free(root);
            return t1;
        }
        else {   /* delete node with left and right child */
            t1 = root->right;      /* make right node new root */
```

```
            tl2 = root->right;
            while (tl2->left != NULL )
                /* find new root's leftmost node */
                tl2 = tl2->left;
            tl2->left = root->left;        /* link-in left node of old root */
            free(root);
            return tl;
        }
    }
    else if (ch == 0) root->left = delete_bintree(root->left, item, freq);
    else if (ch > 0) root->left = delete_bintree(root->left, item, freq);
    else root->right = delete_bintree(root->right, item, freq);
    return root;
}


int remove_tree(treeptr *root)
/* removes a binary tree by deallocating its memory space */
{
    int delete_this_node;

    delete_this_node = FALSE;
    if (((*root)->left == NULL) && ((*root)->right == NULL))
        delete_this_node = TRUE;
    else {
        if ((*root)->left == NULL)
            if (remove_tree(&(*root)->left)) {
                free((*root)->left);
                (*root)->left = NULL;
            }
        if ((*root)->right == NULL)
            if (remove_tree(&(*root)->right)) {
                free((*root)->right);
                (*root)->right = NULL;
            }
        if (((*root)->left == NULL) && ((*root)->right == NULL))
            delete_this_node = TRUE;
    }
    return delete_this_node;        /* return status of tree removal */
}
```

• Listing 9.3. Turbo Pascal source code for the binary tree library

---

```pascal
UNIT BinTree;
{ constant is significant only in rebalancing binary tree }
CONST MAX_TREE_NODES = 100;

TYPE BinTreeStr = STRING[40];
   TreeDataRec = RECORD
      Key : BinTreeStr;
      { ***** put other fields here ***** }
   END;
   TreePtr = ^Binary_Tree_Rec;

   Binary_Tree_Rec = RECORD
      TreeData : TreeDataRec;
      Left, Right : TreePtr;
   END;
   TreeRecArray = ARRAY [1..MAX_TREE_NODES] OF TreeDataRec;

PROCEDURE Insert_BinTree(VAR Root : TreePtr;      { in/out }
                             X   : TreeDataRec { input });
{ inserts new data item X in the binary tree with root node Root }

FUNCTION Search_BinTree( Root            : TreePtr;    { in/out }
                         X               : TreeDataRec; { input  }
                         Occurrence_Num  : WORD        { input }) : WORD;
{ Searches for a certain occurrence number of key X in the
  binary tree. This is based on the assumption that the
  binary tree allows for duplicate keys. }

PROCEDURE Sort_to_Array(     Root  : TreePtr;      { input  }
                         VAR SortX : TreeRecArray; { output }
                         VAR Count : WORD          { output });
{ returns the data in the tree in a sorted array }

FUNCTION Delete_BinTree(VAR Root  : TreePtr;      { in/out }
                            X     : TreeDataRec; { input  }
                            Occur : WORD          { input }) : BOOLEAN;
{ Deletes the key X if present in the binary tree. The occurrence number
  is also specified. }
```

```
FUNCTION Remove_Tree(VAR Root : TreePtr { input  }) : BOOLEAN;
{ recursive logical function used to remove a tree }


{*******************************************************************}

PROCEDURE Insert_BinTree(VAR Root : TreePtr;      { in/out }
                             X    : TreeDataRec { input  });
{ inserts new data item X in the binary tree with root node Root }

BEGIN
   IF Root <> NIL THEN
{ The following code may be uncommented to enable this routine to avoid
  inserting duplicate keys }
{***************************************************************
     IF X.Key = Root^.TreeData.Key THEN EXIT;
***************************************************************}
     { recursive insertion calls to either left or right branches }
     IF X.Key > Root^.TreeData.Key
        THEN Insert_BinTree(Root^.Right, X)
        ELSE Insert_BinTree(Root^.Left, X)
   ELSE BEGIN  { insert new node }
     NEW(Root);   { create a new tree leaf node }
     { assign key value and other possible fields }
     Root^.TreeData := X;
     Root^.Left  := NIL;
     Root^.Right := NIL;
   END; { IF }
END; { Insert_BinTree }

FUNCTION Search_BinTree( Root           : TreePtr;      { in/out }
                         X              : TreeDataRec; { input  }
                         Occurrence_Num : WORD         { input  }) : WORD;
{ searches for a certain occurrence number of key X in the binary tree }

VAR count : WORD;

BEGIN
   count := 0; { initialize count for actual occurrence of X }
   WHILE (Root <> NIL) AND (count < Occurrence_Num) DO
     IF X.Key > Root^.TreeData.Key THEN Root := Root^.Right
```

```
        ELSE IF X.Key < Root^.TreeData.Key THEN Root := Root^.Left
        ELSE BEGIN   { match is found }
            INC(count);
            Root := Root^.Left
        END; { IF }
    Search_BinTree := count { return result }
END; { Search_BinTree }


PROCEDURE traverse_tree(    Root  : TreePtr;          { input  }
                        VAR SortX : TreeRecArray;  { output }
                        VAR Count : WORD           { output });
{ local recursive procedure used to traverse the binary tree }


BEGIN
    IF Root <> NIL THEN BEGIN
        traverse_tree(Root^.Left, SortX, Count);
        INC(Count);
        IF Count <= MAX_TREE_NODES THEN
            SortX[Count].Key := Root^.TreeData.Key;
        traverse_tree(Root^.Right, SortX, Count);
    END;
END; { traverse_tree }


PROCEDURE Sort_to_Array(    Root  : TreePtr;          { input  }
                        VAR SortX : TreeRecArray;  { output }
                        VAR Count : WORD           { output });
{ returns the data in the tree in a sorted array }


BEGIN
    { initialize the number of array members }
    Count := 0; { initialize the number of array members }
    { initiate the recursive traversal procedure }
    traverse_tree(Root, SortX, Count);
END; { Sort_to_Array }


FUNCTION Delete_BinTree(VAR Root  : TreePtr;        { in/out }
                            X     : TreeDataRec;  { input  }
                            Occur : WORD          { input }) : BOOLEAN;
{ Deletes the key X if present in the binary tree. The occurrence number
  is also specified. }
```

```
VAR found : BOOLEAN;
    deleted_node, parent_node,
    node1, node2, node3 : TreePtr;

PROCEDURE AdjustParentNode(NewParentNode : TreePtr { input  });
{ adjusts links with parent nodes }
BEGIN
    IF parent_node = NIL THEN
        Root := NewParentNode
    ELSE IF parent_node^.Left = deleted_node THEN
        parent_node^.Left := NewParentNode
    ELSE
        parent_node^.Right := NewParentNode
END;

BEGIN
    found := FALSE;
    deleted_node := Root;
    parent_node := NIL;
    { search tree for the specified occurrence of the key data }
    WHILE (NOT found) AND (deleted_node <> NIL) DO BEGIN
        IF X.Key = deleted_node^.TreeData.Key THEN BEGIN
            { search key match }
            DEC(Occur);
            IF Occur = 0 THEN      { found sought occurrence }
                found := TRUE
            ELSE   { move down the tree }
                deleted_node := deleted_node^.Left;
        END
        ELSE BEGIN
            parent_node := deleted_node;
            IF X.Key < deleted_node^.TreeData.Key THEN
                deleted_node := deleted_node^.Left
            ELSE
                deleted_node := deleted_node^.Right;
        END; { IF }
    END; { WHILE }
    IF found THEN BEGIN
        IF deleted_node^.Left = NIL THEN
            IF deleted_node^.Right = NIL THEN
```

```
                { node has no children }
                AdjustParentNode(NIL)
            ELSE
                AdjustParentNode(deleted_node^.Right)
        ELSE
            IF deleted_node^.Right = NIL THEN
                AdjustParentNode(deleted_node^.Left)
            ELSE BEGIN
                node1 := deleted_node;
                node2 := deleted_node^.Left;
                node3 := node2^.Right;
                WHILE node3 <> NIL DO BEGIN
                    node1 := node2;
                    node2 := node3;
                    node3 := node3^.Right
                END; { WHILE }
                IF node1 <> deleted_node THEN BEGIN
                    node1^.Right := node2^.Left;
                    node2^.Left := deleted_node^.Left
                END; { IF }
                node2^.Right := deleted_node^.Right;
                AdjustParentNode(node2);
            END; { IF }
            DISPOSE(deleted_node)
    END; { IF }                    •
    Delete_BinTree := found { return function result }
END; { Delete_BinTree }


FUNCTION Remove_Tree(VAR Root : TreePtr { input  }) : BOOLEAN;
{ recursive logical function used to remove a tree }


VAR delete_this_node : BOOLEAN;


BEGIN
    delete_this_node := FALSE;
    IF (Root^.Left = NIL) AND (Root^.Right = NIL)
        THEN delete_this_node := TRUE    { remove leaf node with no links }
    ELSE BEGIN
        IF Root^.Left <> NIL THEN { has left branch }
            IF Remove_Tree(Root^.Left) THEN BEGIN
                Dispose(Root^.Left);
```

```
                  Root^.Left := NIL
              END; { IF }
         IF Root^.Right <> NIL THEN        { has right branch }
              IF Remove_Tree(Root^.Right) THEN BEGIN
                  Dispose(Root^.Right);
                  Root^.Right := NIL
              END; { IF }
         IF (Root^.Left = NIL) AND (Root^.Right = NIL) THEN
              delete_this_node := TRUE;
      END; { IF }
      Remove_Tree := delete_this_node;
END; { Remove_Tree }
END.
```

• Listing 9.4. Turbo Prolog source code for the binary tree library

```
domains
    bintreetype = tree(symbol, bintreetype, bintreetype); nil

predicates
    insert_bintree(symbol, bintreetype, bintreetype)
    search_bintree(symbol, bintreetype)
    delete_bintree(symbol, bintreetype, bintreetype)
    delete_node(symbol, bintreetype, bintreetype)
    prttree(bintreetype)
    tree_driver(bintreetype, bintreetype)
    proc_user(char, bintreetype, bintreetype)

clauses
    insert_bintree(Item, nil, tree(Item, nil, nil)) :-!.
    insert_bintree(Item, tree(Key, Left, Right), tree(Key, Left2, Right)) :-
        Item < Key, !,
        insert_bintree(Item, Left, Left2).
    insert_bintree(Item, tree(Key, Left, Right), tree(Key, Left, Right2)) :-
        insert_bintree(Item, Right, Right2).

    search_bintree(Item, tree(Item, _, _)) :-!.
    search_bintree(Item, tree(Key, Left, _)) :-
        Item < Key, !,
        search_bintree(Item, Left).
```

```
search_bintree(Item, tree(_, _, Right)) :-
    search_bintree(Item, Right).

delete_bintree(Item, tree(Item, nil, Right), Right).
delete_bintree(Item, tree(Item, Left, nil), Left).
delete_bintree(Item, tree(Item, Left, Right), tree(Key, Left, Right1)) :-
    delete_node(Key, Right, Right1).

delete_bintree(Item, tree(Root, Left, Right), tree(Root, Left1, Right)) :-
    Item < Root,
    delete_bintree(Item, Left, Left1).
delete_bintree(Item, tree(Root, Left, Right), tree(Root, Left, Right1)) :-
    Item > Root,
    delete_bintree(Item, Right, Right1).

delete_node(Item, tree(Item, nil, Right), Right).
delete_node(Item, tree(Root, Left, Right), tree(Root, Left1, Right)) :-
    delete_node(Item, Left, Left1).

prttree(nil).
prttree(tree(Item, Left, Right)) :-
    prttree(Left),
    write("Item is ", Item), nl,
    prttree(Right).

tree_driver(OldTree, NewTree) :- !,
    write("Select an option >"),
    readchar(Choice),nl,
    proc_user(Choice, OldTree, NewTree),
    tree_driver(NewTree, _).

tree_driver(_, _).

proc_user('q', _, _) :- fail.
proc_user('i', OldTree, NewTree) :-
    write("Enter item to insert >"),
    readln(Item), nl,
    insert_bintree(Item, OldTree, NewTree).
proc_user('f', OldTree, NewTree) :-
    write("Enter item to locate >"),
```

```
        readln(Item), nl,
        search_bintree(Item, OldTree),
        NewTree = OldTree,
        write("Item found"), nl.
proc_user('f', OldTree, NewTree) :-
        NewTree = OldTree,
        write("Item not found"), nl.
proc_user('d', OldTree, NewTree) :-
        write("Enter item to delete >"),
        readln(Item), nl,
        delete_bintree(Item, OldTree, NewTree).
proc_user('p', OldTree, NewTree) :-
        prttree(OldTree),
        NewTree = OldTree.
```

AVL-Trees

Introduction

In this final section, we turn our attention to a tree data structure that is a powerful extension of the binary trees introduced in Section 9: *AVL-trees*. They are a special form of a type of tree structure called a *balanced tree*, which is based on the principle that for every node in the tree, the heights of its two subtrees can differ by only one level.

We begin our presentation of AVL-trees by discussing how these data structures are represented. AVL-trees require more care than binary trees because of their balanced nature. Each time a node is inserted or removed, the balance of the tree must be examined and the structure of the tree must be altered so it can remain balanced. In this discussion we introduce the algorithms for balancing trees and then write a set of routines in each of the Turbo languages for creating and manipulating AVL-trees.

You'll learn how AVL-trees can be represented with both linked structures and records (Turbo C and Pascal) and recursive domains (Turbo Prolog). Because of the complexity of AVL-trees and the volume of Turbo BASIC code necessary to implement the data structures, we won't present AVL-trees in Turbo BASIC.

Overview of AVL-Trees

Despite being versatile data structures, binary trees lose their efficiency when they become unbalanced. For instance, if the data to be inserted in a tree is already in a sorted order, such as these names:

Alice Barry Lisa Lynn Mary Tom

the tree ends up looking like a linked list, as shown in Figure 10.1. As you can see, the biggest problem with binary trees is that their structure is always determined by the order of the input data. Algorithms used in inserting and deleting nodes from binary trees make no provision to maintain their state of balance. This does not make binary trees completely useless, because binary trees do work well with random (or nearly so) inserted data. However, what we need is a tree structure that can modify its representation to maintain a more balanced state as data is inserted and deleted. That's where AVL-trees come in.

In the early sixties, two Russian mathematicians, G. M. Ade'lson-Vel'skii and E. M. Landis, devised an important enhancement for binary

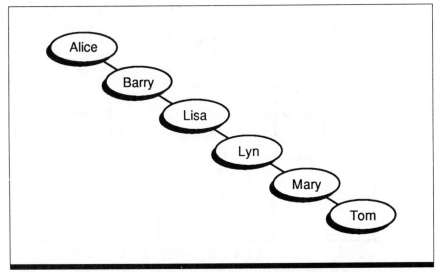

Figure 10.1. Binary tree arranged as a linked list

trees. They suggested a new set of algorithms for node insertion and deletion operations. These algorithms also maintain a state of near balance in the binary tree. This superior type of binary tree is called the AVL-tree in their honor. An AVL-tree is a binary tree that follows these rules:

1. The difference in the height of the main left and right subtrees is not greater than one level.
2. Every node in the tree is also an AVL-tree.

The above explanation of AVL-trees states that a perfect or near-perfect (not exceeding a height difference of one level) balance must be observed throughout the AVL-tree. Figure 10.2 shows various AVL-trees. Whereas AVL-trees are not necessarily perfectly balanced trees, they control and indeed limit the amount of skewness in any subtree. The overhead performed in maintaining the state of near balance is a worthwhile cure for the binary tree's imbalance problem.

Representing AVL-Trees

The basic data structure used to construct an AVL-tree is similar to the one used to construct a binary tree. Each node in the AVL-tree, however, must include an additional field to keep track of the state of balance in its left

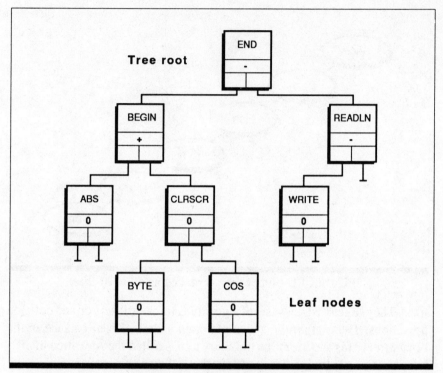

Figure 10.2. Sample AVL-trees

and right subtrees. Three states exist: balance, left tilt, and right tilt. These states may be represented by integers in the range [–1..1] or by using an enumerated data type, such as (left, balance, right).

The basic node structure used in Turbo Pascal is shown here to provide you with a reference:

```
AVLPtr = ^AVL_Tree_Rec;
AVL_Tree_Rec = RECORD
    TreeData : AVLDataRec;
    Balance : BalanceSet;
    Left, Right : AVLPtr;
END;
```

Notice that the field called **Balance** is included to store the balance status for each node. The data type for this component is defined as the following enumerated type:

```
BalanceSet = (left_tilt, neutral, right_tilt);
```

If the node serves as the root of a subtree whose right subtree has the same height as its left subtree as shown in Figure 10.3, the **Balance** field is set to **neutral** to indicate that the node is the root of a balanced tree. If the node is the root of a subtree whose left subtree is taller than its right subtree (shown in Figure 10.4), the **Balance** field is set to **left_tilt**. The last case is shown in Figure 10.5. Here the node is assigned the **right_tilt** value because its right subtree is taller than its left subtree.

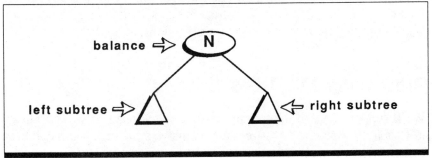

Figure 10.3. A balanced tree

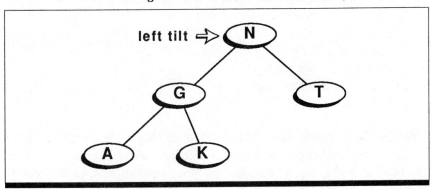

Figure 10.4. A tree with a left tilt

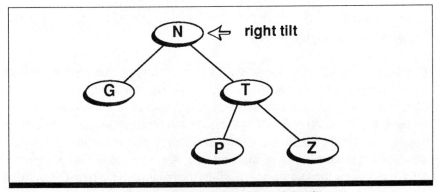

Figure 10.5. A tree with a right tilt

The **Balance** component is used by both the node insertion and deletion operations. In certain cases, after a node is inserted or deleted, it is only necessary to change the balance status of some of the nodes in the tree. For instance, if a tree has a right subtree that is taller than its left subtree and we delete a node from the right subtree, the tree might become balanced. Then the **Balance** component of the appropriate nodes must be set to reflect this new condition. In other cases, the tree must be rearranged and the **Balance** component of the nodes that are moved must be changed. We illustrate how the balance of AVL-trees is maintained in more detail when we discuss the insertion and deletion operations.

Processing AVL-Trees

We'll support most of the tree processing operations that we introduced in Chapter 9. Because AVL-trees are recursive structures just like binary trees, operations such as inserting and deleting nodes in a tree are usually performed with recursion. The operations that we'll implement include the following:

- Searching for a node
- Inserting a node
- Traversing a tree
- Deleting a node

The algorithms for tree traversal and node searching are essentially the same as those used to process binary trees. The insertion and deletion operations, on the other hand, require additional logic to keep an AVL-tree balanced. We'll next discuss how node insertions and deletions are performed.

Inserting a Node

The node insertion operation in an AVL-tree starts in a manner similar to the one used in binary trees. The new node is compared with the AVL-tree nodes until the proper insertion position is found to link in the new node. Because recursion is used to find the insertion position, we're able to keep track of the actual path followed to locate the insertion position in the AVL-tree. After the new node is inserted, the AVL-tree insertion algorithm backtracks along the search path to adjust the balance of the tree. Essentially the goal is to find the closest node with a left or right tilt status, which we call the *pivot node*. Our balancing algorithm must be able to take care of three possible situations.

1. No pivot node is found because every node along the search path has a balanced status assigned to it. We handle this simple case by adjusting the balance status of the AVL-tree nodes on the search path. The balance state of the nodes whose left subtrees are now taller than their right subtrees is reassigned to the left tilt setting. If, on the other hand, a node's right subtree becomes taller than the left, the balance state is set to a right tilt. The inserted node is assigned a balanced status that applies to nodes with either truly balanced subtrees or newly inserted leaf nodes.

2. A pivot node is found, and the subtree in which the new node is inserted happens to have a height shorter than its brother. Fortunately, this type of node insertion improves the balance of the AVL-tree. Therefore, we do not need to rearrange the tree. All we do is change the balance status of each node along the search path, beginning with the pivot node, to the balance (neutral) setting.

3. A pivot node is found, and the subtree in which the new node is inserted is the taller one. The balanced state of the extended subtree now violates the basic rules for an AVL-tree. To restore the balance of the AVL-tree, we perform what is called a *single* or *double rotation*. When a rotation is performed, the structure of the tree is modified. We'll explain how the rotation procedures work with some examples next.

Examples of Node Insertions

Because the first two insertion cases listed previously do not require structural modification of the AVL-tree, we'll examine them first. The first case states that a node is inserted in a tree that is perfectly balanced. Figure 10.6 presents the balanced tree in which we'll insert an element. Notice that the balance state of each node is set to neutral. If we attempt to insert a new node called C, the search path will be G D A. Once the node is inserted, we backtrack along the search path and adjust the balance setting for nodes A, D, and G. The result is shown in Figure 10.7.

To illustrate the second case, we can use the tree in Figure 10.7 because it is not perfectly balanced. We'll insert the node J. This time the search path is G M L. As Figure 10.8 shows, the new node is inserted as the left child of node L. After the node is inserted, the balance states of nodes L,

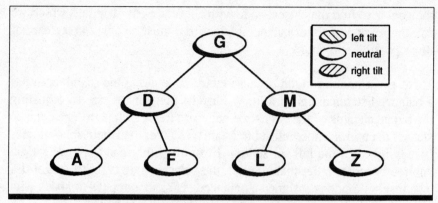

Figure 10.6. Inserting a node in a balanced tree

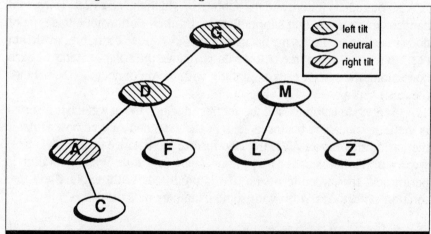

Figure 10.7. The tree after the node is inserted

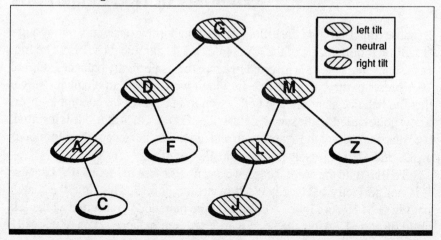

Figure 10.8. The tree after the second node is inserted

M, and G are changed. Notice that the root of the tree, node G, now indicates that the tree is balanced because subtrees D and M are the same height.

The third case for node insertion is much more complex than the first two, because it requires that the tree be structurally modified. As an example, consider the tree shown in Figure 10.9. If we attempt to insert the node C into the tree, the left subtree with root D becomes two levels taller than the subtree with root H. To keep the tree balanced, change the root of the tree by rotating the left subtree.

Let's look at the step-by-step process used by our insertion algorithm. First, we find the insertion position for the new node C. The search path is G D A. As we backtrack along the search path, node A is set to the right tilt balance status, as shown in Figure 10.10. Next, the backtracking takes us to node D, which is set to a left tilt status because its left subtree is now taller than its right subtree as Figure 10.11 illustrates. Finally, we arrive at the root of the tree, node G. The balance status of the root is compared with its left subtree, and because they are both set to a left tilt status, we must change the tree with a single left rotation. The code that actually performs this rotation is shown here in Turbo Pascal for your reference:

```
ptr2 := Root^.Left;
IF ptr2^.Balance = left_tilt THEN BEGIN { rotate once }
   Root^.Left := ptr2^.Right;
   ptr2^.Right := Root;
   Root^.Balance := neutral;
   Root := ptr2
END
```

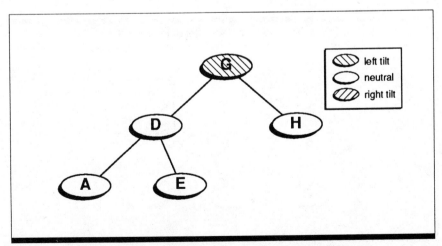

Figure 10.9. Inserting a node into an unbalanced tree

At the start of this code the pointer variable **Root** references the root of the subtree that is to be balanced. Applying this code to our example, **Root** references node G. The variable **ptr2** is set to point at node D, the left child of the root, and because its balance status is left tilt, the **IF** block is executed. This code moves the root's left child so that it becomes the new root of the tree. The old root is then assigned as the right child of the new root. The new tree created from our example is shown in Figure 10.12. Essen-

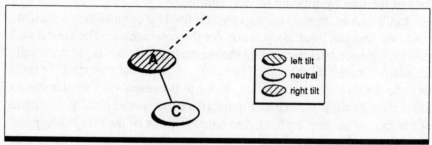

Figure 10.10. First step to balance a tree

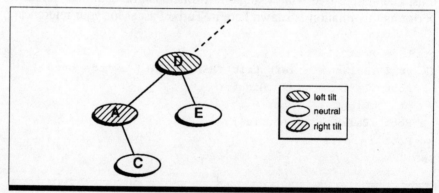

Figure 10.11. Second step to balance a tree

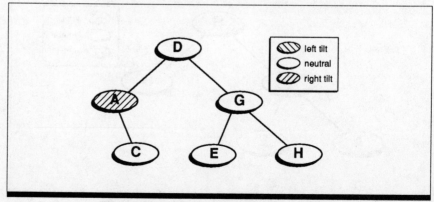

Figure 10.12. Tree after being rebalanced

tially, the node D has been rotated to the left one level, and that's why this operation is called a single rotation.

Our example illustrated how the single rotation is performed to rebalance an AVL-tree. There is, however, a second type of rotation, a *double rotation*, required to rebalance certain types of trees. As an example, consider the problem of inserting node F in the tree we introduced back in Figure 10.9. After the node is inserted, the tree becomes out of balance, as Figure 10.13 shows. Notice that the root of the tree, node G, has a different tilt setting than node D. Because of the structure of the tree, we can't balance it by moving node D to the root as we did with the single rotation example. The correct exchange consists of moving node E to the root. Unfortunately, the code to perform this double rotation is slightly more complex than the single rotation code.

```
ELSE BEGIN { rotate twice }
    ptr3 := ptr2^.Right;
    ptr2^.Right := ptr3^.Left;
    ptr3^.Left := ptr2;
    Root^.Left := ptr3^.Right;
    ptr3^.Right := Root;
    IF ptr3^.Balance = right_tilt
        THEN ptr2^.Balance := left_tilt
        ELSE ptr2^.Balance := neutral;
    IF ptr3^.Balance = left_tilt
        THEN Root^.Balance := right_tilt
        ELSE Root^.Balance := neutral;
    Root := ptr3
END; { ELSE }
```

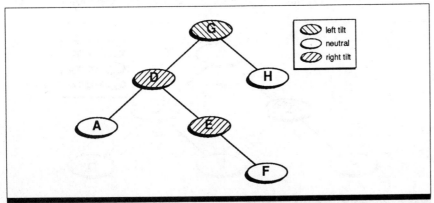

Figure 10.13. Tree produced by inserting a new node

Here we must use two extra pointers, **ptr2** and **ptr3**, to restructure the tree. The final tree produced is shown in Figure 10.14.

Deleting a Node

To delete a node in the AVL-tree, we use an algorithm that is similar to the one used to insert a node. Essentially three main steps are required.

1. Locate the node to delete by searching the tree.
2. Remove the node.
3. Rebalance the tree if it becomes unbalanced.

The first step uses recursion to traverse the tree. Because recursion is used, we're able to keep track of the search path, which we'll need later to rebalance the tree. Once the node is located, it can be removed by reassigning the node's parent left or right link. To properly delete the node, we must consider three factors, detailed in Figure 10.15. The first two cases are easy to handle because the node being removed has only a left or right child. In either case, the node is deleted and its child becomes the new root of the subtree.

The third case, deleting a node that has a left and right child, is more complex. If the left child of the node being deleted does not itself have a right child (such a case appears in Figure 10.16), the left child is moved to the root and its left link is assigned to the original root's right child. If the deleted node's left child does have a right child (shown in Figure 10.17), we must employ a different algorithm. In this case, we go to the deleted node's left child and use the rightmost child of the left node as the new root. In Figure 10.17, notice that node F becomes the new root of the tree.

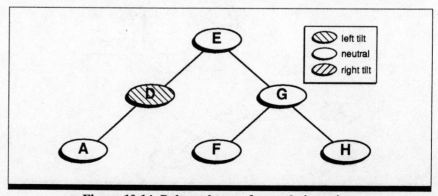

Figure 10.14. Balanced tree after node insertion

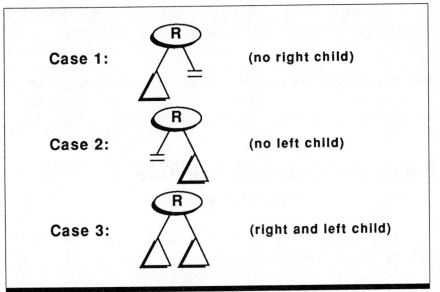

Figure 10.15. Factors to consider in deleting a node

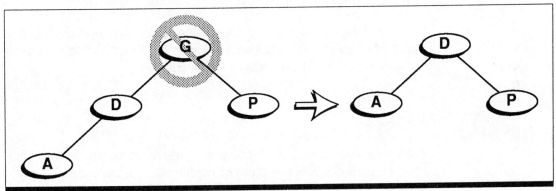

Figure 10.16. Special case for deleting a node

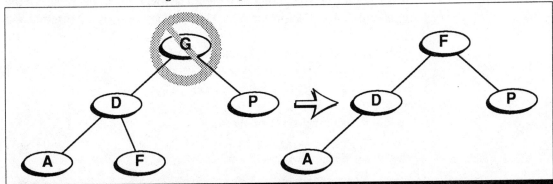

Figure 10.17. The tree after the node is deleted

You've now seen how a node is located and actually removed. The final required step balances the tree. Fortunately, this process is the same as the one used to balance a tree as nodes are being inserted. If we find a left subtree to be unbalanced as we're backtracking along the search path, a routine called **balance_left** is invoked to either set the balance setting of a node or perform a single or double rotation. If, on the other hand, a right tree needs balancing, the **balance_right** routine is called.

Implementations of AVL-Tree Processing Algorithms

The implementations of the AVL-tree processing routines are presented in Listings 10.1, 10.2, and 10.3.

Turbo BASIC

Because of the complexity and code size of implementing the AVL-tree algorithms in a language that does not provide dynamic data structures, we've omitted the Turbo BASIC implementation.

Turbo C

The source code for the AVL-tree processing routines appears in Listing 10.1. This file contains two types of functions: main and local. The main functions are the high-level functions directly called to perform operations such as inserting and deleting tree nodes. The local functions consist of the internal routines used to balance the AVL-tree after nodes are inserted and deleted.

The main structure to represent the AVL-tree is

```
typedef struct avlstruct *avlptr;
struct avlstruct  {
    struct avldatarec treedata;
    int balance;
    avlptr left, right;
};
```

```
struct avldatarec {
    char key[STRING_SIZE];
    /*   put other fields here */
};
typedef struct avldatarec treerecarray;
```

The **avlstruct** is composed of four basic components: the data stored by an AVL-tree node, the status of balance for the attached subtrees, and the left and right node pointers. The **avldatarec** is the simple structure that contains the key data for a node. As with the binary trees, you can customize the AVL-trees by altering this structure so that it can hold other types of data. The array of tree structures called **treerecarray** serves the same purpose as with the binary tree library: to copy the nodes of the AVL-tree to an ordered array.

The functions in the AVL-tree library are described next.

Inserts a new node into the AVL-tree and maintains the status of near-balance in the AVL-tree. This function invokes the routines **rotate_left()** and **rotate_right()** to maintain the balance of the AVL-tree. A 1 value is returned if the element is inserted without an error; otherwise, 0 is returned.

insert_avltree()

Syntax:
```
int insert_avltree(avlptr *root, struct avldatarec item);
```

Parameters:
*root   the pointer to the root of the AVL-tree.
item   the item inserted in the AVL-tree.

Searches for a certain occurrence number of a given key in the AVL-tree. The function returns one of the following values:

search_avltree()

1. A 0 if key **item** is not found in the AVL-tree.
2. The number of times the key **item** is found.

This function assumes that duplicate keys are allowed in the tree. If the library implementation (or any of its customized versions) is edited to guard against duplicate keys, the argument for **freq** should always be 1.

Syntax:
```
int search_avltree(avlptr root, struct avldatarec item,
                   int freq);
```

Parameters:
root   the pointer to the root of the AVL-tree.
item   the item searched for in the AVL-tree.
freq   the occurrence of the searched-for item.

avlsort_to_array()   Returns the data in the AVL-tree as a sorted array. If the nodes in the AVL-tree exceed the storage capacity of the array, the surplus nodes are not included in the array. You can detect this when the returned value exceeds the value of the constant **MAX_TREE_NODES**. The difference between the returned value and **MAX_TREE_NODES** is the number of surplus nodes.

Syntax:
```
int avlsort_to_array(avlptr root, treerecarray *sortx);
```

Parameters:
root   the pointer to the root of the AVL-tree.
*sortx   the array of nodes ordered in an ascending fashion.

delete_avltree()   Deletes the key of **item** if it is present in the AVL-tree. This routine implements one of the most elaborate basic operations for an AVL-tree. It uses the routines **balance_left()**, **balance_right()**, and **delete_both_children()** to perform the delicate deletion/rebalancing of an AVL-tree.

Syntax:
```
int delete_avltree(avlptr *root, struct avldatarec item);
```

Parameters:
*root   the pointer to the root of the AVL-tree.
item   the item to be deleted from the AVL-tree.

Turbo Pascal

Listing 10.2 shows the library unit that implements the data structures and routines for processing AVL-trees in Turbo Pascal. The library exports the following constants and data types:

```
CONST MAX_TREE_NODES = 100;
```

```
TYPE AVLTreeStr = STRING[40];
     BalanceSet = (left_tilt, neutral, right_tilt);
     AVLDataRec = RECORD
        Key : AVLTreeStr;
        { ***** put other fields here ***** }
     END;

     AVLPtr = ^AVL_Tree_Rec;
     AVL_Tree_Rec = RECORD
        TreeData : AVLDataRec;
        Balance  : BalanceSet;
        Left, Right : AVLPtr;
     END;
     TreeRecArray = ARRAY [1..MAX_TREE_NODES] OF AVLDataRec;
```

We are declaring the enumerated type **BalanceSet** to monitor the tilt in each AVL subtree. The **AVL_Tree_Rec** is composed of four basic fields: the data stored by an AVL-tree node, the status of balance for the attached subtrees, and the left and right node pointers. The **AVLDataRec** is the record structure that contains at least the key field that enables the AVL-tree nodes to be placed in order. When you customize the AVL-tree library, you insert new fields or modify the record itself. The array of tree records serves the same purpose with the binary tree library: to copy the nodes of the AVL-tree into an ordered array. The routines of the AVL-tree library are presented next.

Insert_AVLTree

Inserts a new node into the AVL-tree and maintains the status of near-balance in the AVL-tree. It invokes the routines **rotate_left** and **rotate_right** to maintain the balance of the AVL-tree.

Syntax:
```
PROCEDURE Insert_AVLTree(VAR Root : AVLPtr; X : AVLDataRec);
```

Parameters:
Root   the root of the AVL-tree.
X   the item inserted in the AVL-tree.

Search_AVLTree

Searches for a certain occurrence number of a given key in the AVL-tree. The function returns one of the following values:

1. A 0 if key **X** is not found in the AVL-tree.

2. The value of **Occurrence_Num** if **X** is present in the tree that many times.

3. A positive value less than **Occurrence_Num** reports as the actual count of **X** in the AVL-tree.

This function assumes that duplicate keys are allowed in the tree. If the library implementation (or any of its customized versions) is edited to guard against duplicate keys, the argument for **Occurrence_Num** should always be 1.

Syntax:

```
FUNCTION Search_AVLTree(VAR Root          : AVLPtr;
                            X             : AVLDataRec;
                            Occurrence_Num : WORD): WORD;
```

Parameters:

Root   the root of the AVL-tree.
X   the item searched for in the AVL-tree.
Occurrence_Num   the occurrence of the searched-for item.

AVLSort_to_Array Returns the data in the AVL-tree as a sorted array. If the nodes in the AVL-tree exceed the storage capacity of the array, the surplus nodes are not included in the array. You can detect this when the returned **Count** parameter exceeds the value of the constant **MAX_TREE_NODES**. The difference between **Count** and **MAX_TREE_NODES** is the number of surplus nodes.

Syntax:

```
PROCEDURE AVLSort_to_Array(VAR Root    : AVLPtr;
                           VAR SortX   : TreeRecArray;
                           VAR Count   : WORD);
```

Parameters:

Root   the root of the AVL-tree.
SortX   the array of nodes ordered in an ascending fashion.
Count   the number of tree nodes in the array **SortX**.

Delete_AVLTree Deletes the key of **X** if it is present in the AVL-tree. This routine implements one of the most elaborate basic operations for an AVL-tree. It uses the

routines **balance_left**, **balance_right**, and **delete_both_children** to perform the delicate deletion/rebalancing of an AVL-tree.

Syntax:
```
PROCEDURE Delete_AVLTree(VAR Root   : AVLPtr;
                             X       : AVLDataRec;
                         VAR DelOK : BOOLEAN);
```

Parameters:

Root   the root of the AVL-tree.
X   the item to be deleted from the AVL-tree.
DelOK   returns the status of the delete operation.

Turbo Prolog

The source code for the AVL-tree processing predicates is presented in
Listing 10.3. Like the C and Pascal implementations, the Prolog version
also contains both internal and main routines. Because of the uniqueness
of the Turbo Prolog language, we've also included a simple test driver
predicate called **tree_driver** that you study to see how the main tree
processing predicates are called.

The domain type that is used to represent the AVL-tree is:

```
domains
    avltreetype = tree(symbol, avltreetype, avltreetype,
                       symbol); nil
```

This domain type is very similar to the one used to represent binary trees;
however, we've added an extra component to store the balance status for
a node. A tree that consisted of a single node would be represented as
follows:

```
tree(node_1, nil, nil, neutral)
```

where the **neutral** symbol indicates that the node is balanced. If the node's
left subtree has a greater height than its right subtree, the representation
is

```
tree(node_1, Left, Right, left_tilt)
```

If the reverse condition is true, the node's right subtree is greater than its left subtree, and this representation is used:

```
tree(node_1, Left, Right, right_tilt)
```

The Turbo Prolog implementation also uses two database predicates to control how AVL-trees are balanced after nodes are inserted and deleted. These predicates are:

```
database
    insert_stat(symbol)
    delete_stat(symbol)
```

The **insert_stat** predicate keeps track of the balance status of a tree while a node is being inserted, and the **delete_stat** predicate serves a similar function as a node is being deleted. Both of these predicates assert and retract a **true** or **false** symbol. As the recursive levels of the insertion or deletion predicates unwind, the status of these predicates is tested to determine when to stop balancing a tree.

The main predicates in the AVL-tree library are presented next.

insert_avltree   Inserts a new node into the AVL-tree and maintains the status of near-balance in the AVL-tree. It invokes the local predicates **check_lbalance** and **check_rbalance** to maintain the balance of the AVL-tree.

Syntax:
```
insert_avltree(Item, OldTree, NewTree)     (i,i,o)
              (symbol, avltreetype, avltreetype)
```

Parameters:
Item   the item inserted in the AVL-tree.
OldTree   the tree in which the item is inserted.
NewTree   the tree with the item inserted.

search_avltree   Searches for a single occurrence of a given key in the AVL-tree. If no match is found, the predicate fails; otherwise, it succeeds.

Syntax:
```
search_avltree(Item, AVLTree)     (i,i)
              (symbol, avltreetype)
```

Parameters:

Item   the item searched for in the AVL-tree.
AVLTree   the tree to search.

Deletes a specified node from the AVL-tree. This routine implements one **delete_avltree**
of the most elaborate basic operations for an AVL-tree. It uses the local
predicates **balance_left**, **balance_right**, **delete_node**, **rotate_dl**,
rotate_dr, and **set_del_bal** to perform the delicate deletion/rebalancing of
an AVL-tree.

Syntax:

```
delete_avltree(Item, OldTree, NewTree)      (i,i,o)
               (symbol, avltreetype, avltreetype)
```

Parameters:

Item   the item to be deleted from the AVL-tree.
OldTree   the tree containing the item node to delete.
NewTree   the tree with the item node deleted.

• **Listing 10.1. Turbo C source code for the AVL-tree library**

```c
#include <stdio.h>
#include <alloc.h>
#include <string.h>
#define TRUE 1
#define FALSE 0
#define STRING_SIZE 40
#define MAX_TREE_NODES   100
#define LEFT_TILT -1
#define NEUTRAL 0
#define RIGHT_TILT 1

typedef struct avlstruct *avlptr;
struct avldatarec {
   char key[STRING_SIZE];
   /* put other fields here */
};
struct avlstruct {
   struct avldatarec treedata;
```

```
    int balance;
    avlptr left, right;
};
typedef struct avldatarec treerecarray;

/* local functions */
void rotate_right(avlptr *root);
void rotate_left(avlptr *root);
int insert_avl(avlptr *root, struct avldatarec item, int *insertedok);
void traverse_tree(avlptr root, treerecarray *sortx, int *count);
void prttree(avlptr root);
void balance_right(avlptr *root, int *delok);
void balance_left(avlptr *root, int *delok);
int delete_avl(avlptr *root, struct avldatarec item, int *delok);
void delete_both_children(avlptr *root, avlptr *ptr, int *delok);

/* main functions */
int insert_avltree(avlptr *root, struct avldatarec item);
int search_avltree(avlptr root, struct avldatarec item, int freq);
int avlsort_to_array(avlptr root, treerecarray *sortx);
int delete_avltree(avlptr *root, struct avldatarec item);

void rotate_right(avlptr *root)
/* rearranges the nodes in a tree by rotating them to the right */
{
    avlptr ptr2, ptr3;

    ptr2 = (*root)->right;
    if (ptr2->balance == RIGHT_TILT) {   /* rotate once */
        (*root)->right = ptr2->left;
        ptr2->left = *root;
        (*root)->balance = NEUTRAL;
        *root = ptr2;
    }
    else {   /* rotate twice */
        ptr3 = ptr2->left;
        ptr2->left = ptr3->right;
        ptr3->right = ptr2;
        (*root)->right = ptr3->left;
        ptr3->left = *root;
```

```
        if (ptr3->balance == LEFT_TILT)
            ptr2->balance = RIGHT_TILT;
        else ptr2->balance = NEUTRAL;
        if (ptr3->balance == RIGHT_TILT)
            (*root)->balance = LEFT_TILT;
        else (*root)->balance = NEUTRAL;
        *root = ptr3;
    }
    (*root)->balance = NEUTRAL;
}


void rotate_left(avlptr *root)
/* rearranges the nodes in a tree by rotating them to the left */
{
    avlptr ptr2, ptr3;

    ptr2 = (*root)->left;
    if (ptr2->balance == LEFT_TILT) {   /* rotate once */
        (*root)->left = ptr2->right;
        ptr2->right = *root;
        (*root)->balance = NEUTRAL;
        *root = ptr2;
    }
    else {   /* rotate twice */
        ptr3 = ptr2->right;
        ptr2->right = ptr3->left;
        ptr3->left = ptr2;
        (*root)->left = ptr3->right;
        ptr3->right = *root;
        if (ptr3->balance == RIGHT_TILT)
            ptr2->balance = LEFT_TILT;
        else ptr2->balance = NEUTRAL;
        if (ptr3->balance == LEFT_TILT)
            (*root)->balance = RIGHT_TILT;
        else (*root)->balance = NEUTRAL;
        *root = ptr3;
    }
    (*root)->balance = NEUTRAL;
}
```

```
int insert_avltree(avlptr *root, struct avldatarec item)
/* inserts a node in a balanced tree */
{
    int inserted_ok;

    inserted_ok = FALSE;
    return (insert_avl(root, item, &inserted_ok));
}

int insert_avl(avlptr *root, struct avldatarec item, int *insertedok)
/* inserts a node in an AVL-tree (local recursive function) */
{
    int cmpresult;

    cmpresult = strcmp(item.key,(*root)->treedata.key);
    if (*root == NULL) {   /* allocate memory */
        *root = (avlptr) malloc(sizeof(struct avlstruct));
        if (*root == NULL) return 1;   /* memory allocation problem */
        (*root)->treedata = item;   /* store node's data */
        (*root)->left = NULL;
        (*root)->right = NULL;
        (*root)->balance = NEUTRAL;
        *insertedok = TRUE;
    }
    /* the following may be uncommented to enable this
       routine to avoid inserting duplicate keys
    else if (cmpresult == 0) {
        *insertedok = FALSE;
        exit(1);
    }
    */
    else if (cmpresult <= 0) {   /* go to left subtree */
        insert_avl(&(*root)->left, item, insertedok);
        if (*insertedok)
            switch ((*root)->balance) {
                case LEFT_TILT: rotate_left(root);
                    *insertedok = FALSE;
                    break;
                case NEUTRAL:   (*root)->balance = LEFT_TILT;
                    break;
```

```
             case RIGHT_TILT: (*root)->balance = NEUTRAL;
                 *insertedok = FALSE;
          }
      }
   else {   /* go to right subtree */
      insert_avl(&(*root)->right, item, insertedok);
      if (*insertedok)
         switch ((*root)->balance) {
             case LEFT_TILT: (*root)->balance = NEUTRAL;
                 *insertedok = FALSE;
                 break;
             case NEUTRAL: (*root)->balance = RIGHT_TILT;
                 break;
             case RIGHT_TILT: rotate_right(root);
                 *insertedok = FALSE;
                 break;
         }
   }
   return 0;   /* element inserted */
}


int search_avltree(avlptr root, struct avldatarec item, int freq)
/* searches an AVL-tree for a specified node */
{
   int count, cmpresult;

   count = 0;
   while ((root != NULL) && (count < freq)) {
      cmpresult = strcmp(item.key,root->treedata.key);
      if (cmpresult > 0)
         root = root->right;
      else if (cmpresult < 0)
         root = root->left;
      else {   /* match found */
         count++;
         root = root->left;
      }
   }
   return count;   /* number of elements found */
}
```

```
void traverse_tree(avlptr root, treerecarray *sortx, int *count)
/* traverses the AVL-tree (local recursive function) */
{

    if (root != NULL) {
        traverse_tree(root->left, sortx, count);   /* go left */
        (*count)++;
        if (*count <= MAX_TREE_NODES)
            strcpy(sortx[*count].key, root->treedata.key);
        traverse_tree(root->right, sortx, count);
        root = root->left;
    }
}


int avlsort_to_array(avlptr root, treerecarray *sortx)
/* copies the nodes in a tree to an array */
{

    int count;

    if (root != NULL) {
        count = -1;
        traverse_tree(root, sortx, &count);
        return count;   /* number of nodes found */
    }
    return -1;
}

void balance_right(avlptr *root, int *delok)
/* Restores the balanced or near-balanced state of an AVL-tree by
   rebalancing a right subtree. This function is called by delete_avl(). */
{
    avlptr ptr2, ptr3;
    int balnc2, balnc3;

    switch ((*root)->balance) {
        case LEFT_TILT: (*root)->balance = NEUTRAL;
            break;
        case NEUTRAL: (*root)->balance = RIGHT_TILT;
            *delok = FALSE;
```

```
        break;
    case RIGHT_TILT: ptr2 = (*root)->right;
        balnc2 = ptr2->balance;
        if (balnc2 != LEFT_TILT) {
            (*root)->right = ptr2->left;
            ptr2->left = *root;
            if (balnc2 == NEUTRAL) {
                (*root)->balance = RIGHT_TILT;
                ptr2->balance = LEFT_TILT;
                *delok = FALSE;
            }
            else {
                (*root)->balance = NEUTRAL;
                ptr2->balance = NEUTRAL;
            }
            *root = ptr2;
        }
        else {
            ptr3 = ptr2->left;
            balnc3 = ptr3->balance;
            ptr2->left = ptr3->right;
            ptr3->right = ptr2;
            (*root)->right = ptr3->left;
            ptr3->left = *root;
            if (balnc3 == LEFT_TILT)
                ptr2->balance = RIGHT_TILT;
            else
                ptr2->balance = NEUTRAL;
            if (balnc3 == RIGHT_TILT)
                (*root)->balance = LEFT_TILT;
            else
            (*root)->balance = NEUTRAL;
            *root = ptr3;
            ptr3->balance = NEUTRAL;
        }
    }
}
}


void balance_left(avlptr *root, int *delok)
/* Restores the balanced or near-balanced state of an AVL-tree by
    rebalancing a left subtree. This function is called by delete_avl(). */
```

```
{
    avlptr ptr2, ptr3;
    int balnc2, balnc3;

    switch ((*root)->balance) {
        case RIGHT_TILT: (*root)->balance = NEUTRAL;
            break;
        case NEUTRAL: (*root)->balance = LEFT_TILT;
            *delok = FALSE;
            break;
        case LEFT_TILT: ptr2 = (*root)->left;
            balnc2 = ptr2->balance;
            if (balnc2 != RIGHT_TILT) {
                (*root)->left = ptr2->right;
                ptr2->right = *root;
                if (balnc2 == NEUTRAL) {
                    (*root)->balance = LEFT_TILT;
                    ptr2->balance = RIGHT_TILT;
                    *delok = FALSE;
                }
                else {
                    (*root)->balance = NEUTRAL;
                    ptr2->balance = NEUTRAL;
                }
                *root = ptr2;
            }
            else {
                ptr3 = ptr2->right;
                balnc3 = ptr3->balance;
                ptr2->right = ptr3->left;
                ptr3->left = ptr2;
                (*root)->left = ptr3->right;
                ptr3->right = *root;
                if (balnc3 == RIGHT_TILT)
                    ptr2->balance = LEFT_TILT;
                else
                    ptr2->balance = NEUTRAL;
                if (balnc3 == LEFT_TILT)
                    (*root)->balance = RIGHT_TILT;
                else
```

```
                  (*root)->balance = NEUTRAL;
                  *root = ptr3;
                  ptr3->balance = NEUTRAL;
            }
      }
}


int delete_avltree(avlptr *root, struct avldatarec item)
/* deletes a node from an AVL-tree */
{
   int delok = FALSE;

   return (delete_avl(root, item, &delok));
}

int delete_avl(avlptr *root, struct avldatarec item, int *delok)
/* Deletes a node from an AVL-tree. This recursive local function calls
   balance_right() and balance_left() to balance the tree if it becomes
   unbalanced. */
{
   avlptr ptr;
   int cmpresult;

   cmpresult = strcmp(item.key, (*root)->treedata.key);
   if ((*root) == NULL) *delok = FALSE;
   else if (cmpresult < 0) {   /* go to left subtree */
      delete_avl(&(*root)->left, item, delok);
      if (*delok) balance_right(root, delok);
   }
   else if (cmpresult > 0) {   /* go to right subtree */
      delete_avl(&(*root)->right, item, delok);
      if (*delok) balance_left(root, delok);
   }
   else {
      ptr = *root;   /* node found */
      if ((*root)->right == NULL) {
          (*root) = (*root)->left;
          *delok = TRUE;
          free(ptr);
      }
```

```
        else if ((*root)->left == NULL) {
            (*root) = (*root)->right;
            *delok = TRUE;
            free(ptr);
        }
        else {   /* node has right and left child */
            delete_both_children(root, &(*root)->left, delok);
            if (*delok) balance_right(root, delok);
            free((*root)->left);
        }
    }
    return *delok;   /* return status of delete operation*/
}


void delete_both_children(avlptr *root, avlptr *ptr, int *delok)
/* deletes a node with two subtrees */
{
    if ((*ptr)->right == NULL) {
        (*root)->treedata = (*ptr)->treedata;
        *ptr = (*ptr)->left;
        *delok = TRUE;
    }
    else {
        delete_both_children(root, &(*ptr)->right, delok);
        if (*delok) balance_left(ptr, delok);
    }
}
```

• Listing 10.2. Turbo Pascal source code for the AVL-tree library

---

```
UNIT AVLTree;

{ this constant is significant only if an ordered array of the AVL-tree
  nodes is desired }
CONST MAX_TREE_NODES = 100;
TYPE AVLTreeStr = STRING[40];
    BalanceSet = (left_tilt, neutral, right_tilt);
    AVLDataRec = RECORD
```

```
        Key : AVLTreeStr;
        { ***** put other fields here ***** }
    END;
    AVLPtr = ^AVL_Tree_Rec;
    AVL_Tree_Rec = RECORD
        TreeData : AVLDataRec;
        Balance  : BalanceSet;
        Left, Right : AVLPtr;
    END;
    TreeRecArray = ARRAY [1..MAX_TREE_NODES] OF AVLDataRec;

PROCEDURE Insert_AVLTree(VAR  Root  : AVLPtr;        { in/out }
                             X     : AVLDataRec   { input  });
{ inserts data item into the AVL-tree }


FUNCTION Search_AVLTree( Root               : AVLPtr;        { input }
                         X                  : AVLDataRec;   { input }
                         Occurrence_Num : WORD          { input }) : WORD;
{ Searches for a certain occurrence number of key X in the AVL-tree.
  The function returns one of the following values:

  + A zero if key X is not found in the AVL-tree.
  + The value of Occurrence_Num if X is present in the tree that many
    times.
  + A positive value less than Occurrence_Num reports the actual
    count of X in the AVL-tree.

  This function assumes that duplicate keys are allowed in
  the tree. }


PROCEDURE AVLSort_to_Array(VAR Root   : AVLPtr;        { input  }
                           VAR SortX  : TreeRecArray;  { output }
                           VAR Count  : WORD           { output });
{ returns the data in the AVL-tree as a sorted array }


PROCEDURE Delete_AVLTree(VAR Root   : AVLPtr;        { in/out }
                             X     : AVLDataRec;   { input  }
                         VAR DelOK  : BOOLEAN        { in/out });
{ deletes the key of X if it is present in the AVL-tree}
```

```
{**************************************************************************}
PROCEDURE rotate_right(VAR Root : AVLPtr   { in/out });
{ rearranges the tree nodes by rotating them to the right }


VAR ptr2, ptr3 : AVLPtr;

BEGIN
   ptr2 := Root^.Right;
   IF ptr2^.Balance = right_tilt THEN BEGIN   { rotate once }
      Root^.Right := ptr2^.Left;
      ptr2^.Left := Root;
      Root^.Balance := neutral;
      Root := ptr2
   END
   ELSE BEGIN   { rotate twice }
      ptr3 := ptr2^.Left;
      ptr2^.Left := ptr3^.Right;
      ptr3^.Right := ptr2;
      Root^.Right := ptr3^.Left;
      ptr3^.Left := Root;
      IF ptr3^.Balance = left_tilt
         THEN ptr2^.Balance := right_tilt
         ELSE ptr2^.Balance := neutral;
      IF ptr3^.Balance = right_tilt
         THEN Root^.Balance := left_tilt
         ELSE Root^.Balance := neutral;
      Root := ptr3
   END; { IF }
   Root^.Balance := neutral
END; { rotate_right }


PROCEDURE rotate_left(VAR Root : AVLPtr   { in/out });
{ rearranges the tree nodes by rotating them to the left }


VAR ptr2, ptr3 : AVLPtr;

BEGIN
   ptr2 := Root^.Left;
   IF ptr2^.Balance = left_tilt THEN BEGIN   { rotate once }
      Root^.Left := ptr2^.Right;
```

```
        ptr2^.Right := Root;
        Root^.Balance := neutral;
        Root := ptr2
    END
    ELSE BEGIN   { rotate twice }
        ptr3 := ptr2^.Right;
        ptr2^.Right := ptr3^.Left;
        ptr3^.Left := ptr2;
        Root^.Left := ptr3^.Right;
        ptr3^.Right := Root;
        IF ptr3^.Balance = right_tilt
            THEN ptr2^.Balance := left_tilt
            ELSE ptr2^.Balance := neutral;
        IF ptr3^.Balance = left_tilt
            THEN Root^.Balance := right_tilt
            ELSE Root^.Balance := neutral;
        Root := ptr3
    END; { IF }
    Root^.Balance := neutral
END; { rotate_left }


PROCEDURE insert_AVL(VAR Root      : AVLPtr;       { in/out }
                         X         : AVLDataRec;   { input  }
                     VAR InsertedOK : BOOLEAN      { in/out });
{ performs node insertion in an AVL-tree (recursive routine) }


BEGIN
    IF Root = NIL THEN BEGIN
        NEW(Root);   { create new memory space }
        WITH Root^ DO BEGIN
            TreeData := X;
            Left := NIL;
            Right := NIL;
            Balance := neutral
        END;
        InsertedOK := TRUE
    END
{ The following commented ELSE IF clause is used to guard
  against duplicate keys. Uncomment to use it. }
{*********************************************************
```

```
    ELSE IF X.Key = Root^.TreeData.Key THEN BEGIN
        InsertedOK := FALSE;
        EXIT
    END
*************************************************************}
    ELSE IF X.Key <= Root^.TreeData.Key THEN BEGIN
            insert_AVL(Root^.Left, X, InsertedOK);
            IF InsertedOK THEN
              CASE Root^.Balance OF
                left_tilt  : BEGIN
                                  rotate_left(Root);
                                  InsertedOK := FALSE
                             END;
                neutral   : Root^.Balance := left_tilt;
                right_tilt : BEGIN
                                  Root^.Balance := neutral;
                                  InsertedOK := FALSE
                             END;
              END; { CASE }
        END
        ELSE BEGIN
            insert_AVL(Root^.Right, X, InsertedOK);
            IF InsertedOK THEN
              CASE Root^.Balance OF
                left_tilt  : BEGIN
                                  Root^.Balance := neutral;
                                  InsertedOK := FALSE
                             END;
                neutral   : Root^.Balance := right_tilt;
                right_tilt : BEGIN
                                  rotate_right(Root);
                                  InsertedOK := FALSE
                             END;
              END; { CASE }
        END; { IF }
END; { insert_AVL }


PROCEDURE Insert_AVLTree(VAR  Root : AVLPtr;       { in/out }
                             X    : AVLDataRec   { input  });
{ inserts data item into the AVL-tree }
```

```
VAR inserted_ok : BOOLEAN;

BEGIN
    inserted_ok := FALSE;
    insert_AVL(Root, X, inserted_ok)
END; { Insert_AVLTree }

FUNCTION Search_AVLTree( Root            : AVLPtr;       { input }
                         X               : AVLDataRec;   { input }
                         Occurrence_Num  : WORD          { input }) : WORD;
{ searches for a key in the AVL-tree }


VAR count : WORD;


BEGIN
    count := 0; { initialize count for actual occurrence of X }
    WHILE (Root <> NIL) AND (count < Occurrence_Num) DO
        IF X.Key > Root^.TreeData.Key THEN Root := Root^.Right
        ELSE IF X.Key < Root^.TreeData.Key THEN Root := Root^.Left
        ELSE BEGIN { match is found }
            INC(count);
            Root := Root^.Left
        END; { IF }
    Search_AVLTree := count { return result }
END; { Search_AVLTree }


PROCEDURE traverse_tree(VAR Root   : AVLPtr;         { input  }
                        VAR SortX  : TreeRecArray;   { output }
                        VAR Count  : WORD            { output });
{ traverses the AVL-tree (local recursive routine) }


BEGIN
    IF Root <> NIL THEN BEGIN
        traverse_tree(Root^.Left, SortX, Count);
        INC(Count);
        IF Count <= MAX_TREE_NODES THEN
            SortX[Count].Key := Root^.TreeData.Key;
        traverse_tree(Root^.Right, SortX, Count);
    END;
END; { traverse_tree }
```

```
PROCEDURE AVLSort_to_Array(VAR Root   : AVLPtr;          { input  }
                           VAR SortX : TreeRecArray;  { output }
                           VAR Count : WORD           { output });
{ returns the data in the AVL-tree as a sorted array }

BEGIN
    { initialize the number of array members }
    Count := 0; { initialize the number of array members }
    { initiate the recursive traversal procedure }
    traverse_tree(Root, SortX, Count);
END; { AVLSort_to_Array }


PROCEDURE balance_right(VAR Root  : AVLPtr;    { in/out }
                        VAR DelOK : BOOLEAN    { in/out });
{ restores the balanced or near-balanced state of an AVL-tree by
  rebalancing a right subtree }

VAR ptr2, ptr3 : AVLPtr;
    balnc2, balnc3 : BalanceSet;

BEGIN
   CASE Root^.Balance OF
      left_tilt  : Root^.Balance := neutral;
      neutral : BEGIN
                   Root^.Balance := right_tilt;
                   DelOK := FALSE
                END;
      right_tilt : BEGIN
                   ptr2 := Root^.Right;
                   balnc2 := ptr2^.Balance;
                   IF NOT (balnc2 = left_tilt) THEN BEGIN
                      Root^.Right := ptr2^.Left;
                      ptr2^.Left := Root;
                      IF balnc2 = neutral THEN BEGIN
                         Root^.Balance := right_tilt;
                         ptr2^.Balance := left_tilt;
                         DelOK := FALSE
                      END
                      ELSE BEGIN
```

```
                        Root^.Balance := neutral;
                        ptr2^.Balance := neutral;
                    END; { IF }
                    Root := ptr2
                END
                ELSE BEGIN
                    ptr3 := ptr2^.Left;
                    balnc3 := ptr3^.Balance;
                    ptr2^.Left := ptr3^.Right;
                    ptr3^.Right := ptr2;
                    Root^.Right := ptr3^.Left;
                    ptr3^.Left := Root;
                    IF balnc3 = left_tilt THEN
                        ptr2^.Balance := right_tilt
                    ELSE
                        ptr2^.Balance := neutral;
                    IF balnc3 = right_tilt THEN
                        Root^.Balance := left_tilt
                    ELSE
                        Root^.Balance := neutral;
                    Root := ptr3;
                    ptr3^.Balance := neutral;
                END; { IF }
            END;
    END; { CASE }
END; { balance_right }


PROCEDURE balance_left(VAR Root  : AVLPtr;    { in/out }
                       VAR DelOK : BOOLEAN   { in/out });
{ restores the balanced or near-balanced state of an AVL-tree by
  rebalancing a left subtree }


VAR ptr2, ptr3 : AVLPtr;
    balnc2, balnc3 : BalanceSet;


BEGIN
    CASE Root^.Balance OF
        right_tilt  : Root^.Balance := neutral;
        neutral     : BEGIN
```

```
                    Root^.Balance := left_tilt;
                    DelOK := FALSE
                 END;
     left_tilt : BEGIN
                    ptr2 := Root^.Left;
                    balnc2 := ptr2^.Balance;
                    IF NOT (balnc2 = right_tilt) THEN BEGIN
                       Root^.Left := ptr2^.Right;
                       ptr2^.Right := Root;
                       IF balnc2 = neutral THEN BEGIN
                          Root^.Balance := left_tilt;
                          ptr2^.Balance := right_tilt;
                          DelOK := FALSE
                       END
                       ELSE BEGIN
                          Root^.Balance := neutral;
                          ptr2^.Balance := neutral;
                       END; { IF }
                       Root := ptr2
                    END
                    ELSE BEGIN
                       ptr3 := ptr2^.Right;
                       balnc3 := ptr3^.Balance;
                       ptr2^.Right := ptr3^.Left;
                       ptr3^.Left := ptr2;
                       Root^.Left := ptr3^.Right;
                       ptr3^.Right := Root;
                       IF balnc3 = right_tilt THEN
                            ptr2^.Balance := left_tilt
                       ELSE
                          ptr2^.Balance := neutral;
                       IF balnc3 = left_tilt THEN
                          Root^.Balance := right_tilt
                       ELSE
                          Root^.Balance := neutral;
                       Root := ptr3;
                       ptr3^.Balance := neutral;
                    END; { IF }
                 END;
   END; { CASE }
END; { balance_left }
```

```
PROCEDURE delete_both_children(VAR Root,              { in/out }
                                   Ptr    : AVLPtr;   { in/out }
                                   VAR DelOK : BOOLEAN { in/out });
{ deletes a node with two empty subtrees }

BEGIN
   IF Ptr^.Right = NIL THEN BEGIN
      Root^.TreeData := Ptr^.TreeData;
      Ptr := Ptr^.Left;
      DelOK := TRUE
   END
   ELSE BEGIN
      delete_both_children(Root, Ptr^.Right, DelOK);
      IF DelOK THEN balance_left(Ptr, DelOK);
   END; { IF }
END; { delete_both_children }


PROCEDURE delete_AVL(VAR Root    : AVLPtr;       { in/out }
                         X        : AVLDataRec;  { input  }
                     VAR DelOK    : BOOLEAN      { in/out });
{ Performs node deletion using recursion. The balance of the AVL-tree
  is also monitored and adjusted, if need be.}


VAR ptr : AVLPtr;


BEGIN
   IF Root = NIL THEN
      DelOK := FALSE
   ELSE
      IF X.Key < Root^.TreeData.Key THEN BEGIN
         delete_AVL(Root^.Left, X, DelOK);
         IF DelOK THEN balance_right(Root, DelOK);
      END
      ELSE BEGIN
         IF X.Key > Root^.TreeData.Key THEN BEGIN
            delete_AVL(Root^.Right, X, DelOK);
            IF DelOK THEN balance_left(Root, DelOK);
         END
         ELSE BEGIN
            ptr := Root;
```

```
            IF  Root^.Right = NIL  THEN  BEGIN
                Root := Root^.Left;
                DelOK := TRUE;
                Dispose(ptr);
            END
            ELSE IF  Root^.Left = NIL  THEN  BEGIN
                Root := Root^.Right;
                DelOK := TRUE;
                Dispose(ptr);
            END
            ELSE BEGIN
                delete_both_children(Root, Root^.Left, DelOK);
                IF DelOK THEN balance_right(Root, DelOK);
                Dispose(Root^.Left);
            END; { IF }
        END; { IF }
    END; { IF }
  { END IF }
END;{ delete_AVL }


PROCEDURE Delete_AVLTree(VAR Root   : AVLPtr;      { input  }
                             X       : AVLDataRec; { input  }
                         VAR DelOK   : BOOLEAN     { in/out });
{ deletes the key of X if it is present in the AVL-tree }


BEGIN
    DelOK := FALSE;
    delete_AVL(Root, X, DelOK)
END; { Delete_AVLTree }
END.
```

• Listing 10.3. Turbo Prolog source code for the AVL-tree library

```
domains
    avltreetype = tree(symbol, avltreetype, avltreetype, symbol); nil
    symlist = symbol*

database
    insert_stat(symbol) % insert status flag
    delete_stat(symbol) % delete status flag
```

```
predicates
    insert_avltree(symbol, avltreetype, avltreetype)
    search_avltree(symbol, avltreetype)
    delete_avltree(symbol, avltreetype, avltreetype)
    delete_node(symbol, avltreetype, avltreetype)

    % predicates used to balance a tree during node insertion
    check_lbalance(symbol, symbol, symbol, symbol, symbol, avltreetype,
                   avltreetype, avltreetype, avltreetype)
    check_rbalance(symbol, symbol, symbol, symbol, symbol, avltreetype,
                   avltreetype, avltreetype, avltreetype)
    rotatel(symbol, symbol, symbol, avltreetype, avltreetype,
            avltreetype, avltreetype)
    rotater(symbol, symbol, symbol, avltreetype, avltreetype,
            avltreetype, avltreetype)
    set_balancel(symbol, symbol, symbol)
    set_balancer(symbol, symbol, symbol)

    % predicates used to balance a tree during node deletion
    balance_left(symbol, symbol, symbol, symbol, symbol, avltreetype,
                 avltreetype, avltreetype, avltreetype)
    balance_right(symbol, symbol, symbol, symbol, symbol, avltreetype,
                  avltreetype, avltreetype, avltreetype)
    rotate_dl(symbol, symbol, symbol, avltreetype, avltreetype,
              avltreetype, avltreetype)
    rotate_dr(symbol, symbol, symbol, avltreetype, avltreetype,
              avltreetype, avltreetype)
    set_del_bal(symbol, symbol, symbol)

    % internal predicates
    get_tree(avltreetype, symbol, avltreetype, avltreetype, symbol)
    prttree(avltreetype)
    tree_driver(avltreetype, avltreetype)
    proc_user(char, avltreetype, avltreetype)

clauses

/*********** Insert a node ****************/

    insert_avltree(Item, nil, tree(Item, nil, nil, neutral)) :-
        assert(insert_stat(true)), !.
```

```
% insert in left subtree
insert_avltree(Item, tree(Key, Left, Right, Ht1),
               tree(Key2, Left3, Right2, Ht2)) :-
   Item < Key, !,
   insert_avltree(Item, Left, Left2),
   insert_stat(Stat),
   check_lbalance(Stat, Ht1, Ht2, Key, Key2, Left2, Left3, Right, Right2).

% insert in right subtree
insert_avltree(Item, tree(Key, Left, Right, Ht1),
               tree(Key2, Left2, Right3, Ht2)) :-
   insert_avltree(Item, Right, Right2),
   insert_stat(Stat),
   check_rbalance(Stat, Ht1, Ht2, Key, Key2, Left, Left2, Right2, Right3).

% test the balance of left subtree
check_lbalance(true, left_tilt, neutral, Key, Key2, Left2, Left3,
               Right, Right2) :-
   get_tree(Left2, _, _, _, Bal),
   rotatel(Bal, Key, Key2, Left2, Left3, Right, Right2),
   retractall(insert_stat(_)),
   assert(insert_stat(false)).

check_lbalance(true, neutral, left_tilt, Key, Key, Left, Left, Right, Right).
check_lbalance(true, right_tilt, neutral, Key, Key, Left, Left,
               Right, Right) :-
   retractall(insert_stat(_)),
   assert(insert_stat(false)).

% doesn't need balancing
check_lbalance(false, Ht1, Ht1, Key, Key, Left, Left, Right, Right).

% single left rotation
rotatel(left_tilt, Key, Key2, Left2, Left3, Right, Right2) :-
   get_tree(Left2, Node, L, R, _),
   Key2 = Node,
   Left3 = L,
   Right2 = tree(Key, R, Right, neutral).

% double left rotation
rotatel(_, Key, Key2, Left2, Left3, Right, Right2) :-
```

```
      get_tree(Left2, Node, L, R, _),
      get_tree(R, Node2, L2, R2, Bal1),
      Key2 = Node2,
      set_balancel(right, Bal1, Rbal),
      set_balancel(left, Bal1, Lbal),
      Right2 = tree(Key, R2, Right, Rbal),    %build right subtree
      Left3 = tree(Node, L, L2, Lbal).        %build left subtree

% check balance of right subtree
check_rbalance(true, left_tilt, neutral, Key, Key, Left, Left,
               Right, Right) :-
   retractall(insert_stat(_)),
   assert(insert_stat(false)).
check_rbalance(true,neutral, right_tilt, Key, Key, Left, Left, Right, Right).
check_rbalance(true, right_tilt, neutral, Key, Key2, Left, Left2,
               Right2, Right3) :-
   get_tree(Right2, _, _, _, Bal),
   rotater(Bal, Key, Key2, Left, Left2, Right2, Right3),
   retractall(insert_stat(_)),
   assert(insert_stat(false)).

% stop balancing
check_rbalance(false, Ht1, Ht1, Key, Key, Left, Left, Right, Right).

% single right rotation
rotater(right_tilt, Key, Key2, Left, Left2, Right2, Right3) :-
   get_tree(Right2, Node, L, R, _),
   Key2 = Node,
   Right3 = R,
   Left2 = tree(Key, Left, L, neutral).

% double right rotation
rotater(_, Key, Key2, Left, Left2, Right2, Right3) :-
get_tree(Right2, Node, L, R, _),
   get_tree(L, Node2, L2, R2, Bal1),
   Key2 = Node2,
   set_balancer(left, Bal1, Rbal),
   set_balancer(right, Bal1, Lbal),
   Left2 = tree(Key, Left, L2, Rbal),
   Right3 = tree(Node, R2, R, Lbal).
```

```
% change balance setting of left and right subtrees
set_balancel(right, left_tilt, right_tilt) :- !.
set_balancel(right, _, neutral) :- !.
set_balancel(left, right_tilt, left_tilt) :- !.
set_balancel(left, _, neutral) :- !.

set_balancer(left, left_tilt, right_tilt) :- !.
set_balancer(left, _, neutral) :- !.
set_balancer(right, right_tilt, left_tilt) :- !.
set_balancer(right, _, neutral) :- !.

% return components of a tree node
get_tree(tree(Item, Left, Right, Bal), Item, Left, Right, Bal).

/******** search for an element ************/
search_avltree(Item, tree(Item, _, _, _)) :-!.
search_avltree(Item, tree(Key, Left, _, _)) :-
    Item < Key, !,
    search_avltree(Item, Left).
search_avltree(Item, tree(_, _, Right, _)) :-
    search_avltree(Item, Right).

/********** delete an element ***************/

% element found, no right child
delete_avltree(Item, tree(Item, Left, nil, _), Left) :-
    assert(delete_stat(true)), !.

% element found, no left child
delete_avltree(Item, tree(Item, nil, Right, _), Right) :-
    assert(delete_stat(true)), !.

% element found, node has both children
delete_avltree(Item, tree(Item, Left, Right, Ht1), tree(Key2, Left2,
               Right2, Ht2)) :-
    delete_node(Key, Left, Left1),
    delete_stat(Stat),
    balance_right(Stat, Ht1, Ht2, Key, Key2, Left1, Left2, Right, Right2).

% delete from left subtree
```

```
      delete_avltree(Item, tree(Key, Left, Right, Ht1), tree(Key2, Left3,
                  Right2, Ht2)) :-
         Item < Key, !,
         delete_avltree(Item, Left, Left2),
         delete_stat(Stat),
         balance_right(Stat, Ht1, Ht2, Key, Key2, Left2, Left3, Right, Right2).


   % delete from right subtree
      delete_avltree(Item, tree(Key, Left, Right, Ht1), tree(Key2, Left2,
                  Right3, Ht2)) :-
         delete_avltree(Item, Right, Right2),
         delete_stat(Stat),
         balance_left(Stat, Ht1, Ht2, Key, Key2, Left, Left2, Right2, Right3).

% no right child
   delete_node(Item, tree(Item, Left, nil, _), Left) :-
         retractall(delete_stat(_)),
         assert(delete_stat(true)).
         delete_node(Item, tree(Key, Left, Right, Ht1), tree(Key2, Left2,
                  Right3, Ht2)) :-
         delete_node(Item, Right, Right2),
         delete_stat(Stat),
         balance_left(Stat, Ht1, Ht2, Key, Key2, Left, Left2, Right2, Right3).


   % test the balance of left subtree
   balance_left(true, left_tilt, NewBal, Key, Key2, Left2, Left3, Right,
                  Right2) :-
         get_tree(Left2, _, _, _, Bal),
         rotate_dl(Bal, Key, Key2, Left2, Left3, Right, Right2),
         set_del_bal(left, Bal, NewBal).

   balance_left(true, neutral, left_tilt, Key, Key, Left, Left,
                  Right, Right) :-
         retractall(delete_stat(_)),
         assert(delete_stat(false)).
   balance_left(true, right_tilt, neutral, Key, Key, Left, Left, Right, Right).


   % doesn't need balancing
   balance_left(false, Ht1, Ht1, Key, Key, Left, Left, Right, Right).
```

```
% double left rotation for node deletion
   rotate_dl(right_tilt, Key, Key2, Left2, Left3, Right, Right2) :-
      get_tree(Left2, Node, L, R, _),
      get_tree(R, Node2, L2, R2, Bal1),
      Key2 = Node2,
      set_balancel(right, Bal1, Rbal),
      set_balancel(left, Bal1, Lbal),
      Right2 = tree(Key, R2, Right, Rbal),    %build right subtree
      Left3 = tree(Node, L, L2, Lbal).        %build left subtree

   % single left rotation for node deletion
   rotate_dl(_, Key, Key2, Left2, Left3, Right, Right2) :-
   get_tree(Left2, Node, L, R, Bal),
      Key2 = Node,
      Left3 = L,
      set_del_bal(leftsub, Bal, NewBal),
      Right2 = tree(Key, R, Right, NewBal).

   % check balance of right subtree
   balance_right(true, left_tilt, neutral, Key, Key, Left, Left, Right, Right).

   balance_right(true, neutral, right_tilt, Key, Key, Left, Left, Right,
                  Right) :-
      retractall(delete_stat(_)),
      assert(delete_stat(false)).

      balance_right(true, right_tilt, NewBal, Key, Key2, Left, Left2,
                  Right2, Right3) :-
      get_tree(Right2, _, _, _, Bal),
      rotate_dr(Bal, Key, Key2, Left, Left2, Right2, Right3),
      set_del_bal(right, Bal, NewBal).

   % stop balancing
   balance_right(false, Ht1, Ht1, Key, Key, Left, Left, Right, Right).

   % double right rotation for node deletion
   rotate_dr(left_tilt, Key, Key2, Left, Left2, Right2, Right3) :-
      get_tree(Right2, Node, L, R, _),
      get_tree(L, Node2, L2, R2, Bal1),
      Key2 = Node2,
```

```
    set_balancer(left, Bal1, Rbal),
    set_balancer(right, Bal1, Lbal),
    Left2 = tree(Key, Left, L2, Rbal),
    Right3 = tree(Node, R2, R, Lbal).


% single right rotation for node deletion
rotate_dr(_, Key, Key2, Left, Left2, Right2, Right3) :-
    get_tree(Right2, Node, L, R, Bal),
    Key2 = Node,
    Right3 = R,
    set_del_bal(rightsub, Bal, NewBal),
    Left2 = tree(Key, Left, L, NewBal).

set_del_bal(left, neutral, left_tilt) :-
    retractall(insert_stat(_)),
    assert(insert_stat(false)).
set_del_bal(leftsub, neutral, right_tilt).
set_del_bal(left, _, neutral).
set_del_bal(leftsub, _, neutral).
set_del_bal(right, neutral, right_tilt) :-
    retractall(insert_stat(_)),
    assert(insert_stat(false)).
set_del_bal(rightsub, neutral, left_tilt).
set_del_bal(right, _, neutral).
set_del_bal(rightsub, _, neutral).

/************ support clauses **************/

prttree(nil).
prttree(tree(Item, Left, Right, Bal)) :-
    prttree(Left),
    write("Item is ", Item, ": Bal is ", Bal), nl, prttree(Right).

tree_driver(OldTree, NewTree) :- !,
    write("Select an option >"),
    readchar(Choice), nl,
    proc_user(Choice, OldTree, NewTree),
    tree_driver(NewTree, _).
tree_driver(_, _).
```

```
proc_user('q', _, _) :- fail.
proc_user('i', OldTree, NewTree) :-
write("Enter item to insert >"),
    readln(Item), nl,
    retractall(insert_stat(_)),
    insert_avltree(Item, OldTree, NewTree).
proc_user('f', OldTree, NewTree) :-
    write("Enter item to locate >"),
    readln(Item), nl,
    search_avltree(Item, OldTree),
    NewTree = OldTree,
    write("Item found"), nl.
proc_user('f', OldTree, NewTree) :-
    NewTree = OldTree,
    write("Item not found"), nl.
proc_user('d', OldTree, NewTree) :-
    write("Enter item to delete >"),
    readln(Item), nl,
    retractall(delete_stat(_)),
    delete_avltree(Item, OldTree, NewTree).
proc_user('p', OldTree, NewTree) :-
    prttree(OldTree),
    NewTree = OldTree.
```

Index

Disk Order Form

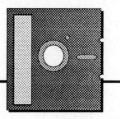

If you'd like to use the code presented in this book but you don't want to waste your time typing it in, we have a very special offer for you. We are making available a set of diskettes that contain all of the major programming examples presented in this book.

To order your disks, fill out the form below and mail it along with $24.95 in check or money order (orders outside the U.S. add $5 for shipping and handling) to:

Keith Weiskamp
Turbo Algorithms Disk
3120 E. Paradise Ln., Suite 12
Phoenix, AZ 85023

- -

Please send me _____ copies of the Turbo Algorithms Disks at $24.95 each (orders outside the U.S. add $5 shipping and handling). Please make checks payable to Keith Weiskamp.

_____
Name

_____
Address

_____
City   State   Zip Code

_____
Telephone

A Special Offer From Wiley

Don't miss out on the only comprehensive reference series on all Borland's high-level Turbo languages.

• Please send me _____ copy(ies) of **Turbo Language Essentials** (1-60907-2) @ $24.95 plus applicable sales tax.

• Please send me _____ copy(ies) of **Turbo Libraries** (1-61005-4) @ $26.95 plus applicable sales tax.

NAME _____

COMPANY _____

ADDRESS _____

CITY _____ STATE/ZIP _____

TELEPHONE _____

Method of Payment (please make payment to John Wiley & Sons)
❑ Payment Enclosed (Wiley pays postage)   ❑ Bill me   ❑ Bill Company
❑ VISA   ❑ MASTERCARD (Sales tax, postage and handling will be added.)

Expiration Date _____/_____/_____   Card No. _____

SIGN HERE: _____
Order invalid if not signed. Offer good in U.S. and Canada only.

--- ✂ --

To get the most out of the Turbo languages, you'll want to add these two books written by the authors of *Turbo Algorithms* to your personal library:

✓ *Turbo Language Essentials* —a complete source to the language fundamentals and advanced concepts of all four Borland's high-level Turbo languages.
✓ *Turbo Libraries*— provides an in-depth look at the major library routines supported by each Turbo language.

To order, fill out the form above and mail it along with your payment to:

John Wiley & Sons, Inc.
Order Department
1 Wiley Drive
Somerset, NJ 08850-1272